For Vista Walker,
      wonderful sleuth for references—
            Affectionately
                  Lois

                        and for Alice, in
                              England.

VULNERABILITY, COPING, AND GROWTH

VULNERABILITY, COPING,

AND GROWTH

FROM INFANCY TO ADOLESCENCE

LOIS BARCLAY MURPHY

and

ALICE E. MORIARTY

NEW HAVEN AND LONDON
YALE UNIVERSITY PRESS
1976

Designed by Sally Sullivan
and set in Illumna type.
Printed in the United States of America by
The Colonial Press Inc., Clinton, Mass.

Published in Great Britain, Europe, and Africa by
Yale University Press, Ltd., London. Distributed
in Latin America by Kaiman & Polon, Inc., New York
City; in Japan by John Weatherhill, Inc., Tokyo.

The research on which this book is based was financed in part by the following United
States Public Health Service grants:
M-680 (I-III): Aspects of Temperament, Mental Health and Ego-Strength in Children,
Especially in Relation to Children's Spontaneous Efforts to Cope with Their Own
Problems, 1953–54, 1954–55, 1955–56.
M-680 (IV–VII): To Study Continuity and Change in Coping Methods (Orchestration
of Outgoing Efforts and Defense Mechanisms) in Primary School Children, 1956–57,
1957–58.
M-4093: Longitudinal Studies in Mental Health Maintenance, 1960–61, 1961–62,
1962–63. Collaborative Studies in Mental Health, 1963–64.
Contract PH43-65-41: Utilization of Research. (Proposal for Development of a Design
for Research Utilization and Demonstration of Improved Techniques for Assessment of
Child Development), 1964–65, 1965–66.
MH 09236-01-02-03: Utilization of Studies in Vulnerability and Coping, 1966–69.

For Gardner

Contents

Preface: The Series of Coping Studies
on Which This Book Is Based

When Gardner Murphy and I and our two children were driving across the United States from New York to California in 1938, six-year-old Midge refused to enter the state of Kansas. We were discussing the proposed route as we drove through Illinois. She would not go through Kansas; she would get out of the car if necessary. She was not going to be blown away like Dorothy of Oz. Since we could not truthfully guarantee that there would be no tornado in Kansas and since it seemed a minor concession to make to a strong-minded child whom we respected, we changed the plan and drove through Nebraska. (Many years later she was quite willing to take the risk in order to visit us in Topeka, where we had moved after she entered college.)

Some years earlier I had observed a small, well toilet-trained and conscientious two year old who was unwilling to leave his play at a moment when he needed to go to the bathroom. He found a small can, put it in a corner of the hallway, and "pee-peed" into it.

In the early 1930s there were discussions of the preschool child's "resistance" to IQ tests—humorless discussions that did not take into account how preposterous the unreasonable series of demands must seem to a small child.

These children were not "naughty." They were doing what made sense to them—they were coping with situations as they experienced them. Who used this term "coping"? Anna Freud, for one, and probably Dr. Spock, our consulting psychiatric pediatrician at the Sarah Lawrence Nursery School from 1937 to 1944. But the term "coping" was not in the *Psychological Abstracts Index,* and I found no systematic discussion of it anywhere. Obviously we needed to explore this aspect of child life, different as it was from "conditioning," "aggression," and other topics then being studied. Most of these studies evaluated children's behavior from the standpoint of the children's "adaptation" to adult demands. Although I made notes on relevant episodes, I had no time to focus on children's ways of coping until I left Sarah Lawrence and accompanied Gardner (to Kansas!) when he accepted an appointment as director of research at the Menninger Foundation.

In Topeka an exciting opportunity awaited me: Dr. Sibylle Escalona with Dr. Mary Leitch and their staff had made uniquely detailed records between 1948 and 1951 of the behavior of 128 infants, 8 boys and 8 girls at each of eight age levels from four to thirty-two weeks. Three simultaneous observers recorded behavior of mother and baby over a four-hour period that included feeding, play, being undressed and dressed, and sleep. Developmental tests and pediatric examinations, movies of a feeding episode, and home interviews were also included in the data. These children were from two to five years old when we began the coping study in 1953.

We were offered the gift of this material with no strings attached: "There is so much there that we could not possibly get in each other's way," Escalona told me. "Do what you like with it." What I found irresistible was the opportunity finally to focus on coping behavior of children at preschool age, and also to try to discover links between their infancy and subsequent behavior.

Equally inviting was the presence of several mature and gifted professionals who were interested in the study and who would be able to free some time for participation:

Dr. Nelly Tibout, training analyst at the Topeka Psychoanalytic Institute and former director of the Amsterdam Child Guidance Clinic, agreed to start us off with weekly conferences for a year to discuss what to look for. We did not commence our observations of the children until after a year of this orientation and sensitization.

Dr. Povl Toussieng, child psychiatrist and director of the diagnostic service of the children's division of the Menninger Clinic, was interested in conducting psychiatrically oriented play sessions with these normal children to provide perspective on his work with disturbed children.

Dr. Walter Kass, director of the psychological services of the same division, administered the Children's Apperception (CAT) and Rorschach tests, sight-touch form test, Bender-Gestalt drawings, and his original application of the Seguin form-board to examine kinesthetic cues in perceiving form and space relationships.

Dr. Alice Moriarty, clinical psychologist and speech specialist, administered intelligence tests: Stanford-Binet (revised, form L), Merrill-Palmer Scale of Mental Tests, and Wechsler Intelligence Scale for Children (WISC). She asked each child to make a drawing of his own choice with crayons and one with water, chalk, and sponge.

Dr. Grace Heider, another experienced psychologist, had also worked with children who had speech and learning difficulties. She made the home visits and handled the scheduling of observation and test sessions of the preschool study.

Dr. Patricia Schloesser, director of maternal and child health for the state of Kansas, took responsibility for the pediatric examinations.

I used my own Miniature Life Toy (MLT) techniques developed at Sarah Lawrence College (Murphy 1956, vol. 1) and the Bon-Hop Playhouse, where the child is left to his own devices to manipulate different latches on doors and to fit forms through holes in the roof. I also used ego-blocking techniques and sensory toys offering different sorts of visual, auditory, textural, and manipulatory values (Lerner and Murphy 1941).

Mrs. Marie Smith, an experienced secretary who had worked with the Escalona–Leitch project, became the permanent project secretary and research assistant after an initial period during which Selma Kraft held that position.

This group made up our basic interdisciplinary research team, all of whom except Dr. Kass participated in certain studies after the preschool phase. Marie Smith, Grace Heider, Alice Moriarty, and I also served as "parallel recorders," along with several graduate students who assisted us the first two years. Appendix 1 gives the complete record of staff members for this and subsequent phases of our work.

The First Phase of the Coping Studies

During the course of our first year of planning discussions we formulated a grant application that stated the following aims: "To initiate the study of children's efforts to cope with their own problems and to explore the relation of these efforts to aspects of temperament and resources for growth." I commented that in the longitudinal studies so far reported, little attention had been given to the ways in which children deal with their problems, or to the aspects of temperament (or persistent physical, mental, emotional characteristics) related to the resources on which each child draws in his coping efforts.

> Buried in research reports, such as the frustration and regression study by Barker, Dembo, and Lewin (1943), we find a significant third of the children who did not regress in response to the frustrating situation, but on the contrary, maintained their efforts or put forth even greater ones. But we are told nothing about these children or what distinguished them from their regressing playmates. . . . The fact that clinical studies, studies of projective methods, etc., fall short of the final predictiveness they would like to achieve may be related to the fact that we have not studied the individual's resources for coping, for helping himself, as thoroughly as we have studied areas of anxiety and conflict.

We proposed a hypothesis-forming study focusing on children's ways of meeting everyday stress, challenge, and opportunities. We also undertook to explore characteristics contributing to the capacity to cope with the environment, and to the capacity to maintain internal integration.

Examinations and tests would not only permit us to see the children in relation to others in the United States but would provide intrinsic challenges. We felt that it was also important to see the children in a variety of situations that would explore their responses to different people in different settings, "natural" as well as "formal." There were trips to the zoo, to the park, and to "parties" at the Murphys' three acres of woods, terraces, and streams. Records of the "to and fro" trips from home to the research center and back included observations of leave-taking and rejoining friends and family. Visits to the home and hospital, participation in birthday parties, graduations, and other family events often added new views of the child and family. In order to allow time for keeping such records we had to limit the number of children we would try to know. We randomly selected thirty-two children (in twenty-seven families) from the Escalona–Leitch group; one of these was the preschool sister of a younger child who had been in the infancy study.

We combined the natural history recording of behavior both in ordinary life situations and during the examinations with the formal records, scores, and other measures from pediatric, psychiatric, and psychological examinations. An adjunctive "parallel" recorder made running records of the ways in which the children coped with the demands of the examiner and the situation.

Method

Our study is sometimes referred to as a longitudinal study, and it is important to make clear immediately that we have not attempted to repeat any of the intensive studies of physical and mental growth, or sequences of problems, as these have been investigated in chronological, systematic fashion by various investigators. Rather, we felt that enough had been done to permit us to build on the important basic findings from such studies and to take a further step, and with a different methodological approach.

Our methods are process oriented, involving the use of very detailed natural history observations along with the pediatric, psychological, and psychiatric examinations at each of four major levels of development after infancy: preschool, latency, puberty, and late adolescence. The tests made it possible to compare our subjects with other groups: for instance, despite their above-average IQ, they were seen on the Rorschach as less ambitious than eastern metropolitan children, though comparable on the Holtzman Inkblot Technique (HIT) to Holtzman's sample of Texas sixth graders (see chapter 5, note 3). The double recording at the preschool phase permitted in-depth study of the child's response to each situation and inferences regarding the way in which he experienced and coped with it. The fact that each child was seen in many situations, differing in structure, pressures, challenges, and sex and orientation of the observers, permitted inferences in regard to both stability and variations in coping behavior.

In addition to examination reports and observation records for situations in which all the children were seen, ad hoc observations in crisis situations, such as hospitals, funerals, aftermath of a tornado and of the assassination of President Kennedy, provided qualitative records of certain children's responses to unusual stress (see Appendix 4 for a list of data-collecting sessions with the children).

You may ask why if we wanted to study the children's reaction to stress, we did not expose them systematically to some experimental stress. We do not believe it is ethically sound to expose children to pain or frightening situations. Those who are confronting new experiences away from their families are forming impressions of the outside world. Destroying their trust is a price we as psychologists could not risk. Consequently we decided to make the most of the ordinary everyday stress conditions under which we would be seeing the children in the course of examination. Since the children ranged in age from two to five when we first saw them, this was for many the first instance of separation from the mother to go with a stranger. In any case the situation of accompanying a stranger for a new examination was strange; for some of the children it was obviously stressful, for others simply challenging. The Sheldon Body Photograph process, which involved being photographed nude, was the most severe stress for a few boys, three of whom cried disconsolately throughout the session. Pediatric examinations involved mild stress for some of the children.

We were interested not only in the specific moment of stress which could be observed in a new situation or under the challenge, frustrations, and difficulty of intelligence tests or psychiatric examinations, but also stresses at home, illnesses, accidents, losses by death or divorce, or moving to another town.

In addition to the examination reports and the natural history records of the children's interaction with the examiners, detailed reports of the children's behavior and conversation as we drove them to the research office, and took them home were dictated immediately. We also dictated detailed records of all of the stressful events we shared with the families. With a few children hundreds of special sessions were carried on to clarify children's ways of experiencing and coping with special problems. For most of the children, forty-five to sixty sessions were recorded in detail, generally with double recording, including tape recording after the preschool years.

The children

All the babies studied by Escalona and Leitch and their co-workers had been selected originally as being free from defect or serious deviations—that is, they were "normal" babies. Grace Heider located through the telephone book those who were still in Topeka, taking them in random order. The original sample included only Caucasian children, and north European names predominated. No professional families from the Menninger Foundation were included, and the fathers reflected the range of skilled workers and small businessmen of the city; there were a few upper-middle-class professional and businessmen in the group. (See Appendix 2 for a listing of the children, siblings, father's occupation, grandparents, and basic intelligence ratings.)

The youngest boys ranged from two years, eight months, to three years, five months, as of 1 September 1953. These included the boys referred to here by the following pseudonyms: Ray (2:8), Lennie (2:10), Brennie (2:10), Donald (2:10), Vernon (3:2), Ronald (3:5).

There were nine two- and three-year-old girls on 1 September 1953: Vivian (2:6), Molly (2:7), Sheila (2:8), Darlene (2:10), Diane (3:5), Sally (3:5), Rachel (3:8), JoAnne (3:7), Daryl (3:10).

The older boys ranged in age from four years to five years, three months: Ralph (4:0), Tommy (4:1), Chester (4:5), Gordon (4:7), Greg (4:11), Martin (4:11), Roddy (4:11), Teddy (4:11), Steve (5:0), Terry (5:3).

The older girls ranged in age from four years, three months, to five years, seven months: Barbie (4:3), Helen (4:8), Susan (4:9), Patsy (4:9), Janice (4:10), Trudy (5:2), Cynthia (5:7).

We decided to use these children even though for us it meant an unusual investment in transportation since they were scattered all over town. The infancy data would provide evidence regarding early factors in the child and also early interactions between the baby and mother or other members of the family.

Escalona and Leitch's sample of 128 babies excluded children of Menninger Foundation clinical staff and families from minority groups. Few were either very poor or very rich. Two-thirds of the families were churchgoers. All the families in this intensive group had lived in Topeka for at least five years, and when the children were ten years old most of them still lived in Topeka. It was a stable group in terms of job and residence. One might consider many of them "core" American families, nonmobile, nonsuburban, even nonambitious. They did not look for more interesting or challenging work or higher salaries. Nor did they move because they would like to live in a different or more pleasant climate or find out what California looks like. They were Kansans. The families were not very competitive. There was only one family that might belong in Whyte's book, *The Organization Man* (1956). Even this family did not fit David Riesman's prototype in *The Lonely Crowd* (1960).

In ability these children were above the norm with an average IQ of 116 at the preschool level, probably the result of selecting babies who had no defects, handicaps, or retardation. There was no intention on either Escalona's part or ours to select superior children, but if all points of retardation in any area are used as a basis for rejection, it follows automatically that the performance of the children selected will range from average on up. The children were not rebellious or aggressive. In some ways they reminded us of Margaret Mead's New Guinea Manus group: realistic, autonomous, competent, sincere in their approach to life in general. They were, by and large, free from pretenses; they lived in neighborhoods and communities where the leadership comes from the middle-class group itself. There was no tradition of the aristocratic family snobbery illustrated in the cliché "the Cabots talk only to the Lowells and the Lowells talk only to God." These families talked to their neighbors, and they and their neighbors alike talked to God. For some of them God was a major support in time of trouble and a constant object of faith, as witnessed in Sally's reply to the question, How are wood and coal alike? "Dod makes it."

Maintaining contact with subjects

We put the emphasis on maintaining contact with our subjects rather than insisting on adherence to a rigid time schedule, which was often interrupted by illness, out-of-town visits, or special family needs. The result was that we maintained contact into adolescence with all but three of thirty-two children studied at the preschool level; because a few of the children had moved to distant states, it was not possible to obtain all data on them in late adolescence. However, all but one of the children who temporarily or permanently moved away from Topeka were able to return for major examinations at the latency and prepuberty periods. Letters, long-distance phone calls, mailed questionnaires, and staff visits supplemented visits of those who had moved.

The observations

During the first year and a half of the study there were over three hundred sessions with the children and their mothers—not by any means limited to "fifty-minute hours" because the extent as well as the timing of the sessions with the small children varied. Some children needed a longer warming-up period and opportunity to get acquainted with the new people who had come into their lives, the new place, the new opportunities, and the new demands that were being made on them. Thus it was sometimes necessary to see the child again and again before completing the observations a given examiner wished to make. Appendix 4 summarizes data-collecting and discussion sessions of that first year and a half.

From our natural history records of behavior we first studied the ways in which the children dealt with challenge in such areas as these:

a) confronting the new and the strange, and separation from the mother (typically occurring simultaneously or in close sequence)
b) confronting challenge, difficulty, and failure in situations calling for cognitive, motor or social skills, or combinations of these
c) experiencing body threat, damage, or pain

Our records invited analysis in terms of coping steps, devices, or operations; processes and styles; changing ways of dealing with the environment; aspects of the constitutional makeup of the child related to his coping methods; aspects contributing to vulnerability as well as to resilience and the child's ways of maintaining equilibrium or internal integration.

After each participant had completed his own examination reports and behavior records independently and without knowledge of the observations of any other participant, the group came together in conferences focusing on an individual child. We also discussed the similarities and variations in the ways the children coped with the widely different experiences to which we exposed them and the relevant influences, both from within the child himself and from the many aspects of his environment, that might have contributed to his coping patterns.

At a later time we collected into one volume ("the bible") all the scores and ratings from the examinations, together with ratings of behavior—those made by individuals on the basis of their own sessions and those made as global ratings for sessions in which three examiners had seen the children. These 640 empirically selected items (Appendix 4) provided the material for correlations between environmental and behavior items, intelligence tests and coping behavior, global ratings of Coping I (coping with the opportunities, threats, and demands of the environment) and Coping II (maintenance of internal integration).

Five major published reports based on this first stage of study are utilized in the present book: *Prediction and Outcome* by Sibylle Escalona and Grace Heider (1959) reported comparisons between Escalona's predictions on thirty-one infants and the preschool observations, together with a discussion of the implication of prediction success or failure. Alice Moriarty's 1961 monograph, *Coping Patterns of Preschool Children in Response to Intelligence Test Demands*, documented the children's ways of dealing with the challenging, demanding, difficult, frustrating, or gratifying aspects of the intelligence test situations. Her 1966 report on constancy and IQ change presented an interdisciplinary approach to influences related to variability and stability in IQ.

I reviewed observations of the children in *The Widening World of Childhood* (1962). The discussions focused on the children's confrontation and mastery of newness and strangeness, difficulties and physical challenges, pain and handicaps. The role of processes of orientation, autonomy, flexibility and gratification in making coping efforts were discussed along with processes of development of coping behavior.

Grace Heider's monograph, *Vulnerability in Infants and Young Children* (1966), compared infancy and preschool behavior. Defining vulnerability as susceptibility to stress, she focused on the contributions of specific aspects of equipment and of environment, and on the child's own management processes.

This book also draws on shorter journal articles dealing with related areas and also the relation of coping devices to defense mechanisms. See the Bibliography of Coping Studies for a complete listing of books, symposium contributions, and articles published by members of the staff.

The Latency Study

The latency study continued with the same group of children. The home visits and most of the preschool examinations were repeated in order to study continuity and change in coping methods in the same children at the primary-school age—from five to eight years. The WISC, Thematic Apperception Test, and Engel Insight Test were added to the psychological tests. In addition, the original qualitative data were quantified by the use of clinical ratings, and relationships between different aspects of functioning and between a child's behavior and aspects of the environment were explored.

Thirty-three additional children randomly selected from the original infancy population were added to the original intensive group (all but one of whom were still available) in order to increase the total sample for a study of perceptual style by Dr. Herman Witkin. The thirty-three children seen only by the Witkin staff were given WISC test, the Thematic Apperception Test, the Rorschach, and the Engel Insight Test in addition to the Witkin Perceptual Battery. This additional group was not seen in formal sessions by the coping staff at this stage, although some members of the staff made observations during the Witkin tests.

At this stage psychiatric examinations on the coping group were carried out by Dr. Keith Bryant. The children who still lived in Topeka were again observed at small "parties" where each child's behavior was recorded by a special observer assigned to him.

We made certain additions to the intensive data. Dr. Tibout and I interviewed the parents of six children in order to explore backgrounds of the parents' ways of coping with stress. I had weekly play sessions for three years in order to explore subjective aspects of the experience of a child severely damaged by polio. Grace Heider administered Rorschachs to eleven parents. One mother of two siblings kept weekly records of stress in the home and the children's ways of dealing with it. These additions to the intensive records provided rich material on background and developmental contributions to changing coping patterns. Budget limitations made it impossible to extend these intensive explorations to all the children.

While natural history records by a parallel observer and detailed notes on each session by the examiner were made again at this stage, test sessions were also tape-recorded, transcribed, and summarized in written reports by the examiners. Detailed notes on the children's behavior and conversations going to and from the research center again provided additional material. Conferences on individual children compared the current findings with earlier records; these conferences included certain interested members of the Menninger Foundation staff (Gardner Murphy, Riley Gardner, Martin Mayman) and also on the occasions of their visits to the Menninger Foundation, Sibylle Escalona, Anna Freud, Robert Holt, Wayne Holtzman, George Klein, and Margaret Mead. Studies of individual children made by different staff members drew on the transcriptions of the tape-recorded conference sessions as well as the total records for each child.

In addition to the original ratings on 134 items dealing with behavior, physiological functioning, and dispositional tendencies of the child (made for the prediction and outcome study) additional items were formulated empirically from the clinical data. Paired comparisons of each child with each other child were made independently by Moriarty and me for Coping I and Coping II, and these were correlated with the other items. Intercorrelations, item analyses, and cluster analyses using an IBM 650 computer at the University of Kansas were made under the direction of Dr. Walter Raine and in consultation with Dr. Philip DuBois.

A first inventory of hypotheses was formulated on the basis of qualitative and quantitative analyses and later extended after further analysis of the material on the children.

The Prepuberty and Adolescent Studies

The prepuberty study was oriented toward mental health maintenance at first, with an emphasis on utilization of the research. This was instigated and supported by Dr. Caroline Chandler of NIMH. A sequel was undertaken by Drs. Toussieng and Moriarty to study the adolescents during their senior year of high school. This phase was included under the general category of studies of vulnerability, since it was (wrongly) anticipated that leaving high school would involve anxiety.

When the children were eleven to thirteen years old, examinations and tests of the children were made by Dr. Schloesser, pediatrician, and Dr. Toussieng, psychiatrist, with me as observer and recorder. At this stage, home visits were carried on by Mildred Faris, chief psychiatric social worker at the Menninger Foundation, while Alice Moriarty administered intelligence and projective tests, and Rosemary Mayman gave the HIT. I made home visits to certain parents whose attitudes toward stress were of particular interest. Test and examination sessions were again tape-recorded, but the use of a recorder in these families' homes was thought likely to inhibit the responsiveness of the mothers; home interviews were dictated immediately after the visit.

Supplementary interviews with parents to explore areas of family activity, communication, discipline, and mother's support of children were made by short-term assistants Beth Koropsak and Diana Dolgoff. Julie Palmquist interviewed mothers in regard to religious practices in the home, participation in the church activities, and religious beliefs.

Two especially stressful events occurred during the adolescence of these children: the assassination of President Kennedy in November 1963, and the disastrous tornado in Topeka in June 1966. In addition, a few personal disasters occurred among the children we were studying: an automobile crash that killed Richard's mother and severely wounded

both his father and him; the accidental drowning death of the brother of
Helen; a tragic fire that killed the mother and five children in Rachel's
family. These public and personal disasters led to efforts to understand
how our children were dealing with them.

During my absence in November 1963 (I was sent to Nigeria for two
weeks of consultations on principles of child development research
there), Alice Moriarty, Sylvia Ginsparg, and C. Joseph Morgan developed and mailed three days later a questionnaire on the assassination
(chapter 9). After the tornado, due to control of the city by the National
Guard and local police and to fallen telephone wires, it was impossible
to obtain as much data on reactions to the tornado as we wished.
However C. Joseph Morgan was able to reach a number of the teenagers
for interviews (chapter 9). During Richard's stay in the hospital, C.
Joseph Morgan made repeated visits, and following his discharge from
the hospital I had an important experience with him (chapter 10).

Alice Moriarty presented a detailed study of continuity and change in
IQ (1966). I reviewed infancy records in detail and added four new
variables to the data pool. These were based on the special study of the
infant's reactions to feeding and included (a) level of demand, (b) level
of gratification, (c) autonomy allowed by the mother in the feeding
situation, and (d) the infant's tendency to protest, resist, or terminate
unwanted feeding. These variables were then correlated with the total
list of coping variables. Dr. Lolafaye Coyne carried out these analyses as
well as studies of correlations between mothers' and infants' ratings, and
also clustering of children at preschool and prepuberty levels.

Meanwhile, continued review of the quantitative and qualitative
records was taking place, resulting in additions to the hypotheses. In
addition to the studies already referred to, Alice Moriarty and I studied
the development of individual children. Vimla Gupta, in weekly
conferences with me, made intensive analyses of the development of four
children. My revised study of Helen, one of these, was presented at the
Hampstead Clinic following its presentation at a conference at the
Menninger Foundation attended by Anna Freud. Two members of the
Hampstead Clinic, Joseph Sandler, M.D., and Humbert Nagera, made
full Hampstead assessments of Helen and Chester following my presentation there. Dr. Donald Winnicott, on a visit to the Foundation, added
to the understanding of Chester with the use of his "squiggle technique."
Dr. Margaret Lowenfeld demonstrated her "world technique" with
Sheila and Sam. I had weekly conferences with Dr. Teresa Bernardez and
Dr. Joan Davidson, psychiatrists in training at the Menninger Foundation, reviewing and analyzing the development of certain girls who had
experienced special stress in relationships with their mothers. Two of

these, Sally and Janice, were discussed in papers by each of these authors (1965 and 1967).

C. Joseph Morgan carried on activity sessions (four hours each Saturday over a period of two years) with three boys who were under special stress during early adolescence. These sessions offered an opportunity to apply understanding achieved through the previous research and also to explore in full detail the experiences, feelings, and thoughts of these boys during their struggle to come to terms with approaching manhood. Dr. Tarlton Morrow and I met with Morgan weekly to discuss and share understanding of the boys' responses. Two reports were based on this work. Dr. Morrow wrote on growth experiences and Morgan described the content of the activity program.

In order to validate one impressive finding from the Rorschach test, namely, the low indices of ambition in comparison with those on metropolitan eastern children, Pitsa Hartocollis gave the Rorschach test to one hundred sixth-grade children in Topeka, confirming the finding (of low ambition) on our small sample.

We had from the beginning regarded our material as a pool of data available on a mutually shared basis for use by others than the funded research group. Thus we had invited participation by Dr. W. K. Sheldon first, and then by Dr. H. A. Witkin. At the prepuberty stage Dr. Riley Gardner of the Menninger Foundation made use of this pool for a study of personality structure in early adolescence. His own staff made examinations on cognitive style, and he enlisted the help of Dr. Moriarty in studying early development of the children for the book *Personality Development at Preadolescence* (1968). Another use of the pool of data was made by Dr. Clyde L. Rousey, who had developed an approach to diagnostic implications of speech sounds. Dr. Moriarty validated the postdicted problems reflected in distortions of speech, *Diagnostic Implications of Speech Sounds* (1965). (See chapter 8, part II.)

A third major study utilizing and adding to our data was Dr. Charles Stewart's investigation of religious views and attitudes. His book, *Adolescent Religion* (1967), made use of tests and interviews that he carried out, interviews of mothers carried out by an assistant on our staff, and the total longitudinal material and case summaries of six children.

Dr. Martin Mayman explored memories of the children as part of his studies of the relation between memory and ego development. The HIT was also given by Rosemary Mayman and results were analyzed by Dr. Holtzman and compared with his test results on a large sample of Texas children. Dr. Gardner Murphy and two associates carried out studies of extrasensory perception with Dr. Moriarty assisting and contributing creativity ratings for comparison with results on the extrasensory perception tests.

In addition to my appreciation for the generous interest and contributions of the people mentioned above, I want to add my appreciation of contributions to group and individual discussions from Joseph Sandler of the Hampstead Clinic, Humbert Nagera, Maria Dale, Margaret Mead, and Margaret Mahler, visiting lecturers at the Menninger Foundation. The late John Benjamin, the first site visitor, gave the project vigorous support. George Coelho was the first intramural NIMH scientist to offer warm interest and encouragement. Lawrence K. Frank was not only an enthusiastic visitor, but had fostered my commitment to interdisciplinary research through conferences he initiated as executive secretary of the Josiah Macy Foundation.

Even more fundamental was the influence of three child analysts: Erik Erikson, whose sensitive observations of the play of disturbed children (reported in a 1935 seminar at the Zachry Institute) inspired my MLT play method with normal children. His discussions of the sense of autonomy and of identity alerted me to the search for earliest beginnings in these areas. Ishak Ramzy opened doors to my explorations of infant experience, and Cotter Hirschberg's understanding of my interest in children's ways of coping bolstered confidence when ridicule from some quarters might have been discouraging. The notes and bibliography will put the reader in touch with the many other investigators who have stimulated my thinking.

I would like to express special gratitude to the perceptive, versatile, and gifted staff who carried on during my absences to NIMH conferences and other meetings in connection with utilization and dissemination of research. Their warmth with the families and one another were basic to the productivity of the studies. Especially crucial was the social sensitivity of Marie Smith, Secretary of the project, who followed Grace Heider's gracious contacts with the families in the beginning and who maintained their active cooperation through all the years of research. In addition to this, her expertise in keeping track of schedules as well as voluminous records made it possible for us all to be where we were supposed to be at the time we were supposed to be there. Among the many careful and expert typists who endured the often tedious work of transcribing tapes and dictabelts, typing lists and tables, and copying revisions of manuscripts were Joan Whitby, Arlene Hamilton, and especially Marge McElhenny, who generously typed some final revisions at home.

For their generous support we are profoundly grateful to Drs. Will and

Karl Menninger and to many people at NIMH, especially Dr. Caroline Chandler, who trusted us to be productive in our exploratory, hypothesis-forming series of studies in what was a new area at the time we began. Lester Roach, Irving Sheffel, and Basil Cole of the Menninger Foundation administrative staff constantly eased our way with appropriate settings. Dr. Karl Menninger's discussions of reactions to stress along with his encouragement of detailed observation contributed substantially to the development of our concepts. As director of research as well as personal friend to nearly all of us involved in the study, Gardner Murphy's inspiration, enthusiasm, and suggestions helped to make the low points of research few and far between.

In addition to the Menninger Foundation and NIMH, financial support came from the Gustavus and Louisa Pfeiffer Foundation, from the Neumeyer Foundation, and from some members of the research group who paid for their own expenses and special assistants at certain points.

Finally, at different stages in the evolution of this book certain readers played a creative role: William E. Henry at the beginning; Wayne Holtzman, a helpful consultant throughout; and L. Joseph Stone during the final draft. Their generous suggestions and friendly criticisms are reflected throughout the book. Of course, in the end, all responsibility for the formulations and hypotheses lies with the authors.

In addition to her contributions at all levels of the research, Alice E. Moriarty contributed the report on speech in chapter 8 and the report on the Kennedy assassination in chapter 9. She read and made suggestions on all chapters of the book as I wrote them. Jane Isay's warm and creative editorial guidance was crucial in the final shaping of the manuscript, and Judy Metro's expertise contributed to clarity at many points.

Lois Barclay Murphy
Chief Investigator

VULNERABILITY, COPING, AND GROWTH

Introduction

One may look at any object—a mountain, an elephant, a growing human being—in any one of several different ways. One may be interested in a detailed examination of mountain rock and its potentiality for producing a desired type of ore; or one may examine its trees and other flora; or one may look at the mountain as a whole; or further, one may consider its evolution and how it came to be. Beyond these, one may be interested in it primarily as one mountain in a range that has a certain contribution to a broad geographical area, such as its role as a watershed.

For one kind of approach microscopes and other detailed measures may be necessary; for another approach a broad review of historical factors; and for another approach an overview of the relation of the mountain to the surrounding territory. We need not reiterate the often quoted allegory of the blind men who try to find out what an elephant is, each by a careful exploration of one part. The prevalent child psychology research orientation, with its emphasis on elegant methodology, instills among some groups a tendency to assume that the only way to learn anything about a mountain, an elephant, or a child is to use the microscope at one point after another. This methodologically "sophisticated" approach has produced a great deal of extremely important and interesting information. And yet the efforts to look at whole, normal children in our culture are still rare; without such efforts, we shall be deprived of guidelines and hypotheses regarding the meaning and interrelations of the variables so beautifully studied. In this book we offer one approach to a view of the developing child as a whole; this leads us to scrutinize the interrelationships of certain key aspects of the child's functioning as these persist or change in the course of development.

We have one broad aim: to increase our understanding of the development of individual children as they grow up in a relatively stable community and as they confront the everyday demands and stresses typical for children in this society. In order to do this we must look first at the setting—neither fast-paced, crowded metropolitan, nor isolated rural; neither hot south nor predominantly cold north—but a middle-sized town in the "heartland" of the nation. We need to look at the culture of this Bible Belt area and at the typical patterns of family life,

3

especially mothering. But then we must concentrate on the children—how they deal with the experiences of infancy and early childhood, how their coping patterns continue or change, and how the latter are related to differences in equipment and in the children's own contributions to their experience. Our interest is in processes of development, and especially in the contributions of coping efforts to these processes.

What processes?

Even a four-week-old baby has had hundreds of thousands of interactions with his environment involving various combinations of basic learning processes: classical and operant conditioning, imprinting, canalization, patterning, programming. Our task does not involve elucidation of these learning processes, which have been extensively investigated by others (Hilgard and Bower 1974). Rather, we are concerned with the more global problem of how a child mobilizes and uses his resources as they are modified by the outcomes of learning processes; that is, how he puts his resources to work to meet his needs and to get along in the environment. This includes coping with obstacles, frustration, and discomfort or pain, and also utilizing existent opportunities (or those he can evoke) for gratification and for growth and support of integration. Our task also involves an effort to understand the integration and transformation of his resources. In chapter 11, for instance, we shall see how in one infant a strong drive to elaborate oral gratification (many mouthing, bubbling, vocalizing activities) in a context of mild deprivation and ambivalence in other zones (tactual, relationship with mother) together with a capacity for elaborating or multiplying patterns of vocal and affective expression, led to a sequence of efforts that used successively: aggressive intrusive impulses in the preschool (phallic) stage, capacities for industrious effort in the school years (latency stage), and sublimations afforded by sports, religion, science, and music in adolescence. At each stage the *style* of elaboration of impulse and effort persisted, but with successive transformations of the modality of expression and with an increasingly socialized modulation of intensity. This is neither drive development nor ego development as such, but an evolving integration of resources utilized by the growing individual to meet needs in ways that increasingly fitted into culturally approved channels. These differentiations, modulations, transformations, and integrations of drives and ego functions led to a characteristic coping style in this socially responsive child.

In scrutinizing the development of the children, we were concerned with continuities and changes both in aspects of equipment and in patterns of coping with the environment that support or contribute to mastery of external pressures. Also, patterns of coping with internal stress arising from sensitivities, difficulties in vegetative functioning, and other vulnerabilities preoccupied our attention.

Background of the Coping Project

On both sides of the Atlantic at about the time we started our work a good many people, including Anna Freud in London and Robert W. White at Harvard, were emphasizing the lack of knowledge of how normal development proceeds and the lack of concepts to deal with the maintenance of normality. All across the United States and outside as well, studies of large samples of children had shown that what we call "problems" actually occur with almost predictable frequency in any group of normal children. It became increasingly clear that there is no such thing as an individual who goes through the complete developmental span from infancy to adulthood without problems. The difference between children who become seriously disturbed and those who remain within the normal group could not be thought of in terms of the presence or lack of problems, but rather the way in which problems are handled.

Studies of mechanisms of dealing with conflicts had been derived from studies of neurotic adults; the mechanisms used were often considered to be pathogenic in themselves, even though Anna Freud, Fenichel, and others pointed to the necessary structuring of personality by defenses through which normal people deal with their conflicts and problems. We wanted to find out, then, what coping patterns were used by children who managed to stay "normal."

We also wanted to learn what we could about factors in individual children that tended to make some rely more on certain kinds of problem-solving methods and defense mechanisms and to make others rely on different ones; in other words, to find out what were the characteristics contributing to different styles of coping. We use the term coping as a general term to include defense mechanisms, active ways of solving problems, and methods for handling stress that do not come under the heading of defense mechanisms and problem-solving methods. The term applies as well to larger patterns of structuring and orchestrating combinations of coping devices and defense mechanisms.

In taking this close look, we have been receiving help in seeing how difficulties in children can be looked at in terms of a continuum. The work of Pasamanick and his colleagues (1956) deals with behavior difficulties and with deviations (such as retardation) that are correlated with disturbances in pregnancy and delivery. Some of the latter are not at all severe, and the behavior difficulties are not necessarily severe. It no longer makes sense to think of children in bipolar groups, for example, normal versus pathological or brain damaged. Rather, the empirical material justifies looking at children in terms of a distribution from optimal normality, on the one hand, through a continuum or series of steps, including very minimally brain damaged, up to degrees of brain damage that interfere grossly with the cognitive, motor, and emotional functioning of the child. The same orientation can be applied to other aspects of vulnerability.

Lacey's work (1952) on individual patterns of autonomic reactivity deals both with degrees of reactivity and with the channels through which autonomic reactivity is expressed. Here again we are no longer justified in thinking of children with normally manageable autonomic responsiveness versus those who are over-reactive in autonomic terms; again there is a continuum of reactivity.

The same is true when we look at the review of biochemical factors that Roger Williams (1956) presents. He puts it very vividly in saying that every individual is deviant in some respects from the norms. And if we look at Sheldon's measurement of body dimensions (1940), we see that only a relatively small proportion of children approximate a balance in the endomorphic, mesomorphic, and ectomorphic areas. Rather we find that many children deviate in one direction or another and that there are extremes in each of the three directions.

Moreover, all studies of growth show that many children have growth irregularities and that the "normal" or average pattern of growth at comparable rates in every aspect of physical and mental development is actually rather unusual. Systematic detailed analyses of Gesell tests and other tests of infants have shown that some children are considerably ahead in certain systems and behind in others: for instance, some children are ahead in social functioning but behind in motor functioning, or ahead in social and language functioning but behind in the adaptive functions that make it possible to handle the stimulation to which their social and language precocity exposes them. In other words, the range of structural and developmental patterns can also be seen in terms of a continuum from well-balanced to extremely unbalanced patterns of maturation.

We did not have adequate data to deal with all these physiological and neurological factors, since we relied chiefly on pediatric, psychiatric, and psychological examinations along with observations of the children in play situations and interviews with mothers. It is doubtful whether one could carry on an adequate longitudinal study of biochemical, autonomic, EEG, and other uncomfortable measurements on a naïve normal group without losing the cooperation of many subjects. The limit of tolerance has to be respected, especially when one is not offering treatment of any kind.

The problem of prediction

The problem of predicting adult personality from childhood behavior is far more difficult than retrospectively sorting out factors that contributed to difficulties, as clinicians do every day. Macfarlane (1972) has illustrated failures of prediction in the careful clinically oriented longitudinal study of a random sample of children in Berkeley. Why can't we predict better? From cultural anthropology we know that by and large children learn to move, absorb, communicate, dress, then reproduce and support their families in ways typical of their own societies. Learning theory supplies some explanations of the conditioning processes that contribute to this process of becoming a member of the culture, and psychoanalytic concepts of identification and internalization, mastering traumata and conflicts, add further explanations. But in the fifties no one predicted that groups of American youth would react to the next decade's war with vigorous, even violent, protests.

To be sure, longitudinal studies have documented individual differences in rate and pattern of physical development (Bayley 1956; Stolz and Stolz 1971). But Macfarlane (1971) notes that 58 percent of children in her longitudinal study changed from 15 to 50 points in IQ between the ages of six to eighteen, and no one has been able to predict which child's IQ will go down or up or by how much. Longitudinal studies point to different patterns of continuity and change in different children and imply a need for further study of dynamics of change and factors in different degrees of plasticity in different children. In short, the assumption of general continuity has to be modified.

The dynamics of development

One difficulty here may arise from the model followed: psychology in the model of classical physics has tended to focus on static principles; in the model of biology the focus is on evolution and growth. Perspectives on any question about human functioning through time may also gain depth from a consideration of the history of cultures; history deals with the interplay of multiple factors contributing to both continuity and change. The history of individuals also involves continuity and change.

The data for this book were collected in the 1950s and 1960s; the analysis and reflection upon the data and preparation of this book continued into the next decade. During these years the Murphys visited India three times and Israel, Egypt, Nigeria, Japan, West Germany, the Soviet Union, Greece, Britain, and many other European countries along with much travel through the United States including Hawaii. Our observations of the demeanor and posture of the children and adults in the many different culture groups we visited gave perspective to our studies of the middle-western children and parents of Kansas, especially with reference to issues of self-respect versus self-denigration, autonomy versus subservience, coping vigor versus passivity. Nigerians are a proud upstanding group who walk with a broad stride and vigorous gait. The people of Israel in 1950 were resonant with vitality and the freedom that comes from new-found safety, autonomy, and coherence of action and belief. Conversely, in the United States one still sees in some states below the Mason-Dixon line the self-denigration in some black hunched shoulders that is comparable only to that of some untouchables in India.

We also observed differences in infant experience relevant to the development of coping. Babies in certain healthy Indian villages we visited rarely cried. Carried in a sling under the shoulder throw of the mother's sari, often with access to her breast, what could one cry about? Any restlessness is quickly felt by the mother, and with all the body contact and rhythm of the mother's movement, soothing does not have to be a special operation. This early experience of instant soothing response by the mother and access to the breast for two or more years may contribute to both the tolerance or patience and the dependence seen by the late Dr. Maiti* as widely characteristic of Indian personality. And the maternal empathy and perceptiveness experienced by the baby are presumably internalized by the baby as well, perhaps contributing to the perceptiveness reported by E. M. Forster in *A Passage to India* (1924) and by others. In those parts of Africa where a baby is carried on its mother's back in a wide sash, there is also much body contact, rhythm, and immediate response by mother to restlessness. In these cultures, does the constant closeness to the mother's body in the early months and the ready feeding contribute to basic security that underlies tolerance for later frustration? Dr. Thomas Lambo says this is so.* We are beginning to get the detailed studies of baby-care patterns among different cultures that could help us answer similar questions (Ainsworth and Bell 1969, Mead 1942).

One is tempted to link the delicate, precise visual differentiation reflected in India's exquisite handcrafts to a maximization of vision

---

* Personal communication.

experienced by babies carried comfortably close to their mothers for two or three years. The carried baby has little opportunity for autonomous locomotion but maximal opportunity for observation and differentiation of observed objects and scenes. That vision and hearing are basic to cognitive development is obvious, and this is confirmed when we find twenty-four babies of Escalona's (1968) sample of thirty-two with both medium to high developmental status as measured by cognitive tests and medium to high importance of distance receptors (vision and hearing). The remaining scattered ratings provide some exceptions that suggest consideration of other factors that may interfere with or support development as evaluated by tests.

Cultural influences are largely mediated by the mother's handling of the baby, as we have just illustrated. As Escalona (1968, chap. 2) has elucidated, the actual immediate experience of the baby is what counts in shaping its development. But in addition to the mother, the baby experiences many qualities of the environment—the space, noise, colors, patterns, movements of family and visitors, exposure to the outside world, as well as interactions with the rest of the family are all important parts of the baby's experience. Extending the concept of ecological psychology developed by the Barkers and their colleagues, we may think of noise pollution, lack of a range of visual stimuli, and even uterine pollution by nicotine, alcohol, and other drugs as aspects of the baby's earliest ecological setting.

Margaret Mead has often said that the whole pattern of a culture is reflected in each area of its life. If this is so, is the middle-western culture reflected in the mother's respect for an infant's autonomy? And what aspects of the culture are reflected in the limits mothers set on a child's experiments with the environment? What do continuities and changes in experience from infancy to adulthood contribute to the middle-western character and its characteristic coping patterns?

All along, we were interested both in differences between children and aspects of their constitutional equipment, and in the relation of their experience to these differences. Experience includes both the ongoing daily pattern of response to stimulation and management of self and the environment, and the punctuating—disrupting or enhancing—special events that contribute to peak experiences, both of trauma and of comfort or joy.

While the primary focus of our studies from 1953 was on the child's coping methods and individual differences in constitution and experience related to these, we were soon impressed with certain ingrained difficulties characteristic of some children, difficulties contributing to vulnerability. Along with this, the resilience reflected in the capacity of some children to cope with their vulnerabilities—and stress often augmented by the vulnerabilities—was equally impressive. Gradually, then, we became aware of (1) the child's effort to deal with some of these basic factors in development and (2) the contribution to the child's emerging personality of efforts to cope with innate vulnerability and their outcome.

In this book we are providing an overview of some results of our studies of children from middle-class middle America. They have grown up able to meet the demands of their families, to complete high school, to establish heterosexual relationships at appropriate levels, and to undertake a vocation. Many of the children received one or more distinctions in school, Scouts, 4-H Club, or other local childhood organizations. Some went beyond this and completed college. In short, they are a competent group. They are now young adults, most of them married, and each one filling a niche in the core society—teaching, repairing cars, running a bookshop, clerking in a store, overseeing accounts in a large agency, and so on. None are delinquents or alienated or radical. Granted, they do not initiate major social changes, but they may well be the ballast that keeps the American boat from rocking too much.

This overview makes use of many separate analyses of the records on the children (see the bibliography) along with new analyses of continuity and change. Within a relatively consistent eco-cultural setting, mothers and babies varied in their adaptational style, their "fit" with each other and their mutual enjoyment. The children varied in vulnerability, in stress from illness, accidents, losses, and environmental pressures; they also varied in resources for coping with both vulnerability and stress. The outcomes of their coping efforts helped to modify the early patterns that reflected constitutional equipment and to shape what they became. In this era when so many children in large cities develop learning problems, hyperactivity, and violent behavior, and when adult anxiety about the economy, housing, world situation, and environment is chronic, it is useful to take a close look at influences surrounding the development of children in a relatively calm setting of comfortable living space, relative economic security, and family stability.

The Challenge of Longitudinal Studies

How does one distill the potentially useful understandings from 50 to 150 one- to four-hour sessions with twenty-five to thirty children over the eighteen-year period from early infancy to high school graduation? Most longitudinal studies have tackled similar challenges by focusing on one or two areas at a time, as with studies of physical development (Stolz and Stolz 1971) and of mental development (Bayley 1949) and of changes in problem behavior over twelve years (Macfarlane, Allen, and Honzik 1954). Studies of important transition phases have included Tuddenham's study of Rorschachs over the early adolescent period. Gesell and Amatruda (1939) early added a review of brief "biographies" of eighty children from infancy through childhood to their cross-section studies of children.

Our own responses to this need have included comparisons of infancy with preschool functioning (Escalona and Heider 1959; Heider 1966); detailed discussions of preschool coping methods (Murphy 1962); a clinical study of continuity and change in IQ (Moriarty 1966); studies of ways of coping with the developmental crises in individuals (Davidson 1967; Bernardez 1965; Morgan 1964; Morrow 1965); case studies of the development of personality structure at adolescence (Gardner and Moriarty 1968); group and individual studies of religion in adolescents (Stewart 1967); adolescent coping styles with biographies of the development of these styles (Toussieng and Moriarty, forthcoming). Most of these studies have included both group analyses and individual biographies from infancy to the age levels on which the authors focused.

Interested readers clamored for something more—"how does it all add up?" Obviously it isn't possible to boil it all down without losing much of the uniqueness of each child at each stage, yet boiling down is necessary. Offering twenty-five or thirty biographies was one possibility, but only at the risk of losing sight of general principles and central concepts that emerged. Moreover, there was an obvious need to integrate findings from our different studies, especially those dealing with continuity and change and with the relationships between later forms of behavior and earlier functioning.

In this book we try to share with the reader some of the main findings on the group—its infancy behavior, then preschool, then continuities and changes from infancy through later development—followed by reflections on stability and plasticity in personality development and processes involved in change. Through this analysis recurrent themes can be seen: the vulnerability of the child in relation to pressures and stress from the environment, and the resources the child finds in himself and in the environment. Consequently, in another section we provide a fuller discussion of vulnerability with a close-up look by Alice Moriarty at the area of speech in which it is reflected; illustrations of responses to two stress situations including Moriarty's summary of the teenagers' responses to JFK's assassination and a close look at factors and steps in resilience and recovery. Brief vignettes of individual children illustrate most points throughout these chapters, and a fuller case study of one child integrates many of the processes we observed.

We present both illustrative case material and analyses of the process of development. Since we are interested in the evolution of the child's coping style, and the process through which the child maintains continuity or modifies his style, we are concerned with individual children and the interaction of aspects of their experience.

What is the place of this study among other studies of the development of personality or of adaptational style? Kagan and Moss in *Birth to Maturity* (1962) offer cogent evidence for continuity in certain aspects of behavior such as aggression, especially between the latency period and adulthood. Robert White in numerous studies, such as *Lives in Progress* and *The Study of Lives*, offers subtle studies of the complex interweaving of drives and capacities as seen from retrospective data. Roger and Louise Barker and Herbert Wright (1954) give us a psychologically oriented view of the ecology and subculture in which a child's behavior is observed at a given time. In none of these do we see the ongoing process by which dispositions are utilized by individual children in meeting adaptational challenges.

The richness in our research derives from the interdisciplinary approach at every level. The limitations are related to the lack of the physiological, neuropsychological depth and other types of technical detail requiring instrumentalized measurements that we could not use.

Contributing to the special character of this study are the availability of unique direct observations in the first six months of life by three simultaneous observers of Escalona's staff; the simultaneous study of intensive multidisciplinary case records and elementary statistical analysis of ratings; the analysis of both correlations between infancy and later data and of records of individual children at subsequent phases; and the qualitative study of processes of development as these appear to have been influenced by the child's efforts to cope with both his intrinsic vulnerabilities and the environmental stress to which he is sequentially exposed.

We undertook this study as a hypothesis-developing exploration, one which could extend our assumptions regarding the process of development. This involved forming concepts and preliminary tools that could be refined for use in further studies by other investigators. These hypotheses and concepts can be found in the reports listed in our bibliography as well as throughout this book.

Here we are attempting to add it up—not all, to be sure, for that would require an unmanageable tome. But we are sharing a picture of growing-up processes and outcomes that has not been generally seen: the child is an active, dynamic creature who quietly or noisily tries to select from the environment what satisfies his individual vegetative, sensory, motor, cognitive, and social needs. The child tries to protect himself and herself from disintegrative reactions to overwhelming or disturbing stimuli and pressures. These are experienced differentially in line with particular sensitivities, vulnerabilities and checkerboards of weakness and strength in the child, and the particular supports, compensations, or burdens provided by the family.

Each child struggles to find solutions and out of these struggles and these solutions develops an implicit or explicit view of life as well as of self. And so the personality is not just a pattern of predetermined (genetic) givens but an achievement or outcome of coping with the challenges and opportunities life has offered. When severe trauma, usually coupled with marked vulnerability, has disorganized the child or blocked development, therapy helps to mend the psychological fences or provide restitution for deprivation. Some vulnerable infants become more vulnerable as they grow; others are slow to develop effective ways of coping with the stress resulting from the interaction of their vulnerabilities with their environment. But when, as with most of this group, a child has been able to muddle through—by some combination of selection, escape, protest, or reconstruction of the situation—tolerance, strength, creativity, or triumph, or all of these, may be the outcome.

PART I
THE SETTING

1

Ecological Setting, Culture, and Development

I was born upon the prairie, where the wind blew free and there was nothing to break the light of the sun. I was born where there were no enclosures and where everything drew a free breath.

Ten Bears, Yamparike Comanche, to U.S. Commissioners at Medicine Lodge Creek, October 1867

Some of this basic experience of freedom to roam in the sun and pure air still belongs to the children of Topeka. The settings in which children grow up vary from culture to culture, and these variations influence the opportunities for independent exploration, the kinds and amount of sensory stimulation, the types of challenge to mastery of the environment, as well as the tempo and rhythm of life and the child's sense of safety or threat in the world around him. Climate, geography, and patterns of child care are all involved here—in short, ecology along with culture, since culture patterns may exploit or be shaped by various nourishing aspects of the ecology.[1] So too does culture modulate, compensating for or protecting from dangerous features of the environment. And the ways of coping with the elements, the givens of the environment, provide models, support, or limits to each child's ways of coping with the challenges of his life.

The ambience of different cultural groups varies with the climate, but we have little hard data on the effect on children. Is the gentle style of native Hawaiians and some South Sea islanders[2] organically related to the smooth, gentle trade winds that caress each body from infancy, bodies unburdened by thick clothing? Does the tenser posture of people of the Plains states evolve from the necessary defense against strong winds? Only Robert Coles (1971), in his descriptions of children in Mississippi and Appalachia, illustrates the meaning and value to children of their closeness to the land, the hills, the streams, the sun.

Compared to the babies whose development we are talking about here, Nigerian babies tied closely on their mothers' backs[3] or Indian babies riding in a sling over their mothers' shoulders must have different

17

experiences of space and visual stimulation, less freedom to move about, more body contact as a foundation of attachment to mothers, less opportunity for infantile autonomy, and more subtle ways of signaling their needs (by a mere wiggle). And the children growing up in large joint families in India, where they hear much talk around them, have a different stimulus for language development from that of babies in Topeka, many of whose mothers talk to them individually from their earliest weeks. Despite the rich reports of anthropologists, we know far too little about the specific contributions of these and other differences in the children's early environments. Without the opportunity for close accurate comparisons, our conclusions have to remain hypotheses.

Conclusions can be drawn from the common denominators of a wide sample of cultures and subcultures (Whiting and Child 1952). Short of this, all conclusions from all research on children have to be seen as relative to the culture, or rather subculture, in which the children were observed. For example, I have seen one year olds on Florida beaches who have already developed skills for avoiding obstacles such as a low fence—skills that I have not observed in one-year-old babies in New York. No taxonomy of coping patterns based on one culture could be assumed to be universal; the coping patterns develop in response to specific challenges, supports, and restrictions.

Our observations of the setting that exposed these Topeka children to a particular pattern of nurturance and obstacles, stress and support, challenge and strengths can, we hope, stimulate others to reflect on the particular balance of positive and negative influences in other settings.

The Kansans are given to understatement, not to rhetoric; they do not express their love of the country in excited ravings over its beauty. Rather, it is implicit in their attachment and their reluctance to move away. Only five of the twenty-seven families in the "intensive" group[4] of our study moved away from Kansas during the childhood of this group, and all of those went to small cities; they are quietly antimetropolis. They value roots and a "settled" feeling. This contrasts with the mobility of professional, military, or business families,[5] whose briefer residence and wider range provides growing children with a different spectrum of rewarding and limiting experiences, of challenge and learning, but also stress, and strain on integrative capacities as they repeatedly confront new styles of life. Kansans' relative stability also differentiates them from both the upwardly mobile climbers of the big cities—those who move geographically, "sent" by their corporations (Whyte 1956)—and migrant workers (Coles 1967). Moves that did occur were on the initiative of the individual and motivated by response to an opportunity for a better salary or a more congenial job and did not take the family to a large metropolis. Many people had ties to rural life and farm relatives to visit, which, along with vacations, extended their geographical range within the huge Middle West.

For our group of children, continuity of home base means continuity of tempo, style, values, and the security of belonging in the larger environment. It may also mean continuity in learning and adaptation where there is congruence between home, neighborhood, and school.[6] A child who has learned "not to talk back" to his parents may be better prepared to learn "not to talk in school unless spoken to by the teacher."

The Uniformities and Continuity of Topeka

In a country as heterogeneous as that of the United States, with life lived as differently as it is from Maine to Key West and from the Bronx to Santa Barbara, it may seem hard to define general criteria of a "typical" American life for children against which to examine the development of children in any one area. Yet the life of children in Topeka is probably characteristic for the huge Middle West—a sizable country in itself.[7]

For Topeka is in the center of the nation and of a large area of the Middle West, stretching north, south, east and west. In 1950, 26.9 million people lived in cities of between 50,000 and 500,000. In 1970, the number increased to 41.5 million.[8] Many of these cities are in a large diamond that excludes the "eastern," "western," "southern" areas and also the northern metropolitan cities of the United States. Here many people are like those in Topeka: churchgoing and family-centered, each family living in its own house, owning its own car, and, in these days of expanded recreation facilities, sometimes a boat. Child-rearing emphases generally parallel those in "Middletown" (Lynd and Lynd 1929), but Topeka mothers place a higher value on tolerance (Appendix 3).

Resources of the setting

Curled in a curve of the Kaw River, the city of Topeka, capital of Kansas, is the home of the Menninger Foundation, Washburn University, the Forbes Air Force Base, the Santa Fe Railway operations, and some large industries such as Goodyear Tires, in addition to huge wheat elevators. Twenty-five miles east in Lawrence, the University of Kansas looks from its hilltop campus over the rolling farms, woods, and creeks that fill the land between the two cities. Here the more ambitious students among our research sample went to college. Sixty-five miles east, Kansas City, the area's big metropolis, attracts the people of Topeka for visits from time to time. A day's drive to the west are the mountains of Colorado, a favorite vacation area for Kansans, including many families in our sample. No farther away are the ranches of Texas, where relatives of some of our Kansas families are engaged in cattle raising or related activity. Even the poorest families of our group visited relatives within this broad area; while few of them traveled to the East Coast, all of them were familiar with the geography of the middle western and mountain areas.

The country around Topeka is neither flat nor empty; not for another fifty miles to the west does the prairie flatten out so that one can see a road for ten miles ahead. While the ground is not yet flat, and the horizon is never a straight line, the skies are open, wide, and deep blue.[9]

Sunsets are ample, often filling the whole sky with a typical Kansas crimson, yellow, or copper glow, sometimes soft, sometimes brilliant. Several man-made lakes are sheltered in the hollows between small wooded ridges and hills.[10] One of them is only minutes by car from the center of Topeka. Families go there to picnic, fish, row, or explore the lake by motorboat. Children keep the steel playground swings creaking on weekends in the often balmy spring and fall and all week long in the summertime. Mothers speak of their pleasure in the lovely landscape.

Space and ease

The century-old main streets of Topeka are wide, six- to eight-lane avenues; traffic is not nervously crowded between uneasily parked cars.[11] The wide sidewalks in the downtown shopping areas allow ample room for pedestrians. Neither the cars nor the children shopping with their mothers squawk impatiently. The age of the town can be gauged by the rows of elms, oaks, maples, and locust trees that have grown so tall that their branches reach toward each other to make cool arcades in the hot spells of summer. The older area of the city is laced with many small parks and playgrounds, all wooded and usually divided by one of the broad creeks that run through the city. In contrast to many parks in big cities in the 1950s, there were no Keep Off the Grass signs. Many parks have play apparatus and game areas available to children; there are also six swimming pools and seven recreation centers that offer craft instruction.

"It's a good little town," one doctor said, when we asked him why he had settled in Topeka to practice. Many of our study group parents commented, "We like Topeka. It's a good place to bring up children," and the children agreed. The unpressured atmosphere doubtless contributed both to the stability of residence among the majority of families in our studies, and to the complaints of some children in the few families who moved away. It is not surprising when these children say, "I wish we could come back to Topeka."

Weather

Topeka weather rarely reaches the outer temperature extremes, but it often varies within short time periods. On a morning in spring, the thermometer may read in the thirties, and then shoot up to the high eighties by midafternoon. The *Encyclopaedia Britannica* (14th edition, 1929) states: "The climate of Kansas is exceptionally salubrious. Extremes of heat and cold occur, but as a rule the winters are dry and mild, while the summer heats are tempered by the perpetual prairie breezes, and the summer nights are usually cool and refreshing."

This exhilarating climate has also doubtless contributed to the vigor, stability, and longevity of the population. There are complaints about the occasional summer heat waves, but the disadvantages are forgotten in the pleasure of exploring the open spaces and lakes. The early spring and the long fall, combined with a lack of heavy long-lasting snow, make it possible for Topeka's children to run around in T-shirts and blue jeans much of the year. There is less need for the cumbersome snowsuits that hamper northeastern children's free movement from November to April.

But despite the advantages of the climate, the changing moods of the natural elements have long posed occasional problems to the town. The Kaw River, which bisects the city, is a shallow overgrown stream, although in the 1850s it was actually navigable. Its rare floods can be torrential, and the worst one of recent times flooded the homes of a few of the families in our group; in one family a toddler was hospitalized for three months at the time of the big flood of 1951.[12] Following this came the preschool years of our group with relative drought and endless days of clear blue sky, days when these children could run free out of doors.

Tornadoes dip into farmlands and towns across Kansas every spring, but only once has severe damage occurred within the city limits. Until then one heard an old Indian legend that "a tornado never hits the town directly." Established residents play down the hazards. "When you've grown up with tornadoes you know what to do [go to the cellar until it passes over]," remarked several mothers in our group. The alertness of well-prepared citizens and the excellent warning system kept the mortality rate very low (only seventeen deaths) in that great 1966 tornado, despite the devastation to property with losses into millions of dollars. This effective warning system may typify a prevalent readiness to cope actively with threat or disaster (see chapter 9).

Economic conditions

In spite of early difficulties in the wilderness, the city of Topeka gradually grew to its present rank of third in population among the cities of Kansas. In 1950 Topeka's population was about 78,800; by 1960 the population had grown to nearly 120,000.[13] New industries, expanding businesses, Forbes Air Base, and low food costs due to proximity of distribution outlets all contributed to the steady annual migration to Topeka. Forbes Air Base at the southern end of the city is a headquarters for jet aircraft development and personnel training. The frequent low-flying airplanes stimulated the fantasy of our study children in their earliest years; a teenager remarked that one of his early memories was that of wondering how it would feel to fly in a plane.

The expansion of the city involved much construction of homes and commercial and industrial buildings. Several fathers among our research group were employed in this expansion as carpenter, electrician, linoleum layer, contractor, and home decorator. Others worked in the Santa Fe shops and various local industries. A small number were engaged in auxiliary white collar jobs. (See Appendix 2.)

The fifties were economically secure years for most of the families. In contrast to the depression years, this era was characterized by increasing wages, production, and stores of grain, rising birth rates and housing, and greater highway construction and automobile traffic on the roads.

Against this background, such unemployment as there was in Topeka in 1952–55 caused little anxiety to families other than the few directly affected.[14] In this atmosphere, unemployment and low wages seemed a matter of temporary bad luck rather than a symptom of an insecure era and therefore a threatening hazard. Relatives contributed food, clothing, and, for at least one family, rent, during the out-of-work periods. The two boys we knew in one of the poorest families were among the most confident in the group in their early years, undisturbed by the mild economic ups and downs.

Our group of children in Topeka was not exposed to the conflicts arising from growing up amidst extremes of wealth and poverty side by side.[15] Whereas children in New York or Boston might see luxurious apartments around the corner from their slum homes, extreme luxury is almost nonexistent in Topeka. Family life centered in the home. (The Russian psychologist A. R. Luria remarked on visiting Topeka, "The joy of America is in its individual homes.")

Inexpensive products from mail-order houses made it possible for low-income families to furnish their homes in good taste and to dress attractively. As Margaret Mead noted while visiting the coping project in the fifties, the working class wives would have been able to step into a major New York hotel without attracting attention as a person "from the sticks" or as different from an eastern middle-class patron. While half a dozen of our families live on unpaved streets, there were so many miles of unpaved streets outside the central areas of Topeka that this in itself does not identify the families as disadvantaged. In fact, some of the more attractive houses in wooded outskirts of the city were also on unpaved streets or roads.

In other words the conditions of life in Topeka were more equalitarian and more like those in a "one class town" such as still exists in the Middle West (Barker et al. 1950). Many working-class families had very few books or magazines, yet all the children had bicycles, and skillful fathers constructed backyard jungle gyms and, later, basketball and other play equipment.

To the older members of the staff who have traveled back and forth across the United States in the twenties and thirties, the middle-class leveling, with its tendency to produce homogeneity in taste and behavior, contrasted with earlier differences between the "hick town" and "big city" styles. Husbands at work, of course, still looked different—with the difference recognized by the terms "blue collar" and "white collar." But these same husbands at a bowling alley with their wives, or on a picnic at one of the large parks, or out in the woods and fields hunting with their eight-year-old boys in the fall, or fishing on a nearby lake, were not easy to distinguish from one another. Neither could working-class and business-class families be singled out easily by the level of enunciation or extent of vocabulary. In many blue collar families the level of wit, fluency, and clarity of speech equaled that of business-class families.

Varying sizes of house, yard, and household equipment for children produced no significant correlations with our measures of coping except for one item: the presence of a piano.[16] Working-class children had play resources and equipment not available to business class children whose fathers were not so "handy." One carpenter father made a boat used for regular weekend boating, water skiing, and swimming activities. Appliances were also available to mothers. In what was probably the poorest as well as the largest family in the group, the father was extremely resourceful in mending cars and obtaining cast-off equipment from junk piles or cheap secondhand shops. In return for repairing his neighbors' cars, neighbors repaired for him an electric washing machine, a dishwasher, and other gadgets that he had selected from junkyards; these facilitated the mother's care of her large family.

These constructive activities gave children a firsthand opportunity to watch and often to "help" their fathers; thus they could learn how to put things together, how to make things, what things were made of, and other facts and orientations important in everyday coping. We do not mean to imply that there were no deprivations for the working-class group; they often lacked money for concerts and even for movies as well as magazines and books.

The subjective concept of "culturally deprived" is sometimes equated with "poor" or with "lower socioeconomic groups." [17] Grace Heider noted that while some families in our group had difficulty making ends meet, only one "felt poor" (this was the family in which the father, out of work for extended periods of time, became depressed and alcoholic, and where the mother was also at times discouraged and limp). The attitude in the other "poorest" family was that of "poor but proud." Most typical were the self-respecting families who felt themselves to be part of the solid working class, proud of their forebears, proud of their extended families, and proud of their children. To have "a fine boy" or "a good child" is a source of great satisfaction.

Finally, these families are not class conscious.[18] They think of themselves as American rather than as belonging to a distinct class. They do not belong to many organizations outside the church, which is the center of their community life as well as the authority for beliefs.

Recreation

Our children were not much exposed to TV until the 1960s. Interest in spectator sports was and still is high. College basketball attracted 125,000 spectators annually and college football ran a close second with 110,000. Almost any summer evening children and adults will convert a vacant lot into a baseball diamond; half a dozen baseball diamonds provide space for Little Leaguers from elementary school through junior high school age. Parents' interest in sports activities is strong, as can be attested to by watching any high school, grade school, or Little League game.

The presence of many lakes and surrounding wooded park lands contributed to the popularity of fishing and hunting in their respective seasons. During the fall, hunting for deer, coyotes, pheasants, and quail was common; by the age of eight or nine some boys had guns to shoot squirrels or rabbits. A bounty was offered for coyotes. Certain boys in our preschool study group told how they would be allowed to go hunting with their fathers when they got to be eight or nine years old, and two boys whose fathers did not take them hunting openly expressed feelings of deprivation.

People of both sexes and all ages go fishing in the many lakes from spring through summer and fall, and fishing was actively promoted by the State Recreation Commission, which stocks lakes and ponds and keeps the public informed as to the type of fishing available at different times in specific lakes. These activities, along with the acceptable and adventurous sports common to the area, continue to provide channels for aggressive drives.

Life for the young children, especially the boys, had a vitality derived from the range of outdoor activities and their freedom to roam as well as from the contact with a large extended family and the lore of the grandparents. The children were, in a sense, closer to certain aspects of what might be termed the "fantasy world"—at least in the sense that they were in the West itself. While to an eastern child the Lone Ranger and Gene Autry were inhabitants of a distant and unreachable land, such figures were not remote to the Topeka children whose friends and relatives lived on ranches. Reality is sometimes heavy competition for childhood fantasy. As two boys said at different times but in almost the same words, "My grandma has a *real* cowboy."

Health care

As the state capital, Topeka is also the headquarters for the State Board of Health and has three large, well-equipped hospitals. Many of the mothers who initially volunteered for the Escalona–Leitch study of infants were contacted through well-baby conferences that provide pre- and postnatal medical consultation. All the babies in this sample were born in a hospital. Medical help is readily available in conferences and clinics, and a substantial proportion of families have, from the infancy of these children, made use of facilities provided by state, county, and city. Failures to carry out routine inoculations and dental care were rare. The parents' relation to the well-baby conference may have contributed to their high degree of persistence in and loyalty to this study.

The fact that in 1950, when our research children were babies, the death rate from TB [19] in Topeka was approximately one-third that in New York City is probably due to a combination of factors: pure air, the absence of overcrowded, filthy slum conditions, the availability of medical care. The last, including prenatal care and well-baby care, may also contribute to the fact that the infant mortality rate in New York City was nearly one-third higher than that of Topeka. However, the death rate from accidents was higher in Topeka (Topeka 53, New York 3,468); one of our group died in a disastrous fire in her home, while another died of a fractured skull in a fall against the curb while playing a daring game of jumping onto the hood of a slowly moving car.

Mental health

Located as it is in "the psychiatric center of the world," Topeka offers a variety of acceptable resources for children and adults who need psychiatric assistance.[20] Taxi drivers, workers in stores, and other townspeople spontaneously expressed appreciation for help made available at the local state hospital. The same can be said for the County Guidance Clinic, which made low cost help available for children and adults. One boy in this study who became embarrassed about his recurrent enuresis (only after he entered school) asked his parents to help him get psychiatric help. Several mothers in our research group who had made use of psychiatric assistance at some time during the childbearing years—in two instances in connection with postpartum depression—spoke of this warmly.

It is not our task to estimate how many others needed psychiatric help. Some mothers felt that "if your religion is good enough, you don't need a psychiatrist." One mother took her child to the minister of their church for counseling after reporting to us her anxiety about the child's unhappiness. One might, however, suggest that two important differences between a medium-sized town in the Middle West and a large metropolitan city on the coast could contribute to differences in mental health (Srole 1962). We noted that a middle-western city like Topeka does not have demoralizing extremes of poverty and luxury side by side. People can be relatively poor by big city standards and yet not be depressed if they can take care of basic necessities of life. And when homes are inadequate, one is not insulted or frustrated by the wastefulness of affluent living around the corner. A second consideration relates to the relative physical stress of life in the two settings: with good air, plenty of sun, a more gentle pace of life, the normal expectable stress may be more manageable—it is easier to cope with life's problems and the fact that a small minority of the families were upwardly mobile or outwardly mobile implies reduced pressures.

Religion

To be sure, this was a bread-and-butter culture where most of the families were busy taking care of basic needs—earning a living, making a home, feeding, clothing, and caring for the children. For a wide group, life centered in the church community, and in the case of those children who went to parochial schools, the church and school communities were the same, thus adding to the integration of the child's experience. Some mothers taught Sunday school or classes preparing children for their First

Communion. Typically, mothers supervised bedtime prayers or said them with their children, and children took turns saying grace at the table. So it was not only a bread-and-butter culture but a religious culture for a large proportion of the families, and when we made plans for a study of children's religious attitudes in adolescence, one mother said, "It's about time the study recognizes the importance of religion in the development of our children" (Stewart 1967). The everyday importance of religious commitment was reflected not only in family devotions, but also in the natural way in which mothers encouraged the children to turn to the Lord in times of stress or hurt.

Religious mentors gave significant support in times of stress. For instance, in one family where an older sibling of a member of our study group "got into trouble" by running away, the parish priest immediately took action to arrange for a period of institutionalization at an excellent nearby Catholic school. This was, of course, possible only as a result of the active participation of the family in the life of the parish, combined with the deep personal interest and readiness for action of the parish priest. Illustrations could also be given of help made available by Protestant ministers. Some teenagers expressed special appreciation for the friendship of their pastors. The fact that the Menninger Foundation has both a division of religion and psychiatry and also open forums and lectures to which the local ministers and parish priests are welcome has contributed to the perceptiveness of some of the religious leaders.

In a number of working-class families faith in God was an active support, and with some of them God was a vivid present reality. Here church membership, attendance, and loyalty were important or basic to every family in the working-class group among our intensive sample. This means that standards, ideals, and the richness contributed by religious tradition, literature, and experiences were contributing to the quality of life and to the development of character in the children. These families regarded some non-churchgoing families of the middle class as spiritually if not culturally deprived.

But religion provided some sources of tension as well as positive contributions. While one independent child remarked on seeing my bracelet, "My mommy says Jesus doesn't like bracelets, but I do," others were constricted by tight religious limits. And the preschool fearfulness of one child who took hellfire literally was intensely reinforced.

Structure and its reinforcement

The limits set by Catholic and fundamentalist Protestant rules were congruent with the strict structures of schools. In first grade at his parochial school one boy confided that his hand was spanked with a ruler when he talked to his neighbor. "And then?" I asked. "You learn not to talk," he said emphatically. Children were divided in their feelings about the legal corporal punishment in school: "I'd rather get the spats than stay after school to write a hundred sentences," Teddy said. But Sally protested, "I'll never let them do that to me—I'll run away." Most children accepted rules and family discipline: "They do it because they want to bring us up right" was a frequent comment; these children seemed to gain security from clearly defined limits. Within the family children were punished for breaking things (low income families cannot easily afford replacements). Noise in the house was often met with, "If you can't be quiet, go out and run," a solution less available to urban mothers.

Destructiveness, rebelliousness, backtalk, as well as excessive noisiness, were promptly curbed. Before school age, nearly half the mothers resorted to sitting the child in a corner or in a chair, with folded hands. Isolating the child in his room was considered unwise at any age by one-third of the mothers, although eight mothers resorted to this disciplinary method before school age. Some of them explained their rejection of this method as not wanting their child to fear or hate his room and bed.

Corporal punishment was general, though mothers differed as to the age when they stopped spanking; the majority continued until the child became an adolescent, even "until they get as big as you are." While spanking with the hand was typical punishment for girls, a belt, paddle, or switch were generally used for boys. About half the mothers admitted they spanked hard—"so they really felt it," or "hard enough to let them know I mean it"—but very rarely "to the point of leaving welts." Nearly half deprived the child of privileges as another form of discipline after the child reached school age; at high school age "grounding"—that is, not visiting friends, going to the movies, or dating—was a typical punishment for misdemeanors.

While almost half the mothers reported that they and their husbands agreed about discipline, one-quarter felt the father was too strict, and among the rest, sometimes the father, sometimes the mother, was felt by the other parent to be too lenient. Barely a quarter of the mothers said they talk about problems with their teenage children—not surprising in an action-oriented culture.

But if punishment was decisive and "permissiveness" unheard of, freedoms and support were equally definite. The same mother who spanked her daughter for angrily smearing food on the table in a moment of frustration, exhausted every resource to help her through critical illness and other difficult periods. Parent–child relationships recalled A. Baldwin's (1945) studies, which found that "warm autocratic" parents had children who developed better than children of "cold democratic" parents. Intellectualized permissiveness may contribute to distancing of parents and children, just as cold autocracy may evoke hostility.

Chores and shared responsibilities

The children were expected to be responsible for their share of chores—tidying their rooms, taking turns at washing dishes, helping in the garden, taking out the garbage, looking after the baby at times, as well as doing errands and assisting parents. All this developed mastery of skills, awareness, and basic competence in handling objects in space and in eye–hand coordination. Four-year-old children volunteered such observations as "our baby can sit up by himself, but we have to help him walk." Such experiences doubtless contributed to their superior achievements on "performance" as contrasted with verbal items on intelligence tests.

A child-oriented town

In contrast to almost any large metropolis, Topeka seemed uniquely oriented toward children in the 1950s. Child monitors as young as nine years old controlled traffic at intersections near their schools, wearing a white shoulder-to-waist band and a large clear sign, "May We Pass?" Newspapers carried detailed accounts of meetings, activities, and achievements of major children's organizations such as Boy Scouts, Girl Scouts, 4-H Clubs, Future Farmers of America. Children graduating from junior and senior high school as well as from college were listed along with their honors. Recipients of prizes in science fairs, county and state spelling bees, and, of course, National Merit examinations for college all "got their names in the paper." So did those in the Topeka Youth Symphony and in school orchestra concerts. A "Teen-Talk" feature presented reports and comments on junior- and senior-high-school life. Still more impressive was the periodic opportunity for children to place their own ads in the paper at no cost: ads about bicycles, rabbits, equipment to buy or sell were placed even by young children, while teenagers advertised their availability for baby-sitting, lawn-mowing, and other jobs.

The zoo not only permitted children accompanied by an adult to enter free, but also contained a "children's zoo," with large animal sculptures on which children could climb, slide, and develop their fantasies. The park also contained a retired but still shiny red fire engine for the children to climb all over.

Consistent with this interest in and recognition of children was the freedom to roam: hedges and fences separating yards 100 feet long and 50 to 75 feet wide were rare, and the youngest children roamed through neighbors' yards and around the block, often "watched" by older children. Outdoor space permitted discharge of tension, channeling of motor drives, thus reducing restlessness and tense clashes between child needs and adult needs often seen in the confinement of city apartments.

Neighborhoods and family life

Neighborhood and family settings for the development of children can differ dramatically in the same city. There are variations in the degree of order versus chaos in the neighborhood; the safety versus threat to life and property; the open responsiveness versus self-protective seclusiveness characteristic of family life; the communication among the people in the neighborhood and from one neighborhood to another, and the degree of cohesion or consistency in the lifestyles of families in the community; the degree of continuity versus change in the neighborhood of which the child and his family are a part; the sense of security or confidence that basic life needs can be dependably met; the stability of jobs; and the optimism versus pessimism or cynicism related to these aspects of life.

It soon became obvious that these Topeka children were growing up in a setting with many common influences, and some of these were different from those to which metropolitan and suburban children in the eastern United States were exposed. Characteristics with so little range in ratings that no correlations emerged have to be considered typical: privacy, availability of other children, and ample play space outside of the house. Moreover, most of the children in this group lived in relatively safe neighborhoods—little traffic and practically no danger from marauders. Ways of life of neighboring families were sufficiently similar so that most mothers permitted the preschool and school-age children to explore freely and to develop friendships with the children in the neighborhood.[21] This meant that it was possible for the child to get outdoors much of the time through his own efforts, even before the age of two, and roam a wide area. Such freedom can be assumed to have promoted the autonomy, eagerness to explore, curiosity, and also cognitive as well as the motor mastery of the environment, as we illustrated in *The Widening World of Childhood*.

All the homes were clean and orderly; most were pleasant, adequate for basic needs of children.[22] This does not mean, of course, that if our sample had included the wealthiest and the poorest groups in Topeka, material variations in living conditions would have mattered so little. Even the homes of most of the very poor in Topeka at that time, however, still had yards up to 50 feet wide and 100 feet deep.

The relative stability, cohesiveness, and continuity in the neighborhoods and families would be expected to contribute to consistency of character development, as shown long ago by Hartshorne, May, and Shuttleworth (1930). All this probably contributed to the fact that most of the children were trusting and trustworthy as well as independent.

Range of experience and spontaneity

It seems fair to say that the spontaneity with which these children approached new situations (Murphy 1962) varied in relation to the range of experience they had had and to the degree of overlap between new situations to which they were exposed and familiar situations previously experienced. For instance, most of the boys who came to a party at the Murphy home in the woods did not hesitate to jump down over terrace walls, explore the stream that ran through the place, and climb up the wooded hillside. This was like exploring the countryside or wooded parks with which they were familiar. By contrast, many of the children showed some anxiety during either the entire intelligence test situation or parts of it, particularly during those sections requiring verbal responses. But consider how very different the intelligence test situation is from the child's usual experience during the preschool years. No mother sits a child down on a chair in front of a table and demands that he show what he can do with a seemingly endless series of novel tasks. With naïve trust, some of the children attempted to reconstruct this situation by suggesting that they might alternate, asking the examiner some questions in turn. Other children were halting, tense, or partially immobilized in this strange setting, despite the unusually skillful and gentle approach of the examiner (Moriarty 1966). In this respect, the behavior of these children and their anxiety and inhibition at times is not different from that reported of children in urban settings when confronted with intelligence tests at an early age (Rust 1932). We are not suggesting that children be given home experiences in the early years that will prepare them for their first Binet tests. Rather, we emphasize the fact that we cannot assume that we have an accurate picture of how the child behaves or would behave in less strange situations.

Family size

With the exception of one family which might be somewhat
doubtfully placed in the "business class" group, none of the business–
professional families had more than four children, and the mode was
two. The average number of children in the working-class families was
four, and the range extended from two to eight. Thus, as is typical
around the world, the families with less money tended to have more
children. For the most part, however, each child did have some private
area in the home as well as his own toys. Even in one of the poorest
families, where four children shared two double-decker beds, each had
his own mattress; there was only one family in which three children
shared one large bed. Moreover, birthdays were celebrated with parties,
although in certain large poor families each child was entitled only to
one birthday party during his school years in contrast to the annual party
provided for children in more affluent families.

Grandmothers and the extended family

Four children (in two families) in the coping study lived with the
grandparents during infancy, and two-thirds of the children enjoyed the
availability of grandparents, especially grandmothers, who lived in town,
often nearby, or in rare cases in a nearby town. Grandmothers visited and
often took care of children when mothers were sick or in the hospital
with a new baby. Thus, separation from the mother, when the child was
in his own home with his familiar and beloved grandmother, did not
generally involve the level of anxiety often observed when a child
separated from his mother is cared for away from home or by a strange
mother-substitute (Robertson 1970). Grandmothers also welcomed the
visits of the children—in a few instances caring for the child in their own
home while the mother was at work outside the home. Grandmothers
visited families or vice versa during holidays. In three instances, there was
a strain between the grandmother and her daughter-in-law, but for the
most part the children were attached to their grandparents, and the
death of a grandparent during a child's growing-up period was deeply
felt. The closeness of grandparents widened the children's range of
opportunities for identification, and provided security in being loved and
cared for. Beyond this, children with grandparents lived in a wider world
than the children who were confined to the stimulation and emotional
experiences of the nuclear family. Where aunts and uncles and cousins
lived in the same town or not far away, visits and reunions extended the
intimate emotional world even further.

This broad world of intimacy and feeling must be kept in mind when we consider the relative mildness of the children's emotional involvement with parents. Serious Oedipal conflicts were rare in this group, although what one might call Cain-and-Abel and Cinderella conflicts were conspicuous in a few instances.

Family unity and stability

By and large, the children were growing up in stable, unified families which stayed together as a family unit year in and year out. In fact, during the first twelve years of the children's lives, we have to think of these families as unusually stable in comparison with the national average during this period. Among the twenty-seven families in this intensive group, only three divorces occurred between 1948 and 1968.

The typical vacation pattern was a trip taken by the whole family to visit relatives or to explore mountains or lakes in Colorado, the Ozarks, or California. In line with this tendency for a family to go on vacations as a unit is the tendency for the family to stay together for the most part during the rest of the year. That is, it was rare rather than typical for parents to vacation together away from the children, or for the mother to leave the family for a visit to her relatives or a vacation of her own.

In other words, children in this group were exposed to few separations, and these few were usually associated with the mother's hospitalization for a new baby or, in a very few instances, illness. At such times a familiar and loving relative usually took the mother's place. The father might use some of his vacation time to stay home with the family, or a grandmother or aunt would come to stay with the children.

Several interviewers commented in regard to families that "theirs was a close-knit family" with strong mutual support and joint participation in recreational activities, church, and the household chores. This fitted with remarks of children from the preschool level to prepuberty: they typically expressed pleasure regarding family reunions, when all available relatives gathered at Thanksgiving or Christmas or during the summer, even mentioning them in their interviews with the psychiatrist, at about the age twelve, as "happiest memories" or the most enjoyable events of summer vacation.

Typical patterns in these families included the mother's reading stories to the children, the father's setting up play equipment, the entire family's going to one of the larger parks for picnics in good weather. Mealtimes were—at least until teenagers began to get jobs—times for the family to be together, except for the few families in which one parent had changing work shifts. And mealtimes were often times for family discussions.

The relation between the father and mother seemed close in most of these "close-knit" families, even where there were discrepancies between the mother's and father's educational level or socioeconomic backgrounds or when they belonged to different religious groups. One husband had only a fourth-grade education while the mother had completed high school and had taken some business college work beyond this. Grace Heider observed that this husband seemed to be devoted to his wife, and during the early years at least there was no evidence of dissatisfaction or frustration with the marriage, although the wife had to struggle with financial stress.

Stimulation in the home

From infancy on, then, the children in multichild families and those with nearby relatives were exposed to the intrinsic stimulation involved in attention from and observation of the comings and goings of familiar responsive persons and their activities. In addition, the family picnics, vacation trips, usually to visit more distant relatives, mealtime conversations, as well as observation of and assistance to parents in their work and stories read to young children all provided varied social, sensory, and cognitive stimulation. At puberty the range of family interaction in forty-four available families was reviewed through questions (in a home interview) about family fun, chores, communication, support to the child in stress, and adaptation of discipline to the child's needs. Twenty-seven families were rated moderate to high in communication; eighteen families were rated moderate to high in all areas, while only eight were rated moderate to low in all areas. The rest were high in certain areas and low in others. It was from this relatively stimulating home atmosphere that these children came, with their average IQs of 116 (Appendix 5).

Stimulation, however, did not include pressure for achievement, for good grades at school, for making a name for oneself, or for a better vocation than the father's. Frankness, tolerance, loyalty to the church were expected, according to the mothers' reports on the Middletown (see Lynd and Lynd 1929) child-rearing questionnaire (Appendix 3).

Parents' support to the child in times of stress

We have noted the range of interplay between parents and children, and this included comfort, reassurance, and other kinds of support to the child in times of stress. In every type of stressful situation reported by more than two mothers, the majority of the sayings offered to comfort or to support the child were religious in nature. "Faith can help us to accept this," and "It's a blessing she's no longer suffering," after the death of a grandmother. Reassuring references to divine support were frequent: "The Lord has been good to us" (in the past, with the implication that He will continue to help) in a time of suffering; "God will answer our needs"; "The Lord provides for His own"; "You know the Lord is with you at all times"; "If you talk to Jesus He will take it away"; "The Lord helps those who help themselves"; "All things work together for good for them that love God"; "God may work for good through a tragic situation"; "God guides us in every decision"; "He will not put on us more than we can bear."

In many other instances, the mother urged the child to pray: "We have to take time and pray about it"; "Now let's say a prayer for . . ."; "All we can do is pray about it"; "Pray about it and you'll feel better." When a child had trouble with homework a mother would say, "Say a short prayer, relax, and then go on with your homework."

Many mothers tried to put things in perspective in one or more ways, showing the relation of the child's situation to that of others, or suggesting that change will come, that the future will be different.

To a child with a physical disability following severe illness: "Everyone has some sort of handicap, and it's just that yours is physical."

After an injury: "It will be better in a minute." "You've got to look forward to tomorrow."

When a girl was excluded by others: "In ten years you won't even know the difference."

In a time of difficulty: "When you get to the bottom, there's no way but up." "Tomorrow it will be different; the picture changes." "Tomorrow is another day." "You've got to look forward to tomorrow."

Perspective in other terms included such thoughts as these: "Material things are not all that is important in life." An effort to help the child accept the balance of positive and negative aspects of life was seen in remarks like, "A bit of the bad goes with the good" (after a hunting accident).

Direct support was reported in some instances: after an injury, "Mommy will kiss it and make it better"; "You'll do fine"; "I'm not angry with you . . . let's wipe the slate clean"; "Whatever you do, don't run away. I'll help"; "I'm sorry about the pain." One father was reported to make the girls laugh at difficult situations and not take them too seriously.

And occasionally, practical remedies were suggested: in a time of physical pain, "Take an aspirin, lie down, and relax" or "Be calm." "Think positively."

Some mothers tried to help the child understand the motivation of others: When a child was upset at the staring from other children, the mother said, "The children are just curious—they don't mean to hurt you."

When a pet was run over: "The man who hit the puppy didn't stop because he must not have seen the dog—he didn't even know that he had hit him."

"We do these things because we care," when a child protested a parent's discipline.

A few instances occurred in which a mother appealed to stoic resignation: "What can't be cured must be endured"; "We can't understand, but this is the way it is" (after Kennedy's death); "Even with this happening, life goes on, we just can't sit down and die"; and after a grandfather's death, "Life must go on for others."

After a serious injury to a brother, the mother said, "It can't be helped and we'll have to make the most of it."

And in a time of difficulty, it would be said, "Well, do all you can and if you've done all you can, that's all."

A process of adjustment was implied when, in a time of pain, a mother said, "This is the way things happen and we'll have to work it through."

Hope was stimulated directly and indirectly: "The third time is a charm"; "We always hope for the best"; "All will turn out okay"; "Maybe you can do it next time."

Maxims used to support effort by a child included: "Whatever is worth doing is worth doing well." "Haste makes waste." "Try to be ready to face life as much as you can." "Hitch to the stars, reach for the highest and the best."

Along with a predominant assertion of the need to face and accept "the way it is," and the fact that suffering is reduced by the passage of time, parents invoked divine support on the one hand and hope, even dreams, on the other hand.

It is in this context of relatively close family life with varied areas for sharing that discipline as discussed earlier (pp. 27–29) has to be understood in this group. We saw that limits were clear, punishment generally immediate, and corporal punishment during the prepuberty years common. Children frankly described spankings, whippings with belt or paddle, as well as loss of special privileges, such as riding a bike. Rarely did a child protest that the mother was too strict. A more common reaction was that mothers punish because "they love you and want to bring you up right." In the puberty psychiatric interviews the children usually spoke acceptingly of the family discipline pattern. However, indirectly and unconsciously on the CAT analyzed by Moriarty, a few young children did reflect feelings that parents were harsh. In some instances we saw a tension between identification with the parents' goals and resentment of harsh methods employed some-times. However, strictness in parents was often a source of pride for children.

Cultural heritage: the pioneer tradition of coping

Most of our intensive group children were at least third-generation Americans. Many families had been in the United States much longer. Ethnic origins were predominantly Anglo-Saxon, with Irish–Scottish–English background; a few included Swedish or German elements, and two claimed a south European or Russian ancestry. Two families boasted of an American Indian background on one side—a matter of romantic pride in this area.

Most grandparents on either the maternal or paternal side—some-times both—came from rural backgrounds, which usually meant a pioneer heritage. Pioneers in Kansas typically began by building a "sod house," [23] then moving, as success in farming and cattle raising made it possible, into a stone house (made of local stone quarried nearby), or a frame house. The pioneer tradition is a proud one; people speak of grandparents who began life in Kansas in a sod house with respect for their courage, vigor, and resourcefulness, and in some families the satisfactions of the rural life are remembered warmly, even enthusiasti-cally.

Self-image of the children

With this foundation for self-respect in their preschool years, chil-dren's awareness of "being poor" emerged only slowly after they got into school, when children everywhere are inclined to make comparisons of the social, financial and other aspects of their lives with those of others.[24] Even so, there was no evidence that the self-image of the few poor children in this sample is depreciated to an extent at all comparable with what is described in reports of studies of metropolitan slum children (Mattick 1967). It is important to note here that many of the disparaging clichés regarding American working-class life did not touch the children in this sample; many of the working-class children had gone to very few movies before the age of twelve and often only to such movies as "The Ten Commandments."

If the culture were lacking in opportunities for enjoyment of a wide range of concerts, opera, museums, and the arts, it was not barren or narrow in its own terms. Along with the emotional life within the extended family and friends in the neighborhood and church commu-nity, there was a warm appreciation of Topeka, the countryside around it, the lakes nearby, and the mountains not far away in Colorado. It was a world with roots and at the same time with horizons that did not seem narrow to the Topeka families, though the eastern metropolis centers seemed remote or even alien, and only one of the families had ever been there.

By and large, then, this group identified with its own image of self-respecting American culture. They generally did not have high aspirations; however 93 percent of the children in the prepuberty years were anticipating going to college or preparing themselves for a vocation distinctly better than that of their fathers. Most of them seemed destined to maintain approximately the same status and to fit into the same stable group to which their families currently belonged. Even their Rorschach tests reflected less ambition than tests of New Haven and Pittsburgh children.[25]

By contrast, cooperation was normal within the extended family, between neighbors, and, in times of disaster, between communities. Older relatives contributed clothing and even food to young, growing families; neighbors and friends brought food and assistance at times of illness, death, or other disaster. When a mother and three children were burned to death in a fire, a neighbor adopted the child who survived. During the 1966 tornado, Topekans who escaped injury formed several "relief stations," and people from all social levels and even communities twenty-five to fifty miles away contributed food, clothing, furniture, and money to supply the victims with basic needs. One village closed down all businesses for a day and sent all of its trucks with workers to help homeless Topekans move into new housing located by an emergency housing office. The Menninger Research Department released a number of its staff to assist in the distribution of supplies and relocation of stricken families. (Here we can recall the pioneer mutual-help patterns, whereby neighbors assisted in plowing, harvesting, and "raising a house," as well as in care of the sick.)[26] Yet friendly cooperation was not limited to times of distress. On moving to Topeka, I repeatedly found shopkeepers in the city suggesting other shops for articles they did not have themselves.

Balances in community life

Every pattern of community life carries its own balance of potentially positive and negative impacts on child development. While the stability, comfort, freedom, and cohesiveness of the middle-western town contributed to certain strengths in the children, it is uncertain how well prepared they were for the changes of coming years. Some social scientists say that in order to be prepared for change children must experience change and learn to cope with it from their earliest years, while others say that the best preparation for subsequent adaptation is a solid foundation, deep roots, and an inner core of stability that contributes strength for coping with external change and threats. But it appears that in this group a balance of structure, consistency, and continuity in family and neighborhood life, together with freedom and opportunities to explore varied experiences and settings, provided a basis for stable development in childhood along with considerable capacity to cope with newness and with stress.

We have seen aspects of life in Topeka that contribute to autonomy and motor discharge of tension; exploratory freedom contributing to the development of a cognitive map and curiosity; chores, responsibilities, and observation of parents' work contributing to the development of skills; family and community patterns contributing to cooperation and communication; homogeneity of the environment contributing to internal integration; and examples of local cultural resilience in reaction to stress. These and related aspects of the development of the children underlie the "core American" personality.

Of course, there are individual differences among the children: we found some were more vulnerable than others (see chapters 8 and 9), and there were variations in openness, spontaneity, warmth, coping capacities, as well as in physical equipment, flexibility, and resilience. In the following chapters we shall be concerned with sources and expressions of some of these differences, continuities and changes in the ways in which they contributed to the children's ways of coping with the external world and with their own vulnerabilities, and the contribution of the outcomes to the evolving personality of each child.[27]

2

Maternal Style and Infant Response

In God we trust
Jesus never fails.
(A motto on one mother's front door)

Mother and family as ecology

What difference could the general ecological setting make to a baby?
A baby knows nothing of the overall community environment, of the
structure of the city, or of the dependability of the police. What he feels
comes from his experiences in his home and neighborhood, from his
mother and others who respond to him. Their level of tension or
comfort, trust or anxiety, flexibility or rigidity, satisfaction or frustration
have much to do with the atmosphere in which an infant begins life.
These are relayed to him through tightness or softness of the muscles
that hold him, feed him, clean, dress, and play with him, the quality of
voices he hears, the patterns of movement he experiences as he is lifted,
carried, played with. Long ago Ann Stewart (1953) demonstrated
differences in mothers of babies who cry much and those who don't cry.
The parents' tension or anxiety level may be influenced by many aspects
of community life of which they are a part—including physical security,
dependability of employment, relative freedom from social competition,
the quality of religious leaders, their confidence in the educational
resources available to their children, and the community atmosphere of
optimism or pessimism.

The baby could not know that when his grandfather moved to Kansas
he first built a sod hut and then built a larger house as the farm
progressed, but his parents' pride in their forebears' resourcefulness is
reflected in their encouragement of the infant's resourcefulness. The

This chapter makes use of Heider's (1966) analyses of mother–infant relations in the
coping sample of 27 mothers with 31 babies; Escalona's (1968) analyses of mother–infant
relations in an independent subsample of the 32 most active and 32 least active infants
from the group of 128 infants observed by the Escalona–Leitch staff; and Sylvia Brody's
analysis of another subsample that included 10 infants in the coping sample. In addition, I
made an independent study of the records on 27 mothers in the coping sample. This
chapter is in no way a substitute for the intensive analyses by these different authors.

baby's mother may transmit the sense of confidence, skill, and ease in handling that she absorbed from experiencing and watching her skillful parents and from her own participation in the household work from the early years. And the mother may also convey the ease, strain, or tension she feels in her setting.

Most of the Topeka mothers were not as isolated as mothers in big cities often are. With nearby relatives (especially the babies' grandparents, see Appendix 2) to give a hand in emergencies, share holidays with, help provide clothes and extras, baby-sit when the mother needed time away, and in a few cases, help pay the rent, the mothers had considerable support from their families. Most fathers were only minutes away from work settings and were able to share in activities, guidance, and discipline of the children and also to give the mother far more daily help than urban or suburban fathers, whose home is often miles away from work.

Thus, most of these mothers shared a sense of closeness and security in a larger world of intimacy than that of the nuclear family unit. In addition to intimacy and support—especially important when the mother went to the hospital for a new baby and the grandmother came to stay with the others[1]—the world of the extended family contributed to a wider orientation of the child from infancy. The multiple mothering, which sometimes involved a change of setting as the infant was left at grandmother's house, and may have involved irregularities in schedule, provided a quantity and variation of stimulation beyond what was experienced by an infant in a nuclear family. This could have contributed to the flexibility we saw in the children in their preschool years.

And the baby's experience varies with the continuity of time with mother. Only two of twenty-seven mothers worked steadily outside the home from the baby's infancy. However, two-thirds of the mothers of the intensive sample contributed financially during the children's prepuberty years, usually by part-time, cash-producing work inside or outside the home, as the needs increased and the mother was freer from constant demands of small children. More than half the mothers had worked as nurse, secretary, or in other roles before marriage and had the security of knowing they "could get a job" if necessary. The mothers thus felt competent and able to contribute to the financial support of the family if their husbands became ill or unemployed for other reasons. The two who worked steadily even from the baby's infancy felt a realistic need to do so because of extremely limited income. A few mothers worked hard at moneymaking activities within the home in response to urgent needs brought on by the husband's periodic unemployment, illness, or limited income during professional training.

This combination of competence and readiness to carry part of the financial responsibility, combined with flexibility and devotion to the needs of the children during their earliest years, was not unusual among mothers in this area. A frequent pattern was to work until the first baby was almost due, then to give up the job until the children were in school. Part-time work, or work in a flexible setting that would permit adequate attention to the children after this age, was often sought by mothers who were devoted to the children's needs and at the same time wanted to contribute greater financial stability. Thus most mothers were providing partners as well as partners in parenthood.

A mother's satisfaction with her marriage is widely seen to be an important factor in her relationship with children, and in the late forties and early fifties special wartime conditions affected some marriages. Under the pressures of the aftermath of World War II there were instances of hasty decisions. For instance, one woman in our study group felt "that I might not have another chance"; another married a nice soldier, still in his attractive uniform but with only a fourth-grade education while she had had some secretarial training after completing high school. Still "the men were men"; although two of the twenty-seven fathers of the preschool children were alcoholic, most of the rest were good husbands and good fathers. Not only did several mothers testify warmly to their husband's encouragement and support in times of stress, but in one instance a father left a preferred job because a new one would enable him to support his family at a better level, and "the family unit is the most important thing," he told me.

Over half the marriages seemed warm, stable, and committed, with problems tolerated and worked at constructively; in a few more, tensions were fairly marked. One-fourth the marriages seemed moderately unhappy. But there were only three divorces in the twenty-seven families over a period of twenty years. In two of these, the mother was hospitalized for mental illness; the third divorce was followed by the mother's stable, satisfying marriage with her new husband. Two other unhappy marriages (though not dissolved) were those in which the fathers were alcoholic. Among the majority of wives in the "good marriages" were those who remarked, "I've always known that life included hardships, and you stand up to them." Such mothers had the strength to tolerate frustration, but we have to add that these mothers also experienced much satisfaction, and most stressful periods were not chronic. Life was a checkerboard of good and difficult times.

The implicit self-respect of these women seemed evident in their appearance: by contrast with the very poorest seen in Topeka's neglected poverty neighborhood, none was unkempt, dirty, or disheveled. By contrast with certain metropolitan extremes, few were defensively or compulsively attention-getting; there was little conspicuous name-dropping, status-shouting, or ultra-high-style clothing. In dress they ranged with rare exceptions from conservative or conventional taste to contemporary modishness—appropriate, neat, and clean. One exception was a young mother who had recently moved to the city from the country and who was at first overly dressed up for the research interviews by the community standards (high heels, much makeup, elaborate dress).

Grant Wood's grim *American Gothic* is an exaggeration of perhaps only one or two rigid parents of our group of babies and has nothing in common with the others. Catholic or Protestant, their earnest loyalty to the church was balanced by empathy, flexibility, common sense, and often humor. Tolerance, durability, and resourcefulness characterized most of the mothers as we watched them cope with the emergencies as well as daily pressures of their lives. They suffered at times but were not martyrs; neither were they "dolls," or restless "women's libbers." H. Leinback's famous sculpture of a pioneer mother* projects the strength of many mothers we knew.

Mothering patterns during the children's developing years

What we saw these mothers do with and for the baby and young child can hardly be summarized in a global concept such as nurturance or authority. While all the mothers were responsible and most were skillful, their expressions of love, support, stimulation, and care varied. Not all the mothers were overtly affectionate, but rarely was a mother seen to reject a child's wish for physical contact. Devoted care was expressed in the exquisite clothes made for babies and small girls by a number of these skillful mothers; they often supported the initiative of the child in "dressing up." Only one preschool girl appeared shabby and unkempt; most of the children appeared at the research center shiningly clean in freshly ironed, if—more often in the boys—worn clothes. This support for the child's self-respect and pride may be assumed to have been important in the strength of these attitudes in the children.

Saying bedtime prayers with the child, talking over the child's experiences at length—whether initiated by the child or by the mother wishing to contribute perspective or offer suggestions—also provided support. An older sister of one of our subjects mentioned that her

* This sculpture, "Madonna of the Trail," is reproduced at twelve points along the Pioneer Trail.

mother often stimulated them with such remarks as "God helps those who help themselves." At the time of the Kennedy assassination, family discussions about it included consulting the encyclopedia or other references to set this event in perspective with previous presidential assassinations.

Children also had opportunities to observe their mothers' capacity to mobilize extra resources at times of family stress; in approximately one-third of the families during the child's first ten years some major emergency arising from illness, father's temporary unemployment, or the great flood of 1951 evoked vigorous efforts by the mother to help the family cope with resulting problems.

Mothers' roles

The voluntary nature of these mothers' participation in this research and their commitment to it over such a long period of time may imply a selective factor that could be responsible for the high proportion of mothers who appeared to have strong personalities and were sometimes the "center" of the family. An example was Mrs. Stevens, who actively reassured, encouraged, and supported her husband and each of their children at their moments of doubt and uncertainty. At the same time, she herself commented most warmly on her husband's capacity to give her support and reassurance during times of fatigue and discouragement. She was able to maintain this role appropriately at each successive developmental stage and in relation to each of the vicissitudes of her family life. By contrast, Mrs. Cooper offered great intuitive support to the children of her large family in their infancy, and in times of crisis, such as when a younger child contracted polio; but she was limited in her capacity to stimulate, guide, and support either their social life or intellectual development in later stages of latency and early adolescence.

Directly and indirectly the mother controls the baby's immediate environment by the setting she provides in the home, the baby's living area, its crib or carriage and by her choice of clothing, toys. Studies of poor children, undertaken in the wake of concern about the rate of school failures, have led to an awareness of the importance of stimulation in infancy, its quantity, variety, timing, and relation to the baby's sensory needs. In many foundling hospitals one can see what constitutes *inadequate* stimulation. Some of the following conditions also exist in poorer households.

Bare walls, no patterned visual stimuli; mobiles not within range of vision; caretakers in white uniforms not contributing to differentiation of persons.

No variety in the environment—babies kept in one area without visits to other areas.

Nothing to explore or discover; visual range narrow and monotonous as with cubicles on a corridor; motor scope lacking in goals.

No response to *individual differences in tolerance of stimulation*, as with babies disturbed by loud sounds, bright lights, vigorous handling, temperature changes, etc.

No suitable toys or other objects that a baby could grasp and manipulate; toys too large or not within reach.

No attention to babies' preferences.

No record player or music available; no mirrors available.

No objects to provide auditory or other feedback when the baby handles them—thus no opportunity to make an impact on the environment or to discover positive effects of action.

By contrast, these mothers had all decorated their homes with colored draperies, rugs, table covers, and pictures; they did not wear white uniforms. They did not keep the baby in one bare area; babies were moved from living room to kitchen to bedroom. Most babies had toys. And the babies were seen, handled by, and could observe other members ·of the family and visitors. They were taken outside the home for visits and medical checkups. The visual aspects of the baby's setting were controlled by the mother indirectly, since she arranged the home for the family as a whole and to suit her taste and that of her husband. But the babies were exposed to a balance of stability and variation in their visual environment, and many mothers were perceptive about the baby's preferences and also their tolerances for bright lights, for instance. The static monotony and visual emptiness characteristic of most foundling homes and homes of some extremely poor families was not observable in these Topeka homes. Patterns, needed to stimulate visual differentiation (Fantz 1963), were everywhere, in both the static and the changing aspects of the home. The adequacy of stimulation supported their development: the average tested IQ at the preschool level was 116.

Some kinds of stimulation were more directly and immediately controlled specifically in relation to the baby's needs and preferences. We can highlight these by another look at the limitations of some foundling homes.

No differentiation in response to baby's vocalization: talking to all babies the same way instead of supporting the baby's vocalization by responding to what the baby initiates, by evoking related sounds, etc.

No differentiation of types of handling related to differences in what a baby "is ready for" or prefers, e.g., protesting against a supine position, wanting leg exercise, wanting baby "games" such as "elevator play," being swung or rocked, etc.

No differentiation of, or response to, disturbed reactions to pain (of inoculation) when one baby continues in prolonged screaming, another loses his appetite, another becomes hyperactive and restless, another becomes depressed.

No provision for independence at the time the baby wants it, e.g., when baby wants to feed himself.

No response to differences in ability to respond to the environment; tendencies to withdraw (which can be overcome by gentle, frequent stimulation by methods preferred by the individual baby).

No differentiation of sleep (duration, frequency of naps, rhythm of sleep needs).

No differentiation of ways of waking babies who shift from sleep to waking very slowly or rapidly.

No response to demand or need-cues from the babies.

No differentiation in length of waiting, frustration, which a baby can tolerate without upheaval, disturbance of appetite, sleep, autonomic nervous system functioning, etc.

No differentiation in making transitions from holding to putting down (some babies "turn to" other visual or tactile contact while some babies "turn off" and withdraw all response to the environment if not actively helped to maintain contact with something).

No differentiation in tempo, vigor, or rhythm of activity with babies, some of whom prefer rapid or energetic movement, while others prefer slower, milder activity.

No awareness of different preferences in exchange of love: some babies enjoy hugs, tickling, vigorous kisses, or poking of abdomen, while others cringe and protest at these and prefer gentle stroking, patting, gentle hugs. Similarly, no differentiation of comfort (if given at all): some babies are soothed by being held to the shoulder and patted, others by swaying, or rocking, or being sung to, or talked to, or played with.

No response to differences in stability, or the needs of some babies for special tension-reducing help.

General tendency to be intrusive and dominating with all babies.

The Topeka mothers, on the other hand, were typically responsive to their babies' preferences and needs, although there were differences from one mother to another, as we shall see in the rest of this chapter.

The baby's first ecological setting

The unborn baby is peculiarly sensitive to the ecological aspects of its mother's womb: infections, any drugs (including antibiotics, sedatives, stimulants, nicotine, alcohol, as well as addictive drugs), or inadequate nutriment from an undernourished, nauseated, overanxious, or hormonally imbalanced mother may produce failures or distortions of development ranging from retardation, autism, deafness, and brain damage to premature birth and skeletal defects. Later difficulties follow: learning, emotional, and behavior problems (Pasamanick, Rogers, and Lilienfeld 1956; Birch and Gussow 1970). The uterus is not soundproof, and babies react to music and sudden noises (Sontag and Wallace 1935). We do not yet know how much prenatal conditioning takes place, but there is mounting evidence for early conditioning after birth (Stevenson 1970). Birth itself puts pressures on the infant's head especially, but also threatens oxygen sufficiency and may offer a severe environmental impact (Greenacre 1952).

While our group of babies was carefully selected to be free of obvious defect, there were, nevertheless, instances of mothers who had difficult pregnancies and deliveries, and these were correlated with mild vulnerabilities in the children. We shall discuss these in chapter 8.

After the baby is born, the mother is for some months the major element in and determiner of what the baby experiences through his eyes, ears, skin, and muscles. The comfort, freedom, available stimulation in and around the baby's crib or bassinet and also in his contact with his mother are controlled by her. How he experiences both this impersonal and personal enfolding depends on his own temperament; his range of sensitivities and related needs; his capacities for selecting, signaling, adapting to, or modifying what impinges on his senses both from outside and inside his body; and his mother's (and others') responsiveness to his needs, his likes, and dislikes. His mother's eyes, face, body, clothes, ways of moving, and talking are important in his first visual, auditory, and kinesthetic experiences.

A mother may be experienced as predominantly pleasurable not just because her milk is satisfying, her breast and nipple easy to manage, but because her clothes attract the baby's eyes, her voice is soothing, she smells good, her way of carrying the baby is comfortable, her bathing and cleaning methods give pleasure, and because she responds to his signals (Ainsworth and Bell 1969).

Some of these characteristics of the mothers are related to their energy, health, sense of well-being, as well as to their bodies and personalities. Of twenty-seven mothers, six had postpartum depressions;* in four instances, the baby in our sample was the third or fourth in the family; in only one instance depression followed the birth of a first baby, and this mother was later hospitalized for mental illness. In most instances the father took over and became especially helpful to the baby, who was somewhat cheated at first of warm mothering.

The baby's characteristics, then, represent the outcome of a very complex and subtle interaction of genetic factors; pregnancy, birth, and early environmental influences; and the successive outcomes of a complex series of interactions. Whatever the origin of the most stable basic tendencies may be, their organization into structural patterns during infancy involves the interaction between these tendencies and the characteristics of the mothers' handling of their babies.

We shall look at both general trends and the characteristics in our group of mothers and also relationships between these characteristics of the mothers and some of the behavior seen in the infants. We are still at a rather primitive level in understanding the many aspects of the mother-baby relationship. Dr. René Spitz, in his 1946 paper on anaclitic depression, commented that the best mothered babies became most depressed when their mothers left. This implies that in the latter part of the first year, maximally gratifying mothering may not offer the child the best preparation for bearing the stress of separation. How do we balance the enriching benefits of warm, close mothering with the need for prerequisites for coping with such stress? In a world with increasing hazards of change, do we not have to rethink our assumptions about optimal, early mother–baby relationships? What experiences contribute to strength, the capacity to meet challenge? What possible answers can our Topeka data offer?

Mothers' ways with babies in this culture

The characteristic behavior of these mothers with their babies differed from the patterns of mothers we saw in India, the USSR, or Nigeria.[2] With small variations certain experiences were common to all the Topeka babies: no mothers bound their babies to cradleboards, or swaddled them; all mothers dressed their infants in shirts, diapers, dresses or rompers, and generally booties. The absence of cradleboard or swaddling allowed for movement, and the recurring physical contact of

* None of these mothers was in the group with previous economic independence and personal job security.

holding, carrying, soothing could contribute to security. At the same time, frequent dressing, cleaning, and changing diapers (ten to eighteen times a day) could involve temporary restriction of movement, at which some babies protested, whimpered, cried, kicked, arched their backs, or strained. Some mothers were notably deft and gentle, considerately minimizing the restriction involved in daily care. These "changes" involving physical contact would be alternated with periods in which the baby was left in a carriage, high chair, or playpen, with an opportunity for visual exploration of his environment.

It was rare for a baby to be carried about or held most of the day by the mother as are babies in parts of Africa and India. Generally the very young baby spent much time in a crib, a bed with limiting fencelike boundaries through whose posts the baby could watch the people, objects, and activities in the environment. However, when not in the crib, the young baby was often held by a member of the family, and this allowed for mutual response of many kinds, including varied visual, auditory, tactual, rhythmic, experiences as the family and baby watched, listened to, played with and adapted to each other. Children as young as four years old were allowed to help with the baby, even to hold it.

The range of experiences varied widely—most conspicuously in the social experiences of first babies at home alone with mother, in contrast to babies with one to three older siblings and live-in or frequently visiting grandparents, uncles, or aunts. Thus one baby's first home might be quiet, with a low level of stimulation, while another baby might enter a complex, noisy, even hilarious and overstimulating household in which mother was the center, but also the object of competing demands.

The range and quality of stimulation also varied with the home furnishings, equipment, and the objects provided by the parents for the baby. One home was rather drab though clean and neat, another harmonious in soft pastels, another vivid and colorful. Some babies had one toy while others had many. But all homes provided more complex stimulation than we saw in village homes in India, for instance, though not so much stimulation as to hopelessly confuse the baby, as we saw in crowded ghetto apartments or in the disorganized, jumbled homes of the poorest families in northern New England.

Mothers' feelings about and enjoyment of their babies differed in intensity and expressiveness, probably depending on a mother's capacity for pleasure in little people, how much she wanted a baby, whether this baby satisfied her hopes for a boy or girl or for a vigorous or "good" or some other specially qualified baby. In a culture where supermarkets provide an astonishing variety of products, it may be frustrating to some mothers to have no choice; when it comes to babies you have to take what you get. Beyond this, in a norm-focused culture where deviance is often regarded as pathology, concern that the baby be "normal" is deep with some mothers, and anxiety or perhaps ambivalence—though not real rejection—was seen in a few mothers who had uncertainties about the adequacy of the baby's developmental pace.

Mothers' ways of enjoying their babies also varied: where one mother gazed and smiled from a distance, others played vigorously, involving the baby in exciting body-play games. Still others took their cues from the baby, thus contributing to a mother–baby duet that developed complex integrations of mutual response. As one reads the narrative of the observers' records of mothers and babies, over and over again we hear echoed the mothers' declarations that "he likes . . ." "he loves . . ." a particular toy, food, type of play and that he is quieted or soothed best in a certain way. Escalona (1968), in summarizing maternal competence, emphasized the freedom from intrusiveness, but she was equally impressed with the responsiveness and sheer skill.

From earliest infancy the baby and his mother cope with varying degrees of the baby's inner distress from hunger, fatigue, colic, or other disturbances of vegetative functioning as well as with distress or pain due to external stimulation. These include difficulty in managing the nipple while feeding, discomfort during bathing, diaper change, or dressing, inoculation shots, sudden loud sounds, bright lights, cold, heat, or overstimulation by experiences which in milder forms are pleasant, such as many playful activities with the family or visitors. Any time from the age of three months on, the presence of strangers,[3] and other environmental changes such as might be involved in vacation trips or even in changing the baby's room, may be sources of distress. In order to prevent disturbed reactions to strangeness when taking the baby away from home, most mothers took his familiar toys, bottle, and so forth to provide continuity. The introduction of new foods was a source of distress for some babies, and most of them had persistent dislikes.

While marked distress expressed by crying or screaming often accompanied pain, severe hunger, or fatigue, babies showed milder states of discomfort by restlessness or fussiness, which mothers sometimes attributed to "boredom." One mother reported changing the baby's location so that he could look at something different; other mothers offered a change of toys, or of posture, or provided other varieties of stimulation. (This need for change or for newness was not recognized as a need for visual, auditory, or tactile nutriment as often as it was recognized as a need for food or, with active babies, the need for freedom of movement.)

Thus while the mothers' contact—ways of approaching, dressing, cleaning—varied in the quality of stimulation, generally they were prompt and effective in soothing their babies in distress, and some were perceptive and resourceful enough to forestall possible discomfort. Most of the babies, then, repeatedly experienced the sequence: distress—relieved by mother's comfort efforts. This was parallel to: hunger—relieved by mother's feeding, and thus part of the basic foundation for the baby's sense of trust in a responsive environment (cf. Erikson 1964).

Along with being attentive to discomfort, many of the mothers were aware of their babies' individual tempos, struggles, and coping resources. In fact, Escalona remarked that some mothers treated their babies like "partners." Furthermore, accelerated development was observed only among infants who had *frequent* tactual and conversational contact with their mothers,[4] and generally a highly stimulating home environment. These were apt to be active babies. (However, as Escalona commented in her subsample, there were irritable babies with both highly competent and less competent mothers [1968, p. 294].)

Mother as a stimulus

A mother is a multimodal stimulus. Visually, by her size, hair, the quality of her smile, the mobility of her face and eyes.* Aurally, by the loudness or softness, tonal and rhythmic patterning, tempo and force of her voice and speech; by her singing and other vocalizing. Tactilely, her firm or soft, gentle or abrupt style. Kinesthetically, by her style of and proclivity for carrying or rocking the baby, along with the forceful or tender, jerky or smooth qualities of her movement. These and other qualities of the mother are part of the baby's ecological setting seen in terms of aspects of stimulation. The selective force of very early conditioning—but not instantaneous imprinting such as experienced by Lorenz's geese (1950)—may have been reflected in Sheila's placid contentment with her obesity at the age of twelve. Her contentment was, we find, sustained by deeply ingrained feelings rooted in early infancy gratification by her endlessly giving, obese mother.

Varieties of mothers

The twenty-seven mothers in our study varied in size, age, education, experience, beauty, strength, health, emotional supportiveness, compatibility and security with husband and extended family, and the level of overall adjustment. They also varied in their satisfaction with and acceptance of the baby's sex and developmental pace, their acceptance

---

* Aldous Huxley, in a conversation in Topeka in the early sixties, commented that our pleasure in jewels probably relates to the nursing baby's fascination with the light of his mother's eyes, which may attract his focal attention earlier than any other part of her face.

of natural functions, attitude toward and success in breast feeding, and feelings of competence with the infant. In addition, they differed in awareness of the baby's needs (for protection, soothing, help with fatigue, hunger, coping with strangeness); in the extent to which their own temperament, vigor, tempo, and style of functioning seemed to fit the baby's needs; in their skill in handling the infant; in the degree of their respect for the infant's autonomous needs (pace and rhythm of feeding, for example); in the amount of attention they gave the baby, specifically in regard to body or tactile contact, talking and visual attention or stimulation.

At the same time, in Escalona's sample, similar maternal styles were seen to be associated with widely different infancy experiences. She notes that "even high maternal intrusiveness could be seen combined with every possible position on the developmental outcome ratings" (1968, p. 294). Still, accelerated development occurred only among infants who had frequent contact with their mother, and a highly stimulating home environment was also associated with high developmental status. It must be remembered, too, that high developmental status was more frequent among *active* babies who were, in turn, more frequently from upper middle class groups in this sample. Yet even the combination of frequent mother–child contacts and level of home stimulation could not *predict* developmental status in this highly selective group with a narrow range excluding low levels of development.

The differing quality of care and devotion to children as infants and at older stages varied so widely and with such important nuances that in trying to rate it we run the risk of blocking some basic understanding of the children's development. For instance, four mothers gave each of their children an extraordinary level of devoted care during periods when illness threatened the development of the child, but consider the difference in quality: Mrs. Stevens, like a tiger mother when her cub's life is threatened, summoned unusual energy to transcend the limits of what the hospital doctors and nurses could do for her polio-stricken child. She persuaded the nurses to teach her how to give Susan the rehabilitative exercises that the nurses weren't giving her because they felt their time should be invested in children who were more likely to recover from polio. Dauntless, and apparently inexhaustible in her passion to save and restore her child to normal life, she actually succeeded—despite doctors' predictions first that the child would not survive, then that she would not be able to get out of bed, and later that she would never get along without crutches. The contagious intensity of the mother's devotion evidently contributed to the special radiance that Susan developed, a quality different from the just normally happy, healthy, sturdy glow that she had when originally seen.

This behavior is very different from the ambivalence with which another mother dutifully tried to get help for the lesser handicap of her small son; it was as if he had let her down after his initial start as a very superior, small baby. And different again from the steady, responsible care given by the mothers of two girls with prolonged illnesses. Susan was the only one of the four who radiated a sense of triumph, although the others were restored to an adequate level of functioning.

A similar quality of intensity was seen in mothers who had experienced a deep loss of their own mothers in infancy, or who had difficulties in carrying a baby to term. Mrs. Nash had been an orphan, and although she was inexperienced in handling babies and seemed to have little of the natural ease with them shown by mothers who had absorbed into their muscles the patterns of good, early mothering, she was devoted to her baby and stimulating in a way that probably contributed to the vividness of Roddy's boyish response to other people. Mrs. Leonard had succeeded in producing a basically healthy baby only after a series of disappointing miscarriages, and her eagerness about Brennie was naturally tinged with anxiety about whether he would develop well. Mrs. Harris, traumatized by the loss of a beautiful baby boy, was skillful and responsible with her little girl Helen but unable to cease mourning for the beloved child she had lost the year before. (Through the years, however, she became very fond of this daughter and deeply appreciated what the child gave to the family.) The quality of each mother's relation to her baby was, then, a product of interacting influences rooted in the mother's skills, including her long past and recent experiences, her feelings about babies in general and this baby in particular, as well as her temperament and style as a person.

The observations of the mothers' ways with their babies can be supplemented by inferences regarding the children's preschool-age perceptions of their mothers. The CAT proved a fruitful source of evidence for these inferences, which we shall now summarize.

Mother–child relation implied in CAT responses

The preschool children's descriptions of the behavior and activities of mother figures on the CAT, as noted by Dr. Walter Kass, give us a glimpse of the children's concepts of mothers and, by implication, their wishes in relation to mothers and areas of frustration. Stories in which the mother takes the children for a walk imply mother–child sharing and interacting in a stimulating way; a mother who stands by and allows the children freedom and autonomy and, of course, the representations of mothers as feeding the children and nurturing them also imply satisfaction in relations with mothers.

But along with the reflections of care by mothers, the children reflected sources of frustration, such as the feeling that there is not enough room on mother's lap for all the children (and especially for oneself). This response was given by Helen, a child with strong affect-hunger, and longing for contact and intimate expressions of affection. JoAnne saw the mother as unable to be both a wife and mother at the same time—unable to give both the children and the husband all that they want. Another child described a mother who goes to town leaving a child at home who wants her to come back. Still another may reflect feelings about the mother's response to our research staff when she describes the divided interests of a mother who diverts her nurturing activities from children to strangers, satisfying the needs of others outside the home. Other children also described the unavailability of mothers when they are out of sight or absent.

Another child depicted the mother figure as having her hands full taking care of very active children who make constant demands for mothering and supervision. This was a mother of four who actually shared management of a shop with her husband, thus having divided interests, but the child did not reflect concern about that. Psychological distance from the children is reflected in comments about mothers' preoccupations with household jobs and taking care of the baby. One child saw the mother as a dependent person with depleted energy, needing rest and withdrawing, so that the child had to intrude upon her in order to get her attention. A vigilant concept of mother is reflected in the description of a restraining person who keeps the child from intruding, who forbids the child to leave the house when it's raining and muddy outside, and even an admonisher who restricts the activity of her child because of concern for the cleanliness of the home.

But Janice represents the little one as showing strong self-assertion and self-determination with artful skill: when the mother took her hand, the little dog* sneaked out of bed and went to play (at the price of a spanking). A note of confusion and vacillation in the expression of conflict of wills between the mother and child runs through Janice's stories: the child's reaction to discipline is a show of resistance, which yields, however, to the threat of force. One boy represented the child as avoiding the mother to escape punishment. Some children saw demands of mothers for grooming, and punishment for failure to keep clean, as

* The CAT assumes that children project their feelings and impulses through animals.

part of an overall pattern of taking care of the children, while others saw these as hostile.

The feeling of being deprived of the mother is associated with the mother's involvement with the father, which competes with the child's need for the mother. Brennie handled this problem at a fantasy level by representing two mothers, one who talked to the daddy while the other took care of the baby. In other instances, the mother becomes part of the sibling rivalry for the father's attention. Or the father competes with the children for the mother's attention. For JoAnne, probably both of these competitive relationships were being experienced at the same time since her tie to each parent was strong.

The amount of time spent with the mother, the degree of closeness, the dependability of her stimulus, support, and nurturance were desperately important to many such as Darlene, who appeared to rely on the mother figure as ego-auxiliary or adjunct of herself for motivation and guidance in achieving integration.

While grandmothers were referred to very enthusiastically by several children, particularly those whose grandmothers lived on farms with cows and cowboys, the grandmother could also be seen in the context of a shifting mother relationship in which the child felt uncertain about the grandparent who would fill the mother's place, or felt shunted over to the grandma while the mother went off with the father. Sometimes, even when the grandmother was a satisfying mother substitute, the feeling of being relegated to her or shoved away by mother crept in.

Mother as "bad object" [5]

In our group of children a few mothers were seen by the research staff as providing marked difficulties for the babies (Heider 1966). These included the overstimulating mother of Daryl, the teasing mother of Terry, the rather abrupt mother of Vernon, the often tense mother of rugged Tommy. In other words, a *few* mothers were judged to be creating difficulties for the baby because of (1) covertly ambivalent attitudes, (2) amounts of stimulation which the baby could not master, (3) insufficient stimulation, or (4) insufficient support of active coping efforts by the baby. Perhaps only in the first three instances would the mother be actually experienced as a "bad object" by the baby. In the instance of the mothers who were somewhat distant even in the act of feeding or of body care, the baby's reaction might be assumed to be more vague or confused; it might not be easy for the baby to connect the vague disappointment that it felt with the qualitative inadequacies of the mother's attention and contact.

We saw the conscious and explicit effort of Daryl's mother to offer herself as a substitute for food when the baby was hungry. If she wanted to postpone the feeding and did not want the baby to have the bottle, she cuddled and played with the baby saying, "If she gets attention, she won't think about being hungry." The mother here assumed interchangeability of herself as object with the food that the baby wanted. Later evidence suggested that the baby did not find this satisfying, and instead of accepting the mother's attention as a substitute for the bottle, she experienced frustration, both in relation to feeding and in relation to the mother. This apparently contributed to the development of covertly hostile feelings toward the mother, feelings that were, incidentally, more characteristic of this child during the preschool period than of any other child in the sample.

All together we see the children reflecting both an awareness of mothers' nurturance and stimulation on the one hand, and what were ambivalently felt to be deprivations at times of mothers' unavailability. Some early sources of frustration by mothers were observed at the time of the infancy study, and we shall take up these next.

Mothers' Style and Infant Behavior

Grace Heider (1966) evaluated a number of the items most directly involved in the mothers' handling of their babies. We shall discuss some of these items in another light.

When we think about the relationship between the functioning of the babies and how they experienced the handling techinques of their mothers, it will seldom be possible to assign priority to either the baby or the mother. Difficulty in delivery may be due to the relation between the size of the baby and the pelvic measurements of the mother, or to any one or combination of factors. Both the contributions from the baby's constitution and from the mother are in all likelihood highly variable. In our discussion we shall sometimes offer suggestions as to possible directions of influence. We hope our readers will think of other hypotheses; in fact, we shall be disappointed if the data do not evoke other possibilities in the minds of our readers.

First, let us have a brief glimpse of one mother's relationship with her month-old baby as excerpted by me from Dr. Leitch's detailed record of this responsive, very stimulated baby.

JoAnne Jackson (later a child with a stable IQ of 100) was seen at four weeks as a lively, socially mature, smiling baby. Even then oral interest was moderate compared to high visual, auditory, motor, and social interests.

Spitting up, which disgusted and irritated her mother, provided a point of tension in the oral area and may have given it a further ambivalent quality which it might not have had otherwise. According to her mother, JoAnne had been taken out frequently, and there was considerable evidence that she had more contact with her mother and other people than is usual for month-old babies. (When the baby was only two weeks old, for instance, her mother took her to see her former boss.) Hence, she may have been somewhat overstimulated.

The baby was awake for a couple of hours in the morning and less in the afternoon. Then the mother "played with her," holding her to her shoulder and patting her. The baby liked being bounced and smiled when this was going on. At the same time, when the baby was content, the mother left her lying alone "for quite a while." The mother very much enjoyed the baby's response to her and said with quiet enthusiasm, "She follows me with her eyes"; the mother also thought that when she was one week old she followed her own hand. The baby's father was proud of her, and the general impression that she looked like him contributed to the father's pride.

The baby liked to be sung and hummed to, especially when her father sang "Bobble-de-bobble-de-boo." With the "boo" he would suddenly lower the baby, whom he was holding out on his arm, and the baby would let out a big grin. In addition to this positive response to sounds such as singing, ML observed that the baby startled at an adult cough and seemed to startle at every noise that occurred. When the mother occasionally jiggled a rattle close to the baby, she thought the baby noticed the noise since she looked about.

When awake, the baby did not like wet diapers; after wetting she waited for a little while, then began to fuss. She reacted about the same way to soiled diapers. She sometimes strained and also fretted over having a bowel movement. The mother reported that JoAnne loved her bath (like most of the other babies in the study). Thus, in both auditory and tactile zones JoAnne found some experiences very pleasant and others very unpleasant. Her reaction was clear-cut in both directions (see chapter 6).

When the baby fussed, sometimes the fussing subsided of its own accord; at other times the mother had to pick up the baby. During the observation period when the baby fussed, the mother picked her up, saying, "Now watch, she'll stop crying," and the baby did indeed stop crying. Evidently by the age of four weeks JoAnne had already learned what was expected of her in this regard, and she cooperated.

During the time sample in the research office the mother stroked the baby's chest while she was crying, then picked her up and held her in a semisupine position in her left arm; the baby's crying subsided a little, then regained its intensity. The mother swayed the baby from side to side and talked to her softly, but the baby cried about as loudly as before. Then the mother brought the baby to her shoulder and the baby stopped crying, and at once the fussing began to subside. This vertical positioning at the shoulder is nearly always effective in soothing babies.

As the mother held the baby out on her arms, supporting her comfortably with her hands beneath her body, she talked to the baby very gently. The baby smiled a little, and the mother kissed her gently. She pointed out that the baby appeared to have dimples. The baby smiled a little and kept her eye on the mother, following the mother's every movement. Mother said that sometimes you could get a very big smile out of the baby; she would "open her mouth real wide and stick her tongue out with it."

The mother said they did not have a rocking chair at home and added, "We don't want to get into the habit of rocking her." (Rocking provides an important soothing experience involving rhythm, contact, and kinesthetic satisfactions, and the lack of it may have contributed to JoAnne's later restless activity.)

Toys, other than the rattle, were not provided as yet since the mother thought that the baby was pretty young to be shown toys. She said she did not want the baby to have too many, it would confuse her. Evidently the mother was more aware of the possibility of overstimulation by objects than she was aware of overstimulation by people.

When JoAnne's head began to slip across the mother's chest, the mother caught it, commenting that the baby acted hungry. The mother brought the baby down to a semisupine position on her arm so that the baby faced her. The baby fretted a little, then as the mother started to sway her from side to side she stopped fretting, turned a little pale, and closed her eyes. She opened her eyes and gave a small yawn, then she started to squirm, drew her legs up, flushed a little, and again cried. Her eyes remained half open.

The mother said she was sure the baby was hungry. She kept adjusting the baby's position and swayed from side to side with the baby. The baby kicked a little, cried, and began to flush again, drew her legs up, and made a few small random arm movements. Her fists opened and closed and her toes curled and uncurled. The mother again held the baby out with both arms and swayed her. The baby was a picture of contentment for a short period as she was being held by her mother. But when the mother put the baby down in order to go and fix her bottle, JoAnne started to cry at once, flushed, and became mottled. Shortly the mother returned to her, picked her up, sat down in the rocking chair to start the feeding, and the baby stopped crying the instant the mother picked her up. (This recurrent flushing, quite marked at times, along with crying, random movements of arms, and leg kicking suggested that JoAnne would show considerable autonomic reactivity, and regression along with definite protest.)

Feeding

After lowering the baby to a comfortable position in her left arm the mother offered the nipple, but when the baby started to cry, the mother immediately withdrew the nipple and brought the baby to her right shoulder. She said to the baby quietly but firmly, "Stop, before I feed you." The mother explained that she did not like to start the feeding until the baby had settled down. She just didn't think you should. Here we see the mother's explicit training procedure when JoAnne was still very young.

The mother brought the baby down into her left arm again and offered the bottle and the baby took the nipple. Her head was turned a little to the left and she kept her eyes fixed on one experimenter. The baby sucked rather gently, but the mother commented that the very first time "she went right to it and moved her head like this," demonstrating how the baby had moved her head from side to side. The baby burped gently and apparently easily and after the feeding seemed very contented. Her mother said that JoAnne was always contented after she ate. Evidently feeding was comfortable and gratifying.

When she had had enough of the bottle feeding, she would "let you take the nipple out real easy, and then she won't let you put it back in, or if she does, she won't suck it any more." JoAnne was as decisive and clear-cut in terminating a feeding when she had had enough as she was in expressing likes and dislikes of other types of stimulation. Illustrating this, the mother gently ran the nipple over the baby's lips; the baby did not open her mouth for it. She always waited a little while, then if the baby cried, she offered the bottle again.

ML commented that the mother handled the baby quite expertly and with great gentleness, except at the end of the afternoon when the mother appeared to be tired and perhaps excessively warm since the room was overheated.

JoAnne and her mother illustrate some of the rich variety of interactions between an active, responsive four-week-old baby and her responsive mother. We shall now turn to an overview of maternal patterns and their relation to their babies' functioning in the group of twenty-seven mothers (with thirty-one babies) that Grace Heider studied intensively (1966).

Attention given by the mother

Since there is so much interest in the stimulus role of the mother (Rheingold 1961; Gewirtz 1965), the importance of her attention, talking to, providing tactile stimulation through her cuddling and baby contact, and her visual (or eye-to-eye) response to the baby, we shall start here.

Few mothers in this sample talked a lot to their four-week-old babies.* But of the twenty-four mothers of babies eight to thirty-two weeks old, seventeen talked to their babies a moderate or high amount. Heider judged that thirteen of these babies also vocalized to a moderate or high degree. But so did six babies whose mothers talked to them least; in four of these instances, fathers and grandmothers were important in the baby's experience. One father later told how he "queened" his baby, and the mother described his delight in their babies. It seems reasonable to infer that being talked to by *someone* influences the baby's own vocalizing. And let us not forget that many adults are easily stimulated by the baby's talk—in fact, the cooing and babbling of an eager baby are hard for many a mother to resist. Five of the six mothers who talked very little to their baby daughters were disturbed with postpartum depressions; in this culture healthy, well-adjusted, middle class mothers generally do carry on mother–baby conversations.

In the coping sample of babies, both extremes of maternal attention interfered with optimal functioning. An excessively high degree of stimulation may contribute to a loss of functional stability. Some mothers react to a baby's difficulties by rocking or caressing too vigorously in their anxious effort to soothe the baby. Babies differ, moreover, in their "soothability": Escalona found that inactive babies were more easily soothed than active babies (1968, p. 119). The success of efforts to soothe a baby also depends on the relation between the soothing pattern or technique and what is actually comforting or irritating to a given baby.

* However, I have seen numerous mothers of my acquaintance who do talk to such small infants from their earliest weeks.

Now let us turn to some other implications of the mothers' ways of handling these babies. The mother's stimulation of the baby with speech and facial expressions is related to some items in the infant's oral behavior: the most significant correlation is with intensity of nonvocal oral behavior but frequency of vocalization is also important (cf. Provence and Lipton 1962). We have seen tragic examples of the negative end of this relationship in babies in foundling homes or hospitals who receive minimal conversation or verbal play from overburdened nurses, each one of whom has to care for eight to ten babies. Many of these babies babble very little and are often emotionally unexpressive as well. This is only one aspect of the inadequate development of babies in hospital situations of this sort, and it may in fact contribute to further difficulties in communication since the child then fails to respond to positive overtures from adults as well as failing to evoke them.

Now we come face to face with a balancing item; we should not think simply of the active stimulation and gratification of the baby's needs. The baby's autonomy must also be respected. Babies have preferences not only in food and toys, but also in tempo of feeding, ways of being held, temperature of their bathwater, what they like to listen to and look at, and a multitude of other details of their environment. We have noted that many of these mothers spoke about the baby's likes and dislikes and respected them: "He likes his green frog best."

The mother's respect for the infant's autonomy correlated significantly with the infant's ability to utilize support from others in the case of the boys, and with oral gratification for girls; the latter relationship, while in the same direction, is smaller for boys.

What does this mean? We are not surprised that the mother's early respect for the infant's autonomy lays a favorable foundation for his response to other helpers and contributes to his trust of adults (cf. Erikson 1964). Allowing for the baby's autonomy in terms of pace, wish to terminate feeding, and so forth, evidently contributes as well to good vegetative functioning implied in oral gratification. The principle implied is that respect for the baby's natural pace and rhythms avoids irritation and autonomic excitation, which could interfere with good digestion and oral gratification.[6]

Mothers' relationships with boy infants

There are substantial differences in correlations for these boys as compared with girls, as in other studies (Kagan 1969; Moss 1967), so we shall discuss further relationships for boy babies separately. While the degree of respect for the infant's needs for autonomy correlates highly with mother's awareness of her infant boy's needs, it correlates negatively with the amount of attention given. This implies that when the mother is sensitive to the infant's need to do things for himself, she does not give him unwanted or excessive attention; the total amount of attention is then less than with the mother whose attitude is that she must do everything for the baby, and that he can do nothing for himself. (Respect for the infant's needs for autonomy also correlates well with healthiness of the mother's goal, her level of adjustment, and her degree of acceptance of the infant as he is, which implies that she is free from anxious needs to demand rigid conformity.)

But beyond this, the positive correlation of respect for the baby's autonomy with success in breast feeding suggests that the mother who is attuned to the baby, accepting and affording autonomy, is also comfortable in breast feeding. Here we come upon an important new item: autonomy allowed by the mother in the feeding situation also correlates significantly with the baby's own termination capacity and capacity to resist and to protest. We are talking about the babies who clamp their mouths shut when they do not want any more food, or who spit, blow, or push out food they do not want, or who protest and resist in other ways. We see here the development of the infant's active expression of his wishes evidently reinforced by the mother's permission to be autonomous; this is congruent with David Levy's observations in *Maternal Overprotection* (1966) that the vigorous, demanding infant is allowed more autonomy by the mother. We shall discuss later on the relationship between this infantile *autonomy, resistance,* and *protest* to the child's coping capacity at the preschool stage (p. 136).

Our description of the mothers themselves emphasized their implicit self-respect, and now we have found how important is the mothers' respect for even a small baby's autonomy. Shall we say with Bettelheim (1950) that "love is not enough?" Or that to lay a foundation for the trust emphasized by Erikson (1964), a mother must not only satisfy the baby's food, sleep, and activity needs, but she must satisfy them in a way appropriate to that baby's style—his pace, his bodily rhythms, his drives and tastes, and his idiosyncratic comfort patterns?

Now we must add a word about the prerequisites for such respect for the baby's autonomy. First of all, the mothers who spontaneously offered respect were aware of the baby as a unique person, to be observed and understood as an individual, not just cared for according to rules or systems. Along with this they had to be, first of all, free from anxiety that would interfere with acting upon this awareness. Also, a mother could respond most appropriately to her baby's style when her own style did not conflict too grossly. Finally, a mother probably needed to have had sensitive perceptive mothering herself—if we can draw this conclusion from the patterns of the unmothered mother.

We did not anticipate that autonomy allowed by the mother would also correlate well with the infant's tendency to delay action until after orientation has been completed. Could it be that the infant who is permitted to be autonomous develops more capacity for control—partly as a result of being more at ease—with the capacity to delay (instead of reacting directly to stimulation) as one aspect of control? Does the combination of appropriate attention, together with respect for the baby's need to decide when he has had enough, guarantee an optimal relationship? Perhaps not, for we found ourselves formulating another item related to the kind of mother and the kind of baby she has.

"Viability of the mother–child relation" is a broad phrase that has to do with the compatibility or attunement of the mother and baby and the extent to which the mother's style fits with the baby's style of functioning. Poor "fit" is seen when the mother is in temperament so different from the baby that her personality does not easily provide what the baby seems to be demanding. The most clear-cut instances of this were found in the case of a mother who had enormous appreciation for a vigorous baby, skill in handling him, and healthiness in her approach to him—but she was herself a petite and gentle person who was not equipped physically to provide the vigor of interchange that her energetic, robust infant seemed to require. At the opposite end of the scale an extremely vigorous, intelligent, in many ways skillful, healthy mother who valued her children, did not have the gentleness of touch needed by a baby of unusual sensitivity.

We note that mother–child viability is negligibly correlated with such characteristics of the infant as activity level, qualities of vocalization, and drive level—variables that are probably more controlled by genetic factors. As we might expect, there were significant correlations between mother–infant viability and other aspects of the mother. These include mother's respect for the autonomy of the infant and mother's level of adjustment. Nor were we surprised that mother–infant viability also correlated with the baby's vegetative functioning. These correlations were consistent for boys and girls, and the correlation with vegetative functioning suggests that the attunement implied in mother–baby "fit" contributes to physiological integration.

Similarly, mother–child viability is related to the infants' capacity to use support from others. However, it is interesting to see that the item "importance of the baby to the mother" gives a higher correlation for girls, while "feelings about her competence" with the infant gives a higher correlation for boys. "Importance of the baby to the mother" is an item of more than obvious interest: in one instance, the baby was intensely important to his mother, who had been adopted in very early childhood and had eagerly looked forward to "having someone of my own blood." In another instance, a boy baby arrived after two girls, and in addition conspicuously resembled the mother's father. Again, a warm, maternal mother felt this would be her last of three babies and so especially wanted to enjoy him as much as possible (and not let him grow up too fast). By contrast, a baby who was a third girl when a son was longed for, or who was an "extra" baby born to a mother who already had four children and had not expected or wanted any more babies, was not as welcome, and not as important, to the mother.

Mother–infant correlations for boys and girls

Conspicuous differences between mother–infant correlations for boys as compared with girls[7] include in addition to those mentioned above:

Higher correlations for girls:
Mother–child viability correlated
with   autonomy allowed

                                                     importance of baby
                                                     to mother

Mother's respect for infant's
autonomy with   oral gratification

Higher correlations for boys:
Mother–child viability correlated
with   her feelings about
                                                     competence with infant

                                                     the baby's utilization of
                                                     support from others

                                                     the baby's vegetative
                                                     functioning

Mother's amount of speech and
facial (expressive) communication
correlated with   infant's activity level

                                                     frequency of vocalization

                                                     nonvocal oral behavior

                                                     drive level

                          (neg.)   tendency to delay

(neg.)	mother's acceptance of the baby's developmental pace
Mother's level of adjustment correlated with	infant's use of support from others, and from self
	oral gratification
Mother's level of adjustment correlated with	infant's sensory reactivity (i.e., implying that maternal tension heightens the baby's sensory reactivity)

We need to learn more about some of these differences that may be deeply ingrained in cultural assumptions about girls and boys. Do girls just not matter as much, even in our culture, as well as in certain oriental and primitive cultures? Are baby boys more difficult to manage and thus a source of greater insecurity for the mother? As to the first question, it is worth noting that of eleven babies who were judged by Heider to be of less importance to their mothers, eight were girls. Correspondingly, of fifteen babies very important to their mothers, ten were boys. The answer to the second question is less clear since in twenty-two instances mothers felt highly competent with their infants. Of only three mothers who felt very doubtful about their competence, two were the mothers of boys.

Mothers' adjustment level

Since adjustment can contribute to freedom from tension and self-preoccupations, and thus to openness, it is reasonable to find that the mother's level of adjustment correlates significantly (from .50 to .66) with (1) the mother's awareness of needs of the baby, (2) degree of respect for the baby's needs, (3) her skill in handling the baby, and only a little less impressively, (4) healthiness of her goals for the baby.

We must be wary of assuming that a well-adjusted mother will automatically be characterized by all the other patterns just reviewed; moreover, the direction of influence can also be the other way around. That is, when the mother wants and/or needs the baby and also has healthy goals for him; is temperamentally compatible with him (so that empathic awareness of his needs is fostered, and she can more easily respect his needs), and is skillful in handling the baby, all these conditions probably contribute to the level of her adjustment as observed and judged in the context of her relationship with the baby. She is apt to be comfortably satisfied and relaxed in a way that is not so likely in a mother who is less compatible with the baby, finds it harder to judge his needs or to handle him smoothly. Here again we find no significant correlations between the mother's level of adjustment and ratings made on such aspects of the equipment of the infant as activity level and sensory reactivity. So we can see that within this small sample of normal babies, while the mother's level of adjustment is closely related to her behavior with the baby, the baby himself is an independent physical unit, some of whose characteristics are not easily shaped by the mother's adjustment or behavior.

Reciprocal relationships between babies' characteristics and mothers' handling

A high correlation (.74) between the infant's drive level and the mother's responses to the infant through speech and facial expression implies that this kind of response from the mother either stimulates and/or reinforces the infant's drive, or that the baby with high drive evokes much response from the mother, or both (Levy 1966). Since drive was also correlated with the infant's frequency of vocalization, we see a possible cluster of expressiveness and stimulation value that could contribute to a baby's "sending power," as Erik Erikson (1964) describes it, and to his stimulation of his mother.

The good correlation (.53) between robustness of the baby and the mother's success in breast feeding implies a possibility that the baby's own vigor (and stimulation to the breast) may contribute to the success in breast feeding (as well as to the possibility that robustness is fostered by breast feeding, or that robust mothers who can succeed in breast feeding have robust babies). These relationships can be seen in two ways: if the mother has a sturdy, healthy baby, it is easier for her to be relaxed with the baby and to have healthy goals for it, and consequently her own adjustment is better. The robust baby nurses well and contributes to the success in breast feeding. The mother is free from anxious reactions to the baby and anxious concern about its development. Or, we may speculate that when the mother's goals are less healthy, when she is more anxious and less well-adjusted, the baby does not nurse so well and does not become so robust. We need to watch both directions of influence.

Correlations between infant girls' ratings and mothers' handling

Robustness in girls correlates positively with ease of mother's delivery. Here, there may be a common hereditary factor (from robust mothers to infants) but the fact that only two out of seven girl infants with high ratings on robustness were primiparae suggests that the greater ease of delivery in later-born babies may be a major factor; ease of pregnancy also correlates with vocal and nonvocal oral behavior. Are well-functioning little girls who enjoyed an easy pregnancy more spontaneously expressive, or do their relaxed, well-functioning mothers evoke more responsiveness?

A significant negative correlation between sensory reactivity and success in breast feeding may imply either that a mother might find it harder to be successful in breast feeding a highly "sensitive" baby, or that failure or difficulty in breast feeding tends to increase sensory reactivity, with the resulting frustration contributing to more irritability and lowered thresholds (or a least increasing activation and thus reactivity) in the baby. On the positive side, autonomy allowed by the mother in feeding is significantly related to adequacy of vegetative functioning in the infant and to the viability of the mother and child relationship (or their temperamental compatibility). Note also the highly significant correlation between girls' vegetative functioning and robustness of physique. This again suggests that the child whose needs for autonomy are respected may be free from the frustrations that could be disturbing to visceral functioning generally. But at the same time the mother may feel more at ease about the robust baby, who can be trusted to use autonomy.

The high correlations between mother–child viability with mother's awareness of the baby girl's needs, with skill in handling the infant, and with degree of respect for the infant's needs for autonomy all imply that the mother's ease in handling the baby girl is highly related to a capacity for empathy, which goes along with the temperamental compatibility.

Mother–child viability also correlates significantly with speech and facial expressiveness of the mother in her relation with the child, with importance of the baby to the mother, with healthiness of a goal for the baby, and with mother's level of adjustment. But we find an unexpected relationship; mother–child viability correlates with the infant's utilization of support from cognitive experiences, that is, from watching and problem-solving experiences. This new finding suggests that the baby who is at ease in a satisfying reaction with the mother will be free from drive tensions and free to use her eyes and ears and tactile exploring resources.

Somewhat contradictory correlations seem to appear when we scrutinize the *amount of attention* that the mother gives to the infant daughter. On the one hand, a positive correlation with degree of acceptance of the infant would seem to imply the positive value of attention given, while a negative correlation with acceptance of developmental pace implies that in this responsible sample the mother gives extra attention when she is not confident of the adequacy of the developmental pace of the child. That is, the extra attention may be aimed at stimulating the infant's developmental pace. (This was most obviously true for the premature girl in this group.)

Individual mother–baby interaction patterns

So far our ratings have essentially confirmed generally accepted assumptions in clinical psychology, namely, that the well-functioning, gratified, steady, stable baby tends to be found with a well-adjusted mother who values her baby, feels attuned to it, is aware of and respectful of its needs, and is skillful in handling it. There is nothing remarkable about this finding except perhaps the fact that some of the correlations are so modest. Obviously we have to say here what we have to say over and over again—that if we were studying a wider range of infants from the very lowest to the very highest socioeconomic groups— that is, including families living under extremely depriving slum conditions and optimally privileged families—we would expect a wider range of patterns among the mothers. Insofar as the good functioning of the baby is actually closely related to the well-being of the mother, there would then be a wide range in the level of vegetative functioning, stability, gratification in the feeding situation, and so on, and we could expect these correlations to be much higher.

We promised at the beginning of this chapter to ascertain what we could learn by scrutinizing individual mother–baby couples in addition to reflecting on group correlations.

Let us consider Roddy's mother as an example of a mother who was intensely devoted to her infant but who lacked complete attunement with him. As her first "blood relation" (because she lost her own parents in infancy and knew no blood relations), Roddy was of maximal importance. Possibly because of irregularities and inconsistent sequences in her own early care and a lack of subsequent experience with infants, she was not very skillful with the baby despite her enormous love for him and the great importance he had for her. Dr. Brody (1956, p. 196) commented:

> Toward the baby she was warm, affectionate, and at times mildly stimulating. Occasionally she handled him rather abruptly, pulling him toward her by an arm or a leg or lifting him very suddenly. In quite a few respects this considerate mother appeared to feel it her obligation to have the baby adapt to predetermined standards. . . .

She did not hesitate to remove the nipple from the baby's mouth while he was sucking because she felt it proper to diaper him then. She arbitrarily took the pacifier from his mouth when she thought he ought not to have it, but if he fussed, she usually restored it. Sometimes she tantalized him by touching it to his tongue but not letting him have it. When taking things from him . . . she always seemed to make up for the deprivation by talking to him in an especially loving voice.

As seen by Grace Heider (1966), Roddy was one of the most vulnerable babies. Yet despite certain inadequacies in the mother's sensitivity and handling of the baby, and the baby's own vulnerability, this boy became one of the high achievers in school and one of the relatively creative children who seemed—during his growing up years—to be maximizing his potentialities. Was it perhaps the challenge presented by these contradictions between the imperfect attunement and the obvious intense regard for him which his mother had that stimulated him to solve his problems and to make maximal effort?

This hypothesis may seem highly speculative and questionable at first glance, and not in line with usual assumptions in clinical psychology. But it is consistent with the thinking of such historians as Toynbee (1972) who put their emphasis on challenge, and we find it in the biographies and autobiographies of a good many distinguished people; it deserves special consideration.

As we consider the pattern of development of such a child in comparison with the development of certain children who began with a most idyllic experience, our hypothesis in regard to the role of challenge seems to gather some support. The very well-balanced Barbie, handled so understandingly and gently by a mother whom she resembled, developed little tendency to make vigorous use of her capacities. Here was a little girl whose early infantile experience was one of optimal ease and satisfaction and little or no challenge at all. Later, to be sure, some tensions arose as she developed into a more active child.

We observed other problems resulting from what appeared to be optimal mothering in infancy—optimal in terms of sensitivity to needs of the infant, attentiveness, acceptance, and other variables dealing with nurturance. In line with Spitz's comment (1946) that the best mothered babies suffered most at departure of their mothers in the latter part of the first year, the excellently mothered Lennie did not thrive after his mother went back to work when he was about nine months old. The pediatrician recommended that his mother give up working until he was older.

Chester's mother was given an A rating by Brody in her study *Patterns of Mothering* (1956). This rating reflected the mother's consistent sensitivity and attentiveness to her baby boy. "She seemed to enjoy physical contact with him. . . . Her movements were never of a confining nature . . . never failing to give adequate support. . . . To an unusual degree her attitude was shielding and protective. Securely and simply she said, 'You can tell when a baby is ready for anything.' She spoke with pride of the baby's good mood." Yet when a baby brother (born when Chester was twenty months old) was being observed, his mother commented that "Ray was good natured, he didn't get mad at every little thing the way Chester did." We shall see more of Chester later (see pp. 105–08).

Now that we have raised the question about the possible role of challenge at a very early level in infancy, we need to define more carefully different degrees of challenge and the kinds of experiences that were involved. The qualities as well as degrees of challenge are strikingly different with different children. In the case of Helen (see chapter 11), we see her in infancy supported by skillful and adequate, yet not fully gratifying, care, in that strong needs for contact were not met. Although she was handled by a responsible mother who was well organized and met very well what might be regarded as ordinary basic needs, she did not handle Helen's peculiar and subtle combination of need for contact and for avoidance of overstimulation in a way that was adequate to satisfy the baby. This is in contrast to the interference and interruptions that were seen with Roddy, and to the teasing approach of Terry's mother.

If we look at these varied experiences through the prism afforded by Erikson's discussion of infancy (1964), we may infer that Helen must have learned from her earliest experience that the universal basic necessities of life could be counted on; that is, she could trust that enough would be given to make it possible to keep going. At the same time, the contact hunger may have contributed a sense of urgency or impetus to reach out for that additional amount and quality of stimulation that she needed for complete satisfaction.

By contrast, we are entitled to wonder whether the constant teasing and removal of stimulating objects to a distance just beyond reach, which did stimulate Terry to make additional efforts, may have greatly reinforced the already high drive of this maximally active infant boy, and in a context which involved for him the orientation that the environment was not going to make things easily available to him. He would have to struggle in order to attain his desired objects.

At the beginning of our research we did not offer a hypothesis that the experience of moderate challenge and frustration in the infants' relation with their mothers (within a context of satisfaction in the basic essentials of life) would evoke and/or reinforce a tendency toward an outreaching effort to reach goals in the environment. This hypothesis actually emerged only after the children had reached puberty and it was possible to see the development of such a trend in certain children whose infancy had been considered less than ideal. In other words, this is a hypothesis *produced by* the research rather than initiating the research. It can, of course, only be substantiated by replication of similar research on other samples of children in which a comparable *balance* of gratification and frustration in early relation with their mothers is seen; also samples in which children exposed to such a balance of gratification and frustration can be compared with children who experience a more nearly totally gratifying infancy on the one hand, or more extremely frustrating and depriving infancy on the other hand. Insofar as other longitudinal studies have comparable intensive data on the mother–child relation in the first six months of life, the hypothesis could be checked by analysis of existing data.

We can also consider this question of balance of gratification and challenge in relation to different cultures.[8] Is the passivity that underlies the limited problem-solving capacities of many people in India or Mexico, and the United States as well, related to gratifying infantile experiences that leave the baby nothing to struggle for?

This hypothesis also implies the crucial question; how do we determine the "optimal" balance of gratification and frustration for the individual baby? Does "optimal" preclude a degree of stress that leads to regression? Or does a modicum of regression followed by reintegration contribute to flexibility and perspective? As we follow the growth of these babies we may find tentative answers to such questions.

PART II
PROCESSES CONTRIBUTING TO
CONTINUITY AND CHANGE

3

Dynamics of Individuality in the Infant[1]

He knew exactly what was going on and was the most active and most knowing participant of us all.

Once he had seen his red sweater, he expected to be taken out and you pretty well had to do it or else there was no living with him. He insisted on my getting him.

Infancy descriptions of Donald
by an observer and Donald's mother

If the ecological setting and culture were the sole determinants of the baby's development, all babies in a given setting would tend to be alike. Then if the different experiences mediated by the mothers were the chief determiners of differences, babies with similar mothers would likewise tend to be alike. Clinical experience with extreme or deviant mothers—such as those who reject babies—apparently provides examples of such similar effects. But this is a mother–baby interaction, as we have just found in chapter 2 and as David Levy showed years ago (1943, 1966). The same mother may be a party to very different styles of interplay with different babies, as she is warmed or turned off, stimulated or resisted, challenged or yielded to by the baby. Babies from the beginning show impressive differences.[2]

A nursery for the newborn provides as uniform an environmental setting as we could find outside a controlled laboratory. Yet even in such a nursery we can see at a glance certain differences between the babies: some babies jerk or cry at a noise (the dropping of a tin cup), while others sleep on peacefully; some babies scream loudly when they are wet or hungry, while others complain in milder tones; some babies cease crying instantly when picked up and soothed, while others quiet down only slowly; some babies seem to wriggle almost constantly when awake, while others are quietly composed.

These and other differences have attracted the attention of investigators of the last fifty years, but a complete inventory of individual differences does not yet exist. And we have only begun in the last two decades to explore sources of these differences in human babies. We are somewhat better informed about baby rats: for instance, the effects on offspring of dire stress experiences of mothers during the gestational period (Thompson and Sontag 1956). To be sure, we have some data about the infancy and later behavior of children whose mothers were malnourished, alcoholic, addicted, treated with drugs that damage the fetus, infected with rubella, or partners to Rh incompatibility (Birch and Gussow 1970). Anoxia during birth due to prolonged delivery or to sedation of the mother has been found to retard reflex functioning such as sucking and also the attention span of the perinatal baby. But these effects have to do with pathology and do not tell us about factors within the normal range of differences. Here some authors assume genetic control to be the major source of individual differences in infants (Stone, Smith, and Murphy 1973, pp. 30–101).

At one month the baby has already been exposed to thousands of experiences, some of which have conditioned him toward certain persistent types of response. Consequently, when we speak of "constitutional" differences in one-month-old babies, we do not imply that these are solely determined by genes, impressive as resemblances to the family members may sometimes be. In the dynamics of infant development a wide range of environmental and genetic factors constantly interact, producing relatively persistent adaptational tendencies. Some of these tendencies have been studied in detail, a few of which we will review at this point.

Margaret Fries's pioneer study of differences in activity levels in young infants (1953) and Mary Shirley's pioneer study of characteristics of normal (1931) and premature babies (1938) following Gesell's early observations of differences persisting from infancy through childhood (Gesell, Amatruda, et al. 1939) opened the door for further study of a variety of individual differences in babies.

Our Sarah Lawrence studies of individual personality in preschool children (Lerner and Murphy 1941) extended the range of characteristics that we in turn wish to explore. John Benjamin advanced an intensive dynamic study of the innate and experiential factors in infant behaviors (Benjamin 1959), and this was paralleled by the Yale studies initiated by Ernst Kris (Solnit and Provence 1963). In these latter studies psychoanalysis of a small number of mothers combined with intensive observations of their babies provided a depth approach beyond the scope of other longitudinal investigations.

In our Topeka research we did not have the opportunity to study dynamics of the development of individuality by psychoanalytic methods. But individual case studies based on observations and examinations of the children in infancy and later, together with correlational studies, have added to our understanding and have extended our hypotheses about the developments of individual adaptational style. In these studies we have been concerned with the interaction of the broader environment, the mother in particular, and the child's range of characteristics. We shall turn to the observations of the thirty-one infants in the group we followed into adolescence.

We have already glimpsed some of the babies' characteristics as they were first seen at various ages from four to thirty-two weeks, when their mothers brought them to the offices of Escalona and Leitch. Now we need a fuller account of these babies. What characteristics might foreshadow their evolving coping resources and adaptational styles at later ages? How do their different tendencies interact with one another and the environment? Escalona's summary sketches in the original records of two of the seven-month-old babies, Vernon and Brennie, provide examples of the range of characteristics observed.

Similarities and differences in two seven-month-old babies[3]

Both Vernon and Brennie were masculine in appearance; Vernon, slender and fair, Brennie, sturdy with "expressive shiny dark eyes and light brown hair." Both were well coordinated, while Vernon had a remarkable capacity to "execute certain activities at a rather high degree of coordination at an especially slow tempo": he could scratch the screen slowly with individual fingers. Vernon could also roll from supine to prone and vice versa with ease, sit up for long periods and while doing so lean forward and reerect himself.

Brennie could also sit without support, and when pulled to sitting, he actively assisted. Furthermore, he was discontented when lying down; when prone he held his head very high, supporting his chest on his extended arms. His mother reported that he could pull himself to standing by the side of the crib. When held in a standing position, he bounced actively, and he jumped when held by both hands. Thus Brennie appeared more vigorous, showed more initiative, more drive to master locomotion skills, and he vigorously strove toward things he wanted, unmistakably rejecting others.

Vernon showed some evidence of visual and auditory sensitivity— blinking at various sounds, including mild ones. He also blinked at sudden motion close to his face. When very sleepy he tended to cover his eyes with his arms as though the light were troublesome to him. He did not seem more than ordinarily sensitive to tactile stimulation.

Brennie's responses were more variable: at times he recognized minimal stimuli yet was able to tolerate intense stimulation at other times. He seemed fascinated but not disturbed by camera noise and did not blink when he rang the bell very close to his ear. Similarly, even the photographic lights did not seem to phase him. He seemed to feel tickling sensations occasionally when his mother diapered him, but he tolerated the prolonged tactile stimulation of the physical examination without tension or any change in mood.

On the whole, Vernon seemed more easily disturbed by stimulation—a tendency that could lead to self-protective devices and avoidance of stimulation he could not tolerate.

Vernon's vocalizations were well differentiated, consisting of mixed vowel sounds and occasionally mixed vowels and consonants, and his expressive sounds ranged from cooing to loud squeals. Vocalizations occurred both in response to and to initiate social contact with another person, but also in accompaniment to pleasurable motor play or expressive movement.

He tended to hold his mouth closed more of the time than did most infants; intensive sucking, licking, or biting on objects was not observed.

Brennie's vocalizations were not as advanced as the rest of his behavior, but though he did a good deal of infantile squealing, Escalona felt that his laughter was more mature than usual for his age. He almost invariably brought objects to his mouth and partially engulfed them, moving his lips over an object, or moving it within his mouth; but he did not suck or bite objects.

Brennie was extremely active, vigorously outgoing, approaching all available objects and carrying out many activities with them. He offered more than usual resistance to having preferred objects removed from his grasp even when substitutes were offered.

Vernon's social responses were varied and sensitive, and they differentiated his mother and the research group: toward his mother his responses were more immediate and vigorous, whereas he was shy with the investigators except for the very gentle Dr. Leitch.

Brennie was very responsive to people, including the investigators after a short time, although his mother reported shyness with strangers. His unusually wide range of expressive behavior included smiling, chuckling, laughing, pleasurable "gurgling," and excited "shrieks of sheer delight"; on the displeasure side, squealing and other irritable and impatient expressions, brief crying spells, and a somber "mildly disapproving" expression when he first awakened from his nap.

We see Brennie, then, as more active, more responsive both to people and to objects, more outgoing, more open, with stronger drive and with less need to protect himself from stimulation. There were other, idiosyncratic differences between the two babies: for instance, Vernon tended to flush when coughing—the flush both arose and subsided slowly. This, along with his blinking at various sounds, his tendency to cover his eyes with his arms as if to shut out light, and his shyness, all suggested considerable sensitivity.

Let us discuss in more detail two of the tendencies we have just noted in Vernon and Brennie, activity level and sensory reactivity, along with certain other tendencies that contribute to the adaptational styles of other infants.

Activity level

Activity level is an area of infant functioning that attracts the attention of almost anyone watching babies and has been subject to research for years, with a highlight in M. Fries's 1953 report. Escalona (1968) has shown that activity level contributes to the range and content of the infant's experience in his environment and his response to adaptational problems: the active baby exposes himself to a wider range of stimulation. A high activity level may therefore be closely related to the capacity for mastery in two respects: the stimulation of cognitive development through the infant's enlarged exposure to the environment, and the overall enhancement of coping through motor resources developed from a wider range of manipulative experiences. Terry's high activity level was closely associated with pleasure in mastery of skills and his determination to reach his goals, like baby Brennie.

The problems, however, involved in adequate differentiation of different *factors* (physiological, psychological, environmental) in activity level have not yet been solved.[4] Moreover, the proportions of babies at different levels vary from culture to culture. I have never seen babies under the age of six months in India as active as some of the babies in this sample.

While Escalona's study of the relation of activity level to the infant's experience emphasizes the wider exposure and richer experience of the active infant, other considerations are also important. During the weeks before the baby has achieved an adequate equilibrium, before vegetative functioning is smoothly established, we can assume that the less active baby is less exposed to potentially disturbing external stimuli and may achieve and maintain better internal integration. At the same time, he has less capacity to discharge tension through motor channels and less exercise of visual-motor and gross-motor skills needed for coping with stimulation. In different babies the balance of these effects varied. Some "quiet" babies have learned very early to protect themselves from overstimulation by inhibiting activity; it seems likely that this was true of the sensitive and quiet Vernon. It is difficult to be sure whether a given baby's inactivity is due to this self-protective control or to a constitutional tendency toward low activity or to a great visual and other sensory interest that can be better sustained in a condition of motor quiet.

Special qualities of motor behavior are also important in individual instances. In *Colin: A Normal Child* (Murphy 1956) we described a small boy who loped over the ground with apparent delight; movement was not just a means to an end, but a pleasure in itself. Similarly, some of our Topeka infants showed delight in movement: Teddy would bounce on his mother's lap to stimulate his mother to bounce with him. (Interestingly enough, this early rhythm may be related to his later career in music.)

"Activity" is far more than locomotion and other motor exploits. Susan at twenty-eight weeks would look at a person, squeal and laugh until the person "was practically forced to pay attention to her." She would selectively go after and pick out toys she liked from a pile, and throw the others aside. On her own initiative she would at times cease her vigorous movement and lie down to rest. When she was not ready for sleep, however, her mother said there was no putting her down, "She would scream her head off." Here was a highly active baby, both motorically and in her dealings with the world.

Sally, at twenty-eight weeks, was another active, vigorous baby who enjoyed locomotion, play with her body, social interaction, and manipulation of toys; she also handled discomfort by actions which she initiated: When she (apparently) experienced discomfort during a feeding, she got up on her hands and knees and burped. When her mother put an unwelcome nipple in her mouth, she repeatedly rolled over and lost it. When she wanted to move around, she slid off her mother's lap and pushed ahead on the floor. From infancy she used her capacity for resourceful activity to meet her needs and to cope with frustration.

Role of stimulation and other factors in activity level

Our discussion above leads to a question that must be raised when we study individual babies: to what extent is activity a reflection of internally generated impulses (tension or restlessness related to gastric or other physiological difficulties, or genetically controlled drive pressures) as contrasted with a marked tendency to react to external stimuli by motor activity? Activity level in some infants appears to be a resultant of interaction between the individual's given thresholds and reactivity tendencies in an environment that offers greater or less stimulation of different kinds; in other infants, activity level may be an outcome of the interaction between certain drives or needs and an environment that rewards the child's efforts to meet these needs. Infants whose mothers avoided overstimulation and who responded to the infants' demands or cues in a gratifying way, show behavior that is probably close to the baby's genetically controlled activity level. However, even an infant of four weeks or younger who spends much time in the care of a constantly stimulating, or restless, or tense mother, may react with greater activity. Thus it is difficult even in the early weeks to separate the possibly genetic activity level of the infant from the level produced in part by the infant's reaction to the mother's activity, or to that of the rest of his family, or by frustrations or internal tensions.

But stimulation is a two-way affair: the behavior of the initially active and responsive infant may evoke the mother's repeated efforts to stimulate more responses from him, and a circular pattern of activity leading to further, or even more intense, activity may result. This pattern was seen in Terry. Depending on the infant's tolerance for stimulation, this heightened activity level may be a positive factor in his development. But if thresholds for loss of coordination under stress are low, the increased stimulation and resulting heightened activity level may exact a toll in decreased smoothness of motor functioning. So we need to look at differences in reactivity to stimulation and their effects.

Sensory reactivity

The study of visual behavior—attention, scanning, pattern vision, and preferences for certain shapes (Stone, Smith, and Murphy 1973, sec. 57–60)—has demonstrated the subtlety of responses to visual stimuli even from birth on: young infants work at bringing order out of the initial chaos or "blooming buzzing confusion," as William James (1962) imagined the baby's first sensory experience. Beyond this, cardiac and other expressions of autonomic nervous system responses testify to the impact of auditory experiences on the total functioning of the infant organism (Stone et al. 1973, secs. 64, 68).

Differences in the pace of maturation of hearing and vision during the early weeks of life, as well as differences in sensitivity or reactivity in these and in other modalities have also been documented (Stone et al. 1973, secs. 41, 43); thus it is not surprising to find variations among our sample of infants. But the place of sensory reactivity in the baby's day-to-day experience calls for study in its own right.

The research setting of the Escalona–Leitch study (1952) offered the sights and sounds of a more or less homelike "laboratory" with four adults present and the stimuli involved in the tests themselves; sounds from outside the laboratory could be heard as well. The three observers watched for evidences of reaction (in all zones of behavior) to both the planned and serendipitous sensory stimuli. Reactivity to visual, auditory, and tactual stimuli in the tests and examinations was observed directly. In addition, some infants were reported by their mothers to be disturbed by changes in temperature, by bath water evidently felt as too warm or too cold, and by other nuances of sensory stimulation. A few babies expressed strong likes or dislikes of specific toys with particular colors or qualities, for instance, the popular bright shiny surface, a preference appreciated and respected by many mothers. (Such distinctive individual preferences could not be handled in ratings on the group as a whole since they varied so widely from child to child.) As important as the infant's preference is the contribution to his feeling about himself, his mother, and the world generally of experiencing support for his earliest choices. Such support, we assume, reinforces the feeling that he is accepted, that his preferences are okay, that he and the world will be in harmony. More than this, we see in the later development of children whose early preferences and interests were supported a quality of freedom to pursue drives oriented to the external world and a steadiness of goal orientation not as well sustained in children without this early encouragement.

Differences in response to specific visual stimuli such as light were observed: some of these babies turned away from bright lights implying that these were disturbing. Other infants seemed fascinated by light. Idiosyncratic responses to specific sensory qualities of objects and of people[5] were also discussed by Heider (1966) in her study of the child's tendency to be vulnerable in certain areas. It is possible, and consistent with some psychoanalytic assumptions (cf. Jacobson 1954), that the four- to six-months stage is critical for the capacity to master, that is, to process sensory stimulation in such a way as to differentiate clearly between inner and outer stimuli, between self and not-self. After the child has achieved this subjective-objective clarification, sensory stimuli may become less overwhelming, may be assimilated with less autonomic or even motor reaction, or may be managed more effectively.

Management of the excitation aroused by sensory stimuli depends both on the baby's resources for motor discharge of tension and on his inner resources for processing and integrating perceptions evoked by stimulation. Terry was one of the babies with high sensory reactivity, *and* he was extremely active; this helped him to discharge tension aroused by his high sensory responsiveness. His tendency to marked autonomic reactivity, however, contributed to Heider's impression of vulnerability, which was consistent with certain of Terry's later difficulties. Still, his strong drive supported continued progress: he has graduated from college with a plan to help others.

It is equally important to watch the children who as infants seemed to find tactile experience unpleasant. This might be expected to color many of their contacts with people and to influence the terms of intimacy. People who as infants were highly sensitive to touch may develop an early avoidance pattern that would actually not be needed when later development modifies the sensory reactivity.

A precursor to ambivalence

We were especially interested in those infants who responded to stimulation in the same modality, especially tactual stimulation, with strong *positive* reactions under certain conditions (or at certain levels or degrees of stimulation) while responding with strong *negative* reactions when the degree or quality of tactual stimulation was at another level, or when it lasted beyond a limited duration time. For instance, Helen seemed to crave tactual contact, and yet she cried after a given period of time (as if she had had too much of it) and at such times seemed to be contented to be left alone in her crib (see chapter 11). In another instance, a child enjoyed vigorous or rough tactual contact, but reacted negatively to mild or gentle contact. The pattern of another child was exactly the reverse. Since so much of the mother's ministration to the infant involves tactual contact, we can see one foundation of a basic pattern of ambivalence in these contrasting responses in the same modality. When such a pattern is established in the early months before much differentiation has taken place, the ambivalence could color many aspects of the relationship, or indeed the general tone of the response to the mother and to other people. Such a precursor of ambivalence is important to follow in the later development of the child: it can contribute to conflicts that stimulate coping efforts, and reflectiveness, as well as shaping the style of social participation. It is probable that some of the adults who respond to opportunities in encounter groups to learn how to touch, caress, hug, and be touched were infants sensitive to vigorous tactile contact, from which they withdrew in self-protection, while still craving the intimate relationship. Some others do not defend themselves in such extreme ways but develop modulated levels of contact, which they enjoy when the partner adapts to these.

Undiagnosed mild visual defects in infancy

Several children with slow or cautious orientation patterns at the preschool level (age three) were discovered upon entering school to be markedly nearsighted. This visual problem had not been diagnosed in infancy or at the preschool level; nor was it recognized at the time as a factor in the slow orientation process these children required at the preschool level.

It is also of interest to note that two children who were reported to be sensitive to strangeness (of place or of people) in early infancy (Molly and Donald at eight and twelve weeks, respectively) and who were among the most shy children at the preschool stage, were later diagnosed as myopic and received corrective glasses. It seems possible that an early visual problem interfered with the process of clarification and differentiation of new faces. Their range of vision would have been narrowed, so that the infant had less opportunity to become oriented to a strange person during the approach from a distance. The perception of strangeness may thus have been more sudden as the new person came within the infant's functional perceptual range.

The drive to increase perceptual clarity is expressed in the baby's incessant staring, scanning, looking at and around (Stone et al. 1973, pp. 618–717). He needs familiarity with the environment; and his exploratory drives also lead to satisfaction of curiosity, which contributes to this cognitive mastery. All this is important in the development of reality testing and is influenced by vicissitudes partly determined by patterns of sensitivity just described. We do not need to assume here that a high degree of sensitivity or even of difficulty in perceptual areas is necessarily accompanied by integrative difficulties or social inadequacies. The *balance* of capacities of the child—whether or not the child has the flexibility and resourcefulness to cope with the difficulty—helps to determine the outcome of experiences affected by visual "sensitivity" either in terms of low thresholds or of high reactivity.

We have discussed individual differences in activity level and in sensory reactivity and the interactions among the levels of an infant's functioning in these two basic areas. Interactions among other aspects of infant responsiveness are seen in psychological tests of infants.

Imbalances in individual patterns on infant tests[6]

Our analysis of Gesell test data on these babies shows a wide range in scores on different items. For example, some sixteen-week-old babies perform at a twelve-week level on some items, sixteen-week on others, and twenty or even twenty-four-week on others. Such differences in maturity of functioning in different areas can be very important for the baby's development.

Coping problems arising from these imbalances can be considered in broad terms: if an infant of twelve weeks is performing on "social" items at a sixteen-week level but on motor and adaptive functions at an eight-week level, the baby may evoke much more vivid and frequent responses from the mother than a less social baby, and we may have the setting for overstimulation, or exposure to intake and exchange of stimulation, far beyond what the infant can handle. For example, some four- to five-month-old babies developed an impressive ability to attract the attention of adults with squeals, smiles, and seductive outreaching of arms. They "love to be played with," but alas, the unsuspecting adult who obliges with vigorous tossing-up games and hugs suddenly finds the baby crying instead of laughing as he did a moment earlier. The stimulation becomes more than the baby can absorb. By contrast, the balanced pattern of development, in which an infant's social, language, motor, and adaptive functions are all maturing at a comparable rate, provides a setting for smoother ego development and more effective patterns of dealing with the environment. Such a child is less likely to expose himself to stimulation beyond a level which he is ready to manage.

Martin was advanced in language and low on adaptive capacities, while Sally by contrast was high on adaptive and motor functioning and low on language; Vernon's pattern was similar to Sally's. Terry was advanced in motor development and low on language, and along with this had rather poor functional stability, with slow decline after arousal of autonomic reactions. Each of these babies grew into a child who aroused concern at one time: Vernon was very reserved as a child, as if he needed more time to integrate action and language respectively; Terry was the first child to initiate therapy. Sally's IQ showed a greater drop than that of any other child—from a preschool Stanford IQ of 136 to WISC IQ of 106 by prepuberty—with a gap of twenty-two points between her lowered verbal IQ of 95 and her performance IQ of 117. It seemed that she was more vulnerable in the verbal area.

Precursors of Vulnerability

The contribution to vulnerability and relevant coping problems (and likewise to coping strategies) of wide variations in developmental level need further study; in particular, differences between activity level, coordination, and capacity to process stimulation can be expected to contribute to coping problems.[7] The child who takes in stimulation faster than he can integrate appropriate responses is likely to be blocked or inhibited, especially in new situations. The problem of integration of functions is important for the long-term development of ego cohesion (Murphy 1972b). A vigorous, active child may have *coping resources* but lack the stability implied in *ego cohesion*;[8] thus his "ego strength" may be differently evaluated when these two aspects of ego functioning are assessed separately.

Integrative functions and capacity

Multiple problems in maintaining internal integration can be illustrated by Roddy, who was seen at twenty weeks:

His breathing was not yet stabilized: the record showed rhythms of excitement and relaxation, apparently partly determined by inner conditions, while excitement was accelerated by external stimulation from the environment.

Sensory reactivity and a tendency to be disturbed by sensory stimuli was documented by his crying at bright sunlight and also by crying or jumping (or both) at a loud noise. His skin was sensitive, but he enjoyed the tactile experiences of his bath and the kinesthetic stimulation of automobile rides quieted him.

He was immediately responsive to people and to objects. Cumulative effects of the sight of people, objects, and his bottle when hungry led to intense excitement expressed in more rapid breathing, pulsing at the neck, flushing, heightened activity, loss of motor coordination, tense postures with fingers spread, and bubble blowing.

Vegetative functioning involved difficulties: breast feeding proved impossible because of the mother's inverted nipples, and his bottle formula had to be changed several times partly because of difficulties in elimination. Although he sucked vigorously he was distracted by activity in the room. Sleep presented difficulties because he stayed awake at night, then slept during the day.

He was *easily fatigued* as well as excitable, but quieted when his mother held him, talked to him, rolled him in his carriage, or offered him a pacifier.

Heider commented that he seemed "at the mercy of stresses from within and without that threatened stability of functioning: both his own functioning and the stimulation imposed by his mother increased the pressures he seemed to create for himself," and his resources for reducing stress seemed fewer than those of many other babies. Heider (1966) considered him to be one of the more vulnerable babies in this sample because of the accumulation of disturbances in functioning.

Coping with Vulnerability

If you protest that most babies would not be able to do more for themselves than Roddy, consider Teddy at twenty weeks. He was also a baby with certain vegetative difficulties and sensitivity: periods of constipation and rectal adhesions with constipation may have caused pain; crying and feeding overlapped at times. Both some visual and auditory experiences seemed unpleasant—he did not like sunlight, and he became sober when lights were bright for photography. He "minded being wet or soiled more than many babies," and was "particular about the temperature and taste of foods." Tension was expressed through fretful vocalizations, a strained facial expression, flushing, postural tenseness with hands tightly fisted, loss of coordination, and loss of differentiation of vocalizations.

At the same time he enjoyed many types of contact including fairly rough play with his father and was interested in observing objects.

He could initiate pleasant experiences on his own, rubbing his face against the person who held him, making advances to his mother and also to staff members. He observed objects carefully before getting involved with them, and when he did become engaged with an object he maintained a fairly long attention span. In addition he showed far more ability than most babies of his age to initiate action to provide relief to his discomfort or tension.

> When he was bothered by the bright lights, he lowered his head, sucked a toy, then held his two hands, fingers interlaced, deep in his mouth.

> When he became excited, then apprehensive, during the psychological test, he turned away from the examiner and faced his mother, relaxing and thus restoring his control.

> With another period of tension, he swung himself back and forth on his mother's lap, stimulating her to resume rocking him.

> Heider also felt that his interest in careful observation of features of the environment helped to reduce tension at times.

All together, then, Teddy was a sensitive baby who at the same time had many resources to restore stability and maintain integration in the face of disturbing experiences.

In line with his early vegetative difficulties, his response to severe stress (divorce of his parents when he was six years old) was to become obese. Turning away from and avoidance of disturbing stimuli at twenty weeks may be seen as precursors for later "forgetting" details of that stressful period. At the same time, his infantile perceptual and cognitive interests can be seen as precursors of his later intellectual competence in college. His early tactile and social responsiveness could be seen as a foundation for his later ease with people, and pleasant heterosexual relationships. He married early "a very sweet girl."

We see then, how cognitive capacities can determine in part the infant's ability to integrate the potentially overwhelming amount of stimulation that low sensory thresholds or a rapid tempo of intake provide some infants. A moderate tempo of response probably contributes to integration, because such a baby is less likely to be swamped by too much stimulation at once. The infant's autonomic stability also contributes to the integrative outcome. A baby who reacts to sensory stimulation with much autonomic disturbance is experiencing stimulation from inside as well as outside—and the resulting agitation, crying, or restlessness gives us indications of "sensory sensitivity." But his sensory thresholds as such may not be lower; it is his reactivity thresholds that contribute to his disturbance.[9]

Early expressions of selection, control, and integration

Individual differences in precursors of, or early forms of, some integrative functions of the ego during infancy are reflected in the decisiveness of preferences or choices that were observed in some babies in the early months; also the ease of control of impulse or inhibition, and complex synthesizing capacities that include motor adapting to adult handling in the early months. Later imitating and identifying also testify to the level of integrative capacity.

Especially important for the latter is the capacity to delay—with its implication of tolerance for frustration, impulse-control, and potential reflectiveness. All the babies in the Escalona–Leitch sample seen at twelve to thirty-two weeks of age who were rated high in tendency to delay were among those who were later among the high IQ children or those whose IQ improved through their growing-up years. This pattern deserved special exploration for its potential importance in cognitive as well as character development: a baby's quiet delay of action permits him to absorb, differentiate, compare, and perhaps even to organize his perceptions—at any rate to develop the inner relatedness that is required for meaningfulness.

Many other aspects of functioning related to adaptational style and coping efficiency, particularly those associated with flexibility, need more study. Among these are the infant's ability to shift attention and the speed with which the infant is able to assimilate impressions and go on to new impressions; this pace of differentiation of surroundings interacts with the tendency to develop strong attachments or cathexis of individual objects of the total pattern of his surroundings.

Differentiation and reactions to the strange

Such differences in the baby's differentiation of objects must underlie differences in reaction to strangeness, including strange people. Two babies in this sample, one at two months, one at three months of age, were frightened by a strange person. (See also Wolf 1952). Another baby we observed was restless and irritable in a strange place even though his mother was present. Spitz (1946) has told about differences in the degree of depression suffered by babies separated from their mothers, and Yarrow (1963) found that babies familiar with more persons than the mothering person were less disturbed by separation from her. In our group the baby most disturbed by absence of his mother had been in her care almost exclusively. Both the ability to accept substitutes as compared with the tendency to cling to the familiar and the tempo of recovery after an emotional upset are affected by the baby's level of differentiation, his reaction to strangeness, and the intensity of his discomfort with the unfamiliar. Some children who were either shy in early infancy (Molly and Donald) or traumatized by separation from the mother as infants, were very shy at the age of three.

When we realized the importance of the many expressions of autonomy, of the range of gratification, and of the capacity for flexible coping as well as the processes of orientation to the environment, we looked for their precursors in the behavior of the infants. The feeding situation was selected as a setting in which likely behavior might be found, both because of the deep importance of feeding in the early months (when a baby has to double or triple his weight) and because ample data were available on feeding during the four-hour observation period. We shall consider this area next.

Oral Drives and Their Integration in Coping

Early expressions of autonomous ego functions such as perception and action interact with various aspects of drive right from the beginning. The same baby who is motorically active enough to wiggle her position to a comfortable corner of the crib while she is still in the hospital as did Vivian in the Escalona–Leitch records, or to bat away covers that are encroaching on her face in an uncomfortable way, may also make motor efforts to retrieve a lost nipple or to hold onto the one she has. The degree of initiative, concentration, persistence of attention span, and ability to maintain effort, characteristic of the baby's response to objects may also find expression in the persistence, attentiveness, and effort in the feeding process. The patterning of feeding, or the total oral zone experience, is then reinforced by other functions that are more or less autonomous in their own right, yet contribute to and are in turn reinforced by the baby's success in obtaining gratification in the feeding experience.

We found differences in the intensity of certain aspects of oral functioning that are involved in oral drive: differences in infantile oral demand; gratification; autonomy in satisfying oral needs; and capacity to protest or terminate unsatisfying oral situations were discriminated. These different aspects of feeding experiences are not necessarily closely parallel: a baby with very high demand level—the avid "little pig"—might not have an equally gratifying experience if he gulped air which in turn led to gas pains, or had digestive difficulties. While intensely eager, he might not have the capacity to pace or space his feeding pattern or protest effectively what he did not like. (See Appendix 6.)

Whatever his pattern, the oral zone provided a regularly recurrent, frequent experience of (a) signaling a need, (b) experiencing a response to the need, (c) controlling to some degree the quantity, quality, and pace of meeting the need, (d) obtaining greater or less gratification. This pattern then contributed to a sense of being able to communicate a need, to obtain a response, to control the input, and to experience gratification.

In the oral area we also have to compare smoothly functioning babies who feed, digest, and eliminate effortlessly and comfortably with others who have to work harder to consolidate sucking coordinations, who struggle to evacuate their bowels, and who may have more digestive difficulty. Those who have to make efforts to consolidate good sucking and swallowing learn literally that one has to work for a living, that struggle brings a reward, as Bernfeld (1929), Greenacre (1952), and others have commented.

On the other hand if, due to gastrointestinal difficulties, the feeding experience is not satisfactory, there may be negative effects on the hitherto autonomous ego functions. Somewhat defeated in their early efforts in this area, ego functions may lose the reinforcement that they otherwise would have had. Or they may actually suffer further losses through frustration or attrition of the effort to cope actively with the feeding problem.

It is obvious that while one can abstract specific aspects of functioning in order to look at such individual differences and their implications for coping, we always have to recognize that in the child's early experiences much of the time everything goes on at once and provides a context for everything else. Only a complete grasp of the specific level of functioning in every area and the interaction of each with the rest can provide an adequate understanding of the internal and external struggles of the child, as these contribute to the infant's adaptational style.

Rest in relation to the capacity for self-regulation

Some aspects of the self-regulation capacity of a child can be observed in infancy and may become increasingly masked as the child develops more subtle and complicated compromises and adjustments with his environment. Reviewing the observations of our sample of the infants, we find differences in babies in terms of their regulation of activity and rest rhythms; some babies easily alternate periods of activity and periods of rest with such efficiency that extreme fatigue is almost entirely avoided, while other babies are not able to control these rhythms effectively and as a result expose themselves to greater fatigue. The duration of effort and tendency of a baby to make sustained efforts to reach a goal or solve a problem are involved here. Where goal-orientation is clear, interest is intense, and the baby is very determined, effort may be continued beyond the point where a shift to rest and recovery comes easily. Ronald at twenty-eight weeks was seen to struggle for thirty-five minutes in his effort to master getting up on all fours. During this period he pushed strenuously until he was tired, then flopped down on the floor, sucking his thumb until he was rested enough to try again. This alternation of effort and rest went on until he finally succeeded.

The amount of time and conditions for recovery vary for different infants. Some become fresh and rested easily within a few minutes after a period of exertion—such as the effort involved in being tested—while others require a much longer time. Some do not become fully rested until after a period of sleep; others rest as they relax in the mother's arms or while they are lying in the crib. In other words, conditions for recovery of energy and a state of equilibrium vary for different infants.

Heider rated the individual infants' patterns of arousal and their "speed of recovery" in infancy. We can diagram some of the different patterns as follows:

Sally Molly	Occasional quick arousal with quick recovery or decline
JoAnne Terry	Frequent quick arousal with quick recovery
Steve	Occasional gradual arousal with gradual but prompt recovery

Diane   Occasional gradual arousal with delayed gradual
         recovery

Stimulus control

Self-regulation of the intensity of stimulus to which the infant will expose himself also varies; we saw that some infants were able to turn away from or shut out stimulation that was too intense. Patsy, for instance, was actually able to withdraw sufficiently to go to sleep in the face of excessively intense stimulation, such as the presence of three members of the research staff leaning over her crib for the period of simultaneous recording.

The capacity of the infant for self-regulation in relation to stimulus intake varies, of course, with the zones of sensitivity of the individual infant. For a baby particularly sensitive to auditory stimuli in contrast to visual ones, it may not be so easy for him to control his own exposure to the stimulus. He can shut his eyes, but "shutting one's ears" is an achievement that may take some years to accomplish. (Granted, some children do refer to this ability, which may practically amount to a capacity for dissociation.)*

Babies can also control the amount, quality, intensity, and tempo of stimulus intake somewhat by narrowing their focus, concentrating on one small area while ignoring everything else.

Another aspect of the self-regulation capacity is the infant's tempo of mastery and level of integration. Some infants, for example, Barbie and Vernon, show, through their constructive use of delay, evidence for a slow tempo of mastery and integration, while at the same time their capacity for a complex level of integration is high. At a later age both of these infants had IQs over 130 and also demonstrated a high degree of precision in many functions as well as a high level of ability in a range of intellectual areas.

A child's ability to maintain his self-regulation capacity and related coping efforts when under stress has to be evaluated separately from the self-regulation pattern used under ordinary conditions: he may balance activity and rest or control his exposure to stimulation and select from the environment what he needs from it under ordinary conditions, but in situations that arouse acute anxiety or severe threats this self-regulating capacity may break down.

This is, of course, most likely to be true when the child is exposed to threats or stress beyond his range of control—when events are imposed

* A child who had been in the Sarah Lawrence College Nursery School later stated that she got along with a cross and difficult fourth-grade teacher by "shutting her ears."

upon him by adults or external circumstances so that it is not possible for him to select, measure, or time the quantity, quality, or tempo of stress. In many areas of a child's life the behavior and attitudes of adults are of crucial importance here.

These resources for self-regulation are related to the infant's foundation for resilience.

Resilience, recovery, and stress-management

During the four hours of observation in the laboratory, the young infants of Escalona and Leitch's study became fatigued, hungry, wet, frustrated, startled, overstimulated, or temporarily deprived, just as they do at times in the course of daily life at home. Crying, jerking, or loss of motor smoothness, evidences of autonomic reactions as in flushing, paling, or drooling were noted. Some became very red. Restless or more vigorous flailing of arms and legs became jerky and irregular with others. Breathing or pulse became more rapid or irregular. Individual infants showed different combinations of these reactions when disturbed. In addition, observers commented on the tempo, intensity, duration of reaction, and the tempo of decline or recovery from a disturbed state, along with observations of the mother's and the baby's efforts that contributed to recovery.

The baby has its own way of letting go of the tensions aroused by such stress. Crying is the earliest device for such discharge and release. Some infants discharged tension by modulated crying or "fussing": Sally "fussed and got over it—she never seemed to get real mad." Others like Molly let out loud cries or screams and then stopped abruptly. These were unlike the differentiated cries mothers learned to recognize as "his hunger cry," "his tired cry," and so forth.

Pleasurable sensory gratifications, as from thumb-sucking or crib-rocking, initiated by the baby also relieve tensions rising from fatigue or frustration. We saw how at twenty-eight weeks Ronald struggled until he was exhausted to get up on all fours. Then he collapsed, lay prone, sucking his thumb until his energy was restored. Satisfactions from these self-initiated devices are often reinforced by maternal techniques, and these in turn lend their potency to symbols of comfort used by children, and by adults, later.

Other infants spontaneously paced their own needs for rest, alternating activity with quiet. Similarly, several infants turned away from apparently overstimulating objects. This strategic withdrawal and ability to pace stimulus-input contributes coping structures available to the child in the future, as with Vernon, although most children develop a wide enough range of coping patterns so that they do not need to rely on these devices primarily.

Thus, from the early weeks, many an infant demonstrates the beginning of his capacity to do something about discomfort and to facilitate recovery. Alert mothers respond not only to his "fussing" or screaming protests, but also to his restlessness, his motor efforts to adjust postures (struggling, pushing), his frowns, his ability to push out distasteful food or objects with the tongue, and other ways of dealing with or communicating discomfort. Records of mothers' ways of soothing babies—patting, stroking, rocking, swaying, "walking the baby," talking soothingly—were supplemented by their comments, such as "he likes to be held to my shoulder to be patted." Mothers also reported differences between their babies in responses to comfort patterns. Some babies were more easily soothed by tactile stimulation, others by rhythm, still others by visual stimuli such as colorful objects or bright lights, and some responded most readily to songs or music. Certain mothers had very individual techniques: for instance, one mother laughed with her baby to induce her to laugh instead of cry. A mother with nurse's training was especially aware of physiological factors in distress and intervened when she interpreted her infant's cries as the reaction to fatigue.

The support of the baby's equilibrium is fundamental to all the rest of his functioning. Thus the mother's success in restoring the baby to a state of comfort, reducing stress from any source, is probably at least as important as her capacity to feed him in a satisfying way. Both food and rest restore energy; the mother's comforting handling does more than give relief and help the child to recover his equilibrium. It provides positive or pleasurable experiences that renew the infant's trust in the possibility of satisfaction and of recovery. We have seen deprived, neglected infants who cry in a hopeless way as if they could not count on a response to their distress. The most deprived institutional babies who give up hope entirely and become apathetic do not cry at all—do not expect anything. Thus we can consider the ability to develop differentiated cries in infancy, as evidence of trustful, meaningful communication between the mother and baby. The baby who protests expects that something can be done to improve his state. When his discomfort is alleviated, many a baby will smile or laugh with renewed energy for responding to the environment.

The model for recovery and resilience, then, is the loss of integration under stress and the regaining of smooth functioning and energy with relief from stress.

Role of tactile responsiveness in recovery

In the attempt to explore possible early infantile factors in resilience, we checked the baby's responsiveness to tactile stimulation (stroking, patting), which plays a large part in the comforting efforts of many mothers. But we cannot conclude that the capacity for pleasurable responses to tactile stimulation is any guarantee of rapid decline from a state of disturbance. A considerable proportion of children who respond pleasurably to certain kinds of tactile stimulation also respond displeasurably to other kinds. Reactions vary at different times as well: in disturbed states, some infants are especially prone to find tactile stimulation unpleasant.

Since all in our sample were at least four weeks old at the time when they were observed, such learning had already taken place. Several babies immediately stopped crying when picked up; here it is important to note that cessation of crying in response to patting or soothing caresses must be distinguished from responses to more gross contact, change of posture, or the presence of the mother and possible expectation of further pleasure involved in being picked up. The capacity of the mother to discover the particular kinds, zones, tempo, and intensity of tactile stimulation that would be comforting to her baby helps to determine the baby's readiness to be comforted by tactile stimulation.

Interactions can be inferred between the infant's level of stability, his speed of decline after arousal, his reactions of pleasure or displeasure to different stimuli, and his intensity of drive. For instance, Susan's low level of functional stability and low tempo of decline in infancy, along with a tendency to experience tactile stimulation as unpleasant, might be expected to lead to difficulties in adaptation. However, these were balanced by her high drive and marked pleasure at vocal (and musical) stimulation. Other combinations and their interactions can be translated from the chart in a similar way.

Other aspects of the infant's experience may be related to resilience: for Terry, Heider judged that locomotion and other movement experiences were the most pleasurable aspects of his functioning and also that he showed intense, immediate, vigorous interest in objects. This would tend to mobilize positive responses to new stimuli and active efforts to reach them. Even though he showed low frustration tolerance and a degree of reactivity that contributed to low functional stability, his quick responsiveness to stimulation and his drive to movement drowned out, as it were, the reaction to frustration. There was always something worth going after. It is interesting that Terry was not easily comforted by others when very disturbed; he made his own fresh start as the crisis passed.

Another example of the value for resilience of responsiveness to objects is seen in Tommy. A baby of high reactivity (low stability) and a tendency to be easily frustrated, he showed quick decline after upheaval and quick recovery; this accompanied his ready acceptance of substitutes and quick reaching out to new stimuli. Like Terry, he enjoyed active movement, in his case, use of his hands to manipulate objects.

The early innate resources for recovery, such as rest or sleep, food, comfort, object-stimulation by mother, are supplemented by use of toys or other impersonal objects. Rest, sleep, and food promote metabolic activities and cell regeneration and contribute energy directly; comfort by mother is relaxing and alleviates tension and pain. Object-stimulation mobilizes pleasurable affect and drive, which evoke new gratification from the environment. The combination of these helps to reestablish the dynamic homeostatic balance.

We find that these early patterns of disintegrative reaction and recovery are programmed during infancy sufficiently firmly to provide an underlying structure that is sometimes modified or overlaid or transformed by sublimation, but seldom completely lost. In our discussion of later processes of resilience, we shall deal both with self-restorative devices and signals to or responses to help from the environment.

Infancy resilience in relation to age

Certain coping capacities important for the early foundations of resilience are demonstrated in different ways, depending on the infant's age. Among their ways of managing stimulation from the environment, Heider judged that most infants (eight to ten) in the 4-, 8-, and 12-weeks-old group could avoid unpleasant stimuli. None could accept substitutes. Six out of ten were rated average or above for protesting. Six out of ten could provide support for themselves by their own functioning, as by sucking fingers or thumb or focusing on interesting visual stimuli. All but two responded to support from others. Only one was rated high on "action to attain."

Furthermore, only two out of ten failed to return to an equilibrium shortly after arousal; and seven of them vocalized with predominantly pleasant affect tone. All were considered moderate or high in robustness and vegetative functioning, and only three out of ten were judged low in drive level. Only two showed low reactivity to sensory stimulation, but four were rated low in overall activity level.

The next group of infants, 16-, 20-, and 24-weeks old, included the same proportion of low-activity-level infants, together with three who were considered fragile, not robust. At this age, three were rated low on sensory reactivity; but by this time defensive gating[10] or resistance could have developed.

At this stage, all but two could protest discomfort or frustration; half the infants could actively reject unwanted stimuli; and four already showed a high capacity to "act to attain" a desired object or posture. All but one in this age group could use support from others. (All but three appeared to experience tactile stimulation as a source of pleasure, though certain kinds and degrees of tactile stimulation could also be a source of discomfort to a few. Soothing techniques used by mothers included patting, cuddling, or other contacts.) Only five were rated high in avoidance, and only one was rated high in accepting substitutes; the latter responses seem to reflect the increasing response to the environment and increasing intensity and selectivity, in response to specific toys, for instance.

All but one infant in this 16- to 24-weeks group were able to comfort themselves or provide support from their own functioning, and three were rated high in obtaining support from cognitive experiences such as watching ongoing activity or observing visual patterns.

Among the ten infants in the 28- to 32-weeks group, again three were rated fragile and four still had difficulties at this age with vegetative functioning. Only three were rated very high in activity level, while two were judged to be very low in activity or inactive; and two were rated low in drive level. Only three were seen to have a high degree of balance in developmental levels, with "language" low in all but two (by the Gesell norms). Four were vocalizing displeasurably more than pleasurably. Functional stability was rated as low in half these infants, and three showed both low functional stability and a slow tempo of decline from disturbance.

Only three babies in this age group showed a high degree of tendency to delay response, a capacity that could assist coping with their instabilities. But management processes at this age showed six babies using a moderate to high degree of avoidance; all but two could and did protest; all but one could reject unwanted stimuli. By now seven out of ten were finding support in their own cognitive experience, while only four were seen to be using support from others. Getting interested in a (new) stimulus had become an important way of coping, and they were resilient enough to use such opportunities.

Summary of Patterns of Infant Characteristics*

Since we are dealing with only thirty-one infants it is possible to mentally group the babies according to the various combinations of characteristics we have been discussing. These combinations, we hope, will evoke images of different kinds of children familiar in the reader's experience and will serve to provide a summary of potential interactions of different characteristics in the infants.

Eleven out of thirty-one babies were rated high on both robustness and good (easy) vegetative functioning, while four at the other extreme were rated as both fragile and having difficult vegetative functioning. Of the latter four, three had high sensory reactivity, suggesting that their fragility and inner difficulties in vegetative functioning may have contributed to their susceptibility to stimulation from the environment and reactivity to it. Of the eleven robust children, three had moderately high ratings on sensory reactivity.

Only four of the eleven robust children with good vegetative functioning were among the eight babies with high activity level. The fact that none of three other robust babies who were seen at four weeks had a high activity level may well have been a function of their age; the large amount of sleep those babies still needed, the relatively smaller exposure to stimuli from the environment or readiness to evoke stimulation, and the limited capacity to differentiate meaningful objects could all prevent the stimulus to activity of the older infants. But four highly active babies between twelve and thirty-two weeks were low in either or both robustness and vegetative functioning, suggesting, as we indicated earlier, that restlessness or discomfort could have contributed to the high activity level.

All eleven children who were considered both robust and having moderate to easy vegetative functioning also had high drive (ratings of 1 or 2 on a 5-point scale); five other babies with high drive had relatively average ratings on physique and vegetative functioning. We assume that all these infants would be well equipped to develop active resources for coping with the environment.

Only four babies of thirty-one were rated as having excellent physique along with excellent vegetative functioning, high drive, and a high level of functional stability—these being the basic elements, we might assume, of optimal development including both the capacity to maintain a general sense of well-being (contributed by comfortable vegetative

* This summary is based on my analyses of Heider's data.

functioning and functional stability) and resources for coping with the environment supported by their high drive.

Nine of the eleven babies with excellent physique and vegetative functioning also showed excellent developmental balance as rated by Heider on the basis of the infancy Gesell tests; this meant, as we saw above (pp. 84 f.), that motor functioning, social responses, (pre-)language, and adaptive functioning had all developed in a relatively balanced way. This recalls Terman's (1925) study of gifted children: he found a correlation between mental, physical, and social development—a tendency for well-endowed children to be well-endowed in all basic spheres.

By contrast, some other children showed superior personal-social development and vocalization or language development with, at the same time, less mature motor or adaptive development or both.

Developmental imbalances often occurred in a context of poor vegetative functioning, although there were three babies with developmental imbalances who were robust and functioning well. We must wonder what specific processes of coping with discomfort or fragility may have contributed to the developmental imbalance. We might expect that where discrepancies between different developmental levels occur in otherwise well-endowed infants, we would find evidence of genetic factors. Imbalance involving less mature language development than motor adaptive was found in three children whose fathers were skilled workers. In two of these instances, mothers were given the lowest rating for amount of talking to the baby; thus the baby had less stimulation for language development. The verbal stimulation received by babies from the age of eight weeks on is of major importance in language development.

Less than a third of the babies, as rated by Heider, showed evidence of the balance in adaptation that is implied in relatively comparable activity levels during sleep and waking. Heider believed that the infant who is very quiet, with a low activity level relative to other infants during waking, but more active than average during sleep, is discharging tensions that could not be adequately discharged during the day. Similarly, a child who has a higher activity level than average during the day but sleeps more quietly than average, may have a need for a deeper level of rest due to overexertion during the day.

Of the eight children showing functional instability after the age of twenty weeks, proneness to infection was characteristic of three, and frequent illness could have contributed to autonomic reactivity. Six were first children who had experienced some birth difficulties. Can we show relationships between functional instability (low threshold for and slow subsiding of autonomic upheaval) and the flexibility or adaptability of the child as shown in other ways? Logically, we would expect to find that the infants whose autonomic upheaval did not subside quickly but persisted, might be hampered in the development of affective flexibility, might tend to show persistent anxiety, reinforced by internal sensations of disequilibrium. Here again, we expect the data to be significant only in relation to the older infants; instability is more typical of the first two months. Consequently, attention needs to be given to six children from twenty to thirty-two weeks of age who showed a slow decline of disturbances of functional stability: either at the preschool or the puberty level, all these children showed more than average tenseness for this group. Three of these tended to be explosive or to have temper tantrums: the other three were among the most inhibited children. Both extremes, then, may be adaptive efforts to deal with autonomic upheaval and inner tensions.

Combination of traits related to coping

Now we can look at some combinations of ratings related to coping in individual babies:

Terry's high activity level was seen in a fragile infant with difficult vegetative functioning; he was also a fatigable baby with poor digestion and poor sleep, and high sensory reactivity in all areas. It looked as if this fragile infant's high activity level were a reaction to the great amount of inner and outer stimulation to which such a baby must be exposed.*

On the other hand, Gordon, who was also rated as having a high activity level, was considered robust, with easy vegetative functioning and low reactivity to sensory stimulation. Thus there is little or no evidence to imply that his activity level was an outcome of the reactivity to internal and external stimulation that we saw in Terry. Gordon was a "mesomorphic," muscular, broadly athletic boy, whose early activity level was evidently an expression of motor drive as such. There were other children with patterns closely similar to each of these, as well as children showing mixed patterns.

When we look at the children with low activity level and high capacity to delay we find children such as Teddy, with favorable or moderate ratings on robustness and vegetative functioning, but with marked reactivity to sensory stimulation; from all the subsequent records Teddy was a child with a strong drive to cognitive mastery, a highly verbal orientation at a later stage, and typically careful appraisal as he entered

---

* He was also the most extreme "ectomorphic" child in this sample throughout his childhood; this was evaluated at the preschool level by an associate of Sheldon's, and at prepuberty by the pediatrician.

new situations. He was never a very athletic boy. He responded to sensory stimulation by cognitive rather than by motor activity.

Janice, who was considered the most fragile infant of the intensive sample, had very difficult vegetative functioning but only moderate reactivity to sensory stimulation and was one of the lowest on activity level in infancy—as if at that time she had limited energy. Janice, like Teddy, developed a primarily cognitive orientation and emerged as one of the good scholars in the group; her low activity level probably permitted ample opportunity for observation and integration of perceptual and cognitive functioning.

We see that poor internal functioning, combined or not with high sensory reactivity in infancy, may be accompanied by either high motor or high cognitive activity and that an extreme level of the latter is not apt to accompany the former. The infant who concentrates for extended periods on achieving perceptual clarity, making a cognitive map, or trying to "understand," evidently inhibits random activity in order to achieve focus.

From our discussion so far it is obvious that an exclusive emphasis on either the baby's assumed genetic tendencies or the environmental influences would lead to a gross oversimplification. From the beginning these interact, modifying the adaptational pattern of the baby and often that of persons in the environment who are in greatest contact with the baby. Moreover, different aspects of the environment impinge differentially on different tendencies in the baby: of two mothers, each of whom has a baby of high activity level and high sensory reactivity, one may limit the activity range by confining the baby within one room or playpen, while overstimulating him with a plethora of toys and play objects with varied visual, auditory, and sensory qualities. The other mother, however, may give the child free rein in a wide area of space and provide only one or two toys. The activity of the first baby is then channeled into mastery of available objects, whereas the activity of the second baby is channeled into exploratory ventures. Such differences were seen between the approaches of the generally more confined Westchester children studied by me at Sarah Lawrence College (Murphy 1956, vol. 1) and the less confined Kansas children, some of whom spontaneously "cased the joint" when coming into the MLT playroom. This last pattern had not been observed in the Westchester children, who entered the room, sat down near the toys, and began to play with them.

The sequelae of early interactions (of the infants' different characteristics with each other and with the different behavior patterns of the mothers) then lead to further modifications of the initial tendencies as mothers exploit, attempt to suppress, or tacitly encourage by their permissiveness whatever pattern is emerging and also as the baby repetitively enhances and generalizes behavior that is gratifying or inhibits or even abandons behavior that is frustrating. Some of these sequelae can be inferred from relationships between infancy and preschool functioning (see chapter 5).

4

Preschool Coping and Vulnerability

*"Write JoAnne Jackson—growing up," this four-year-old girl dic-
tated to the observer who recorded her ways of coping with the
psychiatrist-investigator.*

We have seen what distinct individuals the babies and their mothers
were, even when the babies were in the early months of life. And we saw
how babies and mothers evoke varying kinds of response from each
other. What did this mean for the further development of the children?
And what if any connection is there between this early experience and
the behavior we saw when the children were three to five years old?

First we must focus on the preschool children as we saw them,[1] with
their rich resources for dealing with the environment and managing their
relation to it. In the following chapter we shall discuss relationships
between infant and later behavior and their implications for the
development of coping resources.

None of our team who began to study the children at the preschool
stage had seen any of the children as babies, except for Grace Heider,
who had worked with Sibylle Escalona. And since some of us came from
different American or foreign settings, such as the East Coast of the
USA, India, and so forth, we were in for some surprises. These children
enjoyed freedom of the outdoors and opportunities for exploration not
available to most metropolitan children, while at the same time many of
them were exposed to a balance of discipline and support probably
characteristic of many small-town working-class families across the
United States (Whiting 1963). Although we had seen two year olds
playing and wandering around the block through the unfenced yards of
Topeka neighborhoods, we did not realize what this freedom might
mean for the development of autonomy until we saw the children in the
test settings, at parties, and on to-and-fro trips as we picked them up at
home and returned them to their homes.

My first encounter with four-year-old JoAnne involved taking her to
the research office; her mother stayed at home with the baby brother. En
route JoAnne surveyed me, then warned, "Don't you give me no trouble,
or I'll run home!" Out of the car, nimble and quick, she hopped up and

down from a low stone wall and ran ahead. On another occasion Heider described her behavior as follows:

When I reached the Jackson apartment, JoAnne made a dash for the door, apparently to call her mother to take charge of the baby because she was leaving. Then she ran down the boardwalk from the house and with a flying leap flung herself into my arms. She decided to ride in the front seat. When she was once in, I ran hastily back to deliver a message to her mother from LBM, who had taken her to a previous test. It seems that JoAnne sat solemnly in the car pretending to take notes and proceeded to "interview" LBM and LW [Lila Weissenberg] in a way that made it impossible for them to keep their faces straight. Mrs. Jackson gave no indication that JoAnne had felt any lack of sympathy from the people who took her home.

JoAnne wanted to stand in the front seat. Mrs. Jackson assured me that she always rode this way and was able to hold on perfectly well. JoAnne chattered on: "That house is perfectly beautiful." She asked who would be there to see her today and what she would do. . . . Reaching the research house, she told me to look at the flowers in the yard. . . . She ran down the sidewalk in a light quick way; at one point she fell so that she was almost on her knees, but she was up and running on without quite reaching the pavement. Most children would have had a skinned knee at this point, but she was unmarred. In the house she ran around and, when WK [Walter Kass] called, flew upstairs in her usual, quick, birdlike fashion.

Test session with Dr. Kass:

2:12　JoAnne sat on the floor, and WK began the sight–touch test, giving JoAnne the round form. She said, "it's a moon," and then gave a little jump forward so that she could reach better, and chose the oval; then she picked up others and WK firmly told her to choose just one. . . .

Now she suddenly got up and darted across the room to GH, wanting to have her nose blown, . . . a rather funny performance: "I held the piece of Kleenex for her and she leaned forward placing her nose on it; . . . she blew with tremendous energy. . . ."

After several form-board pieces had been tried, she protested that she wanted to play now, saying, "I don't want to do any more." She walked over to the coffee table, picked up the form-board, and wanted to put the pieces in. As she reached for it she was quite emphatic, "Let me have it." WK continued firmly, "Just leave it

right here, Jo, until we finish with this." "I'm not Jo, I'm JoAnne."
This was said in a defiant tone and, having held her own on this
point, she acquiesced, continuing the task.
2:17 "It's a star," she pointed, "right there." . . . On the second
round she said, "Just one more and that is all." WK: "Just a few
more and then you are going to put them in." JoAnne protested
that she did not like him to hide them as he was doing. WK said,
"I'm going to let you see them in a little while." JoAnne protested
again. "That's enough. I'm ready to put them in now." Then with a
more imperative inflection, "I'm ready to put them in now." WK
continued unruffled and said, "One more after this." JoAnne:
"Then I'll put them in." . . . After WK had given her the last
form, she said, "That's all." WK echoed her words, "That's
all." . . . She now had all the forms in the board and still with a
slight defiance in her voice said, "I'm going to play with them for a
little while." She tipped them out on the table and proceeded to
start again. This was exactly what WK wished her to do. . . . She
finally held the board up saying, "Here it is. A new puzzle. I want
one." . . .

   After the formal session came to an end, JoAnne came to me and
wanted me to write on my pad for her: "JoAnne Jackson—growing
up." I asked how big she wanted to be. . . . She showed me how tall
saying, "about this tall so I could drive a car." As we started she said
in an off-hand, grown-up kind of manner, "I like that guy. He didn't
make me no trouble."

From start to finish, JoAnne was independent, though also cooperative
in response to adult firmness. She asked questions to orient herself and
was observant as well as active.[2] She sought help readily for her runny
nose, asserted her wishes, protested her dislikes, and finally expressed her
image of herself as a girl growing up, along with her warmth toward the
examiner. She was considered a "good little coper."
   Many boys were equally independent and talkative. Here Marie Smith
observes Chester communicating his mingled interest in a large extended
family and their environments, and his mixture of fantasies and
observation of reality en route to a test session with Dr. Moriarty.

   As we passed Washburn University he told us his grandfather
lived in that direction, pointing west. AM asked whether his
grandfather lived on a farm, and he told us that was his Grandmother Chatham; then . . . he had two grandmother Chathams,
and ten aunts and eleven uncles. He had never been to the farm in
Texas but his daddy and Janie (his oldest sister) had been there

when Janie was a baby. He said cowboys "jump on each other."
. . . Indians were nice people, although "they used to be naughty
but now they are nice." At a three-way intersection with a traffic
triangle in the center, he remarked that "it was a point." He
recognized the (research) house as we approached and remembered
the "green house" next door where the "firemen" had been. (A
small fire had occurred in this house the first time Ray and Chester
were with us, and though we saw no blaze, we watched them go in
with the extinguishers, hatchets, etc., and both Ray and Chester
have never forgotten this.)

In the house, Chester laid his jacket on the couch, asking to go in
the other room to see the fireplace. He stood in front of the gas
grate "getting warm." He commented on the clock and its ticking
and the candles both on the fireplace and on the table. He smiled
constantly, definitely enjoying himself, hunching his shoulders in
excitement. On one of the end tables he noticed a lamp held up by
three pointed sticks; he mentioned the "points" and wanted to
know how it worked. I showed him and he turned it off and on
several times. I turned the furnace up to warm up the house. He
told me that we shouldn't forget to turn it down when we left or
"the man might get mad at us." (Meaning the owner whom he had
seen once before.) He referred to AM's walking around upstairs and
seemed happy in anticipation of going up when she would call
us. . . .

Upstairs AM asked him if he'd like to make a picture. . . .
Chester said, "I show you how Ray [his brother] makes a house."
"Oh," AM said, "how do you make one?" Taking a crayon, he said
playfully, "You crayon stay over there!" as one of them rolled in the
box. Now he drew with yellow. "See?" he said to AM. "That's our
house. Our house ain't little—big windows in each one," he said as
he drew. "My daddy works at the Santa Fe," he volunteered. Now
as he drew, "Going to make down in the basement now. There's
going to be two windows down there and a great big hole." "What's
this?" AM asked as he drew the "hole." "A great big hole on the
wall, a mouse dug it," he explained. "Did you see it [the mouse]?"
AM asked. "Yes." "How big was it?" He held his arms out to the
side as far as they would go. She kidded him about that being pretty
big, but he went on saying, "and I kicked it." "Did that kill it?" AM
queried. "Yes," he said quite soberly, "I did it with these shoes,"
and he put his foot up on the chair to show AM and said, "Blood
come out."

Working with chalk in the chalk box: "This crayon [chalk] won't go down in here," he said. AM explained that one was broken so that it didn't fit too well. "You can dump them out if you want to," she said. He did so and then put them back in. "Put in there like tools," he said. . . . "Don't get these mixed up now . . . shut it," he said with a sigh shutting the box. Now he put the crayons and his drawing out of the way at AM's request. . . .

Then he said, "My uncle's baby cow ran away and I had to go out to get him." Again he was talking quite excitedly. He continued, "I didn't know I was going to jump on it," and then, "I can lift my uncle's baby calves." (Chester seemed much more relaxed than before and seemed to want to talk about his different skills.) He answered quite a few of AM's test questions correctly even though he told about his activity with the cows and calves in between. . . .

AM showed him how to build the pink tower. . . . He built the tower very quickly, and then wanted to get all the other blocks out and "stack them up as high as I can." . . . Next was the form-board. He looked it over very carefully before beginning, then began. "Goes right here," he said, "this goes right here." . . . He got every piece in the correct slot the first time with no trials or errors.

At the end of the test, he immediately got his jacket, putting it on all by himself and we left. He ran down the steps ahead of me, opened the car door (front seat), and got in. . . . At the drugstore he told me he wanted chocolate (ice cream) and a large cone . . . "and some gum too," he said, "some black and some white." . . . He ate his cone rather quietly and put the gum in his pocket. He asked if he didn't "get a bigger cone than Ray" and I told him I thought he did. When we passed Quinton Heights School he told me "that's where Janie [his sister] goes to school" with much pride and that was where he would be going some day, and that Ray wouldn't be going for some time.

Here we also saw Chester's orientation to growth steps ahead, his early interest in how things work, in tools, and his identification with his father, who was a semiskilled worker;* we also saw his exaggerated fantasies about his skills with cows and calves.

We observed how, through his fluent conversation, Chester reflected much of his world of reality and fantasy, his preferences, his sense of mastery, his pride in his family, and also rivalry with his brother. And we

---

* These probably contributed to his choice of vocation as a garage mechanic, after one year of college. By contrast, Teddy, whose stepfather was in fact a garage mechanic, completed college as a music major and became a member of the Marine Band.

constantly saw his vivid interest in the world into which we introduced him. By contrast with the modest furnishings of his own home, the clock, decorative candles, lamp, and fireplace in the research house attracted his eager attention. Observant, inquiring, and reflective, he made himself at home in each new situation, relating warmly both to objects and to people. Most of the boys were also just as quick to relate to adults.

JoAnne was by no means the only child with a clear self-image and sense of identity: Chester volunteered impressively: "I am Chester Warren Cooper" when he came to a play session with me. Other expressions of identity and status appeared in such announcements as Sally's "Jimmie is bigger'n me and I'm bigger than Mike and Mike is bigger'n Tommy"—placing herself accurately in relation to her siblings. And Helen's self-image was reflected in her remark, "Wouldn't you like to have two cute little girls like me?" as she snuggled up to me on the front seat of the car.

While JoAnne was especially forthright in expressing her wishes and preferences, most children appeared to assume that these new adults would respect their autonomy, their opinions, their wishes, and their comments about their world—implying their experience of consistent respect from adults at home.

Sex differences[3]

Forthright as the more active girls were at the age of four, they were no match for the boys who loped, jumped, climbed up and down the wooded hillside and over the stone retaining walls at the party on the Murphy place on the edge of town. The relatively quiet but well-coordinated baby, Vernon (pp. 77 f.), had developed into a little tree climber, along with other boys who had been more active babies than he was. The opportunities of Topeka ecology, the freedom permitted by parents, the cultural expectations that boys will run and jump and climb had supported the motor skills and initiative of the boys.

The boys' slacks and blue jeans were suited to boys' activities, but who could scramble through the brush on the hillside dressed as the girls were in full skirts and ruffles? While the girls were growing up in the same ecological setting, cultural expectations for the girls were different, and they were treated differently. Both boys and girls were competent, and as we shall soon describe, able to cope with a variety of challenges. All the boys and girls four years old and older were able to go with a new person to a new place—the research center. Four out of six boys in the younger (two to three year) range clung to their mothers at first, while only three out of nine girls of comparable age did so.

These "good copers" were confident, flexible, resourceful, definite in their use of the environment and management of frustration.[4] Even less skillful or more vulnerable children were not confined to a narrow or mutually exclusive use of active coping or defense mechanisms. Darlene's motor inhibition and fear at the party and in other unstructured situations, particularly at the beginning, made her conspicuous among the children, but Dr. Kass commented, "The number and range of coping devices that she uses is extremely large." And at the end of a play session[5] with her that had begun stiffly I summarized as follows:

She uses a range of coping approaches, from rigid and exaggerated conformity, and assumption of a "little girl" role, to casually bypassing frustrations or difficulties which might be frustrating to others; regressing to a dependent or narcissistic position at times of insecurity, while at other times she is able to let out energetic, decisive, aggressive, competitive efforts with a gay spirit and with an undoubted capacity for strong determination. She could become a demúre martinet. She can look at the world through her own eyes and though apparently devoid of the sparkling or imaginative characteristics of some of the other children, she can, even though awkwardly, go after what she wants with astonishing directness. Darlene may develop some shrewdness out of her forceful determination to master reality.

The same child may, as Brennie did, combine denial or evasion at one time with initiative and direct coping efforts at another time.

Variability

It is easy to be misled by first impressions that certain children are passive or inhibited. While Rachel often made use of avoidance and withdrawal techniques, particularly in unstructured party and play situations that did not provide direct, formal adult guidance or support, she was capable of active responses at home. There she would give her mother an animated and detailed account of everything that had gone on around her. At the end of the play sessions, which had begun with her characteristic immobilization in strange, new experiences, I summarized her positive coping resources as follows:

A remarkable flexibility and resilience enabled her to respond freely once she is out of the immobilizing, awesome, or frightening new experience; a capacity for deep sensuous delight and gratification and for sensitive, nonverbal interpersonal communication through smiles and shining eyes contributes to a genuine relationship; a capacity for resourceful manipulation and problem-solving leads to constructive use of the play opportunity; a capacity for representation and symbolization of disturbing experiences and fantasies helps her to tolerate frustrations and stress.

In other words, while this little girl was consistently unable to move freely into new opportunities without support and guidance, so that externally she seemed to be coping less well with the environment than most children, she was all the time stowing away observations that she could use under circumstances more favorable for response. She might be cautious or inhibited in strange situations to the point of being immobilized, but she was not a profoundly withdrawn child. Within the basically circumscribed and protected area of the MLT play session, in contrast to the large-scale and open, unguided, party session, once she had acquainted herself with the opportunities she showed considerable ingenuity and solved problems with objects successfully. In the more familiar pediatric examination, the body-measurement and photography session, and later in the Witkin Three-Dimensional Embedded Figures test, she was eager, and even proudly ready, to cooperate and do her part. All the latter included active adult direction, apparently the key necessary to release her activity.

A very different pattern was observed in Terry, whose efforts to cope with a strange, new situation, "for him apparently so devoid of guideposts or satisfying patterns of interchange at the beginning, included speeding up, trying to move fast from one thing to another, defensive bravado of manner and a loud voice, and using support by involving the adult through questions and requests for help."

Coping efforts were sometimes highly experimental and varied as in this summary of one little girl:

> She copes with external reality with a variety of trial and error attempts, substituting, combining materials from different sources, adjusting, manipulating, restructuring reality—maneuvers which could be well used to maximize her strength and compensate for or minimize her weaknesses.

We often saw a combination of defensive behavior with direct coping efforts oriented simultaneously toward saving face or maintaining the level of self-feeling while at the same time directly attempting to get the help that would make it possible to function more effectively and realistically.

Coping with Adults

We have already seen many examples of the forthright yet flexible way many of these children dealt with us as new grown-ups offering them varied opportunities, yet also making demands, setting limits, presenting frustrations as well as gratification. Their patterns and sequences of maneuver varied from child to child. In addition to our records of their behavior, we have clues from the CAT (administered by Dr. Kass) that give ample evidence that many of these children at the age of three to five years experience themselves unconsciously, if not consciously, as little people surrounded by a world of big and powerful grown-ups with whom they could, however, deal and compete. Some of the children were cautious in their dealings with us at first. Many, though, never let on that they felt this way, and in fact it is quite possible they shut out such feelings as much as they could in the interest of making use of the opportunities we offered.

Among their different approaches in dealing with adults, we may group together the children who seemed to look for or follow adult cues with an implicit recognition that grown-ups have the upper hand and one might as well find out what the score is, what is expected, and follow cues as they come. This was true of Darlene, although she also had much more capacity for independence than this would seem to imply. Looking for the cues in the initial exposure to a situation seemed to help her to clarify the nature of the relationship with each adult so that she could be freer to be independent subsequently.

Some children routinely complied with the adults' commands or even offered the examiner the deference to authority that the child thought was expected by a "teacher." Thus Cynthia started out by fitting in, and Sheila, with all her autonomy, responded to conventional expectations of order and the like. While Janice was defiant in certain areas at times, in general her resistance was at a token level and was followed by compliance. Barbie went further than this, often doing her very best to respond to the experimenter's urging and to find some answer to satisfy him. Karen included in a wide repertory of ways of dealing with grown-ups a need to know specifically from the grown-up what was expected, apparently in order not to incur displeasure. In the CAT there was even evidence that she looked for a grown-up model for her own behavior.

Actually, while such efforts may seem to reflect considerable dependence upon grown-ups, most children were not as dependent as a few like Vivian, who could not engage in any activity until after she had received warm physical support (being held, hugged, and so on). Body contact afforded support and reassurance for such children and made it possible for them to move more freely. In some instances (Murphy 1962, p. 23) this physical support had to come from the mother in the earliest and newest situations in which the children saw us. It is interesting to note that in some cases the child seemed to be afraid of the situation rather than of the grown-up and appeared to count on the mother to be an ally against the strangeness of the situation as a whole.

At a more mature level was the behavior of children like five-year-old Susan, to whom it was important to sustain interpersonal relationship through constant verbal communication, as did Teddy, in contrast to the children described above who sought body contact.

At the beginning of the MLT session Helen appeared to want to start something, to get us involved in interaction, to make something happen, to have something going on, above all to have almost any kind of lively contact and interpersonal activity. Barbie also wanted interaction of an active sort and seemed to get it from structured games that could bring people together in an understood and comfortable way. This social, sharing, giving-and-receiving-support attitude was also characteristic of Chester; shared events, fantasies, and the constant communication of the world in which he lived were part of Chester's way of maintaining a relationship. While Ronald appeared to be uncertain and even suspicious about grown-ups at first, he did not at any time shut them out or keep his distance; he dealt with his uncertainty by developing a lively relationship that soon included the adult among his supporting resources as he repeatedly asked for clarification, information, or reassurance. In other words, he coped with his distrust by giving the adult ample opportunity to dispel any reasons for it.

With children such as Chester, Teddy, Helen, and Susan the tendency to draw other people into their world appeared to have the value of enriching their own experience. With Brennie, however, his eagerness to develop the social relationship, to win the examiner with sharing or cooperation, may have had the value of forestalling possible strain in his relationship with the adults. This was suggested by the intensity of his preoccupation with relationships, which was so extreme as to prevent the strong investment in objective goals we saw in Teddy and others.

Lennie was outgoing and approached people in a more naïve and primitive way; spontaneous and warm, his eagerness for relationships simply gave him an opportunity to be himself. With a few children such as JoAnne, perceptiveness regarding social situations and role differentiation seemed to go hand in hand with their use of defense mechanisms of avoidance and denial, suggesting that they were oversensitive to the reactions of others.

Terry was sensitive to the total continuity of social interactions of individual participants in roles; he could accurately anticipate and predict consequences of behavior. In Ego-blocking play he sidetracked his cars to make room for mine and in other ways maintained a cooperative relationship. This was different from Teddy's tendency to exchange observations at a rather mature and intellectual level where the purpose of keeping a relationship going may have included an effort to support his own feeling of grown-upness (in contrast to Lennie's primitive direct warmth).

Several of the children who actively maintained a social exchange with the examiners were also children who identified with the adults—with the mother, father, or both, or as in the case of Susan, with the nurturant tender loving care given by both her mother and the nurses who cared for her in the hospital.

It is not too surprising that these same children—that is, JoAnne, Helen, Chester, Ray, Terry, and Brennie—were among those who tended to reverse roles in experiments and games, turning the tables, taking over the experimenter's role, testing the experimenter. Terry, when coming to the MLT play session after his Binet session with AM, suggested to me in essence an intelligence test: "I'll mix them up and you fix them." JoAnne also asked in an adult way, "Do you know what these are about?" with an evident tendency toward role reversal. This aspiration to participate in adult modes of behavior in imitation of parents' actions was even reflected in JoAnne's CAT stories and in her attitude of offering explanations to the examiners. With Susan, and surprisingly, Cynthia, role reversal gave the child an opportunity to control the situation and keep the upper hand.

Other children tried to keep up with the adult world in different ways. Martin and Roddy entered into competition with the adult; Roddy invented a game of dividing color sticks. "You have a turn, me have a turn, we'll see who gets most." With Roddy, being fast so as to get the most appeared to be very important in the MLT session. Martin suggested to Dr. Moriarty that he could beat her in putting the toys away. Even Vernon, reserved as he was, showed considerable interest in winning, in games offering an opportunity for rivalry; Ralph, along with his need for and responsiveness to warmth, was sometimes overdecisively emphatic in his correction of the adult and gave other hints of his competitiveness in his gleeful "I beat you." Barbie, Daryl, and Brennie competed to win from the adult whenever they had an opportunity, while JoAnne represented the baby bear and daddy bear on a CAT as winning out over the mother. Brennie seemed to engage in a constant contest, as if he didn't expect the adult to be decisive enough to carry through a plan. He consistently tried out his own ideas to see whether he could get away with them.

In other words, while these children saw themselves as little people in a world of big people, a number of them were not willing to settle for this state of affairs and constantly proceeded to test the possibilities of extending their power by turning the tables, winning out over the grown-ups, expanding their own area of control. For some of these children (for example, JoAnne, Brennie, and Roddy), this effort to find or maintain an equal level in their relationship with grown-ups may have contributed to the uncertainty that their tension reflected.

At the same time we cannot say that an attitude of identification with and competition with grown-ups inevitably threatened the child's security at this stage, since Susan, Chester, Teddy, and others appeared to be confident children who could compete with a grown-up without feeling insecure on many occasions when it was not possible to win, to keep the upper hand, or to control a situation.

It is interesting to reflect on the fact that while many of the children were so active and assertive in their dealings with the grown-ups, they were generally not belligerent, smart-alecky, or grossly exhibitionistic. Not one of them was obnoxious; on the contrary, the research group experienced them as delightful, interesting, and charming. They evoked respect as well as enjoyment.

Flexible Use of Autonomy

Autonomy was typically balanced by cooperativeness and compliance with mandatory requests, as we saw even with the challenging JoAnne; the children were adequately prepared to fit into the traditional school system with its formal demands. We saw the background for this in the mothers' emphasis on letting the child find his own way in the area of interests and vocational plans, and at the same time learn obedience when it was required. But the demands for obedience were not imposed so constantly as to interfere with autonomy in free or unstructured situations. One or two children, moreover, were inclined to test the adult to see how far they could go. Witness Janice:

While I was driving Janice to the research office, she stood up in the back seat and leaned on the back of the front seat, peering through the windshield. LBM: "Janice, please sit down." Janice: "I don't want to sit down." LBM: "But you just told me you are a good girl." Janice: "But I'm not the kind of good that sits down."

Actually, we found that Janice's point was not as witty as it sounded, but merely matter-of-fact, since other children were also allowed by their mothers to stand up in the car while being driven around town, and standing up did not necessarily involve a breach of being good.

Furthermore, autonomy was flexible—available when the children were sufficiently oriented to the proffered opportunities to run, climb, or explore the park, Murphy woods, or zoo, and in abeyance when a familiar adult-dominated situation such as a pediatric examination was the order of the day. This flexibility was also seen in Darlene, whose religiously devoted mother described her as a good, obedient girl. On observing my bracelet she had remarked, "My mommy says Jesus doesn't like bracelets, but I do"; and a few years later, when she was eight years old, "My mommy's too strict." Obedience to a devoted authoritarian mother did not preclude independence of thought and evaluation of experience.

Moreover, initiative could be used in the service of self-protection in what we called strategic withdrawal (from threats or excessive pressures) and constructive use of anxiety. In short, the children were sensible and practical in managing their relations with the environment—a testimony to the range of experience they had been permitted, and at the same time to the fact that limits had been set.

A Pool of Behavior Records for Coping Analysis[6]

We can see that at the preschool stage these children had a wide range of resources and were involved in a great variety of encounters with the environment, both potentially gratifying and frustrating or threatening. We saw the preschool children in a wide variety of situations, and several different observers reported on them. As a result, a large pool of behavior observations was available, and these were empirically formulated into an inventory of items referring to coping efforts, qualities of functioning and self-feeling relevant to their coping efforts, in addition to scores produced from psychological and pediatric examinations.

How did we now transmute the descriptions into statements about the children's coping methods, and how do we look at their coping patterns in relation to their development through childhood? From the summaries and from the raw records specific behavior episodes were excerpted. Often the observer had described or summarized the coping pattern of the child, and in such instances the coping pattern was

entered on a card. When the behavior was described without formulating a concept referring to the coping pattern, the concept was
provided by me.

Dr. Toussieng's summaries contained a large number of coping
concepts, such as: "reality testing," "forestalls danger," "mastery drive—
struggle capacity—determination," "deals with threat by maneuvering
himself," "is tolerant of obstacles and difficulties," "has ability to
postpone, wait for, gratification," "resilience—recovery from embarrassment," "impulse control."

Coping resources mentioned in my summaries included "speed of
orientation—grasp of situation," "uses environmental areas selectively,"
"ability to integrate modalities," "ability to synthesize thought, affect,
action," "ability to control the impact of the environment," "ability to
accept substitutes," "ability to solve problems directly," "ability to
restructure the environment," "ability to protest actively," "strategic
withdrawal," [7] "has emotional sending power," "ability to evoke desired
response," "flexibility in adapting means to a goal."

Moriarty noted children's ways of coping with difficulties presented by
the structured tests, such as: "mobilizing cognitive resources," "utilizing
previous experience," "concentrating deeply," "surveying, evaluating,
classifying," "using extra care," "creative restructuring," "humor," "using
trial and error," "asking for help," "delaying," "protesting," "resisting,"
"excusing failure," "shifting to an easier task," "criticizing the materials."
In addition, bodily adjustments, sound effects, variations in speech,
affective responses were among patterns used apparently to reduce
tension.

Formation of a Comprehensive Coping Inventory

In addition to the coping items illustrated above, items derived from
pediatric examinations and the medical history, from psychological tests,
and from observations in the home, were included in a Comprehensive
Coping Inventory (CCI) (see Appendix 4).

Allowing items coming from each different source to remain separate
even when they were closely similar, a list of more than six hundred
coping items and contributing factors resulted. These coping items
included both active and passive coping devices and also defense
mechanisms and did not imply any judgments of success. Just as a
general may devise a strategy for attack that fails, a child's coping efforts
sometimes fail. And while some combinations of, or overuse of, defense
mechanisms may interfere with healthy coping, flexible use of defense
mechanisms can be part of it.

In addition, two global variables were formulated: Coping I, capacity to cope with opportunities, challenges, frustrations, threats in the environment; and Coping II, maintenance of internal integration—that is, capacity to manage one's relation to the environment so as to maintain integrated functioning (free from marked tenseness, unmanageable anxiety, loss of motor coordination, deterioration of speech, disorganization of thought processes, and so on). Ratings of each child on these two were derived from a paired comparisons analysis made separately by me and Moriarty.

Correlations of Individual Items with Coping I and Coping II

The entire list of coping items was correlated with each of the global variables Coping I and Coping II; those items correlating at an .05 and .01 level of confidence were sorted out for study. As you can see, these correlations in essence reflected the examiners' implicit evaluation of the contribution of specific coping techniques to overall coping effectiveness. The complete lists are included in Appendix 4. Here we present some examples of items in major zones of functioning that correlated highly with global Coping I.

Aspects of Coping I

Some significant correlations with Coping I for boys and girls together follow. Ratings are by Toussieng (PT), Moriarty (AM), or a consensus of Murphy, Moriarty, and Heider (C).

I. Cognitive capacities
   Item No.
   447 Orientation: speed with which child was aware (new situation, AM)
   168 Alertness to details in the environment   PT
   179 Enjoyment of fine nuances of sensation   PT
   600 Curiosity, finding out   PT
   180 Clarity of perception   PT
   418 Receptivity to environmental cues, moods, qualities   PT
   602 Reality testing, accuracy of perception   PT
   302 Freedom from inhibitions or rigidity in thinking   PT
   334 Knowing the score, grasping sequences   C
   384 Coping concepts, ideas, solutions   C
   408 Ability to synthesize thinking, affect, action   C
   457 Cognitive coping capacity   AM
   596 Problem-solving attitude toward life   C

    473 Has insight into situations, realistic appraisal C
    548 Insightfulness into social situations PT

II. Motor capacities
    164 Freedom to translate ideas into action C
    167 Special vulnerability in the motor area (freedom from) PT
    595 Use of motor skills for coping with environmental demands C
    578 Discharge efficiency for child who has resources for discharge of tension PT
    446 Motor and visual-motor control (in test situation, AM)

III. Affect
    179 Enjoyment of fine nuances of sensation PT
    211 Pleasure outweighs frustration experience C
    204 Degree of differentiation of affect PT
    368 Range of areas of enjoyment, gratification C
    224 Vividness of expression PT
    268 Ability to accept warmth and support C
    269 Gives warmth and support to others C
    270 Is stimulating to others C
    382 Love, aggression balance C
    418 Receptivity to environmental cues, moods, qualities C
    455 Affective coping capacity AM
    480 Positive orientation to life C
    479 Enjoys newness, discovery C
    336 Resilience following disappointment, defeat C
    487 Resistance to discouragement C
    481 Intensity of interest, enthusiasm, etc. C
    482 Has emotional sending power—reaches others C
    483 Range of moods in reaction to stimuli C
    485 Awareness of feelings of others PT
    486 Flexibility of emotional management and control C
    490 Capacity for fun, zest, delight, pleasure C

IV. Coping techniques and ego resources (complex integrative capacities)
    245 Autonomy C
    476 Psychically active orientation vs. let life happen[8] C
    610 Ability to protest actively C
    246 Capacity to mobilize resources under stress PT
    236 Ability to solve problems directly PT
    409 Ability to ask for or get help when needed AM
    187 Creativeness and originality PT

524 Uses environmental areas selectively   C
471 Ability to integrate modalities   C
474 Ability to restructure the environment, create new
    patterns[9]   C
607 Ability to balance self and social demands   C
609 Balance of ego strengths and instinctual strength   C
511 Ability to balance dependence and independence   C
512 Ability to synthesize drives; affection, aggression   C
561 Differentiated response to stress   PT
399 Flexibility in adapting means to a goal   C
529 Constructive use of one's anxiety   C
531 Constructive use of external control   C
530 Child's ability to sublimate aggression   PT
546 Ability to take different roles (freedom to shift)   C
503 Eliciting desired response from others   C

V.   Self-feeling
504 Narcissism, healthy pleasure in being oneself   PT
498 Pride (unassailability)   PT
542 Separation, differentiation of self and others   C
323 Maintenance of self-regard under difficulty
506 Ability to positively assert own needs and preferences   C
507 Ego involvement in own activity   PT
604 Confidence in ability to do   PT
500 Independence, self-reliance, autonomy   PT
366 Courage   PT

Coping I correlated more highly with some motor items for girls. This did not mean that girls had greater motor competence, but reflected their wider range (from good to poor or high to low) in this area. (Some girls were very skillful in using their motor resources in coping, while others were not, and still others were limited in motor capacities.)

Items correlating more highly with Coping I for girls were: *motor coordination, purposefulness of movements, interest in mastering space, eagerly explores environment in new situation, speed or tempo,* and *energy level.* While some girls were as energetic and skillful as most boys, a few were less adequate than any of the boys.

Similarly, certain affective, sensory, and cognitive variables gave higher correlations with Coping I for boys than for girls; these reflected a wider range of levels of functioning among boys, some of whom had affect as deep as the warmest girls and pleasure in tactile experience as great, while others were extremely limited in these and some other areas.

Items correlating more highly with Coping I for boys were: *depth of affect, pleasure in tactile experience, tact, ability to balance gratification and frustration, breadth of perceptual field, clarity of distinction between reality and fantasy,* and *overall ability.*

Thus we could say that the best copers among boys were those who were not limited to so-called masculine skills, but rather those flexible boys who could allow themselves some "feminine" qualities along with their masculinity. Similarly the girls with the widest range of coping resources were those who could enjoy some "masculine" resources in addition to their feminine qualities.

The problem of cultural relativity in children's coping[10]

We did not make scales for these coping items because so often scales lead to a freezing of concepts, a premature finalizing of norms, and blocks to fresh observation and thinking. We felt that coping patterns of preschool children would probably differ in other American subcultures as well as in subcultures of other nations. Chester, Helen, Sally, Darlene, and Terry all came from families of semiskilled or skilled worker fathers—families in which both parents were skilled in management of everyday practical matters, in use of tools, in repairing worn or damaged parts of their homes, and in fixing broken appliances. Since fathers had considerable time at home, children had opportunities to observe them in these activities and sometimes to try out and practice use of tools as well as to develop concepts of protection, fixing, adapting, and substituting objects. Such experiences could lead to a different coping orientation from that of children on a primitive farm in an underdeveloped country, or of children of professional parents in a metropolitan area (children who did not have an opportunity to observe parents at work). We need to study the coping patterns in a wide range of subcultures without being constricted by assumptions or norms for coping in just one subculture. The list above could represent the beginning of a taxonomy of coping with the environment.

Aspects of Coping II

Coping II was concerned with maintenance of internal integration[11] and was thus contrasted with vulnerability, which first concerned us in children with tendencies to lose smoothness of motor coordination, or clarity of speech and perception, and other aspects of optimal functioning. We expected that some aspects of Coping I would contribute to maintenance of internal integration, and this is confirmed by the overlap in Coping I and Coping II items for boys and girls at the preschool stage. Significant correlations (.01 level) with both global Coping I and II (for both sexes) occurred with the following items:

Positive self appraisal
Likes self
Separation of self and others
Resilience following disappointment
Resistance to discouragement
Courage
Constructive use of anxiety
Constructive use of external control
Methods of dealing with frustration by adapting self
Methods of dealing with frustration by adapting others
Clarity of perception

In addition, Coping II was significantly related to cognitive items such as "achieving clear structure has priority over expressing affect," as well as range of fine muscle skills, competence, task involvement, low impulsiveness, toleration or containment of negative feelings, freedom from doubt and ambivalence, forestalling danger, knowing when to stop; sensitivity balanced by ability to control stimuli (and ability to fend off excessive stimulation), ability to facilitate resilience by timing rest, high threshold for frustration and tolerance for frustration, ability to accept substitutes. As well, there is an extra nuance added along with the narcissistic "likes self" that we saw among items related to Coping I, namely, sense of self-worth, comfortable relation to ego-ideal.

Certainly the ability to control the impact of the environment, to limit or fend off excessive stimulation, to forestall danger, and to know when to stop also imply autonomy. But in this case the child's efforts are oriented precisely toward maintenance of integration, in contrast to the many expressions of autonomy defining Coping I.

Certain formulations of criteria for mental health (Jahoda 1958) emphasize autonomy; but here we note a balance of autonomy with sufficient dependency to be able to get and use help as characteristic of the children and, for that matter, of their families as well. We also noted the pleasure in self that accompanied autonomy in many of the children.*

* It is interesting in connection with our observations of the children to consider the adaptational styles of President Eisenhower (Kansas) and President Truman (Missouri)— both practical, sensible, courageous yet unassuming, autonomous but not driven, by and large honest, open, salt-of-the-earth leaders. Eisenhower's quiet charm was not unlike that of certain men and boys in our study, though we had none with Truman's dry wit.

Assuming that many of the responses we observed could be included under the general rubric "psychically active orientation to life" (including cognitive, motor, and affective responsiveness), is this ordinarily thought to imply the abilities to get help when needed, to protest actively, to restructure the environment (implying creating new realities), to constructively use anxiety, and related types of action observed in these children? Are such efforts appreciated by adults who are all too often pressuring children to adhere to preformulated expectations of proper behavior?

The many aspects of coping we have mentioned can be classified into techniques, or devices, and dispositions (White 1974). But as we have already seen, dispositions are often utilized even deliberately in the service of coping, so that functionally the line between coping devices and dispositions may be hard to draw. For instance, sending power, seductiveness, warmth all become part of the child's coping resources, along with cognitive dispositions toward attention to details, which facilitate problem-solving.

"Coping styles" may also be misleading as we saw with Rachel, whose turtle-like behavior in new unstructured situations contrasted with her alacrity, even vigor, in familiar adult-directed situations. Coping styles must be seen in relation to types of situations as these are experienced by the child.

In the *Widening World of Childhood* we saw a sequence of coping styles in Molly as she gradually mastered her fear of thunder between the ages of two and four. Thus coping techniques and styles evolve and change over time. In the following chapters we will find other evidences of change in coping style through time, as time brings both new challenges and new strengths to the child, and also in some instances, new vulnerabilities. The process of consolidating an identity (Erikson 1959) in late adolescence involves a choice of coping styles, but even then evolution continues and the mature person often discovers resources he was not able to use in early adulthood.

Healthy Narcissism

We typically assume that self-respect characterizes the healthy person, but do we include "healthy narcissism," [12] liking oneself, "it feels good to be me"—delight in one's own experiencing, even if not at the level of Whitman's "There is such a lot of me and all so luscious"? "Adjustment" is a pale, thin quality by comparison and hardly implies the dynamic, generative response to life so characteristic of some of these children.

The healthy narcissism of Susan, Chester, Lennie, and other children was not an isolating, thumb-sucking, or withdrawing self-absorption, but rather a contagious evocative quality of sharing the sense that it is good to be, as with Helen's inviting query, "Wouldn't you like to have two cute little girls like me?" It was also reflected in their pleasure in their own activity, and in their appearance and dress, and in their expectation of being liked. And these were often seen in a context of naïve pride in demonstrating their skills.

Coping with Vulnerability

With most children in our culture the preschool stage is a period when fears are at a peak (Macfarlane, Allen, and Honzik 1954;[13] Jersild and Holmes 1935). Going to new strange places with a strange adult without mother (see Murphy 1962, chap. 2 for examples from coping sample), being examined by a doctor even when the mother was present, being pressed to respond to new task-demands such as those in the intelligence tests, the Rorschach, and the CAT, having to take off clothes for a nude photograph in view of other children and several adults—these and other experiences included in the research program evoked some anxiety in many of the children.

Our friendly and gentle pediatrician gave no shots nor did she inflict any pain at all, and yet some children were anxious because of previous painful or uncomfortable medical experiences. By careful attention to areas of bodily reactivity, she noted zones in which tension was reflected in different children: the muscular system, reactivity of pulse, blood pressure or heart rate, flushing or paling, erections in a few boys, stammering, and so forth; crying was rare. At the parties on the Murphy grounds, and later in a park, some insecurity was implied in the caution, withdrawal to a safe corner, hesitation to attempt a jump or a seesaw. Still, all the children had ways of coping with anxiety about newness, fear of failure, fatigue, adult pressure, and other sources of mild stress. No child left any of the situations in which we observed them.

At the preschool stage, any deterioration or inhibition of cognitive, motor, or integrative functioning pointed to vulnerable areas, as did extreme autonomic or affective reactivity to stimulation, and other disturbances in functioning.[14] Such deterioration of coordination in action or speech, and the upheavals or threat of being overwhelmed accompanying autonomic disturbances or extreme emotional responses may be assured to be experienced as unpleasant. Some children developed self-protective preventive devices or compensatory measures to manage such problems.

So our attention was drawn to the group of self-protective resources that stand the preschool child in good stead for coping with vulnerability: the ability to facilitate resilience by timing rest, and the ability to limit or fend off excessive stimulation (and/or, more broadly, the ability to control the impact of the environment), both of which we saw even in some of the youngest infants (p. 92). "Strategic withdrawal" is an important resource at a stage when mastery is limited. Capacities for speedy orientation, to "use delay for appraisal," and to "forestall danger by knowing when to stop" (also to be cautious) would logically be prerequisites for these various ways in which the child limits the environment. These processes are important to "constructive use of anxiety." The child also develops the ability to select, to impose his own structure, and to "restructure the environment"—as we all saw in our various testing sessions and as we illustrated above (p. 113). Children can carry on these operations either self-protectively when coping with vulnerabilities, or as part of a strategy toward positive goals. Realistic appraisal of the environment, acceptance of people as they are, and clear differentiation of fantasy from reality are also obviously necessary prerequisites for managing the environment in ways that are consistent with maintaining one's own safety, integration, and comfort. Underlying these we can think of a drive to maintenance of comfort—not just avoidance of pain and stress.

It is not surprising that many cognitive coping capacities are involved in managing vulnerabilities, and we can spell these out: alertness, clarity of perception, insights, coping concepts, and similar contributions (although IQ, as such, is not among the factors highly related to coping with vulnerability). Especially significant (that is, having higher correlations) are the familiar items—autonomy, range of fine-muscle skills, control in handling things, the smoothness in movement to carry out autonomous intentions, the drive to grow up, and the adequate discharge of tension (see Appendix 4). These would all contribute to the freedom and to the active capacity to implement insight and coping concepts.

A child may have vulnerabilities growing out of sensory or motor handicaps that are nevertheless well handled if the child has balancing capacities such as freedom from a low threshold for frustration as well as tolerance for difficulties and obstacles and a capacity to mobilize resources under stress. Related to such tolerance and flexibility are affective qualities, the most outstanding of which is appropriateness of quality of affect, which implies that the child does not react in exaggerated ways, or with emotional expressions that do not fit the event.

It may be surprising that tolerance of temporary regression protects against vulnerability—in other words, a child who can relax with a familiar comfort device, be it babyish thumb-sucking, lip-play, and the like, or merely nonfunctional tension-discharging like foot-tapping, could thereby allow himself leeway for coping. He could then get along better than if he bottled up his tension in order to behave or appear mature.

We also found some aspects of the child's relation to his home negatively related to (and thus forestalling or coping with) vulnerability. As we would expect, every sort of integration in the home and family—mother–child relationship, the child's own equipment and relation with the environment—either prevents, offsets, or helps the child to cope with vulnerability. Especially impressive are the mother's enjoyment of the child, the adequacy of the child's self-image, security and positive orientation to life along with related items such as pleasure in being oneself, or "healthy narcissism" (Van der Waals 1965), and sense of self-worth.

Other aspects of the mother's relation with her child attracted our attention among significant relationships—for example, the mother's encouragement or support of the child and her active help to the child in coping. But these are not as outstanding as her enjoyment of her child and her acceptance of the child's coping style. Here we are reminded of the current cliché "I'm O.K.—you're O.K." (Harris 1967). But in the case of a mother with a young child, where her enjoyment is likely as not expressed nonverbally even more than in verbal terms, we are led to an awareness of the importance of contagion. While there has been some discussion of contagion between the anxious mother and her infant (Stewart 1953; Escalona 1952), there has been too little emphasis on the integrative contribution of feeling that one is enjoyed. This may be a major factor in Baldwin's (1945) finding better development in children with "warm authoritarian" parents than in children of "cold democratic" parents. It is of course easier for a mother to enjoy a child free of vulnerability, and thus we see the reverse of Gregory Bateson's concept of the schismogenic process (1936, 1965) in which negative interactions may lead progressively to a greater gulf between two people. Would it be possible to electronically measure activation, vegetative functioning, and perceptual response of a mother and child during a period when the mother is in the act of enjoying her child? How possible would it be for either one to be wholly natural and spontaneous in such a situation? How else can we move ahead in our understanding of the dynamic importance, the energizing, releasing effect, of a mother's enjoyment of her child? These are questions for future research.

We began this chapter with a question about possible relationships between infancy and preschool behavior among these children. In the next chapter we explore some of our expected and unexpected findings.

5

Relationships between Infancy, Preschool, and Later Development

"Infancy protest, resistance to disliked foods, and the ability to terminate unwanted feeding" is correlated with the preschool ability "to control the impact of the environment" and "to restructure the environment," and the drive for mastery.

For the preschool coping study (Murphy 1962) we simply focused our lens on the children's behavior, trying to see its meaning in the context of the experiences to which we exposed them within the subculture in which they were living. But soon our appetite was whetted for more: could we add something to our understanding of development by exploring relationships between behavior at successive stages? How much connection might be found between the recorded infant behavior and behavior of the same children at the preschool stage? Could we throw any light on the respective contributions of early tendencies and experience? And could we extend our understanding of the kinds of experience as well as constitutional tendencies that influenced development? More specifically, what would be the contribution of outcomes of coping efforts, of both coping with the environment and with difficulties created by the child's own makeup?

Our first step requires us to look at some of the relationships between infant behavior and later behavior of the children.

Sources of evidence on continuity and change[1]

We had several sources of evidence on relationships between infancy and preschool behavior: (a) predicting from one stage to the next (Escalona and Heider 1959); (b) correlating behavior at the two levels (Murphy 1958, 1961), and (c) following the children's behavior through individual sequential studies (Heider 1966; Moriarty 1961, 1966). It would be expected that both unpredictable experiences and new developmental changes would contribute to difficulties in prediction from infancy to preschool behavior. But some unexpected continuities and relationships between infancy and preschool behavior might possibly

127

be revealed through correlations and case studies. Heider's analysis of the infants included ratings on items related to strength and vulnerability, and I evaluated certain coping behaviors observed during feeding of the infants and compared these with later behavior. Moriarty focused on cognitive functioning and speech. Several members of the research group made intensive studies of individual children from infancy to later stages of development (Davidson 1967; Bernardez 1965; Gardner and Moriarty 1968).

Taking these approaches to continuity in order, Escalona (and Heider 1959, p. 52) predicted behavior directly related to or continuous with basic infancy tendencies and also behavior not directly observable in early infancy. Among her best predicted items were:

Prediction area	*Percent correctly predicted by Escalona*
Motor coordination (pattern)	86
Motor development (maturation)	83
Attention, concentration, involvement	81
Activity pattern and range	78
Expressive behavior	74
Perceptual sensitivity (intake)	70
Intelligence level, pattern	70
Affects (complexity, intensity, history)	69
Decisiveness, goal striving	68
Activity level	67

While most of these aspects of behavior are not described in terms of their use in the child's coping efforts, they are closely related to either prerequisites for or sequelae of such efforts. The continuity in smoothness of coordination, movement patterns, and activity level and range, along with such aspects of mental functioning as perceptual sensitivity, attention, and concentration and certain affect and drive factors, fits with the reports by some others, as in Sheldon's (1940) studies of physique and in Thomas et al. (1963). These aspects of behavior are probably most closely controlled by the biological structure of the child, especially musculature and nervous system.

In addition Escalona successfully predicted the following more complex items:

Sex role acceptance	95
Sex role conflicts (internal)	75
Oedipal conflict, resolution, etc.	82

Relationship to siblings	75
Reaction of staff to child	80
Interest pattern in play	74
Interest pattern (excluding play)	86
Fantasy, imaginativeness (intensity)	73
Fantasy (quality, use of)	67
Use of space (freedom in structuring of)	67

Although we generally assume that such patterns are largely out-growths of the interaction of characteristics within the baby and/or between the child and his environment, these tendencies paralleled the constitutional characteristics in predictive success. In the Escalona–Leitch records comments were very often made regarding the masculine or feminine appearance of the baby in the early months, the infant's attractiveness, the baby's relation with its parents, and its preference for objects versus people. These items were relevant to much of the predicted behavior. Still, successful prediction by a very experienced clinician with both psychoanalytic and biosocial psychological orientation does not guarantee comparable success for less experienced and less knowledgeable observers who have less experience with babies and small children. Graduate students in clinical psychology, for instance, proved generally limited in their handling of this material. By comparing correlations between raters, we found "good raters" and "poor raters."

In contrast to the well-predicted areas, the following were successfully predicted by Escalona only 38 to 50 percent of the time:

Response to the unfamiliar (new situations)	38
Shyness, response to strangers	47
Relationship with mother	47
Basic attitudes and feelings regarding self and the world	50
Achievement needs, competitiveness	43
Response to frustration (internal)	50
Play style (thematic)	48

It seems fair to assume that these aspects of behavior are more susceptible to influence from other stressful and stimulative experiences after the first six months, for example, experiences with the mother, other experiences in the family or in the wider world (visits, excursions, events at the doctor's office) or experiences of illness, accident, or disaster. The related items—"basic attitudes and feelings regarding self and the world," "shyness," and "response to the unfamiliar"—suggest that confidence and openness to new encounters are *not* firmly rooted in the first six months but are susceptible to subsequent influence by success or difficulty in coping with new experiences.[2] When we remember reports of changes in mothers' attitudes as the child changes from a dependent baby to a more actively exploring, challenging, and often frustrating youngster, and how mothers themselves change as they become more burdened with more babies, it is not surprising that "relationship with mother" is poorly predicted. Here are several areas where changes, even transformations, can be found.

Escalona also explored relationships between infancy cognitive functioning and IQs at the preschool level (Escalona and Moriarty 1961). All the infants originally selected as being within the normal range had IQs from the average to a very superior level at the preschool stage and later, although within this range there were many changes in IQs. (Since it is well established [Bayley 1949] that tested IQs at infancy do not correlate highly with IQs at the age of five years, we shall not discuss these here; differences in the functions tested are of major importance.)

Continuity and change in vulnerability

The less successful predictions suggested that some areas of the child's behavior are more vulnerable to environmental pressures than others. So we became interested in relations between the baby's functioning and his later vulnerabilities and ways of coping with the environment. Further explorations of relationships between infancy and preschool behavior proceeded in a series of rather cautious steps. As we have just seen, Escalona was most successful in predicting specific tendencies most closely tied to the physical structure of the child (activity and motor patterns or characteristics of perception). Now Heider (1966) moved into the study of certain global characteristics of the infants such as *robustness,* with its implications of stamina, vigor, energy, resistance to infection; *functional stability,* another umbrella covering freedom from marked autonomic lability reflected in tendencies toward flushing or paling, perspiring, or variability in respiration, heart rate, pulse, blood pressure; *vegetative functioning,* still another comprehensive concept, including evaluation of digestion and elimination (a colicky baby or one that tended to have diarrhea or constipation was rated lower on this factor); *sensory reactivity,* referring to the baby's behavior in response to sounds, sights, and contact experiences of many kinds (jumping, jerking, or twitching at a loud or strange sound, turning away from bright lights, protesting certain ways of being touched, or experiencing textures of materials). Heider thought of these and others as important factors in vulnerability at both the infancy and preschool levels. Vulnerable babies had disturbances in feeding or digestion, in bowel functioning, or in breathing, and generally had low energy, a fragile physique, and, often, developmental imbalances.

All the vulnerable babies also had some inadequacy in attunement between mother and baby. We saw (p. 70) that Terry's mother was attentive but a teaser. Helen's mother was a good mother for several boys but somewhat out of touch with a little daughter craving contact (see pp. 303–04). Roddy's mother was careful and systematic but unaware of his rhythm and inclined to interrupt it. Cynthia's mother was flighty and undependable. The mother–baby difficulties were subtle by clinical standards and within the normal range.

In contrast to Heider's group of vulnerable infants who uniformly had disturbed vegetative functioning and who with one exception were relatively low in energy, none of the *least vulnerable* infants had serious difficulty in gastrointestinal functioning. Slight or moderate gastrointestinal difficulty was counterbalanced in some infants, such as Susan and Molly, by very understanding, consistent mothering and in Molly's case by her own resourceful ways of handling herself. When the distress suffered by the baby is within the range of the baby's ability to modify the stress, this primitive experience of autonomous success in coping can contribute to the expectation that one will be able to cope with other difficulties through one's own efforts.

With the least vulnerable babies, the mothers (except for one who had a brief postpartum depression) were pleased and proud of the sex, appearance, personality, and equipment of the baby. In the case of the one exception, the older siblings made up for what the sick mother couldn't give, treating the baby like a queen. All were attractive and sturdy babies, in some cases outstandingly so.

At the preschool stage, Heider judged five children to be less vulnerable and fifteen as more vulnerable than they were in the first six months of life. Eleven remained at the same level—five being judged as high in vulnerability, five as low, and one as moderate at both infancy and preschool levels. The children who became more vulnerable included five in whom illness had diminished the child's adequacy and seven whose mothers' difficulties (depression or other emotional disturbance, extreme fatigue, or anxious over-restrictiveness) contributed to the child's vulnerability. Less resourceful coping capacities were seen in the children who showed greater vulnerability.

Those who became less vulnerable were able to respond resiliently to new opportunities after better physiological integration as they matured, or in one case with outstanding support from the family. This group also included some of the outstanding "copers"—children who developed excellent resources for dealing with the environment through their own efforts.

In short, we saw children with varying infancy levels of vulnerability, and varying sources of increasing or declining vulnerability, including physiological and growth factors, autonomous coping resources, and family (including maternal) stress or support. Still, during latency, all were able to continue to mature and to develop more resources; but in some instances and for limited periods children coped less well in the prepuberty years with difficulties. The vulnerable children differed in their ability to use new opportunities and also in their ability to ask for help.

We must recognize the assessment problems involved in the appraisal of differences in vulnerability and potential resilience in the early years. Lasting effects of the conflictual and vulnerable aspects of the preschool phase are reflected in later scars or frailties in certain children but not all. Vulnerability cannot be viewed as static; children may or may not continue to be as vulnerable as they were in preschool years and infancy.

Six of the eight preschoolers who were rated most vulnerable by Heider and whom we were able to see through their entire childhood, had later phases of depression, anxiety, or other difficulty sufficient to want or need help. Of fourteen children rated low to moderate in vulnerability at the preschool level, only three sought or appeared to need any kind of help at later stages. Help in both groups included special conferences with the family minister or priest, or special activities planned by us to evoke and support more positive coping efforts by a disorganized or depressed child. Of the total group of twenty-seven preschoolers who were seen through high school, four received some professional help or guidance before they graduated from high school. There was no delinquency and no hospitalization for mental illness among this group; there was only one high school dropout, and he joined the Marines.

Loss of coordination under stress was a revealing aspect of vulnerability. Of the seven preschool children who continued to suffer from this form of deterioration of motor functioning five were subject to periods of depression during childhood (Rachel, Daryl, Gordon, Martin, Ronald); two others were subject to sudden loss of emotional integration—mild transitory panic in one instance (JoAnne) and temper outbursts in the other instance (Susan). Lennie's variability in coordination was thought by the psychiatrist and neurologist to indicate some organic damage probably resulting from his illnesses at two to three years. Thus, persistent or recurrent loss of motor integration may be seen as an aspect of a more general susceptibility to disintegrative reactions. Effects of stress and cumulative trauma were evident especially during critical phases such as puberty.[3] But most of these children were resilient enough to show impressive improvement during their pre-adult years, according to observations of them in their high school years by Moriarty and Toussieng (1976).[4]

Coping with early vulnerability

Changes in vulnerability from infancy to preschool stages as evaluated by Grace Heider also give clues to sources of resilience: ten of nineteen infants showing loss of coordination under stress in infancy did *not* do so at the preschool stage. What happened? Two of them tended to become inhibited, as if they might have learned to avoid the loss of coordination by avoiding movement itself under stress.

In some preschool children inhibition becomes more available as an aspect of their greater capacity for control. If this is so, it can, along with their newly acquired active skills, contribute to the *decrease* of disintegrative reactions and an *increased* capacity to maintain integration.

Nine of these same nineteen infants neither showed any motor disturbance nor became inhibited at the preschool stage. Neurological maturation, improved control, and integration on a physiological basis may be involved here. Several of these children (whose later IQs were above average) had developed a wide range of coping resources, thus channeling energy into constructive directions. In infancy, lack of skills and of goal-directed and problem-solving capacities prevented this type of effective use of tension. Insofar as the decreased tendency toward loss of coordination had a primarily physiological and neurological basis, this improvement can be credited to the self-correcting aspects of maturation. This may be implied in the normal tendency to outgrow early problems and symptoms, a tendency demonstrated by Macfarlane, Allen, and Honzik (1954).

It is unfortunate that our limited capacity for exploring the inner life of the infants and children did not give direct clues to the outcomes of these changes in vulnerability. Darlene's use of inhibition in being cautious and taking time to size up new situations was balanced by the expressive spontaneity of her triumph when she succeeded in jumping. In such instances, the strategic inhibition contributed to excitement in mastery. When increased stability of motor coordination appeared to be a result of neural maturation and improved physiological integration rather than of the child's own coping efforts, we did not see this conscious triumph at the preschool stage.

We were also curious about possible relations between Heider's global infancy variables and characteristics seen by the group of observers at the preschool stage. Here we are looking for sequelae that may be new outgrowths of early tendencies and not merely continuities.

Boys' behavior in infancy and at the preschool level

Some of the most interesting relationships between Heider's evaluations of the infants and their preschool behavior were found with infancy robustness, functional stability, vocalization, and sensory reactivity.

Robustness of boys in infancy is related to their preschool ability to accept an appropriately dependent relationship with the mother and also to balance dependence and independence. Would you agree that it is probably easy for the mother to accept at different times a robust child's pattern of autonomy and his desire for help because she is less likely to have anxieties about him?

Correlations between infant boys' *functional stability* and preschool behavior are of special interest. There is a positive relation between infancy functional stability and the preschool child's "capacity for independence vis-à-vis the mother," "capacity to express independence toward the father" and clarity of self-concept.

Infancy functional stability and preschool expression of anxiety are negatively related. These all contribute to an image of a secure child who is clear about himself and free to assert himself with his parents. The negative relation between preschool anxiety and infancy functional stability is congruent with the converse: extensive evidence from child psychiatrists and analysts that childhood pathology is often preceded by poor infancy functioning and a predisposition to anxiety (Bender 1953; Greenacre 1952; Pasamanick and Knobloch 1956).

The implications are great: the baby who has enjoyed inner comfort and stability is not so easily buffeted by every shift in the wind; he can better tolerate the normal vicissitudes of his life. Infantile functional stability evidently contributes to sturdy ego development, resistance to anxiety, and less need for dependence on parents. Early functional stability facilitates mastery and the resulting confidence in one's own perceptions and resources, and thus the ability to stand up for oneself, to assert independence. Moreover, a positive relation between infantile functional stability and preschool capacity for sublimation—even though not impressive on this limited sample—suggests that functional stability contributes to the ease with which the stable child can direct his energy into relatively mature interests (in contrast to being driven to direct impulsive and affect-laden expressions). Here we are seeing the evolution of mature capacities from early patterns that can be regarded as prerequisites for—not direct precursors of—sublimation.

The significant positive relationships between frequency of vocalization in infancy and the preschool capacity to project conflict, as well as to grasp mature concepts, suggest that expressive and communicative uses of infancy *vocalization* contribute substantially to clear communication of internal conflicts, as well as growth of the child's concepts about the world.

Sensory reactivity in infant boys is related to both preschool rivalry with peers and supportive relations with peers. We can see that a characteristic such as sensory reactivity may have both positive and negative potentialities for the development of the child. On the one hand, it may contribute to differentiation and clarification of perception of differences, but it may also contribute to difficulties through increased likelihood of overstimulation under pressure.

The relation between sensory reactivity in infancy and maturity of concepts at the preschool stage suggests that the reactive child (among children within normal limits) not only continues to seek or participate in active relationships with peers, but learns from this interaction. An outgrowth of this active participation may well be the maturity of concepts and also the capacity to project conflict. Our correlations between infancy sensory reactivity, early activity level, robust physique, and preschool adequacy of functioning suggest that sensory reactivity in a healthy child is a basic aspect of responsiveness to the environment. However, very extreme sensory reactivity would be expected to involve more difficulty with the environment. A positive correlation between sensory reactivity and conflicts about toilet training implies that toilet-training experiences are felt very differently by children of different degrees of sensory reactivity. The more sensitive child could experience greater stress from toilet-training pressures.

Mother–child relationships in infancy and later

Correlations between "mother–infant viability" (or "fit") and the child's preschool behavior are also significant. Among the boys, a relationship between mother–child viability in infancy and clarity of self-concept at the preschool level reminds us of our study of functional stability; the infant who has experienced a congenial and easy relationship in infancy is freer from primary conflict or confusion regarding himself.

When we review the correlations between boys' infantile vegetative functioning and preschool variables concerned with the mother–child relationship, we find a correlation of .50 between smoothness of infantile vegetative functioning and the child's preschool capacity to accept dependence on the mother (or freedom from excessive rebelliousness). This relationship is consistent with our finding that the robust infant is able to balance dependence and independence at the preschool level.

Infancy coping in the feeding situation and preschool coping

Prevailing evidence about the importance of vegetative functioning led me to explore a group of related behaviors observed most clearly during the baby's feedings. These included capacity to protest, resist or terminate unwanted stimulation (food or prodding); demand level (urgency, insistence, intensity of demand); expressions of gratification in feeding (reflected in pleasure sounds, smiling after feeding, evidences of comfort and satisfaction); and autonomy allowed by the mother (letting the infant determine the pace of feeding, interruptions for rest, timing; respecting likes and dislikes). Here we hardly dared to expect relationships between the first six months of infancy and behavior three and four years later, but we underestimated the importance of these aspects of infant behavior (see Appendix 2).

Behavior referred to as *oral protest, resistance to disliked foods, and the ability to terminate feeding* can be one of the most significant characteristics in infancy. It is correlated with preschool abilities to "control the impact of the environment" (as by fending off adult pressures); stubbornness (maintaining a stand despite the consequences); drive for mastery (struggle capacity, determination); and the ability to restructure the environment, to create new patterns as well as to organize and provide one's own structure. Along with these resources, this active infancy variable is highly correlated with preschool impulse control, ability to forestall danger, knowing when to stop, and also strategic withdrawal—that is, adaptive withdrawal appropriate to the threat or the next step in the strategy (see Appendix 2).

The capacity to terminate and to resist unwanted stimulation in infancy also correlates with both clarity of self-concept and maturity of perception at the preschool level. This suggests that this early tendency toward active interchange with the environment contributes to a clarity about self as well as about the environment.

Similarly, the infant's *demand level* correlates significantly with several preschool items: adequacy of self-concept, maturity of perception, and maturity of concepts. These relationships add further weight to the likelihood that a quality of vigor in the child's inner push to interact with the environment and to obtain gratification from it contributes to the process of developing mature perceptions and concepts. The child with high demand level has strong motivation to understand the environment in order to find gratification, perhaps to make more effort, and thus to learn more through his efforts and through the reality-testing motivated by his high demand level.

We can see these early infancy and preschool ways of functioning as aspects of a psychically active, self-directed way of managing one's situation in the environment. It is not surprising to find similar relationships with preschool perceptual prerequisites for coping activities, such as speed of orientation, grasp of the situation, and reality testing, on the one hand, and preschool IQ, developmental level of speech, and "overall ability," on the other.

The active infant coping items are also related to preschool clarity regarding own identity and narcissistic drive. We find it logical to infer that an infant and preschool child who can deter unwanted stimulation and shape his interactions with the environment to his own needs would feel good about himself and, through his successful autonomy, be increasingly clear about himself. Finally, and very important indeed, this child is less likely to lose perceptual clarity under stress. *Evidently success in infant coping reinforces his perceptual clarity as well as the determination that contributed to his success.* These relationships imply, for boys at least, considerable continuity of active mental and motor coping from the first six months of infancy to the preschool level, which in turn may contribute to clarity about self at this stage of development.

Autonomy allowed in the feeding situation by the mothers of infant boys was related to preschool oral gratification independently rated by Moriarty on the preschool CAT. Both the capacity to be appropriately dependent when needing care and help and to be appropriately independent when the situation is within the child's capacity to manage it are healthy aspects of development. It is not surprising, then, that for the boys the correlation between autonomy allowed in infancy and the dependence–independence balance at the preschool stage would also be positive. It is of interest that autonomy allowed by the infant boys' mothers is correlated with clear and adequate self-concept at the preschool level.

The significant negative correlation between respect for the boy infant's autonomy needs in the feeding situation and conflicts about toilet training as judged by the preschool CAT ($-.63$) emphasizes the importance of freedom from preexisting conflict about coercion or pressure. This relationship also implies that a mother who allows the baby autonomy in early feeding experiences is apt to continue respecting his autonomy at the toilet-training stage. This is consistent with Brody's

(1956) conclusion that the mother's behavior while feeding the baby is a good indicator of her ways of handling him in general.

Infancy oral gratification and preschool variables

We can now reflect upon some of the relationships between oral gratification in infancy and behavior rated during the preschool observations (see Appendix 2). A positive correlation between oral gratification and later security confirms our initial expectations. We also found positive correlations with later sense of self-worth and a comfortable relation to the child's ego ideal, along with "adequacy of the child's self-image in the child's social milieu," clarity in sex role, assertiveness and forthrightness, differentiation of self from others, and "positive self-feeling level, it feels good to be." Looking at these positive relationships alongside the negative correlation between infantile oral gratification and tension as rated at the preschool level, we can infer that oral gratification in the first six months tends to leave the baby with a good feeling about itself or with freedom from the tensions that both make it dependent upon constant stimulus feeding from the environment, and also blur its perception of the environment. Such a baby is freer to develop clear awareness of self vis-à-vis others, and to maintain stable positive feelings about self.

More or less consistent with these relationships are the negative relationships between infantile oral gratification and such preschool items as a feeling of being rejected, tendency to be demanding in relation to others, being critical of people, and depreciating others. We can understand these relationships if we assume that oral gratification of the infant makes a basic contribution to general good self-feeling, and that these contribute to clear differentiation between self and the external world, especially other people. Under these conditions the infant does not confuse himself with others and has no tendency to project bad feelings, to blame or criticize others.

This assumption is supported by the finding that infancy oral gratification is significantly related to preschool *clarity of perception* and negatively related to loss of perceptual clarity under stress as rated by Povl Toussieng. This seems to imply that oral gratification in early infancy contributes to physiological integration, which in turn supports optimal early perceptual development. We are familiar with disturbed children whose perceptions are easily distorted under stress; in these children we often find histories of extreme gastrointestinal discomfort and disturbance in oral functioning in early infancy, and in the most disturbed children the bad start is often most extreme (Bender 1953).

One of the strongest positive relations between infancy gratification and other items is with *strength of interests*; this suggests that oral gratification in the first half year reinforces the infant's capacity to respond to the external world in a strong and satisfying way.

A more surprising relationship is that between oral gratification in infancy and the ability to limit or fend off excessive stimulation. This in turn suggests that an orally satisfied baby is relatively free from insatiable stimulus-hunger that would make it hard for him to be selective or active in limiting stimulation. An unsatisfied baby might tend to reach out for stimuli even beyond his own tolerance level. The significant correlation with ability to mobilize energy to meet challenge or stress may not be quite so obvious unless we reflect that the orally gratified baby may be freer from tense defensive structures that could interfere with flexibility and mobilization of energy.

In other words, when our infancy observations dealing solely with children in the early months of life are compared with ratings of the children at the preschool level based on observations by several different people, our evidence tends to confirm the hypotheses of those analysts who assert that profound patterning of the ego is laid in oral experience of the infant in the first six months of life. We have evidence that this influences the foundations for integration, for clarity of perception, and in addition the foundations of later self-image.

Oral gratification in the early months is also positively related to the preschool child's *ability to use strategic withdrawal*. Our tendency to regard withdrawal as a poor way of coping often blinds us to the fact that in early childhood when the scope of free movement and choice is often severely limited by the adults' domination of the environment, strategic withdrawal is a good strategy for the child in certain situations. We could regard this as another evidence of the freedom of the orally gratified child to do what feels best for him in a threatening situation; he is not driven to stay in the midst of things when a situation is overstimulating.

Oral gratification appeared to contribute more to internal integration than to active coping efforts and problem-solving. This is understandable in terms of the integrative contribution of serenity and comfort that accompanies infantile (and later) oral gratification.

Infancy behavior related to preschool courage

Relationships quite different from the group associated with oral gratification are those associated with courage as rated at the preschool level. Here we find significant positive relationships with Heider's measures of motility: motor coordination, smoothness in movements, purposefulness of movements. These do not follow exactly the same patterns for boys and girls.

We saw earlier that several aspects of *motor* behavior are among those best predicted from infancy to the preschool level. We assume that continuity in activity level implies satisfaction en route, and support for motivation for further activity. A high degree of motor activity may also contribute to learning via exploration, experimentation, and mastery, as Escalona (1968) has shown and—looking at other items in this large cluster—it may lead to "knowing the score," ability to mobilize energy to meet challenge or stress, being stimulated to greater effort by failures, and positive self-appraisal. Thus, courage appears to be related to and perhaps involved in two-way influences with competence and confidence. The "experienced child" can afford to be courageous.

Early behavior in relation to prepuberty behavior[5]

The beginning aim of the coping project was to scrutinize and understand children's ways of coping with everyday opportunities, challenges, and frustrations. As we have seen, it provided material for the prediction and outcome study, and studies of continuity and change from infancy to the preschool stage. We had not set out to do a longitudinal study in the traditional sense, but when Riley Gardner and Alice Moriarty carried out the study of personality structure at preadolescence with the coping study sample and additional children, we again found that we had material for comparing early and later behavior. Moriarty's ratings of seventy-five "coping items" at the prepuberty stage were available for comparison with a number of aspects of infancy and preschool behavior.

Infancy developmental pace

Certain infancy information not ascertainable in the early infancy examinations had been added in the pediatrician's preschool interview with the mother, such as when the child started sitting and walking. Let us consider these first.

Within this normal group, correlations between reported infancy *age of walking* show few relationships to later coping resources; however, there is a modest correlation of .44 (.05) with the prepuberty variable *level of activity*. This is reasonable since babies with high activity level could be expected both to be motivated toward locomotion and to develop pre-walking skills and strengths. Similar modest relations to *spatial orientation* and *tendency to take cues* (which may develop out of increased exposure to the environment) represent all that we found.

Very surprisingly, age at sitting[6] is related to more aspects of functioning at prepuberty than is age at walking. We find significant correlations with: *clarity regarding own identity* at prepuberty, *social insight, preference for slightly (or loosely) structured situations,* clarity of *distinction between fantasy and reality,* and *intuitiveness.*

This group of relationships leads us to reflect upon the differences in interaction with the environment that could have been stimulated by sitting up early as compared with walking early. The infant who can sit up but not walk—or the infant who insists on sitting up at an early age—is thereby in a position to observe a much wider span of the environment than the supine or prone baby. Instead of looking at a relatively unpatterned ceiling, he is exposed to a wide range of visual patterns in the environment. He can "see everything," moving and static, not just his mother as she comes to his crib. This variety, we assume, stimulates perceptual interest and cognitive activity.

If a baby is able to sit up early, but walks late, he is dependent on the response of others to bring what he needs. Not only the increased opportunity for observation, but the existence of distances between himself and others, distances that he cannot traverse and thus diminish, could contribute to the differentiation of self from others. His prolonged opportunity for *observation without action* may contribute to the cognitive integrative processes underlying "insight," good spatial orientation, intuitiveness, and clarity or distinction between reality and fantasy.

Infancy reactivity to sensory stimulation and prepuberty behavior[7]

We were surprised to find that infancy *reactivity to stimulation* emerges conspicuously in relationships between infancy and prepuberty functioning. One might have thought that after a dozen years the compensations or defenses and other adaptations would mask the early relationships. But prepuberty ratings of Coping I and also Coping II are highly related to this basic aspect of infant functioning. Prepuberty openness to new experience, pleasure in tactile experience, and a range of areas of enjoyment are parallel and highly related to sensory responsiveness in infancy; their recurrence implies that sensory experience tends to maintain a stable level of importance through the childhood years. A number of cognitive functions are equally related to reactivity to sensory stimulation: curiosity, active orientation, clarity of perception, and attention to fine details. "Knowing the score" and grasping sequences or relationships are also strong and evidently evolve from perceptiveness and sensory responsiveness. When we also find autonomy, the ability to translate ideas into action, determination and mastery drive, and confidence in ability to handle situations, we must reflect on a possible central role of the mastery evolving from sensory reactivity.

Even higher correlations included positive self-appraisal and creativeness; the children who observe alertly develop their own reservoirs of data for their confident conclusions, and at the same time, reservoirs of images for creativity.

These aspects of coping may be considered contributions of perceptual–affective–motor *responsiveness* and ability to handle one's relation with the environment, with resulting positive self-feelings. Or perhaps it would be safer to say that there is probably an interaction between effective capacities for adaptation utilizing resources in all zones and positive self-feeling. We mentioned above that Dr. Riley Gardner's factor analysis of the prepuberty coping items produced, for Factor I, a broad variable described as *"openness to the environment."* This openness, we may infer, may be best reflected in the early months by the infant's reactivity to sensory stimulation. However, since Factor I included a large majority of the coping items, active as well as receptive, "responsiveness to the environment" would probably be a more adequate term.

In contrast to these impressive relationships between reactivity to stimulation in infancy and coping capacities at the prepuberty level, we find no highly significant relationships in the case of infant *physique:* "robust to fragile." We saw that some fragile infants became healthier and stronger, while some robust infants became less so as a consequence of illnesses.

There is only a modest correlation between infancy robustness and prepuberty *"activity level (overall)."* This might be expected from the shifts just mentioned. Moreover, infant *activity level* in turn shows only one significant linear correlation with prepuberty coping, and this is a negative correlation with fearfulness—reasonable enough in terms of the likelihood that a fearful infant or child would be more likely to inhibit spontaneous activity.

Nonvocal oral activity in infancy is not directly related to prepuberty behavior but impressive *curvilinear* correlations were found with many prepuberty items: Coping I, range of areas of enjoyment; clarity of distinction between fantasy and reality, length of attention span, capacity to use delay for appraisal; capacity to sustain effort, determination, capacity to mobilize resources under stress, creativeness, and originality. Nonvocal oral activity includes thumb-sucking, of course, but also bubbling with lips and other mouth play. The fact that we find extremes of this activity may be unfavorable for coping implies that a moderate amount of infancy mouth play and gratification is part of a normal coping foundation. Implied here is the presence of *a strong positive drive broader than orality* but expressed in the zone of the mouth during infancy.

By contrast, the infancy *autonomic reactivity*[8] is related to prepuberty ego restriction, overcontrol, and rigidity of expressive patterns. It is not surprising then to find a negative correlation with such items as freedom from disintegration under stress, realistic evaluation of people, ability to accept warmth, intuitiveness, feeling one's way, adequacy of expression of feeling, and receptivity to emotional impressions from the environment. The rigidity of response, developed as a defense to cope with the disintegrative threat from autonomic reactivity, evidently interfered with warm responses to people and the interactions needed for realistic evaluation of people. Too great autonomic reactivity also interferes with internal integration.

But again we find some curvilinear relationships, as would be expected: infancy *autonomic reactivity* shows significant curvilinear relationships with prepuberty Coping II, *flexibility in adapting means to ends*, and much the same group of functions we discussed under sensory reactivity (pp. 81–82). Here we can infer that a *moderate* degree of autonomic reactivity, like sensory reactivity, contributes to coping.

Vegetative functioning in the infant[9]

In evaluating the baby's vegetative functioning, Heider also considered the adequacy of digestion, elimination, sleep, and general fatigability (p. 130). These aspects of the infant's experiences are moderately related to a few prepuberty functions. Surprisingly these are chiefly cognitive: cognitive coping capacity, speed of orientation, spatial orientation, clarity of perception. In other words, babies who are free of gastrointestinal miseries during the early period when cognitive functions are developing and perceptual patterns are being structured are relatively more free of perceptual distortions later. Why? A baby in distress is sending biochemical products of stress reaction into the bloodstream and thus to his brain, which does not have the optimum conditions for good functioning, as we discussed earlier (p. 138). Along with this, pain is distracting to cognitive activity.

The capacity to delay

This implies a capacity for control of impulse. Among infants and young as well as older children it provides an opportunity to appraise a situation. As expected, there is also a significant correlation between this capacity to delay in infancy and prepuberty "use of delay for appraisal" as well as "cooperation with authority demands." Negative relations between infancy capacity for delay and prepuberty use of denial (.01 level) and tendency to use rationalization (.05 level) imply greater objectivity and realism at the prepuberty level in the child who showed a capacity for delay in infancy! The negative relation between infancy capacity to delay and prepuberty tactile pleasure suggests that tactile pleasure might be related to impulsiveness, hence inversely related to the control implied in the capacity to delay.

Level of vulnerability at the infancy level as Heider judged this (p. 130) correlates *negatively* with many prepuberty characteristics assessed by Moriarty. These included Coping I and II; cognitive functions such as speed of orientation, capacity for freewheeling attention, knowing the score, ability to synthesize thought and feeling and action; flexible action capacities including freedom to translate ideas into action, ability to accept substitutes, ability to organize and provide own structure, capacity to mobilize resources under stress and independence; affective coping; and range of areas of enjoyment. A group of attributes related to the experience of the self included clarity regarding own identity, separation of self and others, positive self-appraisal, level of self-feeling, and pleasure in own body. Freedom from inhibitions, freedom from doubt and ambivalence, confidence, trust, and spontaneity were probably important in the availability of energy.

The still greater relation of *preschool vulnerability* with prepuberty traits (likewise rated by Heider years before the prepuberty items were rated by Moriarty) calls for discussion. The number of relationships suggests that while certain basic trends or elements of a pattern are directly laid down in infancy, the infantile vulnerability pattern presents a challenge that may be met in different ways, with different consequences for the subsequent functions of the child at the preschool stage and later on. Thus the outcome of efforts to cope with preschool-level vulnerability shows more relationships to the prepuberty patterns than the infancy vulnerability pattern shows. This implies also that traumata after the first six months will contribute patterning that greatly influences the later *capacity to deal with stress*, whereas the earliest patterning is basic to the level of perceptual clarity and adequacy of the primary ego functions, including cognitive organization.

Mother–infant interaction and coping at puberty[10]

Amount of attention given to the young infant by the mother (rated by Heider) has a curvilinear relation with certain functions at the prepuberty phase. Here we see that a balanced amount of attention—not too little, not too much—is related to the prepuberty child's orientation, perceptual clarity, internalization of standards, trust, and internal integration. This implies that the baby needs not only attention (with the interaction it involves) but sufficient time to himself for his own cognitive processes to work at organizing his perceptions and internalizing the culture. Too much attention may be a negative factor as well as too little. This is recognized in the opposing concepts of "neglect" and "spoiling," wherein excessive intrusive activity—holding, talking to, giving toys, and so on—deprives the baby of the freedom, and continuity of processing time, needed for optimal coping, and insufficient attention fails to provide adequate stimulus content needed by the child in his own perceptual and motor use of the environment.

Encouragement and support by these mothers includes support of the baby's activity, initiative, and interests. Evidently this kind of support does not constitute an indulgence that would lead to overdependence by the baby and failure to develop coping resources.

It is interesting to find a relative lack of affective and expressive items in the comparisons with amount of attention given in infancy. However, a number of affective and expressive characteristics emerge in the curvilinear relationships between the mother's acceptance of the infant's own developmental pace and the child's behavior rated at prepuberty, although there are no significant Pearson (linear) correlations.

	Eta	*p*
Affective coping capacity	.53	.025
Spontaneity (vs. rigidity of expression)	.61	.005
Warmth, love	.61	.005
Ability to accept warmth	.65	.005
Social insight	.53	.025
Spontaneity (vs. inhibition)	.61	.005
Openness	.55	.025

Here again, too much and too little can interfere with the baby's development. Too little acceptance of his developmental pace may be expressed either by pushing him to achieve or by communicating negative, anxious feelings that inhibit warmth. Too much acceptance may be expressed in a lack of stimulation, a casual laissez-faire attitude.

Moderate acceptance of the baby's developmental pace is also related to the following aspects of infant behavior (in a curvilinear relationship).

	Eta	p
Expressiveness vs. rigidity	.61	.005
Ability to ask for help	.62	.005
Ability to assert own needs	.61	.005
Freedom to translate ideas into action	.54	.025
Ability to organize and provide own structure	.51	.025

Here we see a balance of *expecting help when needed* and *initiative*, along with the freedom to be expressive.

Degree of the mother's "acceptance of the infant" also has significant curvilinear correlations with prepuberty ability to provide own structure; to organize; range of areas of enjoyment; confidence in handling demands of adults; ability to mobilize resources; and cognitive coping capacity. The curvilinear relationships here underscore further the enormous importance of allowing the child an opportunity to struggle for himself, to have problems that need to be solved, and to make the effort to solve them. A moderate amount of acceptance of the infant allows leeway for the development of these various ego capacities. Both inadequate acceptance of the infant and total acceptance may leave him without challenge, without any necessity for making an effort, without, in short, the stimulus for autonomy.

Similarly, degree of respect for the infant's autonomy needs shows highly significant curvilinear correlations with prepuberty trust and ability to accept substitutes. We have suggested earlier that optimal respect for the infant's autonomy evidently gives him a basis for expecting comfortable interactions with the environment, and therefore trust. This in turn can contribute to a favorable attitude toward alternative gratifications or substitutes.

With baby's utilization of support from the mother we again find an interesting group of curvilinear correlations including prepuberty coping with the environment; cognitive coping; ability to synthesize thinking, affect, and action; speed of orientation (grasp of situation or task); knowing the score; grasping sequences and implications; clarity regarding own identity; pleasure in own body (healthy narcissism); identification with own sex; freedom from doubt and ambivalence; available neutral energy; and confidence (ability to handle the demands of a situation).

Why do we find so many cognitive items here? René Spitz's discussion of "fundamental education" (1972) is relevant here: the processes involved in responsive interplay with the mother (and we can add especially those that provide support for the baby's efforts), involve complex learning and the integrations implicit in synthesis of perception, feeling, and action. These provide foundations for further learning, and satisfying results motivate further orienting and mastery efforts. These, in turn, lead to confidence. But too much reliance on mother's support could lead to dependence and failure to learn, just as does too little response.

Mother's enjoyment of the infant is outstandingly important: it correlates with so many prepuberty characteristics that I will list here only those correlations at the highest (.001) level of significance:

Affective coping	.71
Trust	.70
Available neutral energy	.67
Self-feeling level: it feels good to be me	.64
Coping II	.64
Capacity for freewheeling attention	.63
Spontaneity (vs. inhibition)	.62
Freedom from inhibitions or rigidity in thinking	.61
Ability to accept substitutes	.60
Active orientation, "doing to"	.60

We are reminded here of Escalona's emphasis on the importance of the "animating" effect of the mother–child relationship. We see here that mother's enjoyment of the infant contributes to well-being and good functioning even into puberty; trust, internal integration and related free energy, and also spontaneity, freedom, and good feeling about the self. The next group of prepuberty functions related to mother's enjoyment of the infant includes active cognitive and motor coping with the environment; these correlations are significant but not as high as those in the first group.[11]

Our findings as a whole imply that when the baby is enjoyed by his mother (and this probably involves mutual loving and play), the gamut of cognitive and motor resources as well as affective responsiveness are released or mobilized for flexible, spontaneous interaction with the environment. If we watch a mother enjoying her baby, we typically see a playful interaction in which whole-bodied and you might say whole-souled responsiveness of mother and baby evokes a wide range of ego capacities and drive.

I am reminded of a Soviet poster in the Children's Park in Tashkent (seen on a visit in 1960). It shows a young and sturdy mother looking up at the baby she is holding high above her head; each is beaming at the other in an open wide smile. With all the cautions stated in the preceding discussion, it seems reasonable to emphasize the special importance of the vitalizing contribution of the mother's sheer enjoyment of her baby—and in turn of the baby's contribution to the mother. A responsive baby can "send" a responsive mother—or perhaps one could say, in the jargon of the day, they take each other on a wonderful "trip."

"Family unity" [12] as rated by Heider on the infancy records correlates more highly with prepuberty coping than most of the patterns involved in "constitution" or equipment at the infancy level. Significant relationships appear with Coping I and II, cognitive coping, affective coping capacity, and also many others including degree of differentiation of affect, trust, freedom from ego restriction, freedom to translate ideas into action, ability to accept substitutes. Similarly, temperamental compatibility of parents during the infancy of the child correlates significantly with many of the same prepuberty variables we have just reviewed.

These relationships are important to keep in mind since they imply that a harmonious atmosphere in the home may be related to more aspects of the child's functioning than anything else. We have to assume that in normal families such as those in our research sample, this harmony releases or supports many kinds of interaction that can support both cognitive and affective aspects of ego development and related coping resources.

Summary

In this chapter we have seen evidences of several kinds of relationship between early and later functioning:

a) Considerable *continuity* in certain functions from infancy to the preschool stage (Escalona and Heider 1959; Escalona and Moriarty 1961).

b) *Congruent expressions* of general tendencies in infancy and in preschool behavior: energy level (Heider, Escalona); active coping in the infant feeding situation as by demand, protest, termination; preschool active coping and clarity of own identity and of orientation; reality testing and IQ (Murphy); infant robustness and preschool balance of dependence and independence; infant functional stability and preschool clarity of self-concept; smoothness of infant vegetative functioning and freedom from rebelliousness toward mother; frequency of infant vocalization and preschool maturity of concepts, capacity to project conflict; sensory reactivity and preschool interactions with peers. Similarly or conversely we found negative relationships between infant oral gratification and preschool feeling of being rejected, and tendency to be critical of others.

Infant oral gratification was related to preschool strength of interests and clarity of perception; it was negatively related to loss of perceptual clarity under stress; and it was related to preschool ability to limit or fend off excessive stimulation, to use strategic withdrawal and to mobilize energy to meet challenge or stress, and to maintain internal integration.

c) *Sequelae of infant–mother relationships:* autonomy allowed by the mother in the infant feeding situation was related to preschool oral gratification and freedom from toilet-training conflicts as rated by Moriarty on the CAT.

Preschool courage was related to infant motor smoothness and skills, doubtless as a result of successful motor experiences; other sequelae of good infant motor functioning are "knowing the score," being stimulated to greater effort by failure, and positive self-appraisal.

Infancy to prepuberty behavior: these comparisons turned up surprising relationships between age of sitting and prepuberty cognitive functions—doubtless supported by the sitting baby's opportunity for wider observation. This ability to observe but not to reach because of the distances he could not traverse between himself and the environment probably also contributed to his greater differentiation of self from others.

As with preschool behavior, a variety of prepuberty cognitive functions are related to infancy sensory reactivity, including creativity as well as curiosity and clarity of perception. But infancy robustness was not highly related to prepuberty variables, probably because of the many variations in illness that intervened over the years. By contrast, infant autonomic reactivity is related to prepuberty rigidity, ego restriction, tendency toward disintegrative reactions to stress, lack of realistic evaluation of people, and lack of receptivity to emotional impressions from the environment. Still, infancy autonomic reactivity has a curvilinear relation with ability to maintain internal integration.

Similarly, infancy vulnerability is negatively related to a wide range of coping patterns at prepuberty, and preschool vulnerability is negatively related to still more prepuberty items; evidently, sequelae of traumata of the first six years greatly influence the later capacity to deal with stress, while the earliest patterning foreshadows the level of perceptual clarity and cognitive functions.

By prepuberty, we find many curvilinear relationships between the infant–mother relationship—extremes of attention, acceptance, and respect for the infant's autonomy interfere with optimal development. However, mother's enjoyment of the infant, and family unity, are significantly related to a host of later coping assets.

The relation between earlier and later forms of experience and behavior are too complex to warrant our thinking of simple causal relations between what came first and what came later; our concern is with observable relations, not with ultimate interpretation.

Our conclusion is that development is not merely due to the effect of either simple hereditary or environmental forces; at any time the child's response to and ways of coping with these and their complex interactions involves unpredictable emergents.

6

Stability and Plasticity of
Early Coping Style

I'm not the baby no more . . . I can sing—everybody can sing, except babies.

Donald, age six

I'm not little enough to be one of those cute little kids that go around saying cute little stuff.

Diane, age eleven

As we explored relationships between infant and later behavior in the last chapter we found certain tendencies toward direct continuity of traits assumed to be "constitutional," and congruent behaviors at later stages evolved from some of the early tendencies. We also found evidences of outcomes at later stages of early interactions or interplay between the infant and mother. But the correlations, often high and very significant, were never perfect. Even correlations of .60 to .70 can result from tendencies seen in many children but not all. So we have to wean ourselves from a preoccupation with continuity or stability alone and pay attention as well to evidence for plasticity that allows for change. Or rather, we need to look at both stability and plasticity or continuity and change.

Our thinking about the continuity of the adaptational style of the infant has drawn upon several lines of evidence from our own studies and upon some additional data from other research. From the Topeka studies we have already discussed our own analysis of Escalona's predictions of preschool behavior on the basis of the infancy data (p. 128), further study of Heider's evaluation of vulnerability in infants and young children, and correlations between infancy and preschool behavior and between infancy and prepuberty behavior, including correlations between Murphy's infant feeding ratings and later behavior ratings. Case studies used in Moriarty's analysis of continuity and changes in cognitive functioning will add further understanding in this chapter, as will a special profile analysis of the group. But first let us discuss what we mean by adaptational style.

Adaptational style in the Topeka infants

Within the limits determined by a realistic recognition of what can be done with different sorts of evidence, then, we will first consider the "basic adaptational style of infancy" that seems to us to be implied by our studies. To illustrate different adaptational styles of infants let us first scrutinize the behavior at the four-week level in JoAnne and Vivian as they were described by Heider.

At the age of four weeks, Vivian was observed to be a healthy, rather low drive baby of average sensitivity, easy functioning, with balanced developmental pattern, quick responsiveness and moderate autonomic reactivity. Her behavior, which was clear-cut, showed a definite beginning and end. In addition to her relaxed, somewhat delicate manner of functioning, the baby showed an unusually wide and flexible range of adaptive behavior for a month-old infant. On the one hand, she went along with imposed pressures: it was hard to get leg resistance during ratings because her legs followed the direction suggested by the examiner. At the same time, she was already autonomous enough to root around to make a comfortable place for herself in her bed. Moreover, she could reject what she did not want; she refused to suck, or stuck out her tongue when unwanted food was offered. She closed her eyes to avoid light. She was also easily comforted by outside contact with mother or other adults.

Environmental factors were somewhat less favorable; the troubled mother hoped somewhat anxiously that she would succeed in handling this baby better than her first, too fussed-over child. She did not seek close contact with the baby and made little effort to communicate with her, apparently treating her somewhat as an extension of herself to be adorned as a beautiful object and enjoyed with a certain degree of distance. Breast feeding, though somewhat halfhearted, was carried out "because it was easier." A bottle was given before the breast feeding because the milk supply was thought to be decreasing. In summary, Vivian had an unusually favorable equipment balance, a less favorable environmental situation, but unusually useful adaptive techniques—and, incidentally, techniques that did not contribute to conflict with the mother.

JoAnne, at the age of four weeks, was a robust, and in contrast to Vivian, a rather high drive baby who was also an "easy baby" in most ways, though not "easygoing." Like Vivian, her vegetative functioning and developmental balance were good, and her sensitivity or reactivity to sensory stimulation was moderate. She was relatively relaxed, with her hands comfortably fisted while she was in action or feeding. In what may be thought of as the precursors of voluntary activity, coordination was described as smooth.

But, unlike Vivian, she also showed some distinct idiosyncrasies: when she was inactive her limbs were often stiffly extended and there was a marked tendency to nervous reactions of a startle-like type that increased during sleep. (In view of a later tendency to panic, this might be seen as early evidence of a tendency toward loss of integration in the face of overstimulation.)

She was more responsive to social than to nonsocial aspects of the situation. She showed special pleasure in most tactile experience, but occasional discomfort, as with wet diapers. One observer thought that she also showed pleasure in sounds.

Under stress autonomic reactivity increased, but this subsided quickly; evidences of tension were more marked and lasted longer in the motor system, as implied above.

Again, in contrast to Vivian, this baby used fewer adaptive techniques than some. While she rejected unwanted stimuli, food, for example, she simply cried at unwelcome postural changes. She did show marked responsiveness to external support, quieting when picked up, or when movement was induced. Her mother, being young and inexperienced, tended to "show off" the baby at the cost of probable overstimulation. She also stimulated the baby more than usual as she handled her.

In summary, JoAnne was a healthy infant with high drive but with a certain lack of autonomy in managing herself, with a greater than average dependence on external support, and evidence of heightened tension when she was on her own. This baby lived in a situation of some external stress from inconsistency and overstimulation which could have contributed to her marked autonomic reactivity and tendency to loss of motor integration as well as to her tenseness.

Thus two infants of the same age may have many similar traits, yet differ decisively because of variations in a few traits that independently, or in interaction with each other and with the environment, contribute to the development of markedly different adaptational styles.

How stable is the early adaptational style?

In our discussion of relationships between infant behavior and later development we dealt with individual tendencies or traits that showed continuity or that were related to traits emerging later. In view of the thousands of repetitive experiences of even young babies we infer that such tendencies must be programmed within the early months. Burton

White, Ainsworth, J. McV. Hunt, and others (see Stone, Smith, and Murphy 1973) have documented the plasticity and response to stimulation of very young infants; their work has dealt with very specific reactions such as visual focusing, the blink response, the smile, and visual–motor coordination. We are concerned now with the patterning of a group of responses that together constitute the infant's style. We do not assume that in relation to any one of these it is possible to speak of "pure genetic factors," since by now there is evidence for both classical conditioning, operant conditioning, and other forms of learning and change even in the very early weeks. This pattern may be shaped by the earliest interactions of an infant having a given range of potentialities with the quantity and quality of stimulation to which it is characteristically exposed. The threshold for and zones of response resulting from the level and the persistence of both environmental and internal stimulation (people and objects around him) are involved here. This programming utilizes the infant's capacities for assimilation and accommodation discussed by Piaget.

We suspected that the child's subsequent experience is shaped in part by the consequences of use of a function by an infant. Thus we are interested here not only in the amount of activity and its tempo, scope, and smoothness, but in *its use and modification in coping with the environment, and its integrity or cohesion under stress.* If we refer back to the infants summarized above, JoAnne was more active but less resourceful than Vivian in coping with discomfort, and her motor coordination was subject to deterioration under stress; Vivian was less active than JoAnne but more flexible and resourceful in coping with discomfort, and she maintained a smooth level of motor functioning. Would not this pattern tend to continue itself? Would not JoAnne's pattern lead to difficulties? We saw that her mother was more stimulating and less aware of the problem of overstimulation, while Vivian's mother tended to leave the baby alone more of the time. Thus it appears that at four weeks JoAnne's pattern was probably already influenced by overstimulation in the sense that increased autonomic reactivity and loss of motor integration were being experienced too frequently for optimally integrated functioning; she was tense and "nervous" at times, especially when on her own, although she enjoyed much of her experience.

By contrast, Vivian was more relaxed and integrated, and this pattern was on the whole supported by her mother's moderate stimulation and tendency to allow autonomy; her equilibrium was maintained at a milder level of response to the environment, which was also less directly stimulating.

At the preschool stage the contrast was greater. Under threat of stress, JoAnne developed forceful devices to fend off the environment, while Vivian softly evoked help. JoAnne panicked at times. While both were competent, normally developing preschool girls, pretty and feminine, JoAnne's protests were vigorous whereas Vivian gently fitted into situations. When anxious, Vivian's tears leaked out whereas JoAnne cried, sobbing and rushing to her mother, clasping her tensely. Vivian's motor behavior continued to be smooth and graceful. JoAnne became highly active and seemed to need energetic motor discharge of tension in keeping with the high drive, reactivity, and persistence of the motor responses to stress seen in infancy. And so Vivian's coping techniques served to maintain her gentle pattern while JoAnne's motor reactions exposed her to greater stimulation and tension in the very act of discharging tension.

The idiosyncratic patterning of differences can be ascertained only by careful scrutiny of all aspects of the functioning of each child as these interact with one another and with the environment.

We see then that the adaptational style of the child is shaped by four groups of factors: (1) the equipment and functioning of the organism (including strengths and vulnerabilities); (2) the psychological climate, demands, stimulation stress, and growth-supporting factors in the environment and the ways in which these are experienced; (3) the way the child uses his resources in dealing with the environment and his needs; and (4) the effects of these coping efforts. The primary adaptational style is thus an outcome of the interaction (the reactions and counterreactions) of all the various specific factors involved in these groups of forces. Of course this summary oversimplifies while it condenses—the detailed account of each child's development is a unique, many-colored, rich, and subtle pattern of interwoven sensitivities, drives, skills, coping, and defense responses to opportunities, frustrations, pressures, along with needs and understandings that change as maturation brings both internal and external changes. Normal children face many of the threats and conflicts we observe in disturbed children; but the balance of stress and support is different. Normal children develop defense mechanisms as well as active coping strategies.[1] To oversimplify even more, normal children continue to be normal insofar as their coping patterns, including defense mechanisms, "work" in their social setting (Murphy 1970).

Relevant environmental factors

Remember that in our "normal" sample no infant was so neglected or deprived as to fail to develop more or less adequately, and all the children were of normal intelligence as measured by standard tests. But there were wide differences in experience from somewhat excessive or relatively inappropriate stimulation to that which was selectively adapted to the infant's rhythms, demands, tolerance. Inappropriate or unwelcome stimulation included teasing, rigid timing of care, vigorous handling of the baby. We saw that conspicuous favorable factors in the environment of our sample were the psychological climate (unity and compatibility of mother and father, health and adjustment of the mother), the mother's enjoyment of the baby, sufficient (not too little or too much) attention, physical contact, talking, and other stimulation from the mother. As we saw earlier these factors correlated significantly with the child's coping capacities and other strengths, and to a considerable extent with continuity of coping capacity.

Crucial resources of the child: "available energy"

In their study of Escalona's predictions of preschool behavior, Escalona and Heider emphasized the importance of "available energy." When this global variable was correctly foreseen, a number of specific traits were correctly predicted. This variable had been formulated on the basis of Heider's comparisons of personality sketches with the predictions and was then checked by Escalona's separate study of itemized ratings. "Available energy" as conceived in Escalona's analysis (Escalona and Heider 1959, p. 142) was rated on the basis of "energy level," activity level, capacity to mobilize resources under stress, freedom from loss of perceptual clarity under stress and from a tendency to become fatigued. Thus it referred to energy available both for active coping with the environment and also for maintenance of internal integration. When this group of tendencies remained constant the child's development was well predicted. Along with unknown genetic and nutritional factors, available energy must be related to the freedom from excessively constricting defense patterns that even a baby may develop. Changes in available energy were related to marked variations in health and stress in certain children.

It is important to note here a factor analysis of Moriarty's ratings of seventy-five variables related to ego functioning and coping at the puberty stage. Factor I, which accounted for 75 percent of the variance, was described as "openness to stimulation." An important question then is this: Is the extent to which a child can afford to be "open" related to the energy available for coping with widely varied demands, pressures, threats, or challenges? It makes sense to suggest that it is, and that when psychological environments are comparable, less "open" children need to protect themselves from exposure to more stimulation than they can handle (because, in part, of marked reactivity to stimulation and the marked autonomic variability that contributes to disintegrative reactions and difficulty in coping). They may do this by direct devices such as strategic withdrawal or successful protest, or by the development of unconscious defense mechanisms; often the child uses a combination of these. Early patterns of resources and limitations thus contribute both to active coping efforts and to defense mechanisms evolving from internalization of early patterns of coping with vulnerabilities, or with environmental pressures.

Sources of continuity of adaptational style

Given the initial patterning of adaptional style during infancy, the question arises: through subsequent development what is most likely to remain fixed, what is reversible, what is open to other sorts of modification? What processes are involved in change? One of the findings from the Escalona–Heider prediction study suggests part of the answer: not only are some traits or tendencies more predictable than others, but some children are more predictable than others. Assuming that predictability implies either consistency of traits or consistency of growth patterns expected at successive stages for different kinds of children, we can look for characteristics supporting such consistency. These were seen in Moriarty's (1966) studies of continuity and change in cognitive functioning, and in Heider's study of vulnerability (1966).

If we look now at the eleven (out of thirty-one) children who were judged to be in the top half of prediction success both by Heider's method of assessment and by Escalona's methods (1959, p. 113) we find in addition to factors of "available energy" (indicated, for instance, by activity level), unusual balance[2]—that is, freedom from variation in developmental level in different zones. Either because of the intrinsic equilibrium supported by well-balanced equipment, or because of a stable hierarchical organization of traits under the dominance of a strong tendency in one zone,[3] or because of the wide margin of adaptability, some of these children tended to maintain the infantile adaptational style. This group of successfully predicted children also included certain infants who were at extremes of energy and activity level (Terry, Brennie) and who maintained these patterns.

By contrast, children who showed neither stable good balance nor persisting extremes of activity level and energy, were more likely to change unpredictably and to be more variable. One of the clearest pictures of stability versus variability is seen in Moriarty's study of cognitive functioning as evaluated by standard tests (see Appendix 5).[4]

The twelve children who were found in the bottom half of the predictive success by both evaluations were those whose energy level apparently changed from infancy to the preschool stage, whose developmental pattern was more variable, and some whose loss of integration under stress was greater. The latter children suffered more from the cumulative stress due to changing relationships with the family, illness, disasters, and the like during this stage. But certain children changed with improved health and the development of greater autonomy despite marked stress, or following effective coping with stress.

Role of balance in continuity

We have seen that the primary adaptational style of different infants varies in degree of balance, consistency or variabililty (and thus degree of fixedness), and consequently in range of potential future development or change. A balanced, well-knit, and consistent pattern in the baby, when the baby is cared for by a stable mother who respects and reinforces the early pattern, can be seen to provide a foundation for later consistency and continuity in development. This is the pattern we saw in Teddy, a relatively consistent child.

The persistence of an early-programmed adaptational style is also related to the intrinsic cohesiveness of the organism, which is supported by balance of its growth-pattern, to the consistency of basic mother–infant support, and to freedom from unmanageable stress. By analogy, the capacity of a tree to maintain itself against the wind will depend on the texture of the fibre of the tree and the character and persistence of the wind. Some trees are brittle and break easily. On the other hand, a persistent wind will distort the shape of the cypress, whereas occasional winds would not.

Will other studies of continuity in these children confirm this picture? Let us turn to Moriarty's study of continuity and change in cognitive functioning.

Continuity and change as seen through IQ tests

All the babies in this group were judged to be within the normal intelligence range, and so they remained at the preschool stage. But still we found marked variations in IQ level as have other longitudinal studies of test results (Bayley 1949; Sontag, Baker, and Nelson 1958). Alice Moriarty (1966) concentrated on an analysis of continuity and change in IQ levels in this group with the addition of other children remaining in

Topeka from the original Escalona–Leitch group, sixty-five children in all.

She identified four patterns: children whose test scores consistently improved, children whose cognitive functioning slowed down, children whose IQ scores were variable, and children whose test levels remained stable. As we would expect, the children whose IQs were most erratic and those whose cognitive functioning slowed down were those in whom stress disturbed this area more than other areas of functioning (Appendix 5). This did not mean that children with stable IQs were not exposed to equal stress, but rather, that they reacted differently—for instance, with psychosomatic disturbances. The vulnerable zones differed from child to child.

The four groups among her *extended* sample of sixty-five children contained varying proportions of children: 40 percent remained stable; 25 percent accelerated, having increasing IQs; 9 percent were slow, or declined in IQ; 26 percent showed erratic or imbalanced test scores, fluctuating over time (in our "intensive" sample this was a higher proportion).

The fact that a child's IQ increases does not necessarily imply a change in adaptational style; rather, it represents the cumulative effect of an adaptational style oriented toward progress and achievement. Moriarty, like Sontag, commented that accelerating children showed high motivation for active coping efforts, for new learning, and for the expression of intellectual drives. In keeping with these tendencies, they used such defense mechanisms as distancing and sublimation. They had strong drives to probe and to understand interpersonal relationships, and a sense of social responsibility. And they enjoyed their families' approval of their personal aspirations.

Moriarty points out that Roddy's increase in IQ paralleled the exercise of his alert, curious mind and increasingly effective direction of his energy into more direct and steady problem-solving efforts. Increased control at latency was reflected in his improved ability to curb his intensity and to reduce his speedy pace in order to increase his efficiency or to fit in with the demands of a situation. Along with these expressions of increased control were his more sustained attention and his effective efforts toward clarification and making considered judgments. He controlled negative feelings and used his energy to do "the right thing."

In contrast, children who developed slowly, with a decline in IQ, had some combination of the following burdens: prolonged illness, sensory impairments, and greater dependency related to impairment, with a need for support and encouragement. Constitutional weakness, physical immaturity, and related disintegrative or regressive tendencies interfered with their developmental pace. Reactions to these included negative attitudes, inability to allow aggression full discharge, and difficulties both with learning and relationships to people.

Furthermore, the stability of IQ with some other children is not necessarily a reflection of optimal development. Moriarty (1966, pp. 95–96) found that children whose IQs remained constant might be physically intact, free from defect or handicap, but they were relatively noncompetitive and typically had rather low energy. With low overt expression of drive they were restrained in self-expression in contrast to the sublimated and active coping methods of the accelerating children. Their self-protective defense mechanisms succeeded in limiting frustration and anxiety but shortchanged their creative potentialities and the range and richness of their experiences. "Mild, passive Steve always let the world pass him by"; "neither Teddy nor Steve vigorously seized upon his world, yet each, despite some obvious self-doubts achieved an equilibrium which permitted normal, relatively comfortable, and stable growth processes" (p. 97). In other words, continuity here has a quality of maintenance of the status quo, a lack of the progressive orientation shown by the "accelerating" children whose IQs change with their increasing mastery. This picture is similar to observations on "static" versus "progressing" students studied at Sarah Lawrence in the 1930s (Raushenbush and Murphy 1960).

Moriarty's fourth group included the 26 percent of her extended sample whose "test patterns tended to be inconsistent, that is, subject to grosser fluctuations, both in terms of test scores and behavioral manifestations" (p. 184). This group included "children whose IQs moved up and down irregularly, children with marked imbalance in the level of skills on different cognitive tasks. . . . As a group they showed more clinical signs of disturbances." But the direction of shift of equilibrium varied: some children with early disturbances improved by prepuberty, while others with temporary prepuberty disequilibria, combined with concurrent stress, regressed. This "erratic" group showed a greater tendency for cognitive functioning to be disrupted by emotuonal disturbances, in contrast to the stable group whose defense mechanisms protected the stability of cognitive functioning under stress. Her observations of variability in the cognitive zone imply not only greater stress and greater plasticity but, specifically, vulnerability in the cognitive zone to stress effects.

Among Moriarty's "erratic or imbalanced" group whose cognitive functioning was variable were five who had been judged by Heider to be moderately or very "vulnerable" at the infancy or preschool level (Rachel, Daryl, Brennie, Gordon, Janice). Here we would need to test the hypothesis that while variability in cognitive functioning could balance vulnerability when it included the ability to mobilize greater cognitive resources under stress, it could contribute to vulnerability when it involved deterioration of cognitive functioning under stress.

A few of Moriarty's erratic group were vulnerable in the sense that they reacted in a disintegrative way to new inner and outer pressures at prepuberty or in adolescence: Chester's principal feared the eleven-year-old boy could become delinquent; Sally's IQ decreased eighteen points around the time of her mother's depression; Barbie became disorganized in early adolescence as did Diane later. All in this erratic group were in difficult family situations, in which exhaustion, irritability, or depression of mothers played a major part. However all responded to new opportunities and three extricated themselves from early family pressures by marrying young. It is important to remember here that some of the initially vulnerable children, such as Janice, gained strength through their childhoods, and their improved cognitive mastery including marked success in school undoubtedly contributed to and also reflected this increase of strength. We saw earlier that certain infants quieted themselves by concentrating on perceptual experiences—watching objects in the environment.

All together, eleven of the twenty-nine "intensive" children available for the prepuberty study needed special help of some kind before adulthood, ranging from support from a pastor or priest to psychotherapy. Of these eleven, mothers of eight had been disturbed during the child's infancy—that is, depressed or overanxious. Another mother was later excessively strict. In addition, two mothers had been overly ready to anticipate every infant need, and physical factors including prolonged illnesses contributed to vulnerability in six instances.

It is also important to note that none of the adaptational styles represented in the preschool children guaranteed that the child could cope with all pressures without becoming disturbed in some area of functioning. There were no invulnerable[5] children, despite Moriarty's finding that about half of her extended sample remained stable or accelerated their IQs. Some of these children whose IQs were stable reflected effects of stress in somatic or motor zones, in emotional disturbances, or in loss of impulse control.

Continuity and change in profiles

We saw earlier that Escalona found some children more predictable than others, taking the entire range of predicted characteristics at the preschool stage. And so we made another approach to continuity of style seen as the total pattern of characteristics: a study of clusters of children with similar profiles. To what extent do children of similar patterns of functioning at one phase tend to remain together in the same cluster either through not changing or through changing in similar ways? Lolafaye Coyne directed this analysis.

Comparisons of the children on 100 coping items at preschool and prepuberty stages found sixteen of twenty-eight children remaining in clusters at prepuberty with one or more children who had been included in their preschool clusters. To this extent the adaptational style of 57 percent of this intensive sample remained consistent. The rest of the children shifted into new clusters in line with changing balances of cognitive, affect, and motor resources; changing use of their resources; and changing health and environmental pressures affecting their adaptation.

Let us consider the preschool profile clusters in more detail: Group I included Trudy, Teddy, Ralph, Barbie, Sally, and Diane. They were high on smoothness, purposefulness and fineness of coordination, the ability to remain quiet when attention is engaged, the freedom to translate ideas into action, and energy level. Auditory and visual sensitivity were high and these children "were more attached to objects than to people." Impulse control, the balance of pleasure over frustration, and tolerance for unpleasurable situations were high, though tempo of recovery from affective disturbance was low. Autonomic reactivity was low, and their tendency to present management difficulties was moderate to low. They were moderately able to give warmth, and had a high capacity for reality testing. They varied from one to another on the other variables. Of these, Teddy was most consistent over time while Trudy blossomed socially, and Sally's cognitive interests and IQ decreased. Sally remained a very skillful girl in feminine ways. Barbie and Diane became distinctly less stable at puberty, as if cognitive and emotional concerns had not been adequately balanced and integrated.

Teddy's early God-given initiative, clarity, and purposefulness carried him through college and into an absorbing career. His innate cohesiveness, apparently reinforced by his mother's support, carried him through painful vicissitudes of conflict between his mother and his paternal grandmother, his parents' divorce, his leaving Topeka for a period, his mother's remarriage to a man with whom Teddy's father fought, and the problems created by his own obesity—his chief stress-reaction to these vicissitudes. He was one of the most stable children. He was not invulnerable; he suffered through these difficult experiences, but he kept his own sense of direction, his strong cognitive interests, his sense of masculine identity, and also his warmth.

Coincidentally, Group I were all independently classified in Heider's lowest groups (IV and V) on vulnerability in the first six months of life and remained low in vulnerability at the preschool level, with the exception of one rated moderate. All these children in Group I had IQs over 120 at the preschool or latency tests. In nursery school Trudy's teacher complained that her social interests were limited. And Barbie seemed awkward in new social contacts at the preschool stage, just as she had seemed tense when socially stimulated as a baby.

Group II included Molly, Susan, Greg, Terry, Chester, JoAnne, and Brennie. They were also purposive and freely translated ideas into action. They were even less vulnerable in the motor area than Group I, which varied more from child to child. They were alert to details of situations, responded emotionally to a wide range of stimuli in highly appropriate ways, and were high in auditory and visual sensitivity like Group I. They also enjoyed handling materials, were intensely involved in play activities, and were very creative. Correspondingly, they were low in stereotyped use of toys and in preference for structured situations. They were expressive and not defensively inhibited. In dealing with practical tasks they were very able to ask for help when they needed it and could also mobilize their own resources under stress and impose their own ideas on situations. In all other items they varied from one to another, frequently with a range of twenty points, and it is interesting that we find so few moderate items for this group. All these were vivid active copers, as we saw in *Widening World of Childhood*.

Three of these children were classified in Heider's low vulnerability group in infancy, three in her high vulnerability group, and one in her middle group. All the boys in this group needed special help during latency or adolescence; two of these were probably similar to Thomas's (et al. 1963) "intense" children who needed therapy during their elementary school years.

Group III included Sheila, Tommy, Ray, Lennie, Helen, and Ronald. They had an entirely different pattern from the other groups except for moderate vulnerability in the motor zone, but they did not tend to use inhibition as a defense. They generally had high tempo and freedom to translate ideas into action. They were alert, with high visual sensitivity; they enjoyed intense stimulation to a moderate degree, and they could maintain a moderate attention span. They were not constricted in using play space, but they did not develop strong attachments to physical objects; they showed little pleasure in cognitive functioning at the preschool stage, and they were *not* (like Group VI) more given to looking than to action. They had little preference for structured situations, nor did they give high priority to achieving structure.

Their emotional responses were highly appropriate, and they had both a wide affect range and high autonomic reactivity. Of six groups they were one of two that had a relatively high degree of conflict about sex role. Despite conflicts and evidence of lability and vulnerability, they were moderately able to mobilize resources under stress. Four of these children were in Heider's vulnerable group of infants, but only one received special help later, and that was because of sequelae to illness. These were children who did not overinvest in intellectual interests but tended to give themselves moderate leeway for regression and to work through problems actively. We shall see more of some of these children in later chapters.

We omit Group IV because of the indistinctness of its pattern.

Group V included Cynthia, Janice, Martin, and Gordon. They had a moderate activity level wih high purposiveness and fine coordination, high freedom to express ideas in action, and rapid tempo, with moderate energy, and moderate to high attention span. But this group had low enjoyment of new sensations and low tendency to look more than act. They were also moderately creative. Affect range, pleasure in handling materials, vividness of expression, and autonomic reactivity were all moderate, although they offered little warmth. Social sensitivity, enjoyment of social contacts, and also reserve with strangers were moderate. With low capacity to give warmth, they were also low in tendency to be stimulating. They had a high tendency to protest, and were also high in their tendency to impose their own ideas—coping resources that over time contributed to greater strength in Janice and Martin.

Three of the four had been regarded by Heider as vulnerable infants and all four were in her vulnerable preschool group. Cynthia was removed from the research group when her mother was hospitalized; of the remaining three, Janice and Martin steadily gained strength while Gordon, victim of an extremely unstable home situation, needed help, especially at puberty. While Janice retained some underlying vulnerability, the progress made by her and by Martin implies latent potential for coping with problems—a potential not recognized in Janice's infancy, as Escalona commented (Escalona and Heider 1959, p. 177). Both children were ectomorphic in Sheldon's terms (1940) and like others of this group, matured slowly but with increasing stability.

Group VI included Darlene, Vernon, Daryl, Vivian, and Rachel. This group contrasts with Groups I and II in that these children had a low activity level (with varying qualities of motor functioning, ranging over 20 points on a 30-point scale) and high vulnerability in the motor zone, along with a tendency to inhibit motor response under stress. This tendency in Group VI is conspicuous among these groups. These children had no difficulty in remaining quiet; their average level of speed was low, along with low freedom to translate ideas into action. Low enjoyment of intense and new situations and of cognitive functioning generally went along with low explorativeness and creativity and also little appropriate affect; they were sober children with little tendency to clear shifts in feeling. They tended to look more than act, were constricted in their use of space in play, and tended to be rigid. They were also low in giving and receiving warmth and in enjoyment of social contacts; they were reserved with strangers. Verbal fluency was low or did not surpass other abilities, and they were the only group at this preschool level that made little use of fantasy to solve reality problems.

But they had a high attention span and high visual sensitivity. While impulse control was high, they had low tolerance for situations that did not please them, a low level of pleasure as contrasted with frustration, and a slow tempo of recovery. They did not seem to greet new situations with open (or eager) anticipation, but they did show moderate pleasure in handling materials and objects. This group was divided in Heider's infant vulnerability ratings: two were seen as vulnerable, two were rated as very low in vulnerability, and one was in the moderate group. But their vulnerability increased at the preschool level, as a consequence of illness in Rachel's case and as an effect of Darlene's difficulties in coordination. Two needed special help, and Darlene effectively protested her mother's overly strict limits to her social life. Her mother consulted first our staff, then her minister, who recommended that the mother permit the child a wider range of friendships.

The backgrounds of their limited spontaneity varied. We saw that Darlene was inhibited both by coordination difficulties related to her unusually narrow, long, flat feet and by her extremely restrictive mother. Rachel never regained normal infantile autonomy after the months of constraint to protect her from infecting her eczematous skin. Daryl and Vivian had been hovered over by an anxious grandmother as well as by their mother, and Vernon had been extremely reserved from his early months.

*Contrasting directions of change from preschool to
prepuberty: toward control, and toward openness*

The independent cluster study resembled the findings of Moriarty's study of IQs. A second clustering at puberty showed that certain children changed in the direction of greater intellectual involvement (and increased IQs); we also found that certain other children like Diane and Sally became more open or labile emotionally. They remained clustered together and they changed in the same direction in their cognitive–affective balance. Those in Group I modulated their early impulsiveness toward greater control and purposiveness while those in the contrasting Group VI relaxed their initial caution, or inhibition, toward greater reactivity and expressiveness.

Without going into details of these changes, we do need to comment on these different patterns or directions of change in adaptational style in relation to the situation of each child at the early and later stages. Trudy, Diane, Sally, and Darlene were among those who shifted from an early controlled style to greater affective freedom.

Trudy at the preschool stage was caught between two busy parents and a considerably older sister with middle-childhood interests on one side, and a toddler sister and baby brother on the other. She coped by intensely identifying with her older sister and focusing on grown-up interests in puzzles; in nursery school she was considered inhibited and socially remote. Later her intellectual and motor skills together with her blonde beauty made her one of the most popular children in her grade, and she "blossomed."

Diane became increasingly open and reactive, to the point of "trying out" many new experiences in adolescence.

Sally, a vigorous, competent girl caught between younger and older brothers, was a preschool tomboy, but in her words, "I decided to be a girl when I was seven." In line with her mother's wishes, she relaxed her intellectual and motor preoccupations in favor of girlish narcissistic and social interests.

Darlene, hampered by her poor motor coordination at the preschool stage, was more at home in school activities later and became more free to press her strong interest in friends and play.

We have to see in these and other instances that a child is not a bundle of "consistent" or "changing" traits but an adapting, plastic individual finding a way to come to terms with changing pressures and opportunities. The latter are experienced individually and selectively as each child's strengths and vulnerabilities make a given situation a source of threat, deprivation, or satisfaction. The quality of plasticity is itself an aspect of genetic givens.

The adaptational style, then, is a more or less flexible attunement between the range of resources and limitations of the child and the quality of the environmental pressures and opportunities.

Changes toward greater control

While the change from preschool impulsiveness and emotional

excitability to greater focus on skills and competence is expected in our culture, it is worthwhile to look at other supports in addition to the cultural stimulation imposed by school. At the preschool stage, children are often exhilarated by their motor achievements—"Look at me climb"—or tricks, and their new abilities to compete, to leave the babies behind. Their basic struggles for ease in communication as well as locomotion are over, and they are released to use them in discovery, in creating, and integrating a proud sense of self. Emotional responses flow readily. In latency, the early dramatic changes from frustrated inadequacies to triumphant mastery are taken for granted, and pride comes to be attached to group membership, as we saw when the children proudly pointed out "my church" or "my school" or spoke of "our family." The child has become part of a "we" group, or rather, several "we" groups. For the Catholic children, First Communion and Confirmation are honored and proud rituals. Among the Protestant children, Diane passionately "gave her heart to Jesus" at the age of six. Along with these broader identifications, we see the drive for recognition by and leadership of the group, as when Ray became vice-president of his third-grade class, and when later other children were recognized for scientific achievements, or by Girl Scouts, Boy Scouts, or 4-H clubs for their mastery of skills or creative products. The invitation and challenge from the environment is internalized into inner drives, including the drive for intellectual mastery. That marked progress in this zone occurred with only part of the group must be seen in relation to the fact that mothers did *not* consider making good grades in school an important priority in child-rearing emphases, and Sally's mother, wanting a "feminine" little girl, explicitly worked against her daughter's cognitive drives. Most of the children who shifted strongly toward increased cognitive interests were middle-class children or children with mothers who had some professional training.

It happens that all four of the most constricted children at both the preschool and prepuberty levels were Catholic, attending parochial schools, growing up in a very homogeneous family–church centered world with limited exposure to outside opportunities. The relatively static adaptational style of these children may be seen as mirroring the extreme consistency of their environment—a degree of consistency which resembles that of small, isolated communities where children have no access to varieties of life-styles. *The simpler the organism–environment interaction, the greater predictability we can have.*

There is sometimes a fine line between deeply rooted inhibition and the developmentally useful caution (which can look like inhibition) seen in children who are observed to withdraw strategically, as Darlene did at the preschool level in order to give herself time for orientation, cognitive mastery, and emotional acceptance of a new challenge she intended to and did finally master (Murphy 1962, pp. 168–70). As they develop skill, some of these cautious, selective preschool children later "blossom" into more open, spontaneous, responsive individuals coping with new challenges. This becomes possible for them as increased areas of motor mastery and cognitive clarity about their world provide greater coping resources and confidence.

Variability

It is widely recognized that variability in tested IQ reflects the influence of many different factors: differences in functions tested at different developmental levels; differences in state of physiological, affective, and cognitive functioning; differences in rapport with the tester and comfort in the testing situation; differences in achievement motivation at the time, and so on. Differences in other areas of functioning—social, for instance—may also reflect similar influences. In addition, variability ascribed to the child may reflect variability in cultural demands and opportunities and criteria for adequacy, as with Trudy. It is quite common to see a child upset, anxious, or inhibited by placement in a rigid school or in a room with a cross teacher change dramatically when placed in a more reassuring setting. "This teacher understands children much better than Miss Burr," said one boy, whose nausea vanished when he was shifted from a frightening teacher to a warm teacher. "Miss Beyer smiled at me all day long," said another, whose aggression and nail-biting stopped when he was taken out of a nursery school run by a teacher who yelled at the children. Many other situational variations can be documented for any group of children.

In fact, considering the many variations arising from interaction with differing situations observed from infancy to adolescence, it is a wonder that we find any children with stable levels of cognitive, affective, or social functioning, or of coping capacity. But we do. Consequently, we have a realistic question as to factors in the differences in variability and continuity in different children.

It does not take a great leap of the imagination to suggest that some children are like a closely woven textile that does not stretch or shrink much, while others are more elastic and react to the pushes and pulls, the storms and heat waves of life. Or that variability might sometimes be related to the benign quality of flexibility—being able to expand or contract without breaking. Is there a relation between variability and vulnerability, or is variability an expression of responsiveness that contributes to positive resources and strengths?

When we reflected on the clustering of children, we found that some children moved from a rather constricted cognitive and motor orientation at the preschool level to a more balanced cognitive–motor–affective orientation at the prepuberty level. Others were impulsive and dominated by an affective–motor axis in the early years, and modulated to a more controlled affective–cognitive–motor orientation later. In other words, we saw that different children matured along different paths, in one case from early ebullience to later increase in control, while others were cautious, even inhibited, in the early years and expanded to greater openness and activity later on.

We see examples of this along a broader age-range too. Who has not seen impulsive adolescents settle down to wise adulthood, or shy or overcontrolled, even ascetic, adolescents warming up to vivid expressiveness or leadership later on? More surprising are the withdrawn "good boys" who become delinquent or criminal later, but there are none of these in our intensive sample.

Our infancy data contain potentially relevant hints of possible factors of different kinds related to variability, as we saw earlier:

Infants differed in the balance of their scores on early developmental functions; some were at a consistent average level in all areas of functioning, while others were advanced in one area, average or slow in another. The variable levels of functioning tended to contribute to a less cohesive ego structure.

Infants differed in their autonomic nervous system reactivity; variability in this zone can contribute to variability in ego control.

Infants varied in their responsiveness to stress and to soothing; we can include differences in their pace of recovery from stress reactions.

Such tendencies as these could contribute to the shakiness or firmness of controls contributing to stability.

These factors, and other aspects of the constitutional makeup of the child, also influence the degree of impact of the assaults, pressures, and demands of the environment—whether constant, as with a rigid, punitive school or an excessively demanding or stimulating family life, or occasional, as with traumata of divorce, mental illness, or death of a parent or severely threatening illness of the child.

In other words, even if we insist that variability may be partly "in the eyes of the beholder," there is enough evidence of real differences in cohesiveness of the personality structure from infancy on to call for greater sensitivity to this aspect of development.

Since nearly half of our intensively studied group were erratic or imbalanced as described by Moriarty, and these overlapped with Heider's vulnerable preschool children, it is important to explore the implications of vulnerability further, and this we shall do in chapter 8. Meanwhile, we shall focus on the varieties of change and processes involved in these changes in the next chapter.

7

Change and the Role of Vulnerability and Coping

I would be wrong to describe growing up as easy because certainly it wasn't. . . . But people can adjust and take things in stride.

Chester, as a young adult

It would be extremely convenient for everyone working with children if we could make a profile of the child's characteristics—abilities, temperament, coping strengths and weaknesses—in the first months of his life and count on these as being permanent.[1] We might condense this information, engrave it on an expandable bracelet, tag him for life, and save millions of dollars on subsequent tests and examinations. Is the possibility of such a lifetime assessment credible? Some child psychologists imply that a scheme like this might be possible, and it might *if* (a) the child's abilities and temperament were completely ascertainable in his early months, (b) they were unaffected by his mother's (and the rest of the family's) handling and the environment in general, and (c) his own ways of responding to his vulnerabilities, illnesses, other inner and outer stress, growth changes in body and drives, and the demands of the world around him at successive stages made no impact on his initial equipment, that is, did not seriously reverse, modify, or transform his initial patterns.

But we have already seen that many children are unpredictable; their early patterns change in very unexpected ways. A prime example is Janice, a sickly and unlikely coper as a baby who developed into a distinctively resourceful young girl.

Escalona commented (Escalona and Heider 1959, p. 176) that "Janice furnished a good illustration for [the fact that] predictive failures suggest problems of greater interest than predictive successes." In Heider's judgment Janice was one of the most vulnerable babies, and Escalona imagined her to be as a child notably fragile, physically and "psychologically; perceptually alert, with exceptional acumen of vision, specifically color; more vulnerable than average to even minor stress, and tending to regress in the face of stress more readily than is age-appropriate." It was assumed that both in terms of libidinal development and behaviorally she would be developmentally immature and that withdrawal would be her dominant method of coping with situations threatening her equilibrium. These predictions were generally confirmed. But Escalona and Heider observed that the predictions did not take into account Janice's reservoir of energy and capacity to alter the environment to obtain satisfaction. Escalona added that her image of Janice would correspond to fixation at an anal-retentive level of libidinal development with stubbornness and passive resistance, a primary goal to maintain autonomy rather than to strive for remote goals. But, Escalona reflected, actually her five-year-old behavior suggested libidinal fixation at the oral level, greedily seeking material possessions without being pleased with what she got. She could not modulate her desires and was constantly disappointed. I saw her as a "restless searcher for gratification." And her withdrawal, mouthing, and thumb-sucking corresponded to oral defenses.

In critically evaluating her prediction Escalona emphasized the fact that Janice was a "complex, changeable, multifaceted little creature," often babyish, but also mature, even precociously self-sufficient and competent at other times. (For instance, she independently fed herself, undressed, and put herself to bed when the family went on visits she did not want to join. Similarly she would dress herself alone in preparation for a trip to the research center, as Marie Smith vividly reported.) Escalona further expected that significant need deprivation would partially prevent Janice from learning at her potential rate. Actually, with her IQ of 122 she gave every evidence of being a good learner (and in fact continued through school with good grades). At the preschool stage she did not seem to enjoy cognitive mastery like many of the other children, but only because she desperately desired recognition from adults.

It is important to pause here for reflection on the subsequent development of this little girl with a "libidinal fixation at the oral level." She was successful throughout school years, warmly loyal to her church despite her parents' neutral attitude, and she continued to reach out for friends and social experiences during the time we knew her. In reaction to the assassination of President Kennedy she was one of the children who wished she could help (p. 259). Dr. Stewart and others commented on what a fine young person she was at adolescence.

When she was fourteen I discussed with her the fact that her mother had always been unwell and relatively unavailable. I asked her what had helped her to grow up so well. She told me that at about the age of four she had found "another mother" in the mother of her neighbor friend and that this other mother had been very important to her. Evidently relationships and especially a relationship with a good mother-substitute (or "good object") was far more important to her than we knew at the preschool stage. If we had been less research oriented and more active in our relationship with her, we might have found her less restless. The importance of relationships is also relevant to the observation that learning did not seem satisfying to her in its own right but as a means of gaining approval from adults. In view of her continued good work through high school, where personal responses of teachers are far less available than in the primary grades, we would assume that the drive to learn had achieved some autonomy from her oral drive (Ekstein, Rudolph, and Motto 1969).

We can look at Janice's pattern of continually reaching out for what she needed in light of my repeated observations of children in foundling homes. There I have been struck with differences in toddlers' responses to visitors; some are completely withdrawn and pay no attention, others stare wistfully or sullenly, a few reach out to tap the glass of their cubicles or stretch a hand through the fence of their play area. Responsiveness and capacity to show a desire for contact have more chance of evoking some contact from others and thus gaining some support for healthy development. Similarly Janice's persistent reaching out for, seeking, and gaining response was a healthy avenue to the restitution needed for progressive development of a somewhat deprived little girl.

Her continued participation in church and school activities in adolescence as well as her learning successes imply sublimation and use of her ego strengths for satisfaction, over time, of the oral drive that initially sustained her outreaching and demanding. The wish to help and thus give to others in need suggests a transformation of "demanding from" to "giving to"—a motivation probably widespread in many helpers, such as social workers and nurses.

From this point of view her persistent "oral" drive was her salvation; bright as she was, and with good community resources, this drive could gradually be satisfied, sublimated, transformed. But did she completely outgrow her vulnerability? Her initial response as a teenager to the assassination of President Kennedy is revealing here: "I felt as if life wasn't worth living any more." Such anguish suggests the despair she may have felt as a tiny, fragile, often neglected baby; and the fact that it was a father-image who was lost suggests that her father may have been crucially important to her even in infancy. Only the sudden shock of the assassination revealed this anaclitic depression type of despair; this implies the extent of repression probably supported by continuing orally driven efforts to fulfill her hope for satisfaction. The regression[2] in the face of severe stress at this time was a unique confirmation of Escalona's prediction. That she did not remain orally fixated in the sense of dependence in a practical sense is illustrated by her unusual competence and independence in self-care as well as by her firm refusal to obey my request to sit down in the car when in all probability she wanted to stand up in order to see as much as possible and thus gain visual stimulation important to her. Her constant firmness in going her own pace and insisting on her own choices implied a forceful effort to offset her dependency by sometimes aggressive autonomy. If this autonomy pattern had not been balanced by her continuing wish for approval and good relationships, even love, she would not have developed into the likable "fine" young person she became.

We can see in Janice one example of ways in which ego and drives combined to cope with vulnerability and frustration in the environment so as to contribute to developmental progress. Hers was a far more favorable development than was expected at infancy and even in the preschool stage—a socially positive outcome even though vulnerability was not totally reversed.

To be sure, case studies also provided evidence that a sensitive but energetic infant with difficult vegetative functioning, marked autonomic reactivity, and other evidences of precarious equilibrium and difficulties in achieving integration later tends to be easily disturbed. L. Bender (1953) and others have noted similar but more extreme early infantile difficulties in children who developed schizophrenia and other psychotic patterns in childhood. And even Janice, who developed so well in many ways, tended to be overwhelmed by severe stress. However, in our group of vulnerable infants a tendency toward creativity can in some instances be seen as an outcome of the effort to resolve the internal problems of the organism, as with Brennie, a highly creative boy. This observation is congruent with the findings of Barron (1968) and others who have studied creative adults.

In relation to later disturbances, including mental illness and behavior and learning problems, it is important to note the role of infancy imbalances such as combinations of extreme sensitivity, high activity level with poor coordination, high drive with poor capacity for delay and control, and poor "sending-power" (any or all of which may follow from pregnancy or birth difficulties, in addition to possible genetic factors).

A child with marked imbalances, much variability within the range of observed behaviors, and thus *less firm organization* is likely to change, moreover, as changing environmental experiences block, deflect, or reinforce different features of his early adaptational style. And when the imbalances occur in the form of marked variability in the intensity of different drives, or in relative drive strength, conditions exist that are likely to contribute to intrinsic conflicts; the outcome will depend on subtle variations in the child's ways of struggling with these conflicts and on the specific kinds of environmental exacerbation or efforts to help resolve the conflicts.

It is important to note that five infants who showed a considerable tendency to change had mothers who were depressed during the baby's early weeks or months. Depression in mothers was apt to result in less closeness between mother and baby. In a few instances the mothers were judged immature or unstable. It may be inferred that some inadequacy of the mother–infant relationship contributed to the instability of the primary adaptational style in addition to the constitutional variability of the baby.

In the altered or secondary adaptational style, as conflicts were resolved or as new capacities evoked new opportunities, we found unpredicted transformations; or less happily, as the early style proved inadequate to cope with intense conflicts or extreme stress at succeeding years and abrupt changes were felt necessary by the child, we found loss of initial resources.

Early changes in adaptational style that were implied in preschool behavior and that Escalona predicted less well (they changed between infancy and the preschool level) included:

a) behavior greatly influenced by developmental contributions, by increases or decreases in energy, vigor, mastery, and by changes in health

b) behavior greatly influenced by selective identification with certain siblings or other relatives and other unpredictable interactions with the family

c) behavior dependent on covert functions not easily visible at the infancy level, such as fantasy used by Susan for effective coping with her hospitalization

d) behavior greatly dependent on reaction to unpredictable gross or cumulative stress, due either to illness or to external events

We must also note that neither the tendency toward regression, the tendency toward progression in response to stress and challenge, the impact of reaction-formation, nor the capacity for sublimation was fully foreseen or predictable from infancy records.

Here we seem to be speaking deterministically even while we speak of unpredictabilities. But the environment is not able to determine what the baby will do with it.

The baby's contribution to the impact
of the environment

The study of development is plagued by many problems in its attempt to describe the processes involved in continuity and change. Each individual baby to some extent *chooses* the parts of his own environment with which he will interact and the way in which he will do this (see Escalona 1968). Both what he chooses and what he does will influence both the feedback—the satisfactions or frustrations—that come to him from the environment and the resulting inner resources and coping tendencies. In a hospital room for foundling babies we have watched an active four-month-old baby playing with a long balloon attached to the foot of his crib. Lying prone within reach of this toy, he pushed it and it sprang back, he scratched it and the balloon gave out screeching sounds; he rubbed it and the sounds were different. From such experiments he may have learned that he could make an interesting impact on the environment, that he could evoke a variety of effects, and also that he could have fun alone. By contrast, another baby merely looked at his balloon, but he looked intently and long, and doubtless developed a very clear visual image of the object; this process of maximizing visual experience may have been equally satisfying and may have contributed a feeling that visual experience by itself could be gratifying, interesting, even comforting.

Of course the mutual stimulations and mutual feedbacks between mother and baby, or between nurse and baby, are far more complex. In the same foundling nursery we have watched nurses hug, caress, talk to, smile at, and play with (bounce, sway, tickle, rock) babies about whom they would say, "This is *my* baby," implying a special rapport and mutual responsiveness. That baby has evocative power and "knows how to" evoke the wholehearted interest and love of that nurse. In the process, the baby accumulated a repertoire of social responses, including learning to respond to cues. In the same nursery a limp, cross-eyed, unsmiling baby did not evoke that kind of stimulation from any of four nurses during my observations over several weeks; the nurses cared for the baby dutifully, but no one really loved her. Love is not a very respectable word in science.[3] Yet when we observed the difference in spontaneity, vivacity, muscle tone, delight in playful interaction shared by the nurses and babies who were "tuned in" to each other, it seemed obvious that love—with all the cognitive and affective stimulation of the baby and response to the baby which it brings—is an important aspect of early experience and foundations for adaptation. A baby's capacity to evoke such responses is to some degree an aspect of the quality of activity or expressiveness, although not necessarily tempo or vigor. Some quiet babies are very appealing.

Lest we assume that activity level is entirely a function of genetic characteristics, we must note the impressive *changes in activity level* observable over a period of successive days and weeks. In the same foundling nursery mentioned above, we saw both increases and decreases in activity level lasting as much as a week after an inoculation shot. Daily variations were seen in some babies who became extremely active when hungry, or tired, or when there was evidence of gastric discomfort.

In our Topeka research sample, certain extremely active babies had extremely stimulating mothers; the high activity level of these babies may have been at least in part an outcome of their shared interactions with their very active mothers. Even in utero the baby responds to the mother's activity, and both baby and mother are influenced by the hormonal, nutritional, and other biochemical factors flowing through the mother's bloodstream (Stone, Smith, and Murphy 1973, chap. 2). Escalona has traced the differences between mother–baby interactions among most-active and least-active babies in her total sample (1968). We do not want to imply that the baby's interactions with the mother are the only important interactions between the infant and his social environment. Siblings, father, and, in fact, everyone in the baby's world can be very important.

Even in the early months some babies "choose" not only preferred foods and toys, but also preferred people: one baby girl is a "mama's girl" while another is "daddy's girl" (fathers were crucially important from infancy to Patsy, Helen, Sally, JoAnne especially). Similarly baby boys may take to father more than mother. And babies of either sex often become very attached to a sibling. Such attachments provide a foundation for identification and, as in the case of Chester, who had two older sisters, may complicate the process of sex-role development and of identification with the same sex parent. The environment is there, but our notion of "the impact of the environment" must be tempered by a recognition of the child's selective embracing, rejecting, evading, and, indeed, changing different aspects of it. As we saw in the comparison of JoAnne, and Vivian, the range of ways of dealing with the environment and coping with one's needs differs from infant to infant and from child to child and influences the outcome of interaction between environment and child.

Revision of adaptational style
through coping with new problems

We have discussed the primary adaptational style of infancy in the earliest months when the primary drives, aspects of equipment having to do with both reception of stimuli and reactions, coping tendencies, learning abilities, and integrative capacity interact with the environmental stimuli and pressures of that phase. The emergent adaptational style of early childhood continues to evolve as new ego functions, new drive resources, new affective and expressive capacities interact in experiences with new aspects of the environment, including changes in all the new stimulations and frustrations provided by the mother and immediate family as the child matures and is regarded as "old enough" to be responsive to new experience or to respect limits.

From the data on our intensively studied sample we can select the record on Lennie, an exceptionally vigorous, healthy, active, alert infant at the age of four weeks, who was retarded in development and had unexpected difficulties in the second year of life concomitant with his mother's absence from home when she went to work.

Although Lennie's sensitive reactions to her absence were not expected, at least by the family, in view of his early vigor and apparent independence, they would not come as a surprise to a contemporary pediatrician or psychologist acquainted with work done in the last twenty-five years on infant reaction to separation[4] from the mother in the last quarter of the first year of life and in the second year of life (Spitz 1945). Other infants in our group, such as Molly and Ray, had also been essentially healthy babies but were sensitive to separation from the mother in the second and even third years of life.

However, with Lennie, and perhaps with Molly as well, there were certain factors in equipment that may have contributed to their reactions. Both Lennie and Molly had visual problems that were not diagnosed until they went to school. As long as the infant was in an essentially protected relation to the environment, in which the mother was still functioning as accessory ego, present for help in orientation as well as emotional support, the visual limitations might not create marked difficulties for the child. However, at a period when other functions are in the process of emerging and are not yet securely integrated, any defect might well add to the difficulties in integration. And under such conditions separation from the mother could be expected to be even more threatening than is usually true even in children without such special adaptational problems at this phase.

Contributions from new resources

Another major shift in adaptational style may occur in reaction to the emergence of new positive resources in the second half of the first year. Beginning in the fifth and sixth months, the infant's rapidly increasing capacity to maneuver his body, to manipulate objects, to reach potentially gratifying stimuli for himself, to create effects such as noises of rattling of paper, ringing of bells, banging of toys against the crib or banging objects on the tray of his chair, introduces a gross new phase in the child's experience: a dramatic expansion of the area of his own *control over the environment* with a concomitant increase in range of reinforcements for initiative, mastery efforts, and activity in general.[5] This phase of course encourages the child to achieve a vertical position, with an increased range of vision even when sitting, but it provides even greater increased potentialities for visual and tactual exploration as the child begins to creep and walk.

This phase of emergent motor mastery has been equated with the shift from a basically passive orientation to the environment to a more predominantly active psychic orientation. The baby is, by the end of the first year, less interested in food and in other aspects of receptive experience than in active self-initiated exchanges with the environment. The evolution of autonomy in dealings with the external environment is more or less paralleled by usually slow but sometimes more rapid steps in autonomous control of sphincters and management of elimination.

The entire gamut of these experiences of autonomy, whether of body management, stimulus management, interpersonal dealings, management of sphincters and cooperation with social demands, contributes a new dimension to the adaptational resources of the child. Like every other developmental step, this one is accompanied by wide variations in individual children. If from the earliest months the child has been very active in handling his own discomforts, in evoking responses from people around him, and in acting upon the environment, this access of autonomy and initiative beginning from the early stages of increased motor control will appear to be an extension, elaboration, and intensification of an already visible pattern. However, if the child's original ways of dealing with unpleasant stimulation were through avoidance and retreat, and if the infant in the first three to six months showed little initiative in evoking responses from people in the environment, the emergence of a psychically active orientation to the environment, insofar as it does emerge, appears as a new development.

Thus JoAnne, whom we saw earlier as an extremely active four week old, continued in a pattern quite consistent with her earlier tendencies; Vivian, though never approaching the level of initiative characteristic of JoAnne in the preschool years, still developed new resources with successive stages in development.

By contrast with these two children, who through successive phases of emergent capacities and changing drive maintained the primary adaptational style with relatively slight modification, Kent,* originally a "quiet, passive" infant became surprisingly active with the emergence of loco-motor resources.

Individual patterns of change in childhood[6]

Over the years then, many of the children surprised us at one time or another. For example, individual studies showed how a stoic and strong preschooler considered to be one of the "best copers" in many ways, became discouraged, embittered, and poorly controlled at the prepu-berty stage; a very vulnerable infant became an unusually competent, understanding, and well-functioning teenager; a forthright, and at times aggressive, preschool girl became a sympathetic and nurturant child at home and at school; a boy who appeared to be ectomorphic at three became obese in latency; a boy leader at age four later became effeminate and rather isolated; a girl who appeared to be well-organized and integrated at four became scattered and rebellious at the prepuberty stage; an average boy at three became a leader and high achiever during latency years; a boy who was extremely slow to make contact with peers at the preschool stage became an eager athlete during latency years; a thin, vulnerable, ectomorphic "ugly duckling" at five became very active socially and attractive as a teenager; a constricted, hostile preschool girl became a generous big sister in latency; an inhibited girl at four became at eight the most popular child in her class. The sequential study of each child comprises a volume; these highlights are given in order to suggest the range of areas in which change occurred and the sometimes dramatic degree of these changes. (See Appendix 5 for individual sequences in IQ and for other variables rated at preschool and prepuberty.)

Our understanding of processes contributing to such changes was deepened by scrutinizing the changes in the child's vulnerability. We saw that of the thirty-one babies in our intensive sample judged normal by Escalona's team, eight children changed from infancy to the preschool stage two to four points on a five-point scale in the direction of greater vulnerability as rated by Grace Heider. Three children had had

* A child not in the Topeka studies but observed throughout his early years.

prolonged illnesses. With five girls, family difficulties, deprivation, or disturbance were factors.

On the other hand, five children were considered by Heider to be less vulnerable at the preschool stage; this improvement appeared to be a response to improved health, unusual support from mother, great striving and drive to mastery from within the child, or a combination of these; some children showed unusual determination and capacity to gain strength through their own coping efforts. Three were considered to be holding their own despite rather severe family pressures, such as a mother's disturbed mental health in one instance and a separation of mother and father in another—that is, circumstances under which other children might become more vulnerable. From the preschool to prepuberty stage, a number of children progressed, while a few were seen by the psychiatric examiner as more vulnerable. Obviously, in the cases of increased vulnerability we have complex examples of change—change that implies that bodily stress suffered by the child, or tension and anxiety evoked by conflict or by school difficulties, or changes in a disturbed or ill parent's reaction to the child, can increase the child's tendency to loss of equilibrium (increase of disintegrative reactions to stress). Considerations raised by various research studies during the last thirty-odd years, as well as our own findings in Topeka, suggest a variety of hypotheses regarding progress and increased strength, as well as increased vulnerability.

Experiences of growth and change

Growth brings changes in height, muscular strength, and body proportions; but the child's experience of these differs with the child's situation. Entering school as the youngest member of the class, as Ray and Sheila did, can threaten the child's confidence in being able to keep up with the others. When Ray was "kept back" the following year and was no longer the baby of the class, he did well and became a leader. The experience of growth depends on the total situation of child-in-his-social-field, the relation of his growth status to that of others, and the feedback he gets from his family and others. At puberty, vulnerable Gordon's rapid growth resulted in welcome height, giving him an advantage in basketball, a new prestige among both boys and girls, a new investment in high school, and new confidence.

Subjective aspects of experience are probably involved in the five children who showed evidence of greater physical energy at the preschool level than had been predicted. Escalona commented in regard to poorly predicted Janice that her unusual ability to mobilize for action seemed to outweigh her physical energy. However, her improved health, the high level of her school performance, and her social activity in subsequent years reflected increased energy perhaps released by her successes, as well as by the mothering by her friend's mother who gave Janice what she lacked from her own mother.

Along with growth are those evolving processes of unfolding, blossoming, ripening, and the emergence of capacities and energies that at times transform certain children. Changes in level of energy or vigor, and in the direction of use of energy, come with progress through successive psychosexual phases. Conspicuous here are the developments at the early stage of autonomy when certain heretofore passive infants turn into two-year-old steam engines; initiative escalates when some children at the four-to-five-year-old stage overflow with imagination, creativity, and expressiveness, and in some cases, when youngsters flower at puberty.

The development of new talents[7] and with them new orientations (as when Helen's musical talent brought new resources) is often a complex resultant of the interaction of some of the tendencies referred to above combined with changes more or less unique to the individual.

Phases of effortful mastery of specific skills are often followed by quiet periods of integration:[8] a familiar example is the flowering of creativity and fantasy (along with pride and increased clarity about self) in four year olds following mastery of speech and motor skills from the age of one to three years.

After this stage of internal integration the child begins (at age six to seven) to be capable of participating in external complex organizations, such as team games, table games, arithmetic processes, riddles, and dramatic productions. Seeing oneself and one's family in a wider context and making broader comparisons also develops as part of this expanded cognitive integrative process. "We don't have much money," remarked seven-year-old Helen, as she surveyed the ample lunch when we took her out to a restaurant. Thus we saw evidence of important changes in awareness and changing meanings accompanying objective shifts in relative social and physical status.

Growth is not always accompanied by release of energy and increased integration. As children grow from infancy to the preschool level, the development of motor skills and range of opportunities for activity also make new demands. Thus, as with Roddy and Patsy (Escalona and Heider 1959, p. 129), the discrepancy between tendencies to activity and energy resources became apparent, whereas it was not seen at the time of the infancy observations. Also new opportunities and demands highlight previously unnoticed deviations or even defects: that Darlene would have difficulty in coordination because of her long, slender flat feet was not foreseen in infancy, while at the preschool stage when other children are escalating motor skills, her troubles became obvious (Murphy 1962, pp. 168–69). It was harder for her to jump and climb. Similarly myopia and other visual problems were not recognized in certain children until school demands for visual response to blackboards at a distance showed up their deficiency.

Individual patterns of growth

Growth has different designs in different individuals, so that some children seem to change when a new growth spurt brings a sudden loss of equilibrium—awkward coordination or instability of autonomic and affective functioning that require extra efforts at adaptation and new solutions. During these phases of maturation and learning, parents and teachers are often puzzled by apparent changes in zest or concentration as the infant and child move from spurts of growth and effortful learning to quiet plateaus that may seem to involve a shift or loss of interest but that have sometimes been shown to contribute to increased integration. They are often even more disturbed by the irritability and aggressiveness that accompany the period of disequilibrium in some children, as with Ray approaching the age of four and Susan six months before menarche. Whether or not the child has "changed" may depend on the timing of the observation in relation to the varied environmental as well as physical accompaniments of growth.

When the child's body build does not fit the culture's norm, heightened sensitivity associated with a feeling of deviation may alter the child's response to his own body.[9] This occurred with Chester and Sheila, who became obese after their preschool years. By contrast, some initially hyperactive, ectomorphic boys who feel inadequate because of their small size, who are acutely sensitive to stimulation, and who are explosive or demanding during their early years, change as they mature, as they gain in weight, and as they gain control of their bodies and of the environment. The former sensitivity is then utilized for increased insight, which evidently combines with improved control to produce reflectiveness, considerateness, and increased social adaptation, as we saw in Terry.

Situational changes and subjective responses[10]

In the coping study we saw some children switch from "frozen" responses to new experiences to free-flowing responses after they became oriented. Darlene, inhibited to the point of withdrawal during her initial observation of others energetically performing feats she felt she could not manage, would make repeated efforts and yell in triumph after a period of fearful observation led to cognitive mastery (Murphy 1962, pp. 168–70).

Rachel was passive and withdrawn to an extreme in all unstructured situations that required initiative of which she was incapable, but in the familiar medical examination and adult-directed body photo situation as well as in the structured and guided Witkin session with embedded figures (three-dimensional) she was proudly effective. We have seen other children who were more at ease and spontaneous in structured situations as opposed to those who needed open, free, situations in order to be most spontaneous and creative.

Changes in a child's "personality"—including measures of imagination, cooperation, sympathy, aggression, and IQ—were illustrated in detail by "Betsy" when she was shifted from a group in which she was youngest and smallest to a group in which she was oldest if not biggest (Murphy 1937). From being inhibited and uncooperative she became active and outgoing, with improvement in social behavior of many kinds. Evidently her sense of relative competence in the new group contributed to self-assured freedom to participate, which she could not do earlier.

Changes in the larger environment

Molly's intense upset at the family discussion of moving to a new town when she was three years old can be seen in relation to her early (eight weeks) fear of strangers. But she found herself at home in the new setting after the family was resettled with familiar belongings in place (Murphy 1962, pp. 68–69). She took a later move in her stride in response to her parents' description of new opportunities, such as having her own horse.

Roddy, without a background of separation-anxiety or previous loss, responded to his parents' repeated moves by specializing, as it were, in orienting himself to the new place. Janice developed a somewhat similar way of using new resources, going to the weekend parties at each of two churches in her new town. While the loss-vulnerable Lennie slowly outgrew his nostalgia for Topeka, these other children maximized the opportunities provided by new environments. We can examine some of these situations in more detail below.

Major changes in environment sometimes bring new opportunities that are exploited by emerging drives, as when Trudy and Molly moved from a middle-western city to a western community where it was more feasible to have their own horses. At the puberty stage when many children are floundering, beset by pressures from inner-body changes, ambivalence about growing up, and insecurities about the new demands of heterosexual social life, the energies of these vital girls were happily absorbed in caring for and enjoying their horses. The intense joy of this preoccupation gave way by the end of high school to appropriate responsiveness to boys, and to early marriages; only after they had established emotional independence from their families and their home life with their mates was settled, did they become committed to college education. The sequence of these steps might have been very different if they had not moved to the "horse country."

Repeated moving involves another level of change and adjustment: Roddy's family moved five times during his childhood. He entered junior high school shortly after one such move and was soon elected president of his class. When I asked him how he managed when he came to a new town, he said, "Well, I watch the others to see how they do things here, and then I do it their way." This repeated or even chronic need to focus on the external situation can interfere with time for internalization, sinking in roots, and development of a stable commitment to vocation or life-style. Thus Roddy identified closely with a medical uncle when he was within that uncle's range of influence and expressed his intention to become a doctor, a realistic goal in view of his good intelligence; subsequently this image gave way to a local peer-group level of less ambitious goals, and he became a garage mechanic. Riesman's "outer-directed" personality may develop in this way.

But moving to a new home does not always bring new interests. Lennie's family moved from Topeka to an industrial town farther east when he was five, and for the next few years the previously exuberant Lennie expressed his nostalgia for Topeka; he felt it was a better town, it was safer, it had better police. However, when the family enjoyed an opportunity to share a summer cabin in the woods on a lake not too far from their new home, the motor-boating and hunting offered compensations that helped him to overcome his nostalgia.

Changes in response to special stress

The child's changed situation as growth and changing environment proceed is also altered by unpredictable events such as illness and its sequelae, disasters such as the 1951 flood and the 1966 tornado, losses from death or divorce of parents, changing satisfactions and frustrations in school and with friends.

All these experiences involve stress that the normal child meets with some combination of pain and growth. We do not say "trauma" unless there is some prolonged or permanent loss of strength and coping capacity. The depth of pain depends on the relation of the child's previous vulnerability to the intensity, extent, and duration of the stress. Lennie was sad at the divorce of one set of grandparents but almost overwhelmed at the divorce of the second pair of grandparents within a year. He had earlier been unhappy about leaving Topeka when the family moved out of state. Still earlier at the age of three he had been upset about leaving his mother (cf. Murphy 1962, pp. 42–44). And as a sturdy infant of nine months he had ceased to thrive when his mother returned to work. The grandparents' divorces, then, struck his weakest point, separation anxiety. After his first deep sorrow at his grandparents' divorces, Lennie responded to this double loss by greater seriousness and reflectiveness—a thoughtfulness that is not an uncommon development at adolescence, but was especially impressive in a boy who used to say, "I gotta run." Gradually he was able to accept the divorces and to recognize that his grandfather, at least, was happier in his new marriage.

Vulnerable phase, stress, and adaptational crisis

Susan's transition from being "special" to being "a regular girl" would have involved some difficulties under any circumstances. The heroic good sport who burlesqued her chin-to-hip cast so delightfully that other people were amused had naturally been the center of much attention. To be a regular girl free from tags of past stress transcended meant the loss of this attention. Making this transition at the same time she entered a new school meant in addition that no one even knew what she had gone through and triumphed over; they could not know, either, the source of residues of insecurity, anxiety, and fears of being ridiculed or stared at—as had happened earlier when an occasional child called her a cripple or teased her. Along with the necessity of coping with mixed feelings of relief and insecurity, she had the typical emotional instabilities of a prepuberty girl in the phase before a maturing physiological system completes its own transition. Her stand-pat refusal to take on new social activities seemed a healthy way to cope with the multiple stress she had to manage, although it was a marked change from her earlier—and later as well—outgoing responsiveness. She was effectively fending off demands which at that time felt excessive. This is an example of vulnerability related to a developmental phase (puberty) compounded by sensitivity related to long physical threat and by environmental stress at the transition to junior high—stress that created anxiety for many preadolescents. Susan's temporary useful withdrawal was followed by vigorous social activity when she entered college. After graduation she obtained a well-paying job and supported her newly acquired husband in graduate school. From being the lovingly cared-for child she became the devotedly caring-for wife. Susan's insistence on finding her own way in her own good time is probably consistent with Escalona's prediction that she would impose her own organization on the environment.

Sequelae of traumata and deprivation

We may consider as additional complex interactional factors stimulating change through learning and coping efforts the sequelae of subjective and objective traumata, privations, or deprivations. This is especially true when, for instance, an illness of Sally's mother imposed stress and when a death in the family or other source of family disruption intervened to destroy the basic stable child-in-the-environment growth matrix. These disruptions were especially disturbing to certain children when they occurred at a time of developmental change, as during shifting phases of psychosexual development, or during shifts in the environment (however routine) such as entering grade school or changing to junior high school. Teddy's parents separated as he left the preschool stage—a time when suppression and repression become part of the child's repertoire of coping and defense mechanisms. "I've had two lives," he said later. "And I've tried to forget the first—" This repressing pattern served to support his development in other ways.

An accumulation of stress brings, in some cases, changes in the child's level of adaptation and capacity to maintain his usual style of functioning. In our group, depression, exhaustion, or illness in mothers who have earlier been supportive have been followed by drastic changes in the child's style and level of adaptation and even in IQ level.

Still different are those changes consciously initiated by the child himself, as with children who take over the task of modifying their appearance, or with Joyce, who said in early adolescence, "When I was ten I decided to stop being shy." [11] Here self-awareness, assessment, and flexibility take over.

Critical phases

Certain critical or sensitive phases are generally recognized, as, for example, the infants' "eighth-month anxiety" sensitivity to separation from the mother (Spitz 1946; Yarrow 1964), which develops earlier in some infants and lasts varying lengths of time, often through the second year (Robertson 1970). We also recognize critical phases for the emergence, focus, or escalation of drives that need appropriate support if they are to be integrated into normal development. When simultaneous or closely sequential events add cumulative threats to two or more sensitive developmental zones, serious interference with psychic development may occur, as with Rachel. Being confined to a crib (to protect her from infecting her eczema sores) at the stage when new locomotion skills ordinarily support a strong autonomy drive, she failed to develop the independence and initiative characteristic of most of the other children. She was thenceforth immobilized in free, unstructured situations, though compliantly cooperative in her pediatric examination and other adult-directed situations. While still confined to her crib she was abruptly removed to a hospital at the time of the 1951 Topeka flood, which probably reinforced her passive withdrawn reactions to new situations (Murphy 1962, pp. 32, 33, 55). Rachel was obedient but she could not cope without support.

The role of a predisposition to anxiety and conflict

We saw that the child's primary adaptational style in infancy will be largely shaped by the sensitivity, activity level, and reactivity pattern, as these influence goals and persistence toward goals, affect range and intensity, and predisposition to anxiety. Related coping patterns and precursors of defense mechanisms also participate in shaping the early style. Moreover, the interaction of all these tendencies will contribute to different needs and will also predispose the child to certain conflicts more than others, such as the conflict between pleasure and displeasure in tactile stimulation for a child who experiences both in response to similar stimuli. These same factors will also shape the pattern of evolution of the conflict.

Moreover, a child with a marked predisposition to conflict or anxiety, and to the heightened sensitivities that accompany this, may be expected to have more difficulty in achieving an integrated image of the mother. She is more likely to be associated both with painful and with less gratifying experiences than is the case with a balanced, less sensitive, and more serenely functioning child. This difficulty in achieving positive integration of the experience with the mother will affect the pattern of the child's identification; it may, as in Daryl's case, contribute to a more symbiotic dependence and demandingness, rather than to an identification that releases the child for autonomy.

This same process will also likely involve a greater tendency toward projection and distortion in cognitive responses to the environment, as contrasted with the more genuinely autonomous ego functioning found in the more balanced, well-functioning infant. The latter is not so flooded with biochemical products of autonomic upheaval when over-stimulated.

Now it might be expected that a corollary of this interaction that produces an anxious, hostile, and sometimes clinging child would be that an extremely serene interaction with the mother would produce an optimal foundation for later development. But serenity in infancy is no guarantee of healthy development in subsequent years either. For an extremely serene and constantly gratified infancy may not stimulate coping resources, tolerance of frustration, or capacity to delay and to accept or find substitutes needed at later times of frustration and disappointment. It may not stimulate an active, creative effort to do something new with the environment. The initially very serene infant who has not developed enough coping resources may, like Barbie in our sample, be very disturbed when at a later time unaccustomed stress is experienced from the combination of inner and outer pressure.

However, another kind of interaction between the infant and the environment can be seen when we focus on the infants who showed extreme patterns at an early stage but who were exposed to stable, consistent environmental influences. In such instances the extreme pattern is apt to be exposed to pressure toward modulation toward the mean: for example, Terry had a high activity level, high tonus, high vocalizing, and tenseness but also showed a high responsiveness to the social environment (and thus a wish to remain a part of it, to identify with it). He had to learn to control his restlessness, talkativeness, and so on, especially after entering school, and he succeeded in doing so.

Sex-role conflict and parental pressure

Tomboy Sally, agile, skillful, energetic as any boy, and bright, yielded to her depressed mother's wish for a "feminine" little girl at the age of seven. While her IQ declined 30 points from preschool to prepuberty, she became versatile or even precocious in feminine pursuits, with elaborate hairdos by the age of twelve. She married early and had three children, closely rivaling her mother's productivity in children.

Pressure of cumulative conflicts

Chester had not been considered a vulnerable baby, but we saw him change from appropriately active behavior in preschool and early latency to a period of impulse-explosion or destructive "disintegrative reactions" at the prepuberty stage. This outburst of hostile impulses came at a time when unresolved conflicts had mounted one upon the other. He was previously an active, somewhat stoic preschool coper in all the situations in which we saw him—so delightfully effective and boyish that we underestimated the depth of his sex-role conflict. We had glimpses of it in his mother's report that he liked to play with his older sister's jewelry and in his facial resemblance to his mother, but our observations of very masculine behavior seemed to overshadow those clues. However, in Winnicott's "Squiggle" interview[12] at the age of twelve, his wish to be a girl emerged clearly. His father had seemed closer to his younger brother, who did not resemble their mother, and sibling conflicts were intense from time to time, along with the complex oedipal conflict. Approaching puberty accentuated all these interwoven and cumulative conflicts. Chester's attacks on his sisters, his nearly delinquent behavior at school, and the deterioration of his schoolwork as he got beyond the grade level his father had reached, all in different ways reflected his struggle for masculinity and identification with his father. He was so responsive to a male member of the research staff that an extended series of Saturday activity sessions in which he created one after another masculine symbols, from a slingshot to a retaining wall, led to a firm masculine identification and apparent dissolving of the conflicts. He finished high school and one year of college. He is married now with two children, working as a mechanic, much like his father.

The transitory explosion of aggressive impulses—which might actually have led to Chester's delinquency—can be described as a disintegrative reaction (Menninger 1954) to the mounting pressure of multiple conflicts at a time of physiological instability. To us, "disintegrative reaction" is a more accurate term than "regression," since the latter connotes regressing to a previous primitive level of functioning, whereas Chester had not been a conspicuously aggressive child earlier—although his mother had remarked on a tendency to be irritable.

His essential healthiness, capacity to respond to relevant support, opportunities to cope with his need to find a masculine identity, and his available resources for developing masculine skills, contributed to his positive change and to the achievement of a newly integrated approach to his life (Morgan 1964; Morrow 1965).

Environmental stress during physiological change

Gordon was seen as a somewhat vulnerable baby but enjoyed an active vigorous preschool development. However, he became depressed at puberty when physiological instability was combined with stressful changes in his family as his father went through three divorces within a few years. Then he regained his equilibrium as adolescence brought increased height, strength, success in sports, and popularity with peers, and as his father settled into a new and more stable marriage. We saw other instances of collapse of morale in young adolescents when home stress accelerated simultaneously with the child's physiological instability and change.

Sources of change related to vulnerability

The infant may be constantly pressured to change, not only by the conflicting forces involved in constitutionally given imbalances and variabilities, but also by other factors in vulnerability such as sensitivites and ambivalences. We saw that ambivalence appears in that early situation when an infant finds satisfaction in a given area such as tactile stimulation or rhythm but all too easily becomes overstimulated (p. 83). Discomfort results from the same type of stimulus given too long or at too great an intensity. The resulting intrinsic conflict could be seen in some members of our sample to contribute to a predisposition to ambivalence in the intrapsychic sense and also to frustration, since the child is torn between wanting to approach and wanting to avoid.

There can also be a difficult if not destructive interaction of continuities and change-capacities that creates coping difficulties. However, in certain instances, this complexity provides the "anlage" for an active effort that eventuates in creativity, as we saw in three of our most creative subjects, who gave us interesting surprises.

Relation of change to phase-typical resources and vulnerability

We have seen sources of change in the relation of the developmental phase to unpredictable events such as illnesses, accidents, operations, and other body experiences that directly bring changes in the level of energy or in specific capacities and indirectly bring new reactions, struggles, and anxieties. The outcome of the child's struggle with these changes is not easily predicted and in our group could be observed to be related not only to the functions attacked by the event, but also to the stage of drive development that emerged just *after* the stressful event as well as to the deprivation or, in some instances, to the stimulus occasioned by the trauma.

We saw the sequelae of illness disturb the child's functioning, interfere with learning, and disrupt control, as with Lennie, who became hard of hearing after ear infections during the period of acquisition of speech. This impediment interfered with Lennie's normal sequences of development, as seen in his inadequate speech, which in turn was evidently responsible for inadequate concept-formation and the lack of necessary prerequisites for progress in reading.

We saw that when incapacitating illness occurs at a critical phase of drive development, it may prevent normal drive contributions. Rachel's decreased activity and markedly inhibited initiative appeared to be a consequence of her months of immobilization in bed with eczema during the period (nine to twenty-one months) when most children are developing autonomy. Illness may also prevent normal environmental support for important steps in socialization; polio in the preschool stage and years of slow rehabilitation limited Susan's contacts with peers. And in Ray's case, we saw illness produce regression to extremely infantile behavior, while recovery was followed by aggression not seen before.

Illness sometimes mobilizes extra effort toward mastery when it is followed by a stimulating phase, as happened with Ray whose illness preceded the development of the phallic phase with its usual competitive overflow of aggressive, imaginative, and play energies. In other instances, the challenge and support during illness or operations, or the compensations provided afterward, evoked a new level of self-esteem and warm appreciation of the environment, as with Helen and Susan.

At the preschool stage we saw five extremely active children, four boys and one girl. With these children physiological conditions related to illness or functional difficulties were associated with their temporary hyperactivity: upper respiratory illnesses followed by hearing loss in one boy; early infection accompanied by a convulsion in another; poor gastrointestinal functioning and nutrition in two others; and a combination of the latter with upper respiratory infections in the girl. All, after much improvement in health, had achieved surprising control and modulation of the early hyperactivity by the time of the prepuberty examinations; three were among the most ambitious children in our group and another was one of the most creative. The fifth was unusually considerate and socially responsible.

On the surface, the behavior of these children changed. Yet when we consider the factors involved in early hyperactivity, the medical help given, and the children's own efforts toward control and socialization, each child was dynamically consistent in his own way.

Factors contributing to fixation

We know that patterns evolved at any of the developmental phases may become relatively fixed and persist beyond the age at which this behavior is considered appropriate for children in our culture. This may happen under the influence of a combination of factors such as deprivation at the given stage; excessive reinforcement; traumatic illness, separation from parents, or other trauma; or sensitivity to parental disapproval of phase-typical behavior. This fixation may block the transition to the next stage.

Moreover, the degree of anxiety experienced by the child during the period when new capacities are emerging and are still insecurely established is often important as a factor in the susceptibility to disturbance in the new function, and to a degree of fixation that sometimes interferes with a shift to the next phase (Greenacre 1952). A mild degree of fixation so that progress is not wholly consistent with the culturally expected sequence was seen in Donald, whose mother did not want to give up her "last baby." However, school and sports later loosened his infantile ties and in adolescence he insisted on going his own way.

Fixations of shorter or longer duration, then, contribute secondary factors to the primary genetically controlled factors in continuity. The persistence that underlies the subsequent consistency (or resistance to expected developmental change) does not help the child to cope with new cultural demands, although it may be used by the individual child in subsequent sublimations or other adaptations to cultural opportunities. For example, persistent unsatiated oral demand led one of our children to resourceful ways of getting prizes at annual fairs. Another girl considered a greedy infant developed a craving for jewelry and clothes, then multiple social activities.

Variability and change

Change can also be seen when a constitutional characteristic of variability is the outcome of factors related to high reactivity. These factors include low thresholds for motor responses to inner or outer stimulation; low thresholds in one or more sensory areas; tendencies for thresholds to be lowered when new skeletal, muscular, or emotional aspects of maturation are in process; and poorly stabilized vegetative functions, autonomic functions, or affective responses. We infer from observations of our sample as well as from clinical observations that such organismic sources of variability make it hard to achieve cohesion of the ego (the organizing, integrative center) and integration of the personality as a whole. With intrinsic variability, changing external and internal stimuli would be expected to produce more change in behavior patterns through periods of time than we see in more cohesive constitutions.

The range of variability in certain zones, moreover, indicated the scope of changes possible in a child who fluctuated "from stony negation to feminine coyness" within a few moments in the same situation; this moment-to-moment variability persisted through childhood.

Variability that is secondary to disequilibrium of the organism decreases when recovery from illness or relief from stress contributes to a more stable equilibrium. This occurred in the area of cognitive functioning with one boy, in autonomic functioning with another, and in numerous children seen in variously optimal to stressful situations. However, flexibility as a positive expression of adaptive variability can also increase with age, as happened in two children who were constricted at the preschool stage but who became more responsive and expressive later.

Even when we grant the possibility of decrease or increase in the developmental or situational variability in one or another zone of functioning, the range within which change can occur may be relatively limited for each individual. Without the possibility of testing under conditions of exposure to overwhelming stress on the one hand, and to optimal opportunities on the other, we cannot know the potential range of change for any individual. For instance, if Lew, a brother of one of the study girls, had not been exposed to the trauma brought by the fire that killed his playmate, we might never have seen the tic he developed.

Subjective aspects of change

Children subject to acute illness must experience more variations in subjective states in conjunction with the bodily discomforts accompanying illness than children whose sense of well-being is rarely disturbed by the pain or discomfort of illness. What is absorbed into the self-image and the orientation toward life will depend in part on the support, comfort, and compensation given to the child. One little girl, repeatedly ill during her early years, felt that "bad things can turn into good things" (cf. p. 332), evidently as an outcome of the warm consolation offered by her grandmother and similar "good" experiences provided to "make up for" bad ones. Such sequences can contribute to attitudes that become formulated into beliefs, and these in turn stabilize the adaptive orientation of the child.

Other subjective aspects of change include the child's new awareness evoked by bodily and cognitive maturation—consciousness of size, of getting bigger, as we saw with JoAnne who announced, "Write JoAnne Jackson—growing up." Becoming one of the big people who go to school can be a source of pride. Leaving childhood behind at twelve or thirteen brought anxiety and increased seriousness to some children; awareness of new responsibility took the place of earlier dependency and was reinforced by opportunities for effort, choice, decision, work, and influence on the environment. Such changes were notable with Lennie and others in contrast to some whose conflicts held them enmeshed in tense, rebellious dependency.

The role of social learning

Factors contributing to change include those predictable and unpredictable consequences of everyday interaction with the environment, the outcomes of day-by-day learning, adapting, and coping efforts of the individual, and the accompanying unconscious defensive operations that become automatized into defense mechanisms. Change is particularly visible when the latter have included conspicuous reaction-formations against strong aggressive or sexual tendencies; that is, when, as with two of our girls, the aggressive four year old stops grabbing and hitting and becomes generous and sympathetic, and when, as in Brennie's case, sublimations rechannel and modulate the aggression (see also Murphy 1956, vol. 2).

We have seen examples of modulation of aggressive impulses with the help of useful defense mechanisms, by the revision of behavior patterns resulting from active coping and mastery efforts, and by the conscious modulation of response in accord with imposed social demands. "We have rules!" exclaimed my six-year-old neighbor while delightedly explaining what school was like. And when talkative Terry said, "The teacher hits your hand when you talk," I asked, "What then?" "You learn not to talk," Terry replied matter-of-factly, as if I ought to have known. Discipline was often taken for granted: "I'd rather have the spats than write a hundred sentences after school," Teddy insisted. And Chester explained, "They punish you because they want you to grow up right." We must remember that discipline, though firm, was a small part of the gratifying family life as we mentioned earlier.

Steps in progress may be subject to regression to an earlier level, or to failure or breakdown in a disintegrative loss of control and coherent function, and this variability is not necessarily undesirable. Moriarty (1961) shows how regression is used playfully, or restfully and comfortably, by some children in ego-syntonic ways, while some disintegrative reactions are shown to be typically a source of discomfort. In any case, as development proceeds the combination of new levels of complex functioning, together with the possibility of comfortable regression or uncomfortable disintegrative response, extends the spectrum of adaptive resources.

Interaction of change and continuity

Changes brought by maturation, and by new integrations made possible by maturation, include the replacement of early undifferentiated forms of response by complex forms. For instance, the infant's first crude motor-approach efforts are supplanted by well-directed grasping and manipulative capacities (White, Castle, and Held 1964). Primitive babbling evolves into differentiated syllables, first used as signals then combined into words and phrases (McCarthy 1954). Diffuse or explosive aggressive reactions are modulated and channeled into socially acceptable expressions. But the problem of studying continuity and change is complicated by the fact that often the later emergent function has no clear analogue in the early behavior of the child, and the fact that so many early behavior characteristics are outgrown as mature behavior emerges. Helen exhibited elaborate and varied mouthing behavior as an infant. In her case some continuity could be discerned—beneath or through the manifest changes—as the sequences of her efforts toward gratification were followed through successive stages. The very aspect of "elaboration" could be seen in the multiplicity of ways she provoked contact and responses from others when a preschool child, in the many prizes she captured at county and state fairs at the puberty stage, and in her variety of interests. The range of her devices to deal with needs for obtaining gratification, and the energy she displayed, persisted. This continuity in one underlying aspect of style persisted not only through the obvious changes brought by the maturation of skills, but also through her impressive modulation of what was experienced by some adults as her aggressiveness in the preschool years; from being a provocative "nuisance," she became an unusually refined, sensitive, and appealing young person. While this transformation might be regarded as an expression of reaction-formation, she remained outgoing, expressive, warm, and vital in her relationships with us. Her subtlety was perhaps related to her very differentiated, elaborated forms of mouthing. She could make distinctions at the action level that permitted her to be more flexible and discriminating in social behavior than was the case with some other children.

While a persistent constitutional characteristic may show continuity and provide the basis for a predictable style of functioning as long as the environment accepts this style without evoking marked frustration or conflict, nonacceptance may bring changed orientations. Thus one boy who lived in a rather isolated rural area seemed to experience little challenge or threat because of his slow, dull style of response. Another boy who went to a school attended by more active children, many of whom were of a higher socioeconomic status, encountered much more of a challenge, to which was added the teasing of his aggressive older brother. His early trust and contentment gave way to discouragement and feelings of helplessness.

Continuity within change and change within continuity

There are dangers in drawing inferences regarding continuity or consistency in general and also regarding change on the basis of one or a few variables. Change often occurs in one zone of behavior while others maintain continuity. We saw earlier that Escalona's predictions of certain traits were confirmed while others were contradicted (chapter 5). The activity level of some children remained high while the surface level of cognitive functioning as evaluated by intelligence tests changed. One child's level of cognitive functioning remained high (IQ around 140) while she changed from an open, emotional responsiveness to a guarded, reserved way of handling her feelings.

Moreover, forms of expression of reaction changed while the essential reaction continued. Sheila protested loudly, vociferously, and decisively as an infant; at three she was equally decisive in her unequivocal "no!"; by age ten she could cooperate yet still convey her clear negative reaction by "making a face." In other words, feelings and attitude patterns could persist in very different forms. Similar shifts in mode of expression were seen in other children.

Along with tendencies toward shift in drive hierarchy and in forms of drive expression, we can expect to find certain continuities. The merely gay infant may become the four-year-old showoff, to be sure; but the quality of vividness of expression or of social responsiveness may remain much the same. The quiet six-month-old infant boy becomes the outstanding baseball player while the quality of smooth coordination persists (as with Vernon).

So we can sort out basic characteristics of the style of the organism and of responses to the environment underlying the increasing variety of new behaviors available to the growing child as he responds at successive developmental levels to changes in the environment. The environmental changes include changes in the structure of the family and thus in the child's relation to different persons in it, changes in the health, energy tolerance, and capacity of each parent to deal with family demands; changes in school structure and in school demands, and changes in peer-group values at successive stages. Many of these changes might not be reflected in behavior during testing if the immediate test situation evoked a continuity of behavior quite unrelated to the pressures of peer group and of family life with which the child is coping in new ways.

We have seen the distillation of an anticynical life theme in Helen's "bad things can turn into good things." Equally impressive was the emergence of a glow of triumph in Darlene, and though not articulated verbally, in Susan's glow through and after her conquest of polio. From "a nice healthy normal baby" she became an unusually radiant and sparkling personality. These are illustrations of the contribution to development that results from the child's effective coping with vulnerability and stress.

Conclusion

Doubtless much of this chapter sounds like pathology to pathology-minded readers. Yet as we noted earlier, these children are similar to a sample of 400 Texas school children, as well as to a sample of 100 sixth-grade children in Topeka. What we are describing is the spectrum of normal vicissitudes of children growing up in our culture—the "human condition" of childhood if you will. What is important here is that the children were able to struggle through, to cope by taking their time and by temporary withdrawal as Susan and others did; by sacrificing of part of their self as Sally and Teddy did; by flexibly responding to new opportunities as Trudy and Chester did; by even "greedily" making the most of all the environment offered as Janice did; by accenting the positive as Helen did; by gently asking for help as Lennie and Terry did; by temporary regression, then making up for lost time as Ray did; and by many other ways of coping with their vulnerabilities and environmental pressures. What kept them normal was their capacity to confront stress with their own resources, even allowing for transitory periods of withdrawal or regression or disintegrative reactions. They—and many other children like them—could not be understood without giving "equal time" to these flexible coping capacities.

PART III
INTERPLAY OF VULNERABILITY, STRESS, AND RESILIENCE

8

Toward Understanding Normal
Vulnerability

I felt like life was not worth living.

Teenage Janice, judged the most vulnerable infant in the intensive coping sample, in reaction to JFK's assassination. No other teenager experienced such an upsurge of despair in response to this tragedy.

I

We have been looking at questions of stability and plasticity in the development of the children we studied. During our exploration of plasticity we were confronted by the outcomes of the child's coping experiences and also the role of the child's vulnerability in contributing to change. Coping capacity depends on the resources of the child and the relation of the child's strengths to the child's vulnerability to threats and obstacles. We saw examples of difficulties in coping related not only to limited resources but to vulnerability to specific kinds or quantities of stimulation or to slow recovery from disturbed reactions. We saw that problems and successes in coping influenced the direction and pattern of change. Thus, the problem of vulnerability in the normal child compelled our special attention, and this chapter will bring together our different approaches to this aspect of development, and its relation to the child's coping capacity. We shall also focus on one example of a vulnerable area fairly common in this culture, namely, speech.

"High-risk" babies are now receiving special care in many hospitals and from many pediatricians. We recognize that their respiratory or cardiac conditions and other congenital deficiencies threaten their lives unless they are carefully assessed and receive help from the beginning (Apgar 1953).[1] Babies and young children "at risk" for schizophrenia are also receiving special attention. The question arises then, if a baby is not at high risk, is it invulnerable? Does "normal" imply invulnerability?

These babies in our intensively studied Topeka group, originally selected as normal, all proved to have normal or superior intelligence and considerable coping capacity. But as we have seen, several of them needed some sort of help or therapy from adults outside the family before midadolescence, and at the critical prepuberty phase a majority had speech problems to some degree (p. 229). Their susceptibility to difficulties varied from one to another, so that we were forced to think of a "continuum of vulnerability." [2] Each member of the basic research group worked on the vulnerability problem from a somewhat different point of view. We can consider my 1959 Vulnerability Index of potentially relevant constitutional factors an approach to "primary general vulnerability." Heider's 1966 approach involved a broader view of the child in his environment, a Gestalt approach to vulnerability, while Moriarty focused on speech as a particularly vulnerable zone of functioning in this culture (see part II of this chapter). Finally, Toussieng's evaluation of vulnerability was concerned with evidences of mild disturbances in any area of the whole range of ego functions, disturbances which, because they evolved from developmental experiences, could be considered developmental vulnerability.[3] Our final Vulnerability Inventory was formulated on the foundation of all of these approaches; we did not attempt to freeze a scale, because we felt room should be allowed for further observations of children in different settings (Appendix 8).

Along the continuum of vulnerability, children may be distributed in different numbers: few if any are so robust, so completely lacking in small as well as moderate or major handicaps as to be totally free from some zone of vulnerability. Most children have a checkerboard of strengths and weaknesses, or an "Achilles heel," or a cluster of tendencies that interact in such a way as to produce one or another pattern of vulnerability as well as strength. Given an infant of greater or lesser initial adequacy, decreases in vulnerability depend on outcomes of interaction between this child and its environment and the extent to which these outcomes compensate for early deficiencies or allow for progress in mastery. Increases in vulnerability are seen when the interaction between the child and the environment results in new limitations or difficulties, new threats to homeostasis and to integration, new obstacles to learning, increased difficulties in mastering anxiety, or negative expectancies.

Secondary vulnerabilities often develop from self-defeating defense mechanisms, which in therapy can be revised by substituting others that support effective coping. Among random samples of school children, one often finds a child like Lennie whose limited primary visual defect coupled with a high activity level to form secondary vulnerabilities.

Secondary vulnerabilities resulting from developmental damage or from emotional reactions to the frustrations arising from handicaps have been increasingly avoidable as the difficulties of children with specific disease defects, or damage, have been recognized early, and expert ways of helping them have been developed. This applies particularly to deaf, blind, crippled, and cerebral palsied and other brain-damaged children. Therapeutic techniques for helping children who are obviously emotionally disturbed have also been refined within the last generation. But the needs, problems, and ways of helping children with subtle types of vulnerability are only recently under careful study.

Observations of infant vulnerability

Among our normal sample were some infants who had had mild birth difficulties; a few had been colicky[4] babies and were hard to comfort; some showed a labile pattern of autonomic reactivity or slow recovery from disturbance. Some were accelerated in certain areas and average or below their age level in other areas of development, and thus they found it hard to integrate the range of basic functions. Others had zones of high sensitivity (or reactivity to specific stimuli) or of highly ambivalent responsiveness—they were intensely pleased by one level or degree of stimulation, then displeased by a slightly more intense or different level of the same type of experience.

These babies had much in common with babies who at an older age are familiar to clinicians: children with behavior problems, psychogenically retarded (as a result of withdrawal from the environment in order to protect themselves from overwhelming stimulation), "neurotic," or predisposed to anxious, angry reactions to frustration, and so forth. But the problems in our group were milder and more transient. The difference between those who do and those who do not require psychiatric help may be one of degree, or of the child's and the family's capacity to deal with the difficulties.

It is important, then, to review in more detail the weaknesses and their sequelae, as these evolve from the interaction of all the tendencies within the child and his response to aspects of the environment that provide nutriment or support—or, conversely, pressures with which the child tries to cope. We shall discuss responses to stress, resilience, and outcomes of coping with vulnerability in chapters 9 to 11.

The importance of individual differences in *tolerance for stimulation* was seen in disintegrative threats that appear when an infant or young child with inadequate buffering against outside stimulation was exposed to a threat of being inundated by more stimulation than could be integrated or handled. The role of interacting internal and external influences is explicit here. The presence of unusual sensitivities to stimulation needs to be seen, moreover, in relation to Greenacre's concept of "predisposition to anxiety" (1952), which may at first consist (operationally) in the low thresholds predisposing an infant to overstimulation or painful experiences from an unmanageable environment, leading to distress, to disintegrative reactions, and, as the ego develops, to anxiety. The infant with unusual sensitivity is likely to be threatened by intense experiences and to have anxious and defensively hostile reactions to them; these in turn predispose the infant to disturbed interactions with the mother and other parts of the environment.

Individual differences in the degree of lability in cognitive functioning could not be thoroughly assessed in early infancy by the methods available when this study was first undertaken. By quantitative lability in cognitive functioning,[5] we refer to changes in IQ, or tested level of cognitive functioning, as this has been studied through the growth of the child (see Appendix 5). By qualitative lability, we refer to variations in specific functions, such as loss of perceptual clarity, the occurrence of confusion or distortion under stress, or disorganization of thought. We are familiar with these variations in severe mental illness, but they occur in smaller degrees in some children and adults under even moderate stress. Several of the children in our research sample showed a tendency to react to stress with mild disturbance of perceptual and other cognitive functioning, implying vulnerability to loss of control, integration, or ego-cohesion.

Variations in physical and emotional functioning

The lag in application of available techniques for studying both the equipment of the child in all its variations and the problems that his vulnerabilities present to himself, has meant a relative lack of data on the interaction of the entire gamut of constitutional and environmental factors. Pioneer efforts have largely dealt with a single variable such as "activity level" (Fries, and Woolf 1953), or "sensitivity" [6] or with a small group of variables dealing with physical and mental growth (Bayley (1949), considered independently. However, Escalona (1968), Alpert, Neubauer, and Weil (1956), and Ritvo (1963) have provided illustrations of interaction of a range of characteristics.

Individual differences in early integration

We came to realize—through study of both the records of mildly disturbed children and the infancy records of our normal sample—that the pathological tendencies found by Bender (1953) in the early histories of so many schizophrenic children are different chiefly in degree and number from difficulties seen in any random sample of infants.

We could, then, look for a continuum of differences in somatic integration in the earliest development of the organism. Our observations then led us to think of a continuum of vulnerability in broad terms and of the many factors that may contribute to it even at the mild level at which we could observe it. It is unusual, as a matter of fact, to see a child with optimal functioning in every area and optimal balance among different functions.

Evaluation of the level of functioning of children with obvious defects on the one hand, or with generally healthy development on the other, is not too difficult. It is harder to evaluate the seriousness of symptoms in preschool years when a mild or middle range of adaptive difficulties is frequently involved. Moreover, there has been too little study of the influence of physiological variations such as allergies, unusual vitamin and mineral needs, deviant functioning of any of the internal organs as described by Roger Williams (1956); any combination of these with other variations such as high autonomic reactivity or slow recovery time can contribute integrative difficulties.

Vulnerability continuum within our coping sample

We have noted that infants with defects detectable in the pediatric examination were excluded from the Escalona–Leitch study group. Moreover, at the time of the infancy observations there were no current severe physical illnesses or emotional disturbances. None of the infants were living in slums; none belonged to alienated, isolated families. None were members of minority groups. We had a relatively homogeneous sample within the normal range. Thus, what are usually considered "high-risk" infants on the sociocultural dimension, as well as on the organic dimension, were excluded at the start (cf. Drillien 1964). Still, during the fifteen years of our sequential studies, the children had their share of illnesses, accidents, operations, and other sources of stress. Beyond this, and despite their generally adequate level of health and well-being, we found various patterns of vulnerability and ways of handling vulnerability we had not foreseen. We found that most of these normal infants had to deal not only with moderate environmental frustrations, deprivations, and other normal expectable stress, but also with their own frailties. Thus we came to think in terms of differences in vulnerability to both external and internal stress. At one end, we would place the most vulnerable infant, frail, with poorly balanced capacities, and poor vegetative functioning. At the other end, we would place the relatively invulnerable baby, who is so robust, adaptable, active, and resilient that he can survive even considerable deprivation or mishandling (Garmezy 1971). Since extremes of defect and also likelihood of severe mishandling or marked deprivation were excluded from our group, we saw a rather narrow range of vulnerability; yet the very exclusion of extremes forced us to look more carefully, and to consider the implications of the child's subjective situation more patiently.

Once we saw the possibility that an accumulation of mild sources of difficulty or vulnerability could handicap a child's coping efforts, just as Bender (1953) saw how severe cumulative or interacting factors[7] contributed to grossly maladaptive development, we were led to the idea that a "vulnerability inventory" might be conceived. This would be made up of ratings on all aspects of individual equipment potentially relevant to vulnerability. The question of what is relevant could be answered only by further reflection upon characteristics discussed briefly in chapters 3, 4, and 7.

Characteristics contributing to vulnerability at the preschool stage

We can assume that a given aspect of equipment, such as activity level, will in and of itself tend to lead to certain kinds of experience that bring certain consequences of interaction and response from the personal and impersonal environment, with effects on the child leading to certain psychic resultants. This was demonstrated by Escalona (1968). If we assumed a linear relation, then the lowest activity level would lead to the lowest degree of such experiences with their psychic resultants and the maximal activity level would lead to the highest degree. However, some families make extra efforts to stimulate the passive baby, while some families try to quiet or calm down the excitable or very active baby.

We can also assume that the amount of the child's exploration, acquaintance with, and mastery of the environment, with resulting resources and self-confidence, would be related to the level of activity, since greater activity provides more opportunities for contact with the environment, learning about it, and experimenting in ways of dealing with it. As a result, a broader range of skills would be expected to develop, and in turn confidence could result. This is most true when a high activity level is combined with excellent coordination and smoothness of movement and control.

But our observations of the experiences of these children showed us that in this environment there was reason to question the assumption that a high activity level would produce only positive results for development. Some of the most active children were anxious about breakage or injury, resulting in a special need to set limits on their activity.

We were also forced to see that the resultants of a given constitutional tendency depend in part upon the relevant opportunities, threats, and limits in the environment and the values and sanctions in that environment. So we need to revise the assumptions in terms of the expectable results in a given setting. The outcome is always a product of interplay between the individual pattern of functioning and the impinging aspects of the environment.

We can now take the next step and state that in this culture an extremely high activity level may contribute to vulnerability, since it is very likely to expose a child to conflicts with the environment, with resulting punishment, guilt, and anxiety that would undermine the child's security and confidence. This actually happened with Terry, our most active child.

Once we acknowledge the hazards accompanying an extremely high level of activity, can we regard the rest of the scale, from a moderately high level of activity down to the minimal level of activity, as having a consistent relation to some specified outcomes? Our inspection of individual children again raises doubt about this. We find that Steve, with a low activity level, had, to be sure, limited acquaintance with the environment and in general a narrow range of mastered skills. Still he was not as limited as might be expected. This was in all probability due to several compensating factors. He was rather attractive, and being a quiet boy, he was not at all threatening to others; more active people reached out to him. He was quite able to participate when others took the initiative, and when it was possible for him to follow along. Furthermore, even while his activity level was low he was not lacking in other forms of response; his well-organized imagination contrasted with that of some of the more highly active (and impulsive) children. The fact that he did not have a constant, driving need for activity may have left him free for fantasy or clarification of inner thoughts. Moreover, he had other capacities, such as musical skills and some artistic flair. Here the lack of a driving need for activity allowed him time to develop skills in playing his instrument and in drawing. Not being very active may also have contributed to his interest in looking not only at near, but at distant areas; this was reflected in his interest in telescopes and in other visual devices by the time he became an adolescent. Thus he developed positive resources of his own, with a certain capacity for contentment and satisfaction even though he was limited in sports, in his capacity to defend himself physically against attacks from other boys, and in some other ways.

We have to say, then, that our consideration of the resultants from any one variable also has to take into account potential balancing factors. We have to be careful about terms like compensation, however. The interests developed by Steve were spontaneous and grew from his own talents and capacities. While they may have served a certain compensatory role, they did not originate because of a lack of something, but because he did actually have these positive resources, which were also congenial to his artistic family.

In other words, the effects of any one characteristic, even such a basic and important one as activity level, have to be seen in relation not only to the opportunities and demands from the environment, but also to the other resources of the individual child. Optimally, then, we would have to consider each variable in the context of the total resources of the individual child, as well as the total environmental situation in which the child is growing up.[8]

Now let us see whether this formulation seems to fit what we find in studying the effects of another tendency. For this purpose, we select "responsiveness to sensory stimulation," a tendency that may include thresholds for sensory stimulation but that focuses primarily on the motor, emotional, and autonomic responses to sensory stimulation.[9] Here it is not sufficient to say what amount of stimulation a child likes. We saw earlier that we have to distinguish between intensity and complexity, and even between specific qualities (pp. 81 f.). We found such incongruous and unanticipated reactions as these even among young infants: one baby was unpleasantly stimulated by a low sound, but pleasurably stimulated by a definite, moderately loud sound; some babies not only tolerated but actively enjoyed even very loud sounds; and some of them enjoyed making very loud sounds by banging tin pans, for instance, whereas others disliked such noisy activity. In other words, we cannot say that baby A will enjoy a soft sound or a low sound to a certain degree and then enjoy a louder sound more and a very loud sound still more. Some babies do not like the soft sound at all and some others do not like the very loud sound at all. Similarly, some other babies simply dislike certain *kinds* of sounds, such as those made by scratching with fingernails or chalk squeaking on a blackboard. Or in another modality, some babies dislike or feel frustrated by soft tactual contacts while they very much enjoy rough and tumble handling, or vice versa.

In other words, we found that a baby may have very strong positive reactions to certain levels or degrees of stimulation, and very strong negative reactions to other degrees of intensity, or kinds of stimulation, in the same modality. Sometimes, the difference is primarily a matter of duration, as when a small amount of tickling delights the baby, but a continuation proves overstimulating and overwhelming.

It was possible to rate the babies' overall reactivity to stimulation, a variable that referred to the tendency of the baby to be rather easily disturbed by sensory stimulation, whether this was a matter of the modality, intensity, or specific quality of stimulations. This recognizes that some babies are not easily disturbed by the ordinary range of stimulation in different modalities while others are very easily disturbed by one or more types of sensory experience.[10]

Now, it would seem that a tendency to be disturbed by sensory stimulation might be directly related to certain consequences. But from the previous discussion we can already see that the tendency to be disturbed by certain types of stimulation may exist in the same baby who also has a capacity for great pleasure from other types of stimulation. But when these exist as possibilities in the same modality and when a given baby is often exposed to both positive and negative experience in the tactile zone, for instance, we are likely to run into difficulty unless we keep both factors in mind. We then have to ask, what happens when a baby is responding part of the time with gratification and part of the time with disturbance to the same modality of stimulation? It is not surprising that this contributes to what we termed a *primary ambivalence*, nor is it surprising to find later expressions of ambivalence in children with this sort of early experience, and problems in relationship with others related to this basic ambivalence.

Contributions of coping resources

When we then looked for the effects of the tendency to be unpleasantly excited or disturbed by sensory stimulation, we saw wide differences in the capacities of different children to protect themselves from (to shut out, avoid, or reject) unwanted stimulation. Some babies from early weeks or months told the environment what they did not like in no uncertain terms (cf. p. 82). When the environment respects the message, this outcome can contribute to confidence in one's capacity to control the environment, to select what is gratifying, and to cope with the kinds of unpleasant stimulation present in a given environment. At this point, then, we are in the same situation described earlier when we discussed activity level: that is, the effects of a given tendency depend very much on the way in which this tendency is handled both by the child and by the environment.

If we turn, now, to the effects of positive and pleasurable responses to sensory stimulation, what do we find here? Looking again at our babies individually we notice that one baby who responded with positive gratification and pleasure to a given type of sensory experience seems easily satisfied and contented; while with another baby the experience of gratification seemed to lead to an insatiable desire for more. Then what happens? One child who constantly wants more may appear rather resentful at not obtaining it and develop a pattern of grabbing gratification when and where it can be found. Another one (chapter 11) elaborated and multiplied her own resources for obtaining gratifying experiences and never seemed to show the resentment at frustration shown by the other child. Even here, then, we have to look at the child's needs in relation to the resources that the child himself brings to his interaction with the environment.

It is clear that for an adequate understanding of the consequences of a given tendency, or constellation of tendencies, which might be assumed to contribute to strength or to vulnerability, we have to study the individual children intensively. To understand the outcomes of early vulnerability we have to focus on the interaction of different weaknesses and also on the interaction of the vulnerability pattern with the environment and with the child's strengths or resources for managing his vulnerabilities in the environment.

At each step in development we can expect the outcomes to contribute to new emerging patterns of greater or lesser vulnerability or strength, which in turn jeopardize or protect the next step in development. For example, Marjory (a child observed by me in her growing up years), a somewhat fragile baby girl of unusual responsiveness to visual, auditory, tactual, and social stimuli, evoked delighted interest and stimulation from her two young intelligent parents. While she was at times overstimulated by her adoring father, she was able to retreat and went to sleep easily for naps and at nighttime. She flourished on her mother's milk and care until she was weaned at eleven months. At this critical stage, her mother, now pregnant and nauseated, could no longer give the baby the intimate attention to which she was accustomed. At this time the approach of a stranger, or leaving her home, or almost any new experience aroused anxiety, and the formerly gay baby became recurrently anxious, though still happy and gay with her accustomed father–baby play. When left alone she turned to exploring in the grass and shrubs around her house, carefully examining leaves, blades of grass, and flowers that pleased her. This exercised her resource of perceptual responsiveness, which was further reinforced when her mother became preoccupied with a handsome baby boy, and again a year or so later when her father took her on walks and encouraged her observations.

Independent as the little girl now appeared to be, her visual interests did not adequately substitute for the place on her mother's lap of which she had been deprived. She wanted to be picked up and played with by relatives and visitors but—as happened earlier—easily became overstimulated and had to retreat. This led to ambivalence regarding close physical contact and a complex pattern of eager hopefulness with anxious shyness that continued into adolescence along with her active pattern of alert observation, independence, and retreat to sleep.

This is a very condensed summary of interaction between some of the primary coping resources and vulnerabilities of a baby and her parents' responses and deprivations. It illustrates a combination of reinforced vulnerabilities balanced by a combination of coping with deprivations by emphasis on available independent satisfactions, while the child alternately evoked and retreated from the closeness she both craved and feared. Such patterns are not unusual—"normal" people often have comparable balances of strength and weakness that both contribute to and help them to deal with their problems.

Approaches to the Study of Vulnerability

Correlation of Pilot Vulnerability Index rating with other variables

Early in our studies we developed an inventory of coping resources (chapter 4). It became clear that we also needed to clarify patterns contributing to vulnerability.

At first we assumed that a Vulnerability Index—*based on the sum of ratings on extremes, limitations, or imbalances of basic sensory, motor, cognitive, and affective equipment*—should correlate *negatively* with ratings on *positive* variables dealing with coping capacities (Appendix 4). Actually the score on the Vulnerability Index did correlate −.62 with boys' Coping I (see p. 401), the overall capacity to deal with the environment. This implies that the greater the number of tendencies indicated by the extreme (low or high, as the case might be) characteristics checked in the Vulnerability Index, the greater the child's tendency to have difficulty in dealing with the environment.

The Vulnerability Index score for each child also correlated −.54 with Coping II, the capacity to maintain internal integration. Some children succeeded in dealing with the environment at the price of limitations in maintaining internal integration.

In addition to the evaluations of global Coping I and Coping II we had prepared a comprehensive list of 643 variables (Comprehensive Coping Inventory, or CCI, see Appendix 4) and it seemed desirable to use this first tentatively validated Vulnerability Index score to sort out other variables potentially either positively or negatively related to this score on the Vulnerability Index. Positive correlations would provide clues to other possible factors in vulnerability. Negative correlations would point out tendencies that might offset vulnerability. When we correlated the Pilot Vulnerability Index with CCI we found positive correlations of .51 to .72 with certain items, such as impulsiveness, spread of affect, frequency of disintegrative reactions to stress, gives up easily at failure, feelings of rejection.

We found that the Pilot Vulnerability Index score, as constructed in terms of aspects of equipment, sorted out other items that had to be seen at another level: that is, problems in control of affect and behavior, and in integration; interaction problems such as management difficulties; internal problems involving conflicts; and dystonic affects, which we had not seen as aspects of the child's constitution. We may think, then, of *primary vulnerability*, and *secondary vulnerability* developing out of the integration difficulties *contributed by interaction of primary vulnerabilities with one another and with the environment.* This list also includes a few closely related environmental characteristics that may be seen as directly or in a secondary way contributing to vulnerability. As we discussed above, a high activity level may lead to conflict with the environment, and the environment may respond with criticism, blame, or punishment; the latter may lead to feelings of rejection, guilt, or anxiety in the child. Over time, the tension level of the child may be raised, and the child may become preoccupied with moralistic concerns. These are only a few of the secondary outcomes of primary characteristics.

When the child has extreme sensitivities and other extreme aspects of functioning, the outcome of these for his development and integration will be closely related to the extent to which his self-management and his interaction with the environment reinforce, minimize, or compensate for his vulnerabilities. We saw earlier how Darlene's determination overcame the anxiety related to her poor coordination and difficulty in achieving motor skills. The progress of children with much greater handicaps, like Susan after her polio, or children with cerebral palsy or brain damage, also depends on the persistence of the child's effort to master the problem. Strong determination is supported by the child's expectation or hope as well as by the help of adults.

*The psychiatrist's ranking of children
on vulnerability*

Another approach among our explorations in vulnerability was made by evaluating the overall vulnerability of the children as they were seen by the psychiatrist at the preschool stage.[11] This will be referred to as the Psychiatric Vulnerability Rating or PVR. Here we find a somewhat different frame of reference from that of the specific developmental variables we have just been discussing. While the Pilot Vulnerability Index was based chiefly on variables having to do with *primary* tendencies such as basic motor, cognitive, and affective functioning, the characteristics or symptoms in the present group were assumed to be largely outcomes of the interaction between the child and the environment up to the preschool age, at which time the psychiatrist saw the child. His evaluation was completely independent of knowledge of any other records, including home experiences.

As an illustration of various ways of exploring a child's vulnerability and strengths we can describe Sally as she was seen in her early years. We begin with excerpts from a longer report by Dr. Povl Toussieng, child psychiatrist.

Sally is a sturdily built, well-nourished four-year-old girl, small for her age and with immature body contours. Her oval face with full cheeks and a high forehead is mobile and expressive, showing many shades of emotions. Whenever she gets preoccupied with something she presses her lips tightly together, which gives her an expression of extreme concentration.

Her movements are slightly jerky, yet decidedly feminine and effective. Her gross and finer coordination are excellent. Economy in the use of her muscles was apparent in whatever she did whether she hammered the pegs with crisp well-directed energetic blows or fed the So-Wee doll. She is skillful for her age at using both hands at the same time and is quite strong. Surprisingly enough, her postures often are awkward, angular, uncomfortable. They never become completely adjusted, free, and functional. Desite this apparent handicap her balance remains good at all times and she is remarkably agile whenever she changes from one thing to another . . . capable of fast starts and of rapid movements whenever this is required. Yet, she gets easily fatigued and her coordination then suffers. For example, she hit her fingers several times as her play with the pegboard was carried too far, while this never occurred in the beginning.

Her voice is firm, high, flexibile, expressive with definite enjoy-ment of sing-song verbalizations and many shades of emotions. Her speech is well-enunciated, clear, easy to understand despite her many infantile mispronunciations and infantile syntax. She said, "cool" for "school"; "dat" for "that" (being unable to say "th" in general) and made sentences like, "Dey gone." Sometimes she pronounces words better than at other times.

At first Sally carefully stayed away from everything until I had suggested that she approach it. . . . Yet, she never became overly compliant, making it very clear that she was a person in her own right who chose to cooperate. . . . As the session progressed and she felt more at ease Sally seized the initiative and loudly announced her intentions. She thus bossed me around in a definite but friendly and unoffensive way but also could be assured at any time that I could stop her if I should disapprove of her activity. . . .

Her relationship to me was guarded only for a very short time and she soon went into a sharing and enthusiastic interaction with me. Yet the relationship was never permitted to become too personal and in an unobtrusive but very deliberate way I was kept at a distance by a constant subtle control.

Sally is a very sensitive girl in all areas, quickly noticing and enjoying details such as textures, shapes, colors of things. Yet she is even more sensitive in the auditory area, especially when she is not absorbed in some activity. When she is idle, sounds seemed to have a startling aspect. . . . She is one of the few children who reacted to Grace Heider turning a page, and she commented on the high school chimes and voices coming from downstairs. Most impressive was her noticing the absence of the sound from a falling peg whenever I caught it. When she hit her fingers with the hammer she also reacted strongly though she did not seem to mind the hurt so much. There was surprisingly little startle reaction when she played with the jack-in-the-box. No distortions of perception were noted.

Sally is preoccupied with the quality and function of things and with the performance of certain skills. Even in her conversation she was mostly sharing bits of information with me or asking for further details. At times she appeared to nearly "show off" with her knowledge, as when she disdainfully stated, "I know," when I said something which appeared superfluous to her. Fantasy material was totally and glaringly absent. That other preoccupations may have been in the background may be read into the fact that she almost exclusively spent her time playing with masculine aggressive toys and that she stressed size relative to herself rather often. . . .

Sally's emotional life covers a wide range and has many nuances but one could not help but feel in this session that it somehow lacked depth. Several times when she was caught off guard it also appeared that there is an underlying constantly present anxiety which may be the driving power behind her constant exploration of the environment. It is as if she wants to make sure that there are no dangers. It therefore appears that Sally can go through the motions as it were but that huge emotional concerns are left unsatisfied and displaced by a suppressed but considerable anxiety. Aggression was very much absent.

On first glance Sally appears efficient, self-sufficient, poised, fairly sure of herself and of her position in the world in relation to things and other people. Yet there is a remarkable contrast between her considerable coordination skills, her intelligence, and her infantile speech. This causes one to wonder whether this child is basically insecure not only about herself and her own accomplishments, but also about the relative safety of her world.

Sally's identification as far as dress and movements go is definitely feminine but her considerable play with masculine toys may indicate a basic insecurity in this area also. One got the feeling from seeing her feed the So-Wee doll that her mother is an efficient, solicitous person, who, however, doesn't bother much with expression of affection.

In summary, Sally appears to be a child who, despite a fairly efficient, adequate appearing facade and many assets such as great sensitivity, good intelligence, good coordination, considerable charm, and so on, still basically is quite insecure and emotionally immature for her age. It would appear unlikely that Sally as she appears now will be able to find a reasonably satisfactory solution to an oedipal struggle which as yet has not really begun, nor to her problems around her sibling rivalry and her completely suppressed aggression, especially toward an older brother.

Her awkward positions, her relatively quick fatiguability, her slight but unmistakable dysarthria [speech problem], and her restlessness of attention raise the question whether there may be some organic brain damage. Some of Sally's emotional difficulties may be explained as a direct consequence of such damage.

Since contamination of judgments had been prevented by consistently independent recording, Toussieng could not know that Sally's mother had been subject to depressions, had been separated from the baby at times, and had been disappointed that the vigorous little girl "might as well have been (another) boy," or that Sally had three brothers. His perception of some lack in the mother–child relationship was very accurate. His inference that this would lead to difficulties in resolving oedipal conflicts was reasonable. (Indeed, her mother's depression in Sally's seventh year, together with her closeness to her father, intensified this conflict. Moriarty's report showing an 18-point drop in IQ, loss of efficiency, clarity, and enthusiasm along with unprecedented confusion, reflected Sally's near-demoralization at that time. But by prepuberty she was intensely involved in feminine preoccupations and on the clustering she had shifted from the cognitive–motoric group at the preschool level to a group more emotionally open.)

Many of Toussieng's observations of competence were paralleled by Moriarty's independent record of Sally's behavior in preschool intelligence-test sessions; in addition, Moriarty illustrated in detail Sally's balance of cooperation with authority while also maintaining her own autonomy. Moriarty added in a review of Sally's reactions to success and failure that she seemed self-assured, accepted praise as her due, and openly remarked on her limits; faced with difficulty she offered alternatives or casually remarked on her inability to complete a task. Her cognitive efficiency was unimpaired by the insecurity inferred from her behavior. At the same time anxiety was suggested by Sally's deep sighs, dry coughing, tight lips, tension under pressure of speed, and difficulty in leaving mother. As of this stage neither Moriarty nor Heider considered Sally highly vulnerable; as a matter of fact, everyone was impressed by her vigor, efficiency, and self-assurance despite her anxiety.

My Primary Vulnerability Index focusing on constitutional characteristics and predispositions would also emphasize such points as Sally's vigor, activity, intensity, alertness, sensory sensitivity, affective reactivity, and lability. Her feeding behavior as an infant was seen as high in demand level, and also tendency to terminate and resist what she did not want (and with more than average autonomy allowed by her mother). Her activity level, sensitivity, and lability could give a foundation for conflict and for potential loss of optimal functioning, as well as for effective active coping when she was not threatened and demoralized by anxiety. One might expect some conflict around sex role in a little girl of unusual vigor; her sensitivity and emotional responsiveness could contribute to her responsiveness to authority, while her active approach would be expressed in autonomy as well. At the same time, in line with our discussion of likely outcomes of high activity level combined with sensitivity (see p. 82), such a child could welcome limits, rules, and structured situations that would protect her from dangers into which her activity level could push her. As labile or variable as she was, her sensitivity could leave her vulnerable to disorganization by overwhelming stimulation or pressures. Similarly her visual sensitivity and initiative could contribute to awareness of and concern about sex, body differences, pregnancy realities (just where inside is the baby?), as well as the awareness of activities of mothers and fathers, all of which were symbolically reflected in Sally's MLT: four small blocks were placed in a U-shaped structure, as if representing a "tummy" containing the four babies in Sally's family;* a red car was put into the hollow part of the stove, as if representing impregnation of the warm uterus. Five policemen did not prevent the train (of children) from disrupting the house but were upset themselves by the train, as if she felt that the children were stronger than grown-up controls. She twice put a girl doll into baby furniture, a gesture suggesting that she might wish to be a baby again. In the ego-blocking games she crashed my car and won the races repeatedly, and her train ran over or pushed off the doll. All this testifies to the multitude of concerns about what goes on in the family between parents and children as well as between fathers and mothers. Realistically, her capacity to win out over the adult and her feeling of being stronger than the grown-ups was reflected in her successful refusal to come to the last MLT session, because as was later reported, she wanted to stay home and take care of her sick mother.

Heider's approach likewise emphasized Sally's constitutional factors of vigor, activity, and high energy level; good vegetative functioning; alertness; manipulative skill; and in addition variability in cognitive and motor functioning. At infancy Heider considered her high in "action to attain" objects that interested her and in finding support in her own cognitive functioning (visual and tactual exploration). At the time she was observed (twenty-eight weeks) her mother was considered highly aware of Sally's needs as a baby and highly attentive but low in respect for her needs for autonomy. In addition Heider reported that when Sally was three to four years old the mother was unable to cope with four little children, discipline was inconsistent, and home structure was poor. Heider saw her as "more affected by home factors" than many of the children at the preschool stage.

Sources of vulnerability

Sally's sturdiness as an infant, high drive and activity level with a high degree of differentiation and good capacity for delay, her constructive ways of handling stress, and her mother's attentiveness at the time of the

---

* This inference is supported by other instances in which little girls reflect thoughts about babies and other contents of the mother's abdomen.

observations led Heider to consider her one of the *least vulnerable* babies. At the preschool stage, however, both Heider and Moriarty saw her as more vulnerable, that is, in the moderately vulnerable group despite her continued good health and vigor. Moriarty emphasized her anxiety. Heider felt that she was more influenced by home conditions than many other children who had also experienced separations from mother during hospitalization for birth of younger siblings.

It seems probable that the implications of Sally's variability of functioning had not been emphasized enough, and that her variability was in part a result of sensitivity and reactivity to separation, to her mother's ups and downs, and to lack of dependable continuity in the structure of home life. The probable reason that this sensitivity was not understood earlier is that at the infancy stage the dramatic variability in level of cognitive functioning seen at later stages was not discerned. The chief clue might have been her wide range on the Cattell tests, but it was only later that we saw the relation between early variations in levels of different areas of cognitive functioning and later variability in reaction to stress. In particular, implications of the fact that her language functioning was retarded in relation to motor and adaptive functioning were not fully realized. Inadequacies in language that can interfere with early communication could contribute to anxiety, especially in a child as observant and involved with her family as Sally was. The fact that at the infancy stage there was little evidence of autonomic reactivity, together with her overall sturdiness and good vegetative functioning also fore-stalled suspicions of vulnerability to stress. But her startling 30-point drop in IQ between preschool and prepuberty, her early latency disorganization in Moriarty's sessions, and a certain flightiness in some prepuberty sessions all emphasized how overconfident the low and even moderate vulnerability assessments had been. Without the longitudinal sequences we never would have discovered how sensitive indeed this sturdy little girl actually was. (However, her reactivity, drive, and autonomous coping contributed to resilience and her capacity to leave home and begin her own life with her own family.)

We have reviewed the story of Sally in some detail, though greatly condensed from our voluminous records, in order to illustrate how gradually we came to understand some aspects of vulnerability and the children's ways of coping with it.

Cohesiveness of the organism

Learning from Sally we can distinguish different aspects of ego strength: Sally's great competence, positive drive, and relatedness to the external world testified to her positive resources and ego strength in the sense of practical coping capacities (Coping I).

But she lacked cohesion in terms of the capacity to maintain her high level of functioning in motor and cognitive functioning when she was fatigued or under persistent stress. She could not maintain her inner equilibrium in these areas despite her emotional control and apparent autonomic stability. Thus Coping II proved less adequate than was anticipated, and along with great strengths, she was a child with her own vulnerable areas.

The psychiatrist expressed concern about ten of the thirty-two preschool children. He indicated that these ten children showed potentialities for hysterical reactions, character disorders, extreme involvement in conflicts, or other intrapsychic pressures that could lead to future disturbances. (In addition, the possibility of minimal brain damage was suspected in connection with dysarthria and difficulty in motor coordination in a couple of cases.)

The psychiatrist's global appraisal was correlated first with the CCI of 643 items; 33 items showed significant positive correlations with the PVR. These items grouped themselves into the following categories:

1. Disintegrative tendencies: this included tendencies to show disintegrative reactions to stress in motor and speech areas, etc. This group was similar to some of those in our Pilot Vulnerability Index.
2. Impulsiveness, difficulties in control, etc.
3. Tendencies to be defensive, demanding, aggressive, antagonistic; that is, coping patterns that were likely to endanger the child's relationships with others
4. Fatiguability, giving up easily
5. Fears and anxieties
6. Tensions and conflicts
7. Difficulties with peers
8. Difficulties with mother, family, and environment

Thus the PVR sorts out symptoms, behavior difficulties, and problems in dealing with the environment. Also, behavior items from both the infancy scores and ratings and from the preschool ratings are selected by this method, as well as background factors observed in infancy and others reported to the pediatrician during the preschool examination. Although no mothers could be called severely rejecting, we have noted that strains between mother and child appeared when the mother found a child "hard to understand" or "odd" or different from the rest of the family; when the child's sex was not the one most wanted; or when the mother was ill, depressed, or overburdened. In two instances we saw that the infant was temperamentally incompatible with the personality makeup of the mother.

Emotional disturbances of the mother during the child's infancy were especially important in the preschool girls seen as vulnerable by the psychiatrist.[12] The little girl needs to identify with the mother, and unless the child has enormous support from other members of the family and someone else with whom she can identify, she is apt to introject the mother's reaction more than the boy does; he is fortified by his ability to identify with the father.

The group "disintegrative tendencies" includes the systems in which the child showed disintegrative reactions to stress, such as loss of smoothness in motor functioning or speech. Few children showed mild perceptual distortions or loss of contact with the environment, that is, marked withdrawal of attention. We have seen that mild disturbances of motility, marked autonomic reactions, withdrawal tendencies, and so forth could all be observed in infancy and were sometimes precursors of preschool difficulties.

Impulsiveness and difficulties in control at the preschool level seemed closely related to constitutional tendencies since, even in infancy, ease of control versus impulsiveness was observable; however, these tendencies were often modified as the child developed (chapter 6).

In other words, we are concerned here with the outcomes of both cumulative background factors and probably early constitutional tendencies (toward disintegrative reactions, sensitivity, irritability, impulsiveness) and also more complicated resultants to which the constitutional factors in the child, the stress that the child has experienced in the family, the accumulated residual strains from unresolved problems, and uncompensated stresses all contribute. The PVR can be seen as a ranking of the child's vulnerability as it evolved out of all the sequential interactions between the child and his environment.

It is interesting to note here that the item miscellaneous illnesses, which might have been expected to contribute to vulnerability, actually showed a negative correlation with the PVR. In our small sample of children, this is probably due to the influence of the cases where enormous family support and help (as for instance in the case of a child who had very severe polio) actually contributed positively to her development and more than offset the vulnerability that otherwise might have resulted from the illness. This positive outcome of special care and attention during illness has been noted by Anna Freud (1937) and other child analysts. This is a clear example of the potential positive contribution to development from an experience which under less supportive conditions may contribute to regression. The total context has to be taken into account for each stress, not only the additionally disturbing factors, but also the offsetting ones that help to shape the outcome and the resulting coping strengths or limitations.

In comparing the three groups of characteristics represented by the Pilot Vulnerability Index, the psychological functions correlating with that, and the PVR with its correlating items, we see a series of factors involved in vulnerability. The Pilot Vulnerability Index can be considered a list of factors *predisposing* to coping difficulties, whose sequelae may include distortions of behavior and character. The PVR, on the other hand, is an evaluation of the preschool disturbances of the child. Thus it represents another level and deals with outcomes in problem behavior and in character of the interaction between the child's equipment and the early environment. This problem behavior and the potential character disturbances then constitute further aspects of vulnerability that contribute to further difficulties for the child. It will be easily seen that what is stressful for a given child will be determined in part by the interacting facets of the spectrum of vulnerabilities and strengths of a given child.

Heider's intensive qualitative study of vulnerability in infants and preschool children

We have already discussed Heider's evaluations of the infants and their mothers (chapters 2 through 4). In keeping with her Gestalt approach, Heider presented a holistic view of the structural factors both contributing to and offsetting vulnerability in each child seen as a whole; she approached the child in terms of the interaction of his equipment with observed persistent characteristics of the environment, especially the mother. In contrast with the psychiatrist's independent evaluation based only on his own observations, Heider's evaluations were based on her analysis of all the records on the child.

The fact that the child's capacity to manage his needs and the impact of the environment had emerged as negatively related to the Pilot Vulnerability Index was further supported by Heider's integrative approach to the vulnerability of the child-in-the-environment: equipment of the child, environmental influences, and management capacities of the child. Good management capacities of the child himself and good support from the environment could be expected to offset difficulties arising from the child's equipment, so the functional vulnerability of the child would be decreased as we have illustrated earlier.

Heider's (1966) study of the equipment assumed to contribute to vulnerability in infancy emphasized a number of characteristics in addition to overall "sensitivity" of the infant, idiosyncratic aspects of reactivity to stimuli in particular modalities and to special qualities of stimuli. We saw that she evaluated susceptibility to fatigue; fragility as contrasted with overall robustness; vegetative functioning, including adequacy of feeding, eliminating, sleeping, and so forth; consistency of level of performance on Gesell tests as compared with imbalance between areas of relative acceleration and retardation; and drive intensities in different areas: motor, object, social, own body.

Sequences in vulnerability

In her evaluation, Heider considered those characteristics contributing to strength as well as disintegrative tendencies coming from the child's equipment, and the supportive as well as stressful aspects of his relation with his mother. (More comprehensively, we should include the interaction with the entire personal and impersonal environment impinging on the child.) At the preschool level, Heider used essentially the same framework. This had the advantage of providing a basis for comparison.

The usefulness and validity of Heider's preschool evaluation is indicated by the fact that of eight preschool children in her "most vulnerable" group, three subsequently asked for help themselves (Lennie, Terry, Greg), and teachers or parents of three others (Gordon, Darlene, Chester) complained or sought help, and the staff was concerned about another one (Steve). Only one of eight "vulnerable" children at the preschool level made steady progress.

By contrast, of six children in the two groups of Heider's "least vulnerable" preschoolers, only one showed a marked loss of integration at any time during the first twelve years, although a few symptoms were transiently acute in a couple of others. In the case of one initially sturdy boy with optimal infantile experience, considered least vulnerable in infancy and at the preschool level, unresolved oedipal problems exacerbated by the illness of two younger children who preoccupied the mother, and by the father's favoritism for a younger brother, seem to have been a major factor. Oedipal problems in other children were often minimized by great satisfaction in hobbies, sports, achievement in church and school activities, and neighborhood friendships. (The answer to the question whether the child is able to manage the emotional pressure of oedipal conflicts in the early latency years has much to do with his feeling of satisfaction in himself and his own resources, his ability to make investments in objects, activities, and relationships in the environment, and his capacity for sublimation.)

All the children who had prolonged disturbances had had severe or repeated illnesses, which may be seen as undermining their somatic integrative capacities and their sense of well-being or narcissism. The severe or repeated illnesses in themslves might have resulted, of course, from initial somatic reactivity or proneness to invasion by viruses and bacteria, or the proneness to infection may in some cases have been increased by stress in the family atmosphere or in the mother–child relationship. The children who were vulnerable in the earliest years and were also disturbed at later points in development included not only those whose somatic integrity and confidence or sense of well-being had been disturbed by illnesses, but also included the somatic extremes in our group—the most active (an ectomorphic, wiry, slender boy) and one of the most passive girls.

Of the seven most vulnerable infants who later had difficulty, five also came from families with atypical sex-role patterns or living arrangements among the parents and/or had ill or severely maladjusted mothers. In other words, extreme somatic reactivity or sensitivity in the child interacted with the impact of difficult parent relationships.

Among the most well-functioning children, one had sufficiently outstanding somatic stability and stable narcissism to cope with the deprivations involved in early and recurrent depressions in the mother. Another minimally vulnerable and maximally competent child was able to weather the divorce of his parents and the virtual loss of his father with only some temporary obesity as a symptom of the stress he experienced.[13]

Variability in relation to the child's vulnerability

Grace Heider also rated imbalances and variability in functional systems at the infancy level. The latter can be placed on a continuum of variability from high consistency, as in a child such as Teddy, who was most consistent and also accurately predicted by Escalona, to variable children such as Janice, most poorly predicted by Escalona apparently because of her variability and especially, as Escalona later suggested, because her capacity to mobilize energy under challenge and stress was underestimated. We have to be careful, however, not to assume that variability implies only vulnerability. It can also underlie flexibility, the possibility of change and growth, as it did with Helen and others (see chapter 11).

Imbalance in status in functional areas

When the infants were appraised on the examination of four Gesell areas of adaptive behavior, motor development, personal–social development, and prelanguage development, they showed many different patterns of status in the different areas. Only five of thirty-one infants showed a balanced picture with the same status in all four areas. A case in point is Donald, who at sixteen weeks of age was rated at the sixteen-week level on adaptive behavior, twenty-week level on motor behavior, and twenty-four-week level on personal–social and language behavior respectively.

If we compare the amount of shift from the preschool to the latency intelligence tests scores in the children who as infants showed the most balanced ratings on the Gesell areas with the change in IQ from preschool to latency of the children with the greater range of variability in infancy, we find that the children with a wide range of developmental levels in infancy tended by and large to be more variable later and that those who were balanced in infancy tended to be less variable later. Variability at an early stage of development was related to variability over time.

Homeostatic factors and early integration of vegetative functioning in infancy were given special attention by Heider. All the babies in the group she considered to be vulnerable had disturbed vegetative functioning, and all but one had relatively low energy or poor physique. None of the group of least vulnerable infants had marked difficulty in gastrointestinal functioning. Slight or moderate gastrointestinal difficulty was counterbalanced by very understanding, consistent, devoted mothering in the cases of Susan and Molly, and, in addition, by Molly's resourceful ways of handling herself. Parenthetically, we can say here that when the distress suffered by the baby is within the range of the baby's ability to manage itself in relation to the environment in ways which succeed in modifying the stress, we see a primitive experience of successful coping that may lay a foundation of expectancy within the individual of ability to cope with future difficulties through his own efforts. We shall illustrate this in our study of Helen in chapter 11.

We saw earlier that Heider also evaluated numerous aspects of mother–baby interaction. All the vulnerable babies had some difficulty from lack of attunement between the mother and the baby. However, all these mothers were *there*. All cared enough to cooperate with the study throughout its duration. The mother–baby difficulties that were observed seemed subtle by clinical standards and within the normal range.

Structural and dynamic factors in decrease or increase of vulnerability

The group of children whose vulnerability was judged to decrease between infancy and the preschool period includes, of course, the children who were not at the top level of well-being and coping capacity in infancy, so that there was by definition much room for improvement. In the case of Terry, Helen, Brennie, JoAnne, and Tommy, the infancy problem centered around combinations of sensitivity, drive, and lack of control that made the child vulnerable to overstimulation. These high drive, active children seemed to improve by virtue of their vitality and determination to conquer their problems, to find ways of controlling both their own impulses and the impact of the environment sufficiently to keep themselves from being overwhelmed. Confronted with a sink-or-swim problem, they were, in fact, pushed into an early experience of mastery. All these children actually had conflicts which, as seen at prepuberty, could cause difficulty later if the conflicts were exaggerated by too much stress. It is interesting to see that despite their own vulnerability, all in this group except Helen felt themselves to be strong in contrast to their mothers. At the age of four, JoAnne put it, "My mommy's afraid of mouses but I'm not." Brennie's mother was conspicuously frail and anxious, and she sharply limited his aggressive attention toward a brother thirteen months younger than he. Brennie, however, was an advanced baby who had walked very early and talked early and whose ego development was sufficiently far enough along to give him some resources to develop on his own. For instance, while in the preschool stage, he began to look around the neighborhood and found "another mother" who gave him a second breakfast and doubtless much additional attention and interest.

When we look at the children who became more vulnerable between infancy and the preschool level, a number of experiences stand out.

First, we note the severe or repeated illnesses such as we saw with Lennie (p. 132). We may include critical environmental events coinciding with physical difficulties; for example, the disastrous flood experience that occurred while Rachel was having severe difficulties with eczema.

Second, with some children an abundant and generous start during the nursing period together with a supportive and protective environment during infancy changed in a variety of ways so that the environment was less suited to the child's needs at a later time than during infancy. In Vivian's case, we know that as she grew older she offered more competition to her older sister, who dealt with this by handling her with an iron hand in a velvet glove, limiting Vivian's spontaneity very much. Donald's family life was extremely restrictive, preventing this intelligent, observant, little boy from the kind of exploratory activities that most of the Topeka boys enjoyed from the time they could walk.

Third, developmental losses occurred that we cannot always trace completely. In the cases of Vernon, Sheila, and Sally, coping techniques that seemed to serve well when they were infants were not always as effective later; and, despite his high intelligence, Vernon did not develop the wide, flexible range of coping resources typical of a number of the children who had lower IQs. He seemed to concentrate on refinement of concrete cognitive activities at the expense of more flexible, complex, integrative responses to the environment. Sheila's ability to directly communicate her needs succeeded in gaining her mother's help in infancy, but may have prevented the development of a wide adaptive range and flexibility that she needed as she grew older, especially as she moved into latency.

Fourth, infantile conflicts intensified under the pressure of increasing confusion or emotional difficulty for the child in the home. As an infant, Patsy's relatively good physiological balance, her mother's basic care along with her father's interest in her, contributed to a picture of a relatively well-functioning baby; but by the age of four, and increasingly afterward, the combination of deprivation of gratification for the contact needs that were strong with her, together with the emotional involvement with her father and the possible effects of being in her parents' bedroom during her infancy, contributed to the most intense oedipal conflict among the girls. Her richly elaborated fantasy served moderately well to contain her conflicts but did not help her to deal directly with external problems.

Conditions contributing to progress

A too bountiful start may deprive the child of opportunities or the stimulus to develop mastery techniques at the infantile level, as occurred with Barbie. All the children who progressed had a combination of good experiences in infancy along with some difficulties that directly stimulated mastery efforts; thus these children developed at a deep unconscious level an experience of mastery. With some other children there were complicated patterns that sometimes balanced out: certain aspects of the family got worse, while other resources in the child improved with growth.

In some families, the general family situation itself was gradually eased. During one child's infancy the mother was burdened by attempting to contribute to the family finances and care for three little children during a period when her husband was completing his professional preparation. When his degree was obtained and the financial situation improved, the mother had more freedom to plan her time with her family and was able to distribute her support of the children more generously than was physically possible for her earlier.

Vulnerability and problems of integration

We began by observing vulnerability expressed in tendencies to disintegrative reactions, and we found that at the preschool stage these correlated negatively with many adaptive coping patterns. The child who struggles unsuccessfully to control simple coordinations cannot readily initiate resourceful solutions to problems, or solutions that would demand higher levels of control. This suggests that we should look for two major sources of vulnerability in infancy: (1) primary difficulties in maintaining integration in motor responses to the environment and (2) precursors of vulnerability in the ego as an organizing, centrally controlling, initiating, problem-solving institution. Vulnerability in specific ego functions (such as speech, space perception, or memory) can interfere with or block the functioning of the central organizing ego, but it is not the same thing as vulnerability in the sense of lability that undermines complex functions such as planning and resourcefulness. The former is directly tied to constitutional aspects of motor functioning; the latter has a complex origin. In order to get a firmer grip on possible sources of vulnerability of the integrating ego, we can consider some relevant aspects of development in early infancy.

A first source of cohesion versus vulnerability in the sense of labile or insecure integration is related to the basic level of vegetative functioning of the infant: contrast the smoothly breathing, efficiently nursing, rhythmically sleeping, autonomically stable infant with the baby whose functioning is unstable in one or more of these zones. The well-functioning, well-integrated baby has a biological foundation for a well-integrated psyche at its deepest roots. He is free of the perhaps toxic biochemical flooding stimulated by upheavals of the autonomic nervous system—a flooding that fills the bloodstream, and hence the brain, during the early months when perception is emerging. The well-functioning body provides the ego with the conditions necessary both for the development of truly autonomous ego functions and for a cohesive organizing ego.

We know from other research that in the early months infants cry more from internal stimuli, whereas later on external stimuli provoke more crying. By the same token, sources of internal distress responsible for early crying may be assumed to evoke feelings, however vague, of anger, rage, or anxiety; Greenacre (1952) has discussed this aspect of distress. When such feelings predominate, we infer that the infant has less experience of harmonious well-being, serenity, or bliss, and since feeling miserable tends to evoke further feelings of anger at the miserable self, the implicit struggle contributes to conflict about the self, or rejection, or a split between the sometimes comfortable self that one wants to perpetuate and the distressed self that one would like to get rid of.

It is, of course, utterly impossible to discuss such infantile experiences in appropriate words; the only language we have is that of the adult. But the test of our notion was in evidence from a later stage that very uncomfortable, distressed infants subsequently had more conflict, more tendency toward self-rejection, as well as greater vulnerability of cognitive functioning both as to level and quality.

Three approaches compared

Each of the three different approaches to vulnerability briefly reviewed here involves a different emphasis.[14] My first Pilot Vulnerability Index focuses on early equipment of the child; Heider's deals with early interactions of aspects of equipment, its use, and the responding environment in infancy and the preschool period; Toussieng's is concerned with the integrative and functional liabilities which (he would readily grant) are the outcomes of the above as they contribute to the intrapsychic organization, conflicts, and resolutions as seen at the preschool stage.

In view of this, my early approach could be referred to as *primary vulnerability* (avoiding the term "constitutional" or "genetic," which is narrow and excludes those irreversible early patternings that occur during pregnancy, birth, and early infancy). Heider's approach may well be called the *organism—environment vulnerability* of the child, implying that in different environments the given equipment would contribute to different outcomes. Toussieng's approach could be termed *vulnerability of the ego*, as it developed from the early and emergent givens of organism and environment.

Finally, Moriarty focuses on speech as a vulnerable area in this culture, where, in contrast to multiple motor freedoms, there is more suppression by the environment. Part II of this chapter reviews her approach to this expression of vulnerability.

II. Speech and Language as Indices of Vulnerability

Many of the preschool children were verbally clear, forthright, and open in communicating with us. Still, there was a wide range in the quality of speech and language functioning, and to our surprise half the children showed some kind of speech distortions, predominantly errors in articulation, during the routine psychological testing. Most of these articulatory errors were age expectable and ordinarily spontaneously dropped away. However, in a few children articulatory errors in combination with other problems, which we shall illustrate, were at least potentially serious deterrents to total coping efficiency, and specifically to communication. Though the etiology and effects of poor speech varied, speech problems of any type sometimes reduced adult understanding of what was said, limited the children's self-expression, and to some extent contributed to their frustrations and sense of inadequacy in this area. Poor speech was both a reflection of stress and a source of vulnerability, particularly in perceptually alert children with high drive to communicate thoughts and feelings. At the same time, poor speech necessitated, and in many cases was ingeniously handled by, coping maneuvers generally consistent with the child's overall individual style.

A case in point was Terry, an alert, highly active boy who had from early infancy shown great urgency to vocalize. He produced sounds that suggested understanding of words in the first year, but these were interpretable only by his mother. By the age of five years, when speech therapy was begun, he was said to have difficulties with *L, S, Th, Ch, Sh,* and *R* sounds. In our tests, at age five years and nine months, he responded with intense eagerness and impatience to show what he knew and to express his many ideas. He spoke rapidly in very loud, ringing, high-pitched tones, accompanied by quick vigorous gestures and ever-changing facial expressions. Every part of his body seemed to be in continuous movement. Instructed to draw, he addressed the examiner: "I know, I know, I know (with increasing intensity) . . . Hold it . . . Hook (look). Am you teasing? It's a hongtong for kuddoo (meaning unknown) . . . It's real heasy . . . I twy (try) . . . It's a bawn (barn) with hanimals and stuff . . . All bawns are most of the time bwack (black) . . . I think they are . . . That's a muddo (mother) cow and here's the faddo (father). And here's the hittle (little) one . . . Oh, here's a hee-haw (donkey) . . . Something is the mattah . . . Oh, here, I'm getting it . . . How do you like that?"

Part II of this chapter was written by Alice Moriarty. It is a synthesis of her informal observations of speech during preschool sessions and of Dr. Rousey's formal speech examinations of the same children in their prepuberty years.

Occurring less frequently than articulatory distortions, but often in the same children, were deviations in rhythm, intensity, or inflection (stammering or repeating sounds in three children; inappropriate changing of pitch or loudness of the voice in relation to meaning in four children; lisping in three children) and word-finding difficulties in two children.

For example, three-and-a-half-year-old Lennie, an effervescent and engagingly responsive child, eager to explore all aspects of his world, suffered from a series of eye and ear infections resulting in later learning disabilities. As a preschooler, he coped with gaps in his knowledge by offering multiple substitute responses. Among these were pantomime or demonstrations of motor skills to substitute for words missing in his vocabulary. He also struggled to think out what he meant to say, and sometimes came up with quite poetic alternatives. "I don't know. I twy think . . . Well, fish don't fly except fly fish. Those darn fly fish." (The latter seemed to be a displacement of his own sense of inadequacy into disparagement of the offending creature whose behavior he was unable to identify.) At other times, he simply said sadly, as though strained by his own limitations, "I'm screw (through)."

Four children spoke with a pitch that seemed inappropriate for their age and sex (that is, higher or lower than expected); and in twelve children who were ordinarily capable of producing recognizable and adequate sounds, speech seriously deteriorated under stress, such as that of meeting unfamiliar people for the first time, or when required to achieve, to deliver learned information, or to express their feelings. In these children, demands for verbal performance in psychological tests were met with a good deal of resistance and with considerable apparent discomfort on the child's part. We noted alterations in pace of motor activity (either becoming increasingly restless or nearly immobile) and in quality of facial expressions (grimaces or stoniness) and hesitancies to verbalize, usually speaking very softly in as few words as possible, or sometimes remaining almost totally silent.

For example, Donald, at three years and five months when he was ushered into the examining room for the first time, stood very stiffly and soberly, keeping his distance and finally retreating behind his mother's chair. He accomplished some of the simpler motor tasks, such as bead-stringing, only through his mother's intercession, carefully avoiding the examiner's gaze and usually standing with his back to her. He was able to give one-word identifications of familiar objects by whispering softly, almost inaudibly, and directly to the mother, as though consciously excluding the unfamiliar adult. After close to one hour, he reached in slow motion for drawing paper offered him by the examiner, but he carried it to his secure place on the floor close to his mother and did not respond to the examiner's inquiry as to what he was doing. Later, with some relaxation of his vigilant refusal to communicate, he allowed the examiner to sit beside him, even once smiled at her, but continued to use only single words as he faced his mother. It was as if he could then allow the examiner to hear, but avoided a personal interchange with her.

Like Donald, most children who showed this kind of initial inhibition in a new situation were willing to attempt tasks that did not require verbalizations. Few were as totally silent and motionless as Donald, and most were quicker to warm up to the examiner and to the appeal of the variety of test materials (Moriarty 1961).

In striking contrast to these preschool children with recognizable problems in production of sounds or in emotional reticence to interact verbally with a stranger, roughly half of our sample verbalized clearly, fluently, and spontaneously.

For example, Chester, a sturdy, bright-eyed youngster of four years and eleven months, handled his body skillfully, appearing to be totally confident and proud of his competence in meeting verbal requests in the examiner's tests. He was equally free to modify these adult directions to his own liking, or to accept some restrictions with good humor. He enjoyed poking fun at himself or at others and was prone to tell tall-tales, smiling mischievously in full recognition of the exaggeration. For him, the cooing of a pigeon outside the window sounded "like a lion." Unlike the more reticent children, he verbally explained whatever he was doing, and on trips to the research building he talked comfortably about the passing scene, his family, or recent experiences.

We might have considered such observations as these as only interesting clinical anecdotes, as expressions of individuality, or as indices of normal immaturity had we not several years later been exposed to the theoretical framework of hypotheses developed by Clyde Rousey.[1] There hypotheses proposed that articulatory errors, as well as deviations in voice quality and auditory intake of sound, may be used predictively to assess such dimensions of adjustment as transmission of sexual and aggressive drives and style of interpersonal relationship. With these formulations in mind, Dr. Rousey examined and tape-recorded the speech of twenty-four of our subjects (then of prepuberty age) and from these recordings made a large number of predictions about current and earlier adjustment. These predictions of adjustment and coping styles, validated by me against clinical findings independently analyzed by other staff members, were impressively accurate for the majority of the children. This fact, plus the unexpected finding that 75 percent of our normal children in their prepuberty years demonstrated deviations serious enough to interfere with communication of others, forced us to think further about the meanings of speech problems. Clearly, we could no longer dismiss our observations of speech problems in the preschool years as solely a function of immaturity, particularly since in many cases vulnerability in the area of vocalization and speech extended backward in time to the infancy years[2] and continued to be present in the prepuberty years.

That persistence of vulnerability in the speech-language area might have constitutional or temperamental bases was suggested by the fact that the majority of the children judged to be most vulnerable in verbal functioning at prepuberty had been independently rated as vulnerable in this area both in their infancy tests and in preschool observations of them. On the other hand, it was equally clear that changing developmental pressures and conflicts, as well as family stresses, particularly from relationships with mothers, contributed to continuing vulnerability in speech. To assess how all these things affected speech development and functioning, we shall want to look at differences between children with good and poor speech at prepuberty. However, as a background for such differential assessment, we need first to think about the role of speech in development, particularly as it promotes or interferes with self-expression and relationships with others.

Speech development and sources of vulnerability

To learn to respond to, understand, and later to initiate verbal communication with others is a vital part of human development and is the fundamental difference between human development and that of the lower animals. Furthermore, though individuals vary as to exactly when these skills are tried out and perfected, they seem to occur in a relatively uniform hierarchical sequence.[3] For instance, within minutes of birth, most babies make their presence known by crying, and for some months a major way of getting attention is through crying. Voice quality and tempo are important even to young babies. In the early months, infants, barring auditory handicaps, differentiate the mother from others first by the sound of her voice. Visual discrimination of the mother follows later.

In our own study, some four-week-old infants were seen to be quieted by a mother's familiar voice, or even by the sound of her approaching footsteps. Nearly all appeared to turn toward sources of sound by four or five months; some were capable of remarkable differentiation, both in expressing their own needs and in response to familiar and unfamiliar sounds. For instance, Donald's mother reported that he had even in the first few months smiled in response to gentle sounds such as tinkling of bells but cried and stiffened his body when he heard loud or sharp sounds. Having been frightened at four months by the loud voice of an elderly unfamiliar neighbor, he continued to be fearful of older people for a long period of time. These remarks by the mother, though perhaps colored by her pride in her closeness and sensitivity to her infant, were in part verified by our observations three years later that he was unusually slow and cautious about relating to older staff members. In his mother's opinion, Donald clearly made differential cries signaling hunger, sleepiness, pain, fear, or a wish for attention, and she was equally alert in responding to these signals. Quite clearly, her relationship to her child affected his responsiveness to others.

Gradually in the first six months most babies, including those observed by Escalona and Leitch, can be seen to widen their repertoire to include cooing and babbling, as well as practice of sound effects of different intensities and physical wave lengths. With increasing capacity to differentiate sounds, babies are able to become increasingly selective in the sounds made and the sounds responded to. By seven to eight months a baby is normally ready to respond behaviorally to single words, especially if these sounds—made by the familiar mother—are accompanied by pantomime.

Paralleling cognitive and sensory development, the baby learns to repeat those sounds he hears and eliminates those sounds that have no identifiable association in his experience. Reinforced in this process by parental recognition and approval of meaningful sounds, he learns successively to combine sounds into single words to identify familiar objects or people (usually by the end of his first year) and into simple combinations of words (sometime in his second year of life). Early efforts to express ideas and feelings may be limited primarily to nouns and confused in articulation and grammar, but they are forerunners of sentences insofar as they reflect complete ideas, beyond simple identification. As the vocabulary grows, in relation to level of maturity and experience, sensory intake and capacity to differentiate between and imitate sounds, his speech becomes more complex. By the kindergarten years, most children are able to use more or less correctly some pronouns, adjectives, and verbs.

If a child has, by virtue of auditory impairment or dysfunction, a temporary or permanent inability to differentiate the sounds he hears, his developing speech may be faulty in articulation. If he has, through limited environmental experience and stimulation, illness or visual dysfunction, been deprived of optimal opportunity to explore the world visually, his functional vocabulary may be limited. (Lennie suffered limited but permanent visual damage and temporary hearing losses.) If he is temperamentally, or as a result of family inhibition and overprotection, prone to delay or avoid personal contact, he may be slow to involve himself in verbal interchange. In some children, such as Donald, apprehension stemming from such environmentally or self-imposed restrictions appears behaviorally as temporary or more persistent negativism and resistance. In our earlier work, we suggested that such behavior may also have the positive coping value of delaying response to clarify or to gain time for integration (Moriarty 1961).

If a child is overstimulated, or erratically stimulated or restricted (as was the case with Terry), he may develop articulatory "symptoms" or problems in integration. Furthermore, given an urgency to explore and/or to communicate, unmatched by developing skills or opportunity, he is subject to expressive difficulties, leading to frustration and insults to self-esteem. If any or all these conditions exist, speech and language suffer; they are then a source of vulnerability and a deterrent to optimal or potential coping.

While professional observers from many fields (including psychiatrists, psychologists, educators, speech pathologists, and linguists) have known that content of language[4] can be used as an index of dynamic processes or style of thinking and perception, there has been less awareness of the apparent meaningfulness of distortions in perception and expression of sound (that is, the faulty intake and production of sounds expressed in misarticulation, inappropriate voice quality, or rhythm). It is this relationship that Dr. Rousey's hypotheses proposed, specifically how particular disturbances in speech can be used diagnostically to understand how children have learned or are able to experience interpersonal relationships, and how they express their natural sexual and aggressive urgencies. In other words, our prepuberty speech examinations (see Appendix 10) allowed us to predict or postdict with considerable success some important aspects of coping and to further assess sources of vulnerability. Hence, we regarded speech not only as a potential source of vulnerability, but also as a useful index and an available avenue for the expression of vulnerability. We should emphasize, however, as we have noted earlier, that vulnerability may appear in many other guises. Motor awkwardness or poor coordination, integrative problems in thinking, slowness to learn, impulsiveness whether of emotional or neurologic background are a few of the other ways in which vulnerability may be expressed. Hence, it is important to state that while speech distortions of any type appear to reflect certain developmental or adaptive weaknesses, the absence of speech problems does not imply optimal functioning in all areas.

Early precursors of vulnerability in speech

Seeking to understand how vulnerability in speech came about, we looked at our infancy records to see whether we could find early systematic differences between those with good and poor speech at prepuberty. These explorations suggested a cluster of styles or behavioral qualities in the infant himself and in the mother's way of communicating with him. Like Heider (1966) we found that those children who continued to be vulnerable in the speech area had as infants exhibited high drive for active exploration of the environment; a wide range of intense preverbal and nonnutritive oral activity; unusual sensory sensitivity (at either extreme of the continuum); and irritability or disturbance in vegetative functioning. In other words, unusual physical–physiological problems or extremes in reactivity were associated with later vulnerability in speech functioning.

Along with these characteristics in the child, certain characteristics of mothers were associated with vulnerability in children's speech at prepuberty. These included lack of congruence between temperamental style of mother and infant (reflected in maternal speech that was too verbose or too infrequent, too loud, or too fast for the baby's tempo); conflicts between or differences in mother's aspirations and expectations for her child and those of which he was capable and desirous of accomplishing; maternal strengths intellectually and/or emotionally of a relatively higher degree than found in father; moderate to extreme dissatisfaction of mother with father's intellectual aspirations and economic status.

Furthermore, high frequency of vulnerability in speech at all ages reflected both the nature of our group of children and some community attitudes in regard to child-rearing. Having, as preschoolers, only recently acquired speech, they were more likely when under stress to show disintegration in this new skill than in the generally excellent, earlier, and more firmly established motor coordination. Since most of the children had few experiences apart from their mothers, as for instance in nursery schools, the mild apprehension and reluctance to interact verbally with a stranger, which we observed in most of the children at times, was not unexpected.

In addition, the culture was one that placed relatively higher value on motor development and achievement (athletic skills were particularly valued in later years) than on academic learning or highly differentiated verbal conceptualization. And as we have described earlier, outdoor space allowed for much free movement and exploration. By contrast, parents with several children in small indoor space were apt to limit noise from loud childish voices. The culture also sets strong taboos against the expression of physical aggression toward persons or property; and sexual feelings, usually considered to be minimal in these young children were, if present and recognized, likely to be restricted and controlled. While experiencing much freedom, these children were expected to be obedient, respectful, cooperative, and emotionally self-controlled. Even in infancy, some mothers were able to discourage crying by frowns, and in the preschool years high exuberance was disapproved by parents and other adults. For instance, one child was "expelled" from Sunday school by a teacher who saw his boisterous gaiety as inappropriate in the religious setting. Another child was thought by grandparents, and occasionally by parents, to be too eager to approach and to talk to strangers.

Conversely, incomprehensible speech was seen as normal, something that would be outgrown or that was not too different from speech of relatives. Originality and vividness in speaking was not particularly encouraged; "sassiness" and "talking back" were vigorously put down. For all these reasons, it is surprising neither that speech was vulnerable in the face of continuing or age-related stresses, nor that it was an area open for expression of whatever tensions and frustrations accumulated. And, of course, by the prepuberty years, when speech was well established and gross apprehension in new situations was no longer present, the speech area was still an available avenue for release of tension from the expected biological and social pressures of early adolescence. Still, we could not believe that these new pressures were quite enough to explain the increased vulnerability in the speech area: whereas 50 percent were considered vulnerable in the preschool years, 75 percent were considered vulnerable in the prepuberty years. To understand these findings, we again turned to our clinical data. Specifically, we asked what were the deviations in speech and how seriously did they affect communication?

Differences in children with good and poor speech at prepuberty

Looking first at individual children, we saw that none of them exhibited anything like a total communication breakdown, though eight children were found to exhibit three or more speech symptoms of at least mild severity. However, with four exceptions, despite distortions in articulation, pitch, and rhythm, all were able to communicate well enough to make themselves understood, and to express their thoughts and feelings relatively clearly. (This, of course, does not imply that they were without the usual defenses when talking about touchy subjects.) Hence, we felt that poor speech, though not grossly handicapping, was a reflection of moderate to extreme residual or current conflict, which incidentally was strongly supported in their retrospective reports of their prepuberty years. In their later adolescence, many of these youths clearly stated that the junior high school years were the most anxiety laden, the most pressured, the least emotionally comfortable of any time in their lives. It was then that they felt most constraint in themselves and from their parents. It was then that they focused most intensively on themselves, and felt least able to communicate. At a time when they faced new and more demanding teachers in a freer, less personal environment, when they were undergoing physiological changes, facing new temptations in a broader social environment, many struggled to find an identity distinct from but incorporating parental values. From these perspectives, our findings of increasing vulnerability in the speech area made a good deal of sense and clearly indicated how very sensitive speech and language functioning is to pressures, whether they be internal, external, or more likely some combination of both.

Aside from this later retrospective evaluation by the youth themselves, we found other evidence that speech served as an available tension outlet in our earlier clinical observations. Looking at the records of the eight children who were judged in their prepuberty years as most vulnerable in the speech area, we found, for example, that seven of the eight had been judged by Heider to be high in drive level in their infancy.[5] These were alert, active infants with unusual urgency or intensity in their interaction with their environment. They ate avidly and moved vigorously, and in their intensity occasionally became tremulous despite ordinarily good motor coordination. They were infants who seemed impatient to be fed; who made it clear that they wanted to be held upright to see the world; who had clear preferences for food-and-care techniques; who looked searchingly and seemed to experience every human contact intensely. They were in no sense moderate in relating to their world, and they acted upon it as much as it acted upon them.

Not unexpectedly, those with later speech problems (which incidentally continued consistently over time from infancy through prepuberty in those considered most vulnerable) were unusually sensitive and highly differentiated in their responses to stimulation in one or more sensory areas. For instance, Greg as an infant was unusually sensitive to changes in intensity of light and could be fascinated by the rays of the sun, by shadows, or dispersion of light. Terry and Roddy could be soothed, excited, or displeased with sounds of differing intensity in familiar or unfamiliar settings. Martin was very early reactive to social stimulation, and his responses varied from intensely pleasurable involvement to discontented and highly critical verbal protests in the preschool years. Rachel, Lennie, and Vivian were remarkably aware of surface texture, and also keenly perceptive visually.

These were babies who experienced sights, sounds, tactile, and kinesthetic sensations vividly—either very positively or very negatively. They were rarely indifferent to sensory experiences and could be unusually excited or happy and equally sad, withdrawn, or overwhelmed. In their intensity, they enjoyed extreme pleasure, but they also suffered from overstimulation at times.

Furthermore, the eight children judged in their prepuberty years to be most vulnerable in the speech area had suffered early physical or emotional trauma, such as long hospitalization in infancy, repeated illnesses, marital discord or instability, inconsistent maternal handling, temporary loss of mother, or maternal care style mismatched with babies' needs. And in these inherently vigorous, highly reactive, sensitive babies, these conditions were particularly frustrating. They were stymied by conflicts between their own strong urgencies and uneven capacities, and by conflicts between their own and their mother's needs and styles. For example, Greg's devoted mother struggled to support her child without a father and fluctuated in her needs to keep the child close to her and to encourage his independence. Rachel's mother, herself partially deaf, was warm but unable to provide enough close dependency in a large and unstable family with an undependable husband and a mentally ill sister adding to her burdens. Lennie's loving but anxious mother, like Lennie himself, was frustrated with his slow developmental pace during the preschool and latency years. Donald's mother, who had been somewhat dissatisfied that she had not had a girl, and who also found infancy the most rewarding period in her relationship with her children, managed to prolong infancy and to delay an independent masculine orientation. Though theoretically claiming that timing of toilet training should be "up to him," she deliberately delayed toilet training as she had also done with weaning. Furthermore, for economic reasons, she dressed the child in the preschool years in homemade clothes which were distinctly less masculine than those of most of the boys in the sample. Vivian's mother consciously chose to develop independence in a growing family with upward mobile orientation; for Vivian, who seemed to need a longer period of dependence, this was frustrating. Martin's mother pressed the child by overprotection and her clear preference for him, thus feeding into sibling rivalry with a sturdier and less alert older brother. Roddy's and Terry's mothers were impatient, overstimulating, and inconsistently inhibiting, perhaps partly because of their own ambitions and the demands of outside jobs that reduced their patience, energy, and opportunity for regular and uninterrupted enjoyment of their children. Nonetheless, all these mothers were responsible and loving and provided their children with competent care, which was rewarded by generally good academic performance and by acceptable social behavior.

In contrast, those children who showed little or no distortion in their speech at prepuberty had in their infancy relatively quieter, less pressured lives. Less vigorous, less intense, and less sensitive, they were not as often in conflict with their environment.[6] Hence, they were less often frustrated, less often protested, and less in need of control. They were the modulated, well-balanced babies, who perhaps enjoyed less but also suffered less from frustration and conflict. They were variously described as more passive, more compliant, more stoical, more self-contained.

Interesting, too, was the fact that those children with little or lesser degrees of speech distortions were offspring of mothers who were at least in the children's early years more contented or satisfied with their lot in life (though it ranged from affluence to marked economic limitations) and who were for the most part satisfied with the father's aspirations and status. They were also more satisfied with the sex, health, and capabilities of their children. Thus, they were in the children's early years during the time when speech was developing, less demanding, less impatient, and more willing to let their children grow at their own pace and in their own style. Feeling relatively little harassment, these mothers were able to be more moderate in the demands made on the children. It is, of course important to point out that in some children, changes in maternal behavior and/or in the child's needs, though probably affecting total coping styles, were not direct sources of vulnerability in speech functioning.

In general, then, the children who were vulnerable in the speech area included those who because of their native high drive, high sensitivity, and continuous mild to severe experience of conflict or distress were rarely free of tension. Those with structurally clearer speech were not necessarily better copers, but they coped with fewer pressures and were less frequently at odds with differences between their own needs and capacities, or between their own needs and parental demands. Less intense in their urgency to communicate, they were less frequently or less severely frustrated, and presumably therefore enjoyed more uninterrupted conflict-free experiences, facilitating smoother speech development as well as other learned skills. Their own modulated temperament and coping style both contributed to and were enhanced by their environment.

Thus, to turn the coin, we can say that when speech distortions are present, we can assume that some incongruities or conflicts, as well as constitutional weaknesses, have been present from infancy and probably continue to exist. On the other hand, we cannot assume that freedom from speech distortion necessarily implies total lack of adaptive problems. The quieter, less intense and less vigorous unprotesting child may or may not be vulnerable in other areas of his functioning. His problems, if they exist, are expressed in modes other than in his verbal communication with his world.

9

Responses to Expectable and
Unusual Stress

*I've always known that life contained some hardships and that you
stand up to them.*

Topeka mothers

I. Reactions to Topeka Tornado

Expectable stress

To be sure, city life in this century is less strenuous than in the past:
central heating keeps people warm in winter, plumbing contributes to
increased sanitation, the availability of a wide variety of food from
distances improves nutrition, and nearby doctors and medical facilities
improve health standards. But tornadoes have not yet been controlled,
and as we know from Dorothy of Oz, Kansas is in the middle of tornado
country. Even though, according to an old Indian legend, Topeka is
protected by Burnett's Mound on the southwest edge of the city and had
never been struck by a tornado, the people of the city were watchful.
They were trained to listen for the warnings "tornado watch" and
"tornado warning: take cover." The unexpected-but-expected actually
occurred at 7:15 P.M. on 8 June 1966, when our children were fifteen to
seventeen years old.

This devastating tornado, the worst disaster in Topeka's history, tore a
half-mile swath over twelve miles of the city, leveling or severely
damaging homes of nearly 2500 people, including 90 members of the
Menninger Foundation staff. It destroyed Washburn University, numerous businesses, and thousands of trees, along with hundreds of automo-
biles and seventy-one of the seventy-five city buses. Potentially lethal
"hot wires" draped the streets as power lines were ripped from their
supports, and communications were interrupted as thousands of telephone poles were torn from their footings.

Due probably to the early alert by the local TV–radio station WIBW
(which preceded the police sirens by several minutes) and the take-cover
warning that followed (fourteen minutes before the tornado struck),

along with years of training in regard to the danger, deaths were limited
to seventeen, although hundreds of people barely escaped with their lives
by dropping into an available ditch or other basement shelters. Several
hundred people were injured.

While all citizens were urged to remain indoors except doctors, nurses,
police, firemen, and other workers needed to protect the area from
vandalism and further accidents, assistance was quickly mobilized.
Forbes Air Base servicemen, National Guard, county and state police
were assigned roles in guarding all devastated areas and directed traffic
through safe channels. Churches, schools, and the Municapal Audito-
rium offered immediate shelter. Local disaster agencies, civil defense,
and the Red Cross set up relief centers to provide food and clothing to
victims of the tornado. Nearby towns sent workers and trucks to help
remove the rubble from clogged streets and to assist relief workers in
collecting and distributing clothing and other needed supplies.

The population as a whole mourned the deaths, the devastation of the
city, the destruction of the university and of thousands of noble trees
planted almost a century earlier. There was no escape from the impact of
the disaster for those whose daily routes to work carried them within
sight of the burning mounds of trees whose smoke masked the evening
sunsets, the bizarre angles of amputated tree trunks still holding parts of
one or two naked main branches, or the unmasked desolation of
pathetically inadequate, now demolished homes of the poor, formerly
shielded from view by the luxuriance of the trees. For others whose
routes took them past the southwest end of the city where blocks of new
apartments were pancaked and splintered, the image of lost homes and
possessions was equally overwhelming.

Yet the children and teenagers, confined within their own home zones,
had individually diversified and modulated experiences of the event. Of
course we tried as soon as possible to ascertain the impact of the tornado
on our subjects—an almost impossible task because the markedly
incapacitated phone system interfered seriously with communication
inside and outside the city. Access to many living areas was blocked by
the police. So our data are imcomplete.

Fortunately, few of our subjects lived or found themselves in the
direct path of the tornado, and none was seriously injured. The home of
one family was damaged, and the following is an excerpt from C. J.
Morgan's report on the family's reactions to the tornado damage:

> The Dickinsons' home in the northeast area of the city was
> considerably damaged. Trees were down everywhere and because of
> all the destroyed houses and debris, police and National Guard were

keeping cars and people out of the area. Telephone wires and other electrical wires were down; power and gas were turned off.

In order to reach the Dickinson home, it was necessary to literally climb over, under, and around large uprooted trees, one of which lay across the front of their house, near the front porch; the normal entrance was completely blocked. Another large tree lay partially on top of an old car parked in the driveway so that it was impossible for anyone to emerge from the front door.

Mr. and Mrs. Dickinson, their son, Donald, and the younger boy were standing outside. Mr. Dickinson did not seen unhappy or really concerned about the damage but said he didn't see that there was much they could do. He said that they were staying with his wife's mother. I mentioned to Mrs. Dickinson that she must have heard the awful noise made by the tornado and she said, "We certainly did," in a rather flat voice, without affect. She is usually rather vivacious and expressive, but now seemed to be in a mild depression. But the other members of the family, Mr. Dickinson, Donald, and the younger boy, seemed to be almost the same as I had seen them on other occasions, and pleased that I was there. Talking about how to cope with the damage, Mr. Dickinson said that if they got a tarp to cover the roof, weighted it down with bricks, and nailed some boards up over the knocked out window, they could live in their home. His chief concern was to protect the contents from being ruined in case of rain. But he wanted to wait until an insurance claim adjuster came out before he started any repairs. His mood and that of his sons seemed to be that of people out on an overnight camping trip, roughing it; and well, this is what is to be expected from this kind of experience. They were not at all unhappy or shocked by it, but making the best of the situation.

Mr. Dickinson showed me different remarkable things that happened to the house: a window knocked out of its casing while the glass in it was not even cracked; the master bedroom was not even touched. He showed me the inconsistency in what the tornado had done—a lot of damage in certain parts: something had come down through the roof and gone back out again, tearing a big hole so you could look out and see the sky. He felt that it was positively amazing that the tornado should do this and yet at the same time leave other parts of the house completely untouched. Everything had been thrown out of the kitchen into a little hallway; a loaf of bread and a bread box lay on the floor with a few little unbroken jars of jam, lying just as the wind had left them. In the living room the piano was intact, and the book of music on the piano was still open to the page to which it had been turned, although five feet away something had come down through the roof and gone back up again leaving the big hole. Their utter amazement at the way the storm acted seemed to be their major reaction.

Doubtless the insurance was one reason for Mr. Dickinson's casualness; they are well covered, so that even though Mr. Dickinson built the house himself, it will not be necessary for him to make his own repairs.

At the back of the house no trees were standing; we saw a little squirrel scampering over a fallen tree and Mrs. Dickinson in a quiet and apathetic manner spoke about the poor little squirrel not having any home to go to now. She told with much empathy how the squirrel used to come up to them, and how tame and friendly it was, how it would come to the back door and you could feed it from your hand. She ceased talking about it as abruptly as she had started.

The lack of self-pity of this family was typical for the city as a whole in the observation of the writers. Even those who lost everything were "so glad to be alive," and felt that "well, we can just pick up the pieces and start over," or "we take our losses along with everyone else," or "we've always known this could happen, and now it has." A prevailing stoicism was balanced in middle-class groups, after initial rescue and shelter by friends or relatives, by immediate efforts first to salvage anything that could be discovered in the rubble to which a home had been reduced—an address book, a wedding picture, a drawer of a bureau that escaped demolition—and then by plans for rebuilding or home finding. But one outstanding medical leader who with his family barely escaped annihilation in a demolished building of the university admitted to still feeling shaky twenty-four hours later, and other professional people turned away inquiries from social scientists eager to get their story, implying that they needed their energy to keep functioning at work and did not want to relive the shock.

As indicated earlier, our teenage subjects escaped severe personal loss. Still, their reactions varied widely. A sense of challenge, curiosity, the wish to see the tornado was the dominant reaction of several, as shown in these excerpts from C. J. Morgan's reports:

Janice and two boyfriends heard the tornado warning and dashed up to Burnett's Mound to get a good view. What they saw was so frightening they dashed down the hill, banged on the doors of the nearest house to no avail, rushed to another two doors down and got into the basement just in time to see [from the basement window] the first house demolished.

Martin was about half a mile from the area first hit by the tornado. He went into a friend's basement, watched from a window, and when it had gone by went outside to watch it further. He said it was "white in front and black in back with lots of dirt and stuff flying around." In his area, windows were broken and some rain came in, but there was no other damage. Later he watched TV and saw for the first time how bad it had been, but he added that he couldn't "really believe it, since I haven't seen the damage myself and I probably won't be able to really believe it until I can get out and see it." He was most concerned about the *damage to cars.* He added that everyone he knew was getting busy cleaning things up and planning to rebuild . . . none of his friends who suffered from the tornado were discouraged or hopeless.

Many other teenagers "wanted to watch it" and did so from a distance of a few blocks or half a mile. One teenager in therapy reported that she and her family watched it from their home a mile west of its path, "and it was a lot of fun." A matter-of-fact "business as usual" attitude was typical of some who could see the tornado at what they considered a safe distance of a half-mile to a mile:

Gordon was up on the roof pounding down some loose shingles. He saw the tornado from the roof and "was not concerned or frightened." The noise sounded to him like a jet plane. He described the tornado vividly, saying that "it was a circular cloud moving kinda fast, it looked pure white" to him. He said that if it hadn't been for Burnett's Mound and the fact that the tornado "kinda skirted around and headed more into the city, it probably would have gone right through" his area of town and destroyed it. His matter-of-fact talk about this gave an impression of some denial of concern and fear. The day afterward, Gordon helped friends in a badly damaged area salvage some belongings and clean up the mess.

Ronald was working at a grocery store about a mile east of the tornado's path. When he heard the tornado warnings he "just kept on working." At the store the radio was on, and the workers heard the reports of the damage left in the path of the tornado and were "kinda shocked but not afraid." He agreed that it seemed like "just another tornado warning." He helped a friend clean up his home; this friend, whose roof was damaged felt "pretty lucky" since the house next door was ruined—"walls down and everything else." He was most concerned about his friend's *car* being destroyed. Ronald said the people he knew expected to rebuild probably on the same foundation of the house that had been destroyed.

Routine protection measures were taken by some who regarded the alert as "one more tornado warning" so "we went to the basement as we always do." "We kept the TV on and didn't pay any special attention to it, down in the basement," one girl said.

Still others felt unwary of danger and ignored the warning:

Chester and his siblings were at a shopping center a mile from the tornado's path. His sister was under a hair dryer; she stayed there and didn't come home until after her hair was dry, but the rest of the family came home and went into the basement where their father made them stay until the tornado was past. Chester "didn't think too much about the tornado warnings. . . . Heck, they have them all the time." He said later he would have liked to get out and watch it. Afterward they went down to the Washburn University area and helped direct traffic away from the zone of destruction. An aunt's house was in one damaged area but only her trees were destroyed; he and his father and brother went there to clean up the debris, chopping up the fallen trees with an ax for better removal by the debris crew.

While Chester *never openly admitted fear of the tornado* he laughed about it nervously, but his brother Ray did admit that he was scared but "not terrifically"; the basement "was a good place to be in." Both boys said they had been surprised at all the damage in the city and "just couldn't believe it." Neither one showed concern over the people who had lost their homes. They were interested in the odd pattern of the storm, leaving a refrigerator full of mud and yet dresser drawers intact in another room; they were also impressed by objects found 30 or 40 miles away.

The unusual things about the storm, the force of it, plus the fact that it hurt some areas and yet didn't even touch adjacent areas—these oddities seemed to be the things that Gordon found interesting while he was a little disbelieving. When asked about his reaction to seeing the devastated area around 29th and interstate 70 he ejaculated, "W——ugh!" as though he were vomiting . . . and I said, "It kinda makes you sick?" and he said, "Yeah." He talked about his friends who had lost everything. They had no clothes, no furniture—nothing. Yet, he talked about this matter-of-factly; there was some empathy but not emotional contagion in his voice as he talked about the predicament his friends were in, and of his efforts to help them.

I asked how his friends in the damaged area were feeling about the destruction of their homes and the loss of all their possessions. Gordon said spontaneously, "Well, they sure weren't feeling sorry for themselves. They seem to be trying to get things cleared up and locate what they had; the biggest problem was where to stay." I asked him if they all had some place to stay for the time being and he said, "Yeah, with either relatives or friends." I said, "I guess you mean the problem of finding some place to stay permanently." He agreed: "Yeah . . . after you get things cleaned up and find out where your stuff's at—where you're going to live?" There was considerable empathy for the friends who really lost their homes.

Gordon also expressed concern over the loss of all the big trees. He talked about how Washburn had been "such a pretty campus with all the big shade trees," and in other areas of the city there had been "these enormous big nice trees." . . . He seemed to really like them and now they just weren't there.

By contrast with the immediate active realistic response of so many teenagers and adults, small children showed more tendency to be disturbed. A three-year-old girl in a day-care center lost previously firm urinary control. In talking with me about her current feelings she was able to convey her anxiety about a teacher whose home had been destroyed by the tornado. Some sleep and behavior disturbances were noted in other children who were not shaken by direct experience of the tornado, but by the stories they heard of what happened to others. Still others "played tornado," building structures with blocks, then destroying them.

Six weeks after the June tornado there was a daytime take-cover warning. In one day-care center, the little girls wrapped up their dolls and hid them under tables; the boys dashed around destroying block building and making a mess of the center. In the other center, a teacher panicked; she had been traumatized by the total loss of her property and near loss of her life in the June tornado.

It seems probable here that the following factors were involved: the preschool children felt helpless to do anything for the people whose sufferings they heard about—they could often not even talk about it since the adults were too preoccupied with their own active coping efforts to pay attention to the children's concerns. For the small children no avenues of discharge were open except fantasy and play. Beyond this the first child described conveyed that she was afraid her teacher might not come back, and another child in the same group reflected the same worry when his own teacher left for the day. Here the little children felt threatened by the potential loss of support and care at a time of threatened helplessness. This was not observed in any of the teenagers, most of whom were already well along in detachment from dependency on the grown-ups and able to give active restorative help.

Through the experience of the teenagers themselves, and through their observations of others, we saw the ways in which this potentially disruptive event was experienced by children at different stages of development and with different prior experience or orientation, and the ways in which the impact was modulated by years of preparation.

Evaluation of stress

Evaluation of stress experienced by an individual child is difficult. Is a child who screams experiencing more stress than a child who stoically masks his anxiety? Is a child who does not cry but whose pulse or blood pressure changes dramatically consciously experiencing more stress than the child who lets out feelings? Does the child whose speech is blocked experience as much stress as the child whose motor coordination deteriorates? Or, if we turn to the potentially stressful event, how do we measure the relative stress of a long illness such as hepatitis against that of a tonsillectomy?

Our evaluations are admittedly intuitive and subjective and more confident chiefly at the extremes. Even here there are difficulties since the special devoted attention received by most of the children who experienced long or severe illnesses seemed to reduce the stress or at least to evoke an awareness of pain balanced by relief or even pleasure (see chapter 10). Sudden unexpected and unfamiliar stress can evoke individual differences most clearly, and this will be seen in the discussion of the teenagers' reactions to the assassination of John F. Kennedy.

II. Reactions to the Assassination of a President

The sudden unexpected violence of the assassination of President Kennedy and the succeeding events placed the children under considerable stress, common to the entire group, and more emotionally laden, more dramatic, and potentially more threatening than any previous event in their lives. We were, of course, in a position to gather a special kind of information about the experiences of these children we already knew well. A detailed questionnaire (Appendix 11) sent three days after the assassination evoked reports of their feelings about the tragedy and related events—feelings that were generally consistent with the individual adaptational styles already documented at this stage but highlighted by the emotional impact of the immediate situation. The striking directness and honesty with which children responded gave new focus and emphasis to individual reaction patterns, including quality and range of affect, capacity to integrate and assimilate feelings, interpretations, and impulses to deal with a situation. Certain individuals reflected long-suppressed anxiety, depression, vulnerabilities, and ways of coping with them. As a massive shared insult to the status quo and to the usual sensibilities about the destruction of human life, the assassination seemed initially to arouse widespread feelings of disbelief and underlying insecurity. Beyond this, we found individual reactions related to feelings about their own fathers, about death or personal losses; the intensity of feeling was in proportion to the degree of identification with President Kennedy, who in his person perhaps symbolized for many the vigor, intelligence, sensitivity, and manliness of the ideal father. A man whose personal life was known through mass media, he must have been as real to our children as the local mayor or pastor. Yet President Kennedy was not the father, relative, or even personal acquaintance of any of the children, nor was he in any way directly involved in their immediate lives. The events of the assassination, despite their dramatic impact, were remote, not intrusive or directly personal. Beyond a natural disbelief and horror, there were no standards of how to behave or how to feel. Therefore, the feelings they expressed tapped basic underlying impulses and understanding of such broad issues as attitudes about authority, law and order, capital punishment, and personal responsibility in the complex world in which they lived. It is perhaps this combination of strong feelings and personal remoteness that contributed to the uniqueness of the children's responses, which though consistent with earlier observations, in many cases more openly expressed primitive or habitually inhibited feelings.

Part II of this chapter was written by Alice Moriarty.

The major feelings expressed by the children

Hearing the news within minutes of the event, when most were in school, the children shared with peers and familiar teachers initial denial that such a thing could happen in our civilized world. Following this, some were overwhelmingly sad; some felt physically ill; others sympathetically wished they might soothe the bereaved family, particularly the President's young children; a few were angry and vengeful. The intensity and kind of feelings expressed were, of course, to some extent a function of their feelings about the President during his life, but more important than partisanship were their efforts to be themselves, to be sober, vague, or intellectually oriented as was their wont.

For example, Melvin's outright denial ("I couldn't believe that he had been shot. I felt someone was pulling a fast one") coincided with our psychiatrist's view of this bright but affectively cautious and overly repressed boy as one who "takes a very sober view of his environment, and avoids anything which will stimulate impulses or emotions too much." Cassy also wanted to disbelieve the news, but the intensity of her feelings showed up in misspelling, poor grammar, and verbal confusion, which was not ordinarily characteristic of her. She wrote, "Disbelifle that it anything like that couldn't in this day and age."

Both of these answers differed from the more sophisticated cognitive control of Teddy who said, "I was stunned and in disbelief, as I never conceived the possibility of Mr. Kennedy being assassinated. As his death was not announced until 1:40, everything seemed to be utterly unimportant besides the President's life." Clinically, this answer resembled similar reactions to more direct personal stress in a very intelligent, serious, and thoughtful child whose emotional responses, though inwardly intense, were typically contained and usually expressed in carefully worded phrases without overt indication of cognitive distortions or loss of emotional control.

A few who saw the bullet wound as probably not serious were in a sense deferring judgment or delaying emotional feeling until they were clear about facts. Later, markedly angry vengeful feelings on the part of some children appeared to reflect their efforts to control the intensity of their feelings, either because intense feelings were in themselves painful, or because too strong feelings threatened internal integration. This interpretation fitted our earlier observations of Vernon, whose self-control and poise at times covered feelings of great depth. Likewise, Janice's temporary self-reassurance that the wound might not be serious seemed to cover both intense anger and a considerable sense of loss in a child who had suffered both severe physiological distress in infancy and considerable affective harshness from her mother. Her remark, "I felt like life was not worth living," emphasized the extent to which these feelings were revived.

The highly individualistic implications of overt denial were further indicated by the responses of five other children who preferred initially to believe the President's wounds were superficial. These children included a boy who had grown up without a father, a boy whose mother was seriously ill with an incurable disease, a girl who frequently silently delayed reacting to the world, a girl who had learned to handle stress by turning bad into good, and a girl who was concerned not because of the loss of a president of whom she disapproved but because of potential violence resulting from the event.

Equally self-expressive was Daryl's reply, "I felt all sick inside. I just could not believe that the President was really shot." Daryl's intellectual denial, combined with her physical reaction, implied a split between her cognitive and affective response, which was not unlike a long history of similar reactions to her mother's many pregnancies.

Political concerns for the country and fears of aggression were combined with shock in the response of Nancy, who remarked, "I was terribly shocked and I prayed to God that he would live. Also, I was terribly frightened about who shot him, because if he was a confirmed communist, I was afraid people might catch him and get violent." Nancy's replies to other questions were forthright in expressing her disapproval of the President's viewpoints and suggested her attempt at or search for intellectual appraisal, but these efforts were not entirely successful in dissipating her fears, as was indicated by her use of the words "frightened" and "afraid."

It thus became obvious fairly early in our analysis of answers to the questionnaire that we were seeing massive shock, common to both adults and youth, in response to this national disaster. It seemed equally likely, and more dynamically significant, that individuality of response could be regarded as a sensitive indicator of children's evolved orientation toward life and of their defensive or coping styles as these were magnified in response to the unusual and powerful stress of the assassination.

When it was definite that the President was dead, sadness increased, particularly for those who had experienced loss of close relatives through death or divorce. Then, the sense of loss was experienced as more personal. For example, Teddy, though still immersed in the tragedy, reported his difficulties in striving for assimilation over a period of time. "Everything was obliterated but the voice on the radio and the possibility the report was wrong. It took me nearly a week to fully assimilate the fact, however."

Claudia's feelings of personal loss were referred to her bodily self. Whereas she had first felt "as if one of my close relations had been badly injured," she now remarked, "I felt as if a living part of me had died." One could not miss the parallel between these feelings and her own probable reactions to the recent divorce of her parents and the fact that her father, who no longer lived with her, was experientially "lost" to her.

Equally strong feelings were expressed by motherless Brenda, by Greg whose father was dead, by Ronald who had in the latency years been pressured by the possible separation of his parents, and by Milly whose prepuberty relationship to her mother was somewhat tenuous and in a state of flux. In other words, it seemed as though the national tragedy revived deeply personal feelings that were the more intense because the children's empathic reactions were similar to those they had felt in response to realistic stresses in their own lives. For example, Brenda said, "I had an empty feeling like when you try hard to win something and then lose." It was as though she were saying symbolically that she had tried hard to win the love of her mother and had experienced the mother's death as a personal insult. Less directly, Milly avoided the strictly personal and focused instead on national deprivation. ("I felt that we had lost one of the best leaders of our times.") However, in other responses, she showed deep sympathy for the President's family; hence, her initial reaction appeared to be a kind of intellectual distancing in a self-protective way, not unlike her overall affective style.

Shifts and combinations of feelings could be traced in responses of many of the children. For example, Daryl moved from generalized somatic malaise to overt aggression: "I was filled with sadness and disgust. I hated the man who did it." Roddy's initial anger was followed by sadness and disbelief: "At first I felt anger, then I felt sad and disbelief." Delbert's initial shock, merged with hopefulness, was later differentiated into grief, anger, and concern for the country: "When I heard that JFK was dead, I was grieved and perhaps a little angry that a thing like this could happen in my country." In other words, a close review of children's responses suggested that disbelief, though very common, tended to be an initial protective reaction, covering complex, multiple underlying feelings that were extremely meaningful in terms of the child's total adjustment. For most, shock decreased and feelings of sadness increased when they could no longer hope the President might recover.

Feelings about the reactions of the Kennedy family

The majority of the children saw Mrs. Kennedy as sad, or as having suffered irreparable loss, though they differed in their feelings about the intensity of her feelings and the meanings of her outward self-control. For example, Claudia wrote, "I cannot express how Mrs. Kennedy and her children feel because President Kennedy was not my father or husband, but I think Mrs. Kennedy feels as if the world has almost come to an end and that there is no place for her in her opinion, since the death of her beloved husband." Equally intense but more definite was Delbert's comment, "Mrs. Kennedy is of course grieved and lonely." Although Claudia expressed strong feelings, she prefaced them by indicating that she could not really say how Mrs. Kennedy felt since the loss was Mrs. Kennedy's and not Claudia's own. Chester, too, was unwilling to commit himself to a definite stance: "I thinck that they would feel as anyone would feel if they lost a friend or relative. But I thinck that they took it very well." His and seven other children's admiration for Mrs. Kennedy's emotional control seemed to reflect high value on self-control, in some a kind of temperamental stoicism, and in others an expression of strong family pressures to control feelings.

On the other hand, some children saw Mrs. Kennedy's control as numbness, as an index of depression, or as too lacking in feeling. And in each case, these perceptions paralleled their own experiences. For example, Greg saw temporary depression as compensated for by earlier happiness. "I'm sure that Mrs. Kennedy is terribly sad and depressed, but she should remember that her ten years with Mr. Kennedy had been filled with more happiness than most women have in a life time." A sensitive, intelligent child who was deprived of his own father at an early age, he appeared to relive his own depressing efforts to reassure himself that his life was full and complete, despite his lack of a father and some major developmental difficulties stemming from this lack.

Darlene, who had struggled to be self-expressive in a restrictive environment said, "I think Mrs. Kennedy was very grieved. I think it would maybe had been better had she shown more emotion. I almost felt that she didn't care an awful lot." Here, Darlene seemed to be saying that strong feeling is present only if it is expressed, raising questions about the pressures she felt from her own mother's personal style of rigid control of her own feelings, and her suppression of many of her daughter's feelings. Overtly a highly constricted and unfulfilled child, she was apparently suffering considerable strain and conflict in these years, as she retrospectively described vividly in adolescent interviews with her.

More than half felt that Caroline and more especially John were really too young to fully understand the long-range implications of the tragic events. For some, attributing deeper feelings to the older child picked up feelings of sibling rivalry. Others attributed differential feelings to Mrs. Kennedy and the children in relation to the role of the deceased as father or husband. They assumed the loss of a husband would be different from the loss of a father. These were especially sensitive children who were deeply aware of status and privilege in relation to age, and of their own roles in their particular families.

Feelings expressed about Kennedy's assassin

Of special interest to us were their attitudes toward law and order, standards of justice, capital punishment, and their appreciation of mental health problems. We asked ourselves whether these feelings were generalized or specific to the particular situation. Did they feel differently about the appropriate treatment of the President's assassin and the murderer of his assassin? How much did the children identify with Ruby, who committed an act they might have condoned or even wished to commit themselves? When we asked, "What do you think should have been done with the killer?", nearly two-thirds favored merciful or impartial treatment of the President's assassin by the usual legal means. However, close to one-third focused on execution and punishment. Of these, several felt uncertain or ambivalent about how the assassin should be treated. For example, Gordon approved commonly accepted legal procedures, but he also suggested that the crime should be punished in a painful way. He wrote, "I think he should have had a trial and if found guilty sentenced to a slow death." It occurred to us that he perhaps was responding to inner hostility derived from a need to avenge injustice in his own experiences. Jay, on the other hand, upon reflection tempered his immediate anger with a sense of justice. He wrote, "I first thought the police should of hunt this man down and shot him, but after thinking it over I thought he should be given a fair trial."

One could contrast both of these responses with that of Darlene: "The killer had a soul and needed God and needed a chance to give his life to God, although he probably wouldn't have. Yet, one would feel he should be treated as he had treated JFK. But God said in the Bible that we are to love our enemys and pray for him that dispitfully use us, and that we are not to return evil for evil. So I'm not sure exactly what I think should have been [done] to him." Each of these answers suggested some ambivalence about aggression. However, Jay expressed and then retracted his aggressive feelings; Gordon abided by social standards and secondarily added feelings of hostility. These sequences were perhaps most meaningful in relation to other data about these three children. As already indicated, Darlene was a very constricted child who had been forced to suppress and indeed did repress many intense feelings. Jay overtly conformed to society's demands and was in fact quite successful in sublimating aggression in sports, but his internal conflicts, presumably in relation to parental divorce, were not entirely eliminated. Gordon's tendencies to act out against a society which had not always considered his needs were balanced by his positive response to some supports in his environment.

We might contrast these responses with those of Daryl who said, "I think the killer should have been brainwashed." With no inkling of feelings of justice or mercy, she focused entirely upon deserved punishment for aggression. In a somewhat less concrete way, Sally recommended more internalized punishment: "I think the killer should have suffered than [been] killed for what he did." The omission of several words here suggested the depth of her feelings, with the distinct possibility that she perceived death in itself as less painful than the mental torture of having to come to terms with one's misbehaviors. Each of these children had experienced considerable aggression from the environment, as well as frustration in working out positive resolutions. Sally, capable of resolving her own problems more positively than Daryl, could give up physical torture, since she clearly felt that the toll for unacceptable behavior resides within the individual.

Feelings about Oswald's murder

While half expressed regret that Oswald had been killed, these feelings were less intense and involved more intellectual curiosity about facts and motivation. Some, for instance, raised questions about the sanity of both killers. One-quarter of the children appeared relatively indifferent to the shooting of Oswald. A few others reported feeling glad that Oswald had been murdered. Still others were concerned about the killing, not so much because of injury to the individual, as because of the potentially harmful effect on the country.

What should be done with Ruby?

Consistent with these feelings was frequent advocacy of just treatment of Ruby. However, the quality of justice differed for different individuals. While nearly three-quarters felt that Ruby should be shown justice and treated like any other killer, some recommended minimal punishment, while others favored maximal punishment. Adele, recommending minimal punishment, said, "I think they shouldn't do much because he would have been killed anyway." There was a kind of resignation in this answer, which was perhaps significant in a child who had been subjected to especially unstable family experiences over which she had little control. All who recommended maximal punishment had themselves experienced generally fair but formally strict and rigid discipline.

In summary, we noted that a majority of the children favored justice in any instance. They were more comfortable when justice was meted out by legal means. On the other hand, nearly a third would have preferred some kind of retribution and punishment, and all of these either had themselves been treated with some harshness, or were still in the process of resolving conflicts about aggression.

Evaluation of the probable effect of the President's death

As a part of our investigation of reactions to the death of a President, we hoped to examine maturity of thinking, especially in regard to responsibility and the consideration of the larger implications of the tragedy. How does the prepuberty child, as exemplified by our sample, see his own role in society? How does he evaluate the effects of such an unusual event, and are these effects viewed predominantly in terms of personal emotional reactions or in relation to the political and economic status of the United States as a world power?

Appraisal of personal effects

Looking first at their remarks about personal effects, we found that about half felt either that there would be no lasting effects or that any effects would be minor. On the other hand, almost the same number of children indicated that effects would be far-reaching, have lasting affective impact, or might lead to personal improvement. A few deferred judgment. Typical responses indicating no lasting or important personal change were those of Chester, "No effect that will harm"; of Ray, "There won't be any effect of the President's death on me, but it will effect the country very much"; of Bertha, "I *hope* there won't be any effect"; of Sheila, "I *think* I'll get over it." Of course, even here we could point to qualitative differences between the two boys' quite definite statements, and the girls' margin of doubt in their formulations ("I hope" and "I think").

Quite different in feeling tone were the responses of children who indicated strong affective reaction, such as Rachel, who said, "It is a sadness which I will never forget"; or Gordon, "I was a little sick and mostly sick"; or Sylvia, "It saddened me and I cried."

Still different in implication were the responses of children who saw the effects of the assassination as leading to personal improvement, largely in terms of increased maturity and responsibility. These included answers such as those of Helen, who said, "It will make me think more"; or of Brenda, who wrote, "It will make me appreciate the President more even if I don't like the way he runs the country"; or of Delbert, who said dramatically but obviously sincerely, "Part of me died with him, but because of him I strive with increased determination to be in private what he was in public." In this boy, who had more seriously questioned community and parental standards and whose behavior had been moderately delinquent, urgencies to find an adult model were especially poignant.

On the basis of our knowledge of these children, we felt that those who expected a lasting emotional impact were capable of greater affective differentiation or had achieved a higher level of cognitive maturity. Those who saw no lasting or significant change were on the other hand either more emotionally contained and/or less reflective.

Appraisal of national effects

A third of the children foresaw no real change or only minor effects on the country. Half saw more lasting or significant changes, such as improvements through more national unity and determination in handling national problems. Most felt that the emotional impact, though intense, would be short-lived.

A small number foresaw changes that would be detrimental to the United States or that would place the country in a vulnerable position. Rachel, who had herself experienced a good deal of insecurity in relationships with others, worried about insecurity in the nation. She wrote, "Their may be more deaths or shotings in the other states." Similar doubts and insecurities were expressed by Darlene, who pessimistically added that probably things would not really be very different; her response reflected the ambivalence so highly characteristic of much of her prepubescent thinking: "I have thought maybe it's the way for communism to take over our country. I do think it is communism that caused it, but other than maybe this, I think our country will go on pretty much as it has been." Brenda modulated her pessimism by possible improvement. "It will make people wonder what our country is coming to and help everyone be more patriotic." This attitude of meeting pressures directly, and of using them to gain personal strength, was highly characteristic of this particular child. Jay, who was distinctly interested in politics remarked with some uncertainty, "I believe this event will either bring our countrymen closer together or perhaps weaken us. I think it will depend on how other people support President Johnson."

Appraisal of international effects

While the majority did not anticipate widespread or continuing impact on the world, close to a quarter were concerned about shifts in world power or international relationships. Gail's response was typical: "It's one less worry for Mr. Khruschev and one more for the countries under our later President's foreign plan." This response was apparently a part of her realistic effort to evaluate the situation without emotional involvement, and to assimilate her negative attitudes toward President Kennedy as a person and a political figure with her strong positive attitudes about justice for the killers. Overtly, she maintained that the President's murder, though undesirable, had been no more of a tragedy than the death of any other individual.

Only two girls (Helen and Brenda) anticipated improvements in themselves, the nation, and the world, a fact perhaps reflecting the prominent capacity in both of these girls to assimilate negative aspects of their own lives and to develop ego strength from earlier vulnerabilities and pressures.

Thus, for most children the emotional impact of the assassination was highly personal. While some were concerned about temporary national disorganization, few foresaw widespread or lasting effects on the wider world.

Activity and passivity in dealing with stress

The ramifications of the responses cannot be treated extensively in a brief summary of the data. Nor can we present here more than a superficial picture of the striking fashion in which individual replies highlighted both specific vulnerabilities and individual coping styles in response to stress. However, we should like to illustrate and discuss some of the ways the children chose to deal with their feelings, some by active efforts to assimilate, dissipate, or contain feelings; some more passively minimizing or becoming overwhelmed by feelings. These differences were most prominent in response to a question asking whether they had a desire to do anything after the death of the President.

We found close to half reported no desire to do anything. These "passive copers" included some who appeared to let the impact of the assassination flow over them because they felt emotionally drained and were immobilized. Typical of these were Sylvia, who said, "No, just cried and felt very sad"; Melvin, who wrote, "No, I was so dumbfounded that I couldn't really think very clearly"; or of Kitty, who remarked, "I felt like being alone."

Other "passive copers" tried to view the situation realistically, implying either that there was nothing *anyone* could do, or that there was nothing *they personally* could do, or nothing they *wanted* to do to ameliorate the situation or to cope with the pressures of an uncontrollable environment. These children gave relatively undifferentiated negative replies with somewhat less affective intensity. They included personal overtones, varying from child to child, but they were alike in quietly focusing on their own feelings, rather than mobilizing actions to reduce their feelings or to act upon the situation in ways that were characteristic of the more "active copers." Norma quite directly said that she did not know how to behave: "I didn't really want to do anything because I really didn't know what to say or do." Bertha's passive acceptance seemed to reflect more generalized feelings of inadequacy and helplessness in any difficult situation: "No, because there wasn't anything I could do."

Slightly more than half of the children took a more active stance, by either thinking about or mobilizing their feelings in various ways. Some did this by seeking support through prayer—either for the dead President and his family or for their own peace of mind. Others sought to understand through concentrated listening to newscasts or reading about past assassinations. Several children would have magically revived the dead President. Still others expressed feelings of sympathy and a wish to be helpful, either through expression of warmth and sympathy for the Kennedy family, or by their efforts toward self-improvement, as a kind of monument to make up for the loss of a great man. A few others expressed strong feelings of hostility and a wish to achieve vengeance.

The helpful and sympathetic children

Of particular interest were the responses of nine children who reported that they wanted to be helpful or sympathetic, or somehow be better, stronger individuals to make up for the death of the President. These answers varied from the need for direct expression of sympathy (expressed by Claudia: "I felt like I wanted to be there at that very moment and do something for Mrs. Kennedy"; or by Corliss: "Anything that would be of help") to efforts for self-improvement (expressed in Brenda's remark: "It made me want to be a better citizen"; or in Diane's comment: "Yes, I don't know. I don't think there is much we can do. More than anything I want to go straighten out this mess of a country, but I'm afraid I'd put it in even more perilous position").

Efforts to be helpful and sympathic were sometimes spontaneous expressions of warmth, as in the case of Helen, who said, "Yes, I felt as if I wanted to take Carolyn, John, and Jackie into my arms and comfort them." In other children, positive maneuvers emerged as a final result of working through the emotional impact and of attempting to handle it. This was true of Diane, who first cried, then asked a good many questions, and finally discussed the issues quite thoroughly with her own family. Next, there followed a period in which she wanted to be alone, and finally she tried to understand by looking up historical facts about earlier assassinations. It was partly this effort that led to a determination to participate in national affairs even though she was not altogether certain of her own adequacy in this regard.

The vengeful children

Distinctly different were responses of those eight children who focused upon the aggressive act, by directly or indirectly expressing a wish to retaliate against the killer and to achieve vengeance. One of the most outspoken expressions of hostility and anger was that of Daryl: "My heart was filled with hatred and I wanted to kill the assassin." Significantly, this remark was made by a girl who had throughout her life expressed a great deal of passive aggression toward adults and considerable overt aggression toward her siblings.

These ways of coping with feelings were not, of course, mutually exclusive, though one affective tone tended to pervade the entire series of responses for a particular child. Speculating that the children who responded sympathetically and those who responded with hostility were fundamentally different in many aspects of their development, particularly in typical and pervasive coping styles, we made a special study of the two groups.

Differences between helpful and vengeful children[1]

The "helpful" children were judged by experienced observers of their infancy behavior to be higher in drive level than the "vengeful" children (significant at the 5 percent level). There was also a hint that most of the helpful children experienced greater viability with the mother, who in turn was more likely to view the father as an adequate individual.

Preschool ratings showed greater sensory reactivity on the part of the vengeful children (significant at the 2 percent level) and greater tendency to be overwhelmed by sensory stimulation. That is, the vengeful children were more likely to be uncomfortable and irritated by intense sensory stimulation, whereas the helpful group, though not insensitive, were generally more positive in their response to sensory stimulation. The helpful group was also judged as more capable in the preschool years of coping with practical aspects of problem-solving and more likely to have achieved internal equilibrium. Probably important in this more comfortable adjustment were temperamental compatibility with their mothers, more positive relationships with and greater support from the fathers, and more indications that their mothers were satisfied with fathers' vocational achievements.

At prepuberty, the helpful children were not more capable of handling overt problem-solving, but they continued to be more internally balanced and more satisfied with themselves as individuals. They were also more likely to believe or trust in the integrity of significant individuals in their environment.

Turning to the Rorschach[2] data on these children, we found in protocols taken at preschool, latency, and prepuberty, consistently greater homogeneity of response in the vengeful group as compared to greater diversification in the helpful group. This suggested that in the vengeful group, generalized hostility interfered with discrimination and differentiation. It was also clear that the "helpful" children were more likely to anticipate positive outcomes, even from such negative experiences as the assassination. Furthermore, behavioral observation and analysis of the projective test data showed that the children who in adolescence responded to the Kennedy assassination with a desire to offer help had already at the preschool age been significantly more productive, more cooperative, better able to relate to others, and to achieve self-expression both affectively and ideationally. Perhaps as a corollary to the preceding, they were less hampered by ego constriction than were those who later responded with a desire for revenge.

By latency, the helpful group reduced their involvement with others, apparently as a part of the process of achieving latency, whereas the vengeful group continued to be fixated in their earlier ambivalent relationships.

By prepuberty, both groups concentrated primarily on details in the Rorschach cards, with the vengeful group making slightly more global responses than the helpful group. The differences then were not so much quantitative as qualitative. The vengeful children were more likely to perceive vague, amorphous, or inaccurate global percepts, while the helpful children were better able to achieve a synthesis of the selected details of a situation. Most important of all was the greater capacity for differentiation and reintegration in the helpful group. While each of the children in the latter group gave some responses of this type, none of the children in the vengeful group gave any such responses. This finding, in the tests obtained nearest in time to the assassination, suggested that those children who responded sympathetically were better able first to organize parts of a stimulus situation, then to respond to a situation by breaking it down into its component parts, and finally to reorganize these parts to derive new meaning. The children who responded to the assassination with vengeful feelings, on the other hand, were more likely to respond to any situation in terms of its emotional impact with either little or inaccurate regard for the intellectual aspects of the situation.

Furthermore, ratings[3] based on the Rorschach responses showed higher level of overall creativity, greater capacity for self-expression through communication of thoughts and feelings, and greater tolerance for primary process or unrealistic thinking in the helpful group.

The consistency of these differences over time seemed remarkable and implied better integrated, more flexible, and certainly more effective and personally rewarding cognitive and emotional functioning in the helpful group. In turn, their positive, effective coping styles were associated with greater stability in their early family relationships and with higher self-regard. The helpful children were those who most nearly maximized their own potentialities and were least vulnerable to disintegration in the face of environmental pressures. Thus, once again, the children's responses to the impact of the assassination were clearly related to established adaptational styles and to personal outlook toward their lives, as these had been developed out of significant early experiences, and the quality of their self-regard.

Summary

We believed that the emotional impact of the assassination and related events was sufficient to create temporary imbalance in internal organization, which then forced those who experienced it to assimilate feelings by defensive and coping processes that were temperamentally suitable and habitual.

While the responses on the questionnaires sent to fifty-seven children showed a predominance of feelings of denial and shock, these feelings were combined with other feelings in highly individual ways. Most children were genuinely concerned that justice be administered by legal means, and some children were acutely aware of threats to national stability.

Most significantly, children's responses to our questionnaire reflected differences in their characteristic ways of handling their feelings, particularly in regard to how they had learned to mobilize their energies in relation to stress, and their capacity for resilience.

10

Resilience: Steps in Recovery and Development of Strength

As you encounter one stressful experience it strengthens you, like a vaccine, for a future crisis. One acquires a callousness and builds up a sort of reserve. When you're young there is a natural ability to survive crisis, you aren't as deeply involved; even though a minor crisis may seem great or is exaggerated, it disappears quickly. As one grows older, the natural ability to live ahead and forget diminishes, but experience and living give you a maturity that takes the place of your natural ability to survive—in something like the Topeka tornado; you have to bounce back or you couldn't go on.

Karl, fourteen years old*

Karl had been considered a vulnerable infant and had struggled through childhood with certain recurrent functional difficulties more than balanced by marked gifts. His immunization concept of resilience has something in common with the concept of learning from shock developed on the basis of studies of rats.[1] And it is relevant as well to Macfarlane's (1963) observations that children who have coped with stress in early years are better copers in later years.

Resilience has both a biological and a psychological foundation; after commenting on the former, we will review psychological forces, including coping devices of the child, contributing to recovery from different kinds of stress experienced by these children.

No less miraculous than the capacity of living organisms for reproduction is their capacity for self-repair and recovery from periods of malfunctioning. The simplest organisms share this potential quite as fully as complex mammals; witness the worm, which, when cut in half, completes itself. This achievement is as striking as the recovery to normal thinking and feeling of a mentally ill person who has been harassed by wild delusions and impulses. But although the study of mental illness is nearly a century old, the processes of recovery are only partially understood. One factor promoting recovery is the tendency of the organism itself to reestablish wholeness; another factor is the tendency to

* A boy observed periodically from birth, not in the Topeka sample.

maintain the dynamic, flexible balance necessary for coping with vicissitudes of daily life. Contributory metabolic processes involve biochemical factors, and, supported by the interaction of cortical, subcortical, autonomic, and glandular activity, psychophysiological forces mobilize regenerative powers. Probably these both respond to and evoke hope, the drive to get well, determination to struggle against odds. Thus, the capacity to recover, to master vicissitudes, to be resilient, is rooted in biological human nature, that is, in the tissues of the body. Rhythms of rest and sleep aid recovery from fatigue due to activity or stress and support the capacities of cells to regenerate tissues damaged by illness or accident. Rest at a time of depleted strength or energy may be followed by a resurgence of vigor, zest, tempo, and interest or cathexis. External assistance, whether it involves surgery or therapy, aids in the restoration of diseased or damaged tissues. In modern medical care, pathology-reducing agents (antibiotics, specifics against inflammation) are used to diminish the stress; restitutive agents (vitamins, hormones, selected foods) are used to assist recovery of losses. In addition, nursing care furnishes soothing or discomfort-reducing activities (massage, warm or cold applications, or medication for pain) and activities directed toward restoration of function (exercise). In World War II, "t.l.c.," or the tender loving care long characteristic of good nursing, was seen to assist recovery even from severe injuries, supporting hope and the expectation of renewed well-being.

Somatic resilience and emotional recovery may go hand in hand. In human beings the unconscious and physiological self-restorative processes may be stimulated both by support from others and by the individual's conscious steps toward recovery; the expectation of recovery, which is supported by favorable messages from the environment, may in turn evoke autonomous efforts toward recovery.

While some of the psychophysiological processes referred to above are generally involved, our observations deal primarily with some of the *steps* toward recovery from stress, and with evidence of some aspects of development contributing to increasing strength, or toward decreased vulnerability.

Energies provided by growth itself contribute to the vitality of effort. In *The Widening World of Childhood*, chapter 8, "The Process of Mastery," records steps by which each of several children struggled to master a physical challenge, alternating effort and rest with unflagging persistence until the desired coordination or skill was achieved. One can observe similar examples in any group of young children during phases of early growth; the path to the goal may be pointed out, encouraged, or reinforced by the adult, but it has to be felt by the child as his goal and his path. Individual differences in this drive to mastery are seen very early; we noted (pp. 136–37) correlations between infancy coping and later coping resources. The intensity of the drive to mastery differs from child to child both when he is coping with stress and when he is trying to master skills.

The spontaneous efforts of the child to bring himself back to a state of equilibrium and to restore his level of available energy also vary from child to child. Some children take a rest from developmental challenges and tasks until phase-specific, growth-stimulated hormones provide a new access of physical energy and, with it, morale. Some children regress to a less demanding level of functioning, and simultaneously evoke the tender loving care (soothing comfort and encouragement) needed to assist recuperation. Discharge of tension in crying, angry protests, non–goal-oriented motor patterns, and so forth in early years yield to more constructive management of tension as motor skills increase. Compensations or comforting objects (toys, teddy, doll, blanket) that symbolize past and hoped-for future gratification all have restitutive value nourished by the child's own drive to grow. In this chapter we shall document these and other processes involved in resilience and recovery.

Observations of resilience in children from preschool to prepuberty

As mentioned in the introduction, we were not willing deliberately to expose our subjects to any sort of severe stress. But when they were three or four years old all the children in our studies experienced mild stress in new situations as the result of demands made by adults in test situations; the threat of or actual failure in test situations; the pediatric examinations and nude body photographs; and the probing, sometimes threatening questions involved in interviews and the like. These were described in *The Widening World of Childhood*. In addition, the child's illnesses, operations, and accidents and family vicissitudes contributed to the normal expectable stress we discussed earlier.

In order to learn how children dealt with these disturbances or crises at home, we relied on chance and family cooperation. Some parents spontaneously phoned us at times of stress. In other instances, we learned from the local newspaper, for example, of an accident or a death in the family and followed it up. Whenever possible, we kept as closely in touch as we could—visiting the hospital, or home, or attending the funeral, for example. We responded to cues from the children, visiting a cemetery when a child wanted us to accompany him. We invited the grandmother of one child to lunch in order to get some view of her personality as background for better understanding the child's disturbed reaction to her divorce.

The following summaries of steps and processes in recovery are telescoped from the detailed records in our files. After describing our experiences with some of these children, we will give brief illustrations of some of the major processes that contributed to resilience in other children.

Recovery from trauma of a multiple disaster

You will remember Janice, the fragile, vulnerable baby who as a preschool child had the energy and drive to manage her environment to suit her own needs and who at adolescence was doing well in school and in her social life. Because she had inconsistent support at home, her resilient progress seems to be energized by forces within herself. To some extent this was true of most of the resilient children. But a violent multiple trauma may not leave energy for coping, and the child then has to evoke help, as we shall see in the following accounts.

Richard, aged twelve, was seriously injured in a flaming collision of the family car with a skidding oncoming car. Both of his legs were fractured. His mother, to whom he had been very close, was killed. His father, also severely injured in the accident, was in the same hospital but unable to go to Richard in the children's ward. C. J. Morgan of our staff visited Richard and talked to the supervisor of pediatrics, who reported that the boy had been in pain, was under sedation, and was "apparently confused," since he continued to ask for his mother after he had been told of her death, occasionally had a nightmare, and often called out in the night for her. He also seemed angry at his father and blamed him for the accident. He was upset by the brief visits of relatives who spent much more time with his father than with him. One nurse felt that Richard was babyish, wanted to suffer, and wanted his father to know it. Another nurse, however, said that although he complained a great deal, she did not feel he was complaining excessively for a boy in his condition. He had sobbed when talking to her about the loss of his mother. She said that once Richard remarked, "I wish you were my mother." This nurse felt that his situation was hard, as he did not have the support of either parent and had to bear the loss of his mother as well as his physical pain. To still another nurse, he complained of pains in his stomach that "he forgets when he is played with."

In bed with his legs in traction and a trapeze to help him maneuver around a bit, Richard was in pain, yet he quickly responded to Morgan's interest and to a model airplane, a puzzle, and a book his grandmother had brought about a boy's fantasies of interesting monsters living in a tiny pond. He showed Morgan a small transistor radio and a rented television set. "He didn't seem to care for flowers but it seemed to mean something to him that people cared enough to send something to indicate they were sorry." During this period of absorption with Morgan's companionship, he did not cry or complain. This we saw as illustrating his capacity to make use of new relationships and to shift his attention from pain to gratifying stimuli.

Morgan told Richard about the "Secret Life of Walter Mitty" and reported that "he seemed to get a kick out of it." His teacher had mentioned the previous year that he had seemed immensely interested in any little fairy tale, but he had outgrown this. Morgan observed that he appeared to have *regressed* to it. We have found in other instances that temporary regression can play a useful role in recovery.

"Now he began to participate in games—older boys in wheelchairs were running back and forth bumping into each other; Richard blew a whistle he had adapted from a plastic cap off a hypodermic needle, told the boys they had been speeding, and was going to give them a ticket. One boy agreed to a fine; he was to give Richard two chess lessons. Richard also had a long plastic back scratcher he had asked his sister to bring so he wouldn't have to call nurses or other people to scratch places on his legs that itched," thus showing more independence in coping with discomfort. In these activities, he demonstrated an active problem-solving capacity, a resourceful ability to restructure a situation, as well as to use peer relations in the absence of family support. He also welcomed help in adjusting his posture, relieving discomfort in his back. Richard talked about his memories of the accident—the fire, his fear of an explosion if the fire had reached the gas tank, his father's injury from the steering wheel, and the fact that he himself would probably have been killed if he had been in the front seat. He did not mention his mother. After this brief talk he quickly switched his attention to the boys across the room. This conversation implied both his capacity to assimilate and reflect on some of the experience, along with his suppression of the most painful part of the disaster—the loss of his mother, as revealed in his nightmares.

Morgan asked further questions about games Richard liked and promised to look for some of the number games, picture puzzles, and model airplanes Richard mentioned. In the afternoon he returned with a paper cup full of candy similar to those the children had arranged for themselves after research sessions. At this, Richard's eyes lit up in apparently delighted recollection, mentioning these previous occasions, and spotting a new type of candy that he planned to share with the nurses. Apparently, he was still child enough to enjoy oral pleasures along with the activity stimuli to which he had responded earlier. He then spent a full hour eagerly putting together a toy hot rod, fascinated by its little electric motor and gears. This mobilized his own special interest in electronics, a favorite hobby that renewed maximal interest and investment of effort.

Richard expressed his grief, anger, loneliness, and pain directly and indirectly. In view of the cumulative impact of injuries and loss of his mother along with the inaccessibility of his father, this open expressiveness seemed therapeutic; but the insufficiency of this mode to deal with all his physical and mental pain was indicated by his nightmares, night crying for his mother, and continued sobbing and complaining.

His ability to talk to the nurses, to get needed help but also to try to meet some needs independently, to mobilize energy, to shift attention and respond happily to new stimuli, to sustain prolonged effort in solving puzzles and making models, to engage in playful, gratifying fantasy with other boys, and to respond to Morgan's offered companionship were all factors in his resilience.

Support for working through loss: Richard's visit to his mother's grave

Another instance of Richard's seeking help was seen later in the quiet communication of his wish to visit his mother's grave. Having been confined to the hospital, he had not been able to attend her funeral. I will quote a digest of my notes on this episode: As he came out of Dr. Toussieng's office after he was able to get around on crutches, I said, "Richard, I'll be taking you home this time, that is, if you'll show me the way, because I don't know it."

As we approached the cemetery on the way home, Richard said proudly, "When my mother was buried here they had a great big tall wreath of flowers and a cross, and the Girl Scouts made a big wreath." I commented that the Girl Scouts must have thought a great deal of his mother to make such a beautiful wreath for the funeral. Richard did not reply, but he looked very hard at the cemetery, evidently trying to find the grave. Suddenly he said, "Oh, it's over that way, it's over there near the tallest tree." He seemed to feel so deeply that I asked, "Would you like to drive over there?" A little surprised, as if he hadn't expected anyone to understand what he might want, he said, "Oh, yes, *would* you?" Then he pointed out the driveway through the heavy blanket of snow on the ground.

I drove slowly as he tried to identify the exact location, with a little trouble at first. Then he said, "Oh, it's over there where the blue wreath is." I finally saw a very pale blue plastic wreath at one end of a grave, near an Austrian pine in a pleasant spot. He was very eager for me to see it. I commented that the wreath would probably last a long, long time. He added as if comforted that it was made of plastic and it would.

As we drove out of the cemetery, he said meaningfully, "It was awfully nice of you to take me there," again as if he hadn't expected that anybody would want to take him to the cemetery. Evidently the grave and the beauty of its location meant a great deal to him.

I was astonished to find him completely relaxed in the car after such a bad recent experience. So I asked whether he had been afraid in a car after the accident. "Yes, for a while." And when I asked him how long, he said, "Oh, for a few days" and then added, "We were driving around with friends all the time"—as if implying that feeling safe with them he soon got over the fear.

I asked how his seventeen-year-old sister managed in taking care of the house now with all of her high school work; was it quite hard for her? Richard said most enthusiastically, "I think she's *amazing.*" As we reached his home he said sincerely but brokenly, "Thank you . . . for taking me to the . . ." and I finished "cemetery." Here Richard had initiated an experience that helped him to assimilate the loss of his mother.

In the next months he made a complete physical recovery, but his intense hostility to a new mother when his father remarried a year later pointed to deep undercurrents of blame or resentment toward his father. Undoubtedly, he could have used therapy to deal with these emotional pressures, but this was beyond the scope of our resources and the family's readiness.

Richard's disastrous accident occurred at a sensitive phase of prepuberty; insecurity about body integrity and about one's capacity to manage alone sufficiently to leave childhood dependence behind are typical of this phase. His cries, protested by an intolerant nurse, were not just a regressive reaction; they were a communication—a plea for help and support. When Morgan, a congenial, understanding young man, brought him this support in the form of companionship and electronic materials of maximal interest for him, he responded quickly and constructively. The support relevant to his favorite activities evoked his own resources.

Similarly, when he hesitantly indicated his need to come to terms with his mother's burial and I made this possible, he responded warmly and deeply, if quietly. It was doubtless important to him to share this experience with a mother figure.

Coping methods contributing to
recovery from a short-term trauma

A clearer example of regression under stress was seen in Grace Heider's visit to Ray* when he was in bed with a broken leg.

Ray, the fourth of five children in one of the poorest families in our sample, was considered by Heider to be one of the less vulnerable infants. But as a result of simultaneous pressures (illness, a broken leg, and his mother's preoccupation with a seriously ill baby and a new pregnancy) when he was three and a half, he was rated more vulnerable at the preschool stage than at infancy. His behavior was immature, and he seemed to feel inadequate. Yet later he recovered resiliently and in school became successful socially and academically.

In the winter before the injury and illness Ray seemed unusually well coordinated, especially in walking and mounting stairs, which he did with marked ease, bodily control, and good balance. His finer (finger) coordination was adequate for his age. He was very open to the world of stimuli. His skin and auditory sensitivity provided much gratification: with tremendous joy or enchantment he hugged and listened to our musical dog. He preferred strongly colored toys. He was not much interested in organized cognitive experiences, though he was moderately capable of dealing with them.

Ray cooperated willingly and wholeheartedly with the examinations; he felt free to ask for and accept help. He seemed to get somewhat tense when the tasks were difficult, and he did not strive for achievement. He had the usual masculine interests of a boy his age; he was honestly interested in all the materials, in how things work, how they fit together; he liked to try things out and was curious. But even before his illness and accident, mild stress was seen to produce considerable deterioration of his functioning.

The fracture of a leg in April changed, for a short time, Ray's situation in the family. For the time being, *he* was his mother's baby. In the first days he seemed to be happy and enjoying a comfortable period of regression: he "apparently at first allowed himself to slip completely into a state of babyhood, lying passive in the crib, fingering toys while his family hovered about, eager to please." Suddenly he had found himself the focus of attention and care of which he had been moderately deprived earlier. To a degree this method of dealing with his illness has a restitutive value then, as well as balancing his discomfort with gratification.

* This study of Ray makes use of a report by Ralph Sherfey.

But soon he lost most of this attention and care because of a new baby's needs. This was reflected in the second MLT session with me in June. Here Ray included a great deal of baby-feeding activity and mother–baby care; he looked at the observer wistfully when putting the baby in the mother's arms and squeezing them together. He appeared "soft and infantile, suggesting that he hadn't had as much babying as he could use" and apparently was feeling deprived all over again. Projecting his longing in play did not meet his need adequately.

Some changes in activity level and reality-orientation seemed to express his weakness. Observers were impressed by his sleepiness and dreaminess; even when he was doing things with the toys, nothing much happened. He also showed less effort at control than earlier.

Ray had a mild case of polio during the summer; since it was not reported to us, we did not see him until some months after this. At the age of four years and one month, the experimenter observed a "failure of maturation in the ten months since we saw him first." Moreover, his behavior revealed a much higher degree of background stress than in the earlier sessions. In the previous winter he had become very much at ease in the test situations, but now his whole appearance was different; he seemed to consider himself a small, inadequate person. At the same time, he was newly aware of achievement and seemed to be motivated more by this than by his interests. There was less communication with adults. His main problem now seemed to be his position between big and little, his struggle between dependency and independency needs. Since the summer he had recovered some physical strength, and in his dealing with people he was now more active and assertive, but at first unproductively.

With a male psychiatrist Ray tended to more effortfully show himself as a "man" while at the same time struggling against and attacking the real "man." He expressed a masculinity that to him seemed to be connected with ruthlessness and violence. On the other hand, a strong need for tender contact would break through at moments and cause him to lean affectionately against the examiner's knee. But in another moment he would turn against the examiner, attacking him aggressively. It appeared that Ray made a point of being negativistic and naughty and was torn between needs to be dependent and to be aggressive.

The whole situation seemed to involve a great deal of stress for him. Throughout the hour much anxiety, insecurity, and tension were revealed in fears, especially of noises outside the examination room— noises to which he had not reacted so intensely in the spring. We may guess that Ray was so insecure in this situation not only because of the trauma of illness and the accident, but also because he no longer knew what position he had in his world after his mother's preoccupation first with a sick baby and then with a new one. His world had a character of unstructuredness and unreliability, and he seemed to feel very inadequate to deal with his problems in his changing world.

Emergence of an active response to tension and insecurity

While his awkwardness, resistance, and control under tension continued, there were new observations of wild and uncontrolled activity, fighting in a manner that approached "drivenness." He was now described as irascible and stubborn when tension mounted, and also aggressive. His mother too saw him as more irritable than he was before. (Earlier she had considered him very good-natured and easygoing.)

The active side of his potentialities now seemed to have more impetus than before. He developed better coping methods, such as humor and doing things to change the situation. Direct expressions of needs, struggles, vigorous action, and a certain flexibility were seen more clearly in the session with the male observer, whereas in sessions with women he showed more resistance, rigidity, and control.

It is interesting that a rise in his IQ from 92 to 102 occurred at this time. He seemed now to mobilize resources of energy and to apply them more strictly on the reality level.

From regression to progress through aggression

Ray's shifts during nearly a year of varied stressful experiences (broken leg, polio, sick sibling, new baby) and his start toward recovery reflected his capacity both to make good use of temporary regression and to mobilize aggressive energy for progress. A similar pattern was repeated during his first year of school when, as one of the youngest children in the group, he was not functioning at his best. His mother and teacher agreed that he should "stay back" and repeat the grade. This time around, with the advantages of both his previous learning and his now superior status in the group, Ray became a good scholar, maintaining a good level of achievement throughout his school years, and also showed a moderate increase in IQ. In addition he was popular with his peers; in second grade he was vice-president of his class.

Rebound

Ray's resilience may have included an element of "rebound" after the period of regression and static functioning; this may have been facilitated by a real satiation of needs to play the baby or to maintain a dependent role. Moreover, his accident and illness occurred just prior to the onset of the phallic phase, with its typical surging competitiveness, intrusiveness, and zest. A marked stimulation of competitive drive and aggression in the phallic phase after his illness was inferred from subsequent evidence.

Ray gave himself leeway to be a baby again, and his thumb-sucking must have been consoling, judging from his contentment. The play session testified to the fact that he needed more mothering than could be provided by his busy mother. While this retarded his progress, it also left him to his own resources—in time, to pull himself up by his own bootstraps.

In contrast to the motherless Richard and to Ray, whose mother had more problems than she could manage, we see Susan, whose parents left no stone unturned to help her recover from a near-fatal case of polio. They offered her sensitive support, endless love, and tireless attention. Instead of dying or becoming a permanent cripple, Susan seemed to absorb vitality from her devoted, strong parents, and, with the care of imaginative nurses and skillful doctors, she gradually recovered normal functioning over a period of ten years.

The role of love

We noted earlier the built-in regenerative and recovery processes provided by nature. The doctor cannot create new cells where tissue has been burned, torn, or cut away; he can only make it easier for the body to use its own regenerative processes. But with human beings and some animals we have to go beyond the organic and biochemical factors in resilience, beyond even the sheerly medical care provided to assist natural forces in recovery. Marasmic babies do not die solely from lack of nutrition. Also involved may be a mysterious deficiency that we call "loss of love," without understanding exactly how this works (Spitz 1945). There are many reports of death in both animals and people following the loss of a loved object, most often a mate.

The counterpart of this phenomenon is the recovery promoted by love, or tender loving care. When I observed Susan at the age of six years acting out fantasies and vivid though not consciously remembered experiences in the hospital three years earlier, she placed the "sickest baby" in a corner by itself and remarked, "They love the sickest baby best," as she proceeded to give it "special" care. The sense of being loved, the tender soothing bodily contacts, apparently activate sensory—cortical, thalamic, autonomic, hormonal, biochemical—processes that facilitate recovery. I have observed this process at first hand in several instances of severe illness where doctors felt that "death could happen at any moment" or where a thyroid or ulcer operation was thought to be necessary. In these cases total mobilization of special loving care was followed by recovery, without the operation. We can agree that "love is not enough" (Bettelheim 1950) and also recognize that sometimes drugs and medical apparatus are not enough without love.

Interaction of supportive love and the drive to mastery

A fusion of new growth energies in a propitious phase, along with natural recovery processes and the mutual reinforcement given by these when combined with gratifying external stimulation were seen in preschool Susan after her polio. But Susan's crisis was much more severe and prolonged than Ray's. The polio that left her back and muscles very weak was followed by years of hampered locomotion and a long struggle first to master sitting up, then to master the use of crutches, and finally, after hospitalization and fusion of nine vertebrae, to master as many forms of movement as possible. Her own energy, zest for life, coping resources, and drive to recover were great; but there was also the stimulus of the devoted care of nurses and parents, from whom she perhaps "borrowed strength" during the most severe part of her illness. Their support included *demands* to do everything that could help her to get well, and when she faltered, their determination held her to the effort and kept the goal of recovery in sight: "If we keep on with the exercises, you can dance at parties when you are sixteen."

Discharge of angry reactions to frustration and pain

The role of love and of positive gratifications is only part of the picture with Susan. During a long struggle for recovery from serious illness, enormous frustration was involved, with inevitable angry reactions. Here she was probably helped by the fact that she could allow herself periodic open discharge of anger in occasional explosions and crying. In time, as she was able to sit up and handle her body more freely, the piano and music came to be an outlet, which we can relate to her earlier use of fantasy.

One boy remarked that "when you're young, crying is one method of letting out your fantasy—after you've gotten rid of the outburst, you can more easily get back to reality." (This is a child whose mother commented when he was a preschool child that a spanking seemed to relieve his tension.) We also saw in our children examples of techniques of modulation of anger, as with Teddy's way of grinding acorns under his heel during a party that he found frustrating. Mild mock fighting is another device not unusual among children who are able to modulate active expressions of aggressive tendencies, as we saw with Teddy and Steve at the preschool "parties."

Reduction of pain through decathexis via fantasy

As part of her effort toward mastery, Susan also had a capacity to minimize pain through participation in fantasy and games initiated by hospital nurses—a resource used by Sam and his mother at the time of his treatments for an injured finger (Murphy 1962). A similar capacity was noted in Richard in the hospital. The process involved here appears to be that of decathecting the pain; attention is fully absorbed in the gratifying, amusing fantasy or activity, and the fact that it can be "forgotten" permits energies to be mobilized for constructive use.

Other roles of fantasy: retaliation and promise

Susan's fantasy was also used in another way. At one time she was angry and humiliated at the cold, impersonal way she was exhibited by one doctor at a medical conference discussing sequelae of polio. Afterward she retaliated in fantasy by playing that a tornado demolished the doctor's house.

Seven years after the polio damage, when Susan had to go to the hospital for an operation on her back, she took to the hospital her very worn little baby doll which she had kept from her earliest childhood. It was as if this doll had survived with her through all the vicissitudes of her entire life and to have her near would be perhaps a way of sharing, and also a promise of further survival. The doll was evidently a *symbol* of her continuity and her hope.

This special, highly symbolic fantasy device of Susan's might be compared to Sam's use of his mother's gift of a little elf doll "Woody" (Murphy 1962, pp. 124–25), so tiny that he could always have it with him on his visits to the hospital for painful treatment. What Woody really represented was not the personal survival apparently symbolized by Susan's "baby," but the active resourcefulness of his mother—Woody meant most to him when his mother was not allowed to be at his side. Years later he remarked to his mother, "Woody was really you."

Fending off intolerable demands

Sturdy as Susan was, she consistently protected herself from embarrassment or humiliation in situations involving bodily exposure: she simply refused to participate in the preschool body photograph sessions and also in the prepuberty pediatric examination. She avoided reliving unpleasant memories or submitting to disturbing questions by refusing to talk about polio. She never passively complied with demands that she felt she could not handle. These refusals, and her relative confidence that they would be respected, helped her to maintain her equilibrium in all social situations. At the same time, her refusal to comply never became generalized to a wide range of situations; she participated actively in play and sports activities to the point where she successfully mastered bicycle riding, horseback riding, swimming, and dancing. In other words, she clarified what she could and could not manage both physically and emotionally. She protected the process of her recovery by not attempting so much that she would be overwhelmed.

The propitious phase

Ray's and Susan's stressful experiences occurred at the age of three to four years, after basic motor and language skills had been established. We noted also that the period of regression following Ray's broken leg doubtless satisfied some residual needs for babying. His recovery began as he was on the threshold of new emerging energies of the phallic phase, when small boys typically do become more aggressive and more aware of their masculinity and of their progress beyond babyhood. The release from constraint and from the pain due to the illness and the broken leg, the temporary gratification from infantilization (being babied), and the new upsurge of growth energies all contributed to heightened activity and then to more resourceful coping methods. If the multiple stress had occurred in the more vulnerable phase of the second year of life when locomotion, speech, and other functions were less secure, it is doubtful that such good progress would have been made. More than this, the sequence of broken leg, polio, and competition from a new baby could have been traumatic for Ray.

Several young children who suffered severe illness, accident, or other bodily insult at the age of three showed similar resilience in recovery from these stressful experiences in contrast to the lag in development of important functions in certain children who were immobilized by illness during the second year of life, as occurred with Rachel and Lennie.

The common element in the resilient three year olds is the fact that the child's illness with its temporary regression occurred *after* speech, motor development, and basic coping resources were relatively well integrated; in other words, these functions involved in communication and self-management in the environment were sufficiently well developed and organized so that no permanent or severe losses in these areas were experienced as a result of the illness. In addition to the fact that the illness did not occur at a critical phase for development of such functions, is the fact that following the illness the child was *entering* that period of normally zestful expansion, curiosity, intrusion into and dominance of the environment, emergence of rich emotional responses and of fantasy known variously as "the phallic phase" (Freud 1953) or "the first adolescence" (Gesell and Ilg 1940). That is, the normal rebound instituted by the child's bodily recuperative processes was augmented or reinforced by the new energies released at this stage and perhaps also by an intensified impulse to grow, which in many children, becomes intense and contributes to conscious coping efforts at this stage.

This contribution of new phase-specific growth energies after a period of immobilization, helplessness, regression, defeat or frustration at the age of three, was illustrated in several children. This was especially clear in the case of Colin, an initially cooperative little boy who also experienced an acute illness, though one of short duration (Murphy 1956, vol. 2). During this, he had experiences of dizziness and, we infer, helplessness, along with some confusion that was evidently intensely distressing. After recovery the drive to mastery evoked by a need to conquer the feeling of helplessness was expressed in new and extreme aggression. This required special controls from his teacher and eventually brought a modulation and thoroughly constructive channeling of activity drives. The point here is that the occurrence of Colin's illness, just before the emergence of vigorous phallic energies meant that recovery from the illness-imposed passivity was facilitated by the new aggressive impulses and the accompanying drive to mastery.

Both principles outlined above—a fusion of new energies with natural recovery processes, and the mutual reinforcement given by these when combined with gratifying external stimulation—also applied to Susan whose polio occurred when she was three. *Thus, the propitious phase can be as important for recovery as a sensitive or critical phase is for trauma.*

In these illustrations we have seen the interaction between the child's capacity to respond and to use multifaceted support, and the adults' understanding of what help is most relevant for each child. Other forces were at work in some of the instances of resilience we saw over the years; in certain instances, assistance in achieving understanding can be crucial.

Recovery from sudden trauma through understanding*

Five-year-old Lew accompanied his family to church one Sunday.

* From a report written by Lew's mother, whose two daughters were in the intensive sample.

After he had gone in to Sunday school, his parents learned that the five-year-old son of the rector—who lived near Lew's family—had suffocated in a fire during the previous night. When they picked the children up after church one of the older children asked what was wrong with everyone. Mother said, "Bobby Smith died last night in the fire at Grace and Steve's house. I don't really know much about it, but that's 'what is wrong' with everyone."

Lew apparently paid no attention to this, but his mother felt that he could probably see that both she and her husband had been crying. He did not mention it the rest of the day, and his parents did not refer to it again since Lew did not seem particularly bothered at that time. When his mother put him to bed he seemed calm, but she noticed that he did not go off to sleep immediately, as he usually did; he seemed a bit restless. However, he settled down in about fifteen minutes and she left.

In about twenty minutes one of the older children came to her saying, "The little's man's crying just like his heart would break." Mother went in to him, held him, saying, "Son, what's wrong? Tell Mother and I'll help you." Lew said, "Oh, I'm just so unhappy." "Why?" she said (thinking it might be about the death of the child but not wanting to emphasize the matter if that were not the case). He did not answer but continued to cry. Mother rocked him comfortingly, and after about fifteen minutes he went to sleep.

The next morning his mother noticed that he had developed a tic; he would blink his eyes for a moment as though the light hurt him or he didn't like what he saw. Again that night he had difficulty going to sleep. His parents felt that Lew might be fearful of dying in his sleep, perhaps imagining that this was what had happened to Bobby. They decided that it would be better to tell him more about the child's death, as probably nothing they could tell him could possibly be as bad as what he was imagining.

The next day they discussed the matter with each other in Lew's hearing; they could see he was listening intently. The father commented that the fire that killed the child had occurred because of defective wiring (something Lew understands). The father also said the the house Bobby lived in was old and that fires due to defective wiring seldom occurred in houses that were new "like ours." Then the mother said that Bobby had *not* been asleep when he died but had become frightened and locked his door, so his father could not get to him to carry him downstairs. Lew was listening carefully to all this though apparently playing with some soldiers. The father concluded by saying that Bobby's bedroom was upstairs, whereas "all our bedrooms are on the ground floor, so we could jump from the windows if we ever *should* have a fire."

That afternoon, the mother overheard Lew talking to the cat. He said, "Now I'm going to tell you just what happened to that boy." He proceeded to tell the entire story, in almost the exact words his parents had used. He ended up by saying, "That boy *didn't* die when he was sleeping, he died from the fire." Lew went to sleep peacefully that night. The next day he was still blinking his eyes occasionally, but not for a long period of time. In a few days he stopped this entirely. He has never referred directly to the incident. Here the reduction of personal threat by clarifying the reality seemed to be the core process in recovering.

The role of adult help in understanding

Lew's symptom developed from anxiety due to misunderstanding and confusion. At his age the confusion could be clarified by the understanding explanation from trusted parents, and with this clarification the symptom vanished far more quickly than would be expected at a later age. His parents' help was as impressive as Lew's need to know and his use of what he knew.

We also saw in *The Widening World of Childhood* (chapter 6) Sam's endless questions reflecting his need to understand and clarify every detail of the surgical work in repairing his amputated fingertip.

Thus, recovery from disturbance—emotional upheaval, disintegrative reactions, loss of both equilibrium and smooth functioning—may be seen to have cognitive as well as drive aspects. These include such capacities as the readiness to recognize change in a situation or in the child's relation to a situation as this relationship changes when new coping skills are developed. Cognitive factors involved in resilience also include sheer awareness of, clarity about, and capacity to mobilize problem-solving possibilities.

Mothers' methods of support to evoke resilient coping

As of this writing we know of no study about how the parents of American children teach them to accept pain. Anthropological reports deal with this subject periodically (Mead 1935). In our group, some teenagers reported that while their mothers took adequate care of any wound, they were taught to be brave about pain. Such advice as "this is a hard life and you might as well get prepared for it" was used by some parents.

In situations that commonly arouse fear or anxiety in young children, sympathetic mothers, nurses, and doctors utilize some combination of support and soothing techniques to relieve the child's discomfort. Anxiety, and the subjective sense of stress, can be alleviated by gratifying experiences. These range from oral gratification in the form of candy, gum, or the promise of an ice-cream cone to reassuring conversation with the child and pleasure-evoking tactual stimulation such as caresses, stroking, and patting.

Evidence of soothing support successfully reducing the level of anxiety was seen in the comfort Sam received from his mother at the time of his accident (Murphy 1962, p. 123) and in the support mothers gave to preschool children beginning their research sessions (ibid., pp. 23–24).

Narcissistic rewards and resilience

During the hospital experiences of both Sam (Murphy 1962) and Susan there was, in addition to the loving care of parents, the vivid appreciation of nurses and doctors who regarded each of these children as heroic. This gratification acted as an additional motivating force to these children in strengthening their own drive to recovery. Both children also responded positively to other childlike gratifications in the form of oral delights and special gifts. New stimuli, such as Helen's trip to Disneyland after her tonsil operation, probably also gain their memorable and engulfing happiness quality from the resurgence of global infantile pleasure in response to new sensory experience. Consolation and comfort are the more effective when they are provided by parents who are also able to deal with their own needs and stressful experience and those of the family.

Parents' example

Assumptions of the possibility of progress were expressed by parents who directly improved living conditions for the family. The families of nearly two-thirds (nineteen of thirty-one) of the children of the intensive group either moved to a better home in Topeka or built or enlarged their homes themselves (seven). Improvements also included decorations, furnishings, and appliances handmade by one or both parents in many of the families. Thus, the process of making life better in a material way provided an immediate model for progress as the children were growing up.

Identification with resilient models

Because our sample did not include families from the most disorganized low-income group, the children were growing up in families whose adult members were able to cope with most of the problems they confronted. Depressive tendencies were rare and most often relatively transient. Disturbed mothers required only a few weeks and a small amount of psychiatric support in order to return to their family responsibilities. Some mothers paid warm tribute to the helpful support of husbands at times when the mothers themselves felt overwhelmed. They expected to be able to manage whatever stress life brought. However pressured they might feel, many of them took assurance from the fact that their forebears had survived greater stress. The children, then, were growing up in an atmosphere where resilience and the capacity for recovery, mastery, and progress were expected, if not in fact an obligation. Identifying with a resilient coping style was part of the process of growing into the culture.

The ways in which the child has coped with stress, in terms of response to and extent of internalization of support from the mother, as well as in terms of spontaneous efforts the child himself can make, have a bearing on and must include the pattern of defense mechanisms integrated with active coping efforts of different kinds. Here we saw the effort of Susan's mother to substitute laughter and positive affects when her seven-month-old baby was crying. This was followed later by Susan's capacity for clowning, burlesque, and other gay and humorous ways of dealing with stress of polio, along with tendencies toward temporary denial and hiding. The defense mechanism of denial was accompanied by a broad capacity to mobilize many kinds of positive gratification from toys, pets, and pleasant tactual stimuli to her use of piano playing and music at times of stress. Active efforts combined with useful defense mechanisms contributed to her success in mastering the stress involved in physical suffering, difficulties with physical skills, and occasional ridicule of peers.

Restitution

The need for restitution where emotional and material deprivation has played a part in a child's disturbance has been discussed by Alpert (1959). We too found that recovery was facilitated by the provision of new resources to a boy whose level of school functioning had deteriorated. Many factors were involved in Chester's declining level in schoolwork and deteriorating relation with his peers at the age of eleven: his poverty and poor clothes, his feeling of neglect by his father, and his mother's emotional instability and violent punitiveness at a time when she was overwhelmed by family burdens. However, he responded eagerly when he was given special attention by a parent surrogate from our staff and an opportunity to learn how to make good fishing flies, a crystal radio, a boat and other objects of special interest to him. Then he began to make a new place for himself in the schoolroom, bringing things he had made to his teacher, explaining how he had made them, letting her show them to the class in the "show-and-tell" period (he was still too diffident to show them to the class himself). He progressed to being able to give the explanations while she showed the objects he had made and then before long was able to show these things to the class by himself. These progressive steps—in common with other new outlets for his interests and stimulation for improving his schoolwork—led to improvements in his grades and in his relationships with the other children at school, as well as with his teachers.

Substitute parent

Another kind of restitution involved providing a "substitute" parent for Gordon, whose mother had been removed from him because of mental illness. His father's work was such that he was busy especially on weekends and evenings and had little time for the boy. Gordon's schoolwork was also deteriorating badly; his relationships with teachers and children were poor; he seemed utterly discouraged, defeated, and bitter. Again C. J. Morgan from our staff, who became both parent surrogate and companion, provided gratifications and opportunities to develop new interests and skills. This led to improved work in school, better relationships with teachers, an important place for Gordon among his peers in sports, and a beginning of good heterosexual relationships. Profound discouragement and depression that threatened his outlook a couple of years earlier yielded to a forward-looking orientation toward solving his problems.

Integrative processes and defenses used for resilience

Resilience often involves complex integrative patterns. Special processes were at work in Susan's humorous dramatic burlesquing of herself when she was still crippled, projecting the role of a damaged clown, and in Helen's conceptualization of the sequences of her experience as "bad things can turn into good things" (see pp. 332–33). Both processes were seen in latency and both bespeak a capacity to formulate fantasies or concepts that can contain the experience, objectify it, and universalize it—an important process to accomplish especially in Susan's case, where active rumination regarding causes of her disaster, resentment against it, and fantasies of possible neglect by her parents were still present. Her humor helped to keep her feelings sufficiently flexible to permit ultimate working through and revision of her accusations of her parents. Susan's defensive clowning actively helped her to get through the awkwardness of a period of convalescence. Subsequently, after an operation when she was encased in a cast from chin to hips, she burlesqued her rigid posture by "queening it" as she held her head high, thus amusing her peers and gaining their respect for her pluck, along with their help in situations she couldn't manage herself.

Selective retrospective denial

At the sixth-grade level, anxiety about going to junior high school was observed in many Topeka children as part of a broad uneasiness, insecurity, or discouragement about themselves at the transition from childhood to adolescence. However, at the completion of senior high school, they could retrospectively see some positive values in their struggles, although that early period still seemed the most difficult and unrewarding of their lives. It made demands on them which in anticipation seemed unmanageable, such as adapting to the hourly changes from one room to another, from one teacher to another, none of whom were really acquainted with the children; individually keeping track of one's belongings as they were selectively removed from or returned to the locker for a given class period; changing to new groupings of students; and losing contact with old friends. Yet, after recovering from their anxiety, what they remembered was the relief in being able to move around more as they went from class to class. The more distant relations with the teachers came to be seen as part of their welcome detachment from adults in early adolescence.

Repression

Lazarus states (1966): "There has been uncertainty over whether to treat repression as a separate defense parallel with other defensive strategies or whether to treat all the defenses as forms of the one basic process, repression. It is not clear which defenses go together in the same individual or in a given form of psychopathology. Nor is there agreement over whether the choice of defense is linked to the degree of threat, is specific to the threat content, or is a dispositional property of personality itself."

In our children we saw instances of persistent tendencies to use one type of defense and of certain kinds of defensive maneuvers to be used in certain typical stress situations. At other times we observed defensive behavior related to the threat content, for example, the frequency of slightly exhibitionist clowning in nude body photograph and group measurement situations. In other instances, the choice of defense seemed to be linked to the degree of threat: denial or negation may be used initially, with escape, suppression, or repression in order to totally avoid the threat when the denial is ineffective. Teddy appeared to deny conflict between his parents as a preschool child. Some years after their divorce he "just tried to forget it"—a process that seemed to help him to continue his own maturing at a steady pace, although he paid a price in decline of memory of other events as well. In different personalities different combinations of active coping and defense are seen and with different patterns of variation and effectiveness.

The role of challenge

Toynbee's *A Study of History* offers a hypothesis about the waxing and waning of civilizations: a challenge to growth and activity has to reach a certain critical degree of intensity if there is to be anything more than mere carryover from generation to generation. It is only when men encounter a failure in the use of available techniques that they invent and carry through new creative ideas. If, on the other hand, the challenge is too strong, it may actually crush the best efforts that can be made. There is a rather narrow critical band between the "not enough" and the "too much." The challenge may be repeated frequently and in some civilizations there may be continuous or stepwise progression in which a great individual necessarily plays an important part, but in which the objective character of the tasks to be surmounted is paramount.

This may be seen in relation to children who solve problems easily, conform, and are under no challenge to progress. A well-behaved, well-adjusted child may appear static by college age, as studies of Sarah Lawrence students illustrated (Raushenbush and Murphy 1960).

In the course of our exploration of steps in recovery, we have seen illustrations of relevant help and of the child's own coping efforts and struggle for mastery of useful defense mechanisms, sometimes temporary as in Ray's regression, sometimes permanently woven into the child's character as with Susan's humor and fantasy. We come now to the question: What are the outcomes for the child's development? At the beginning of this chapter we quoted the conclusion by one boy—that working through a crisis strengthens one to meet future stress. We can reflect now on various ways in which this comes about.

Desensitization and "getting used to" stress

Just as illness, accidents, and other traumata sensitize the child and result in decreased control, including the capacity to shut out or gate stimulation, increased health and certain aspects of growth (including neural maturation) and useful coping techniques contribute to desensitization. The "stimulus barrier" (Tennes 1972) may be strengthened; the capacity to selectively shift attention so as to reduce stressful stimulation may increase; sensitive zones may be selectively decathected; attention may shift to the outer world and possibilities of actively managing it or exploiting its potential gratifications; interest may shift from the narrow and often very conflictive world of family to new relationships in the broader world outside.

Reduction of stress reactions to intense stimuli, pain, or frustration by coping devices is also assisted by some additional processes. *Familiarization* decreases the threat perceived in an originally new stress. A few children who were initially fearful in coming to psychological test sessions lost their anxiety after the first one or two visits and became actively interested. Only one child did not respond this way and was dropped from the sample at his mother's request. Familiarization contributes to cognitive mastery, knowing what to do, feeling secure and thus free to enjoy the new experiences. *Negative adaptation*, or getting used to a stimulus of some degree of unpleasantness, is recognized in the psychology of smell, but a similar process occurs with many children in relation to such experiences as getting shots. "I'm used to it now," the child says. *Mastery of specific tasks and skills*, experiences of success, and so forth decrease the threat of failure and thus anxiety.

Other initially stressful stimuli to which the growing child becomes accustomed or which he "learns to conquer" include: the unpleasantness of cold water in infancy or when he begins to learn to swim; fear of strangers, the mastery of which Bühler (1930) considered a positive indication of expected developmental progress at ten months; "shyness" in new situations; and other fears such as of jumping, climbing, or dogs.

In overcoming these fears a combination of several processes is involved, among which are the release from anxiety about the unknown aspects of the real or imagined threat; the development of new coping techniques, ways of handling the situation; and changes in the physical relation of the child to the stimulus, as when a child gets enough taller and stronger so that the dog is realistically less able to knock him down when it jumps on him. Thus, different kinds of learning combine with a real change in his relation to the stimulus to produce affective changes and reduce apprehension. The universality of these processes is seen in the reports of changes and outgrowing of fears in longitudinal investigations (Macfarlane, Allen, and Honzik 1954) and cross-sectional studies (Jersild and Holmes 1935; Jones 1924) of children's fears.

Other contributions to desensitization include (a) improved defenses, such as gating out the stimulus, temporary healthy or unhealthy use of denial and minimization of danger or pain ("whistling in the dark") and (b) mobilizing compensatory or masking comforts. In our children these desensitizing processes reduced anxiety, released the children for free enjoyment of gratifying experiences and active exploration of the potentialities of the situation, and led to new experiences of mastery. These positive consequences of desensitization may be assumed to reinforce the child's willingness to try new experiences even when some threat or pain is involved.

Increasingly mature cognitive appraisal also contributes to desensitization. Some very young children in our day-care centers cried or screamed when the tornado "with a roar as loud as five express trains all together" tore through Topeka. But we saw that some teenagers either stayed on their jobs, found a place to watch it from a distance of half a mile to a mile, or took shelter as ordered by parents. "We're used to them, we've grown up with them, and we know what to do" was a common response among those questioned after a serious tornado watch that preceded the historic tornado.

In *Children of Crisis* (Coles 1967) we read of mothers remarking of the desegregation stress, "It's a fact of their young lives, not something strange and impossible [to cope with]," thereby desensitizing the issue by calling attention to the everyday reality the desegregation process had become. In a somewhat similar way a teenager spoke of "taking each day as it comes." Another youth was described as able to "concentrate hard on the intense moment and the distant future's promise," like his mother; he was also able to use some of his father's ability to shrug off the "useless baggage of anxiety" inherited from a world shadowed by fear.

Effects of exposure to manageable stress
and resilient mastery

One of the boys in *Children of Crisis* remarked of his desegregation experience, "That school glued me together." He thought it made him stronger than he ever supposed he could be. Dr. Coles also described a black boy, Fred, who had developed stubbornness, staying power, a capacity for control and modulation, will and endurance through his early conquest of polio. Dr. Jean Macfarlane (1963) concluded from her longitudinal studies that children who met stress earlier were better able to cope with the difficulties of college years than were those who had had less experience of coping with stress in childhood. Studies of rats have led some authors to overgeneralize this point; rats subjected to a certain degree of electric shock in infancy were better learners than comparable rats who had not been shocked. The children we have described are those who were able to experience gains in coping capacity following early mastery of manageable stress. In recognizing the positive contributions to future resilience and resources for mastery of stress, we must not forget the differences between these children and those for whom stress experiences have been overwhelming and traumatic and have led to disorganization, familiar to every clinical worker.

In comparing the steps and processes contributing to recovery from major stress with the coping devices observed when children were confronting challenging new situations and opportunities that involved the mild but real threat of the unknown, we note the narrower range of coping resources in the former. The reasons seem obvious: a child in a hospital, or at home with a broken leg, or in a body cast, is inherently less able to "impose his own structure on a situation" or even to "fend off pressures from the environment." Protests and demands are of little use all too often. He is largely at the mercy of the hospital routine; at home, he has to fit into the convenience of the family and the medically prescribed schedule. Coping includes very few active possibilities for a child in these situations. Still, the consequences of adaptation to such situations vary enormously, depending in part on the extent to which long-enforced passivity becomes an internalized pattern, as it did with Rachel in contrast to Ray and Susan, who became more active after the period of regression. Moreover, some children, especially during the highly motoric preschool years, seem to find it impossible to fit into a scheme of inactivity even when they are very ill with a high temperature. Maggie,* an active five-year-old, vigorously protested, and rebelled against, being kept in bed for scarlet fever and played games of outwitting her nurse.

If the early experience included a balance of gratification in both an oral-receptive-passive context and a psychically active problem-solving (or a challenge-mastering or struggling) context, the child may be able to both extend the range of resources for gratification and also utilize and respond to, or even seek, a challenge. Weissenberg (unpublished) showed that children valued objects that were the results of their own efforts more highly than objects that they had acquired effortlessly. Some children in our sample performed better on difficult structured tests than they did on the easier ones; several children even succeeded on a difficult test after having failed an easier one of the same series. This, of course, is in line with the observations of many teachers that children find challenging tasks more "interesting" and attack such tasks more vigorously than those that present no problem.

* A child not in this study but observed from infancy on.

Thus, the child not only continues to enjoy and to feel good about appropriate receptive experiences at each new level but also "likes himself" when engaged in problem-solving efforts to master a challenge. A drive toward progressing and toward meeting new challenges then comes to be established as a deep motive within the child.

Residues of resilient experiences and self-image

Clinical discussions have analyzed the effects on character formation of cumulative trauma (Khan 1964), and it is clear that to be disorganizing stress does not have to be initially overwhelming if it is prolonged.

Recurrent experiences of resilience may, however, leave positive residues. The child learns that while he may get sick, or hurt, he "always gets well"; or that while he may fail in one task, he will be able to succeed in another. Thus confidence in his own resilient capacities is reinforced and breeds further resilience. The common prescription to get on the bicycle again immediately after a tumble carries the implication that it is important to avoid jelling an experience of failure and to erase it, as it were, by a new experience of success. Coping with the failure produces greater strength.

Self-image and self-feeling

In *The Widening World of Childhood*, we saw how the impact of a new challenge intensified the child's awareness of himself; his capacity to meet such a challenge enhanced his pleasure, his sense of adequacy, and his pride. Through experiences of mastery of new demands and utilizing new opportunities for gratification, the child extends and verifies his identity as one who can cope with new aspects of the environment. Through his coping experiences, the child discovers and measures himself and develops his own perception of who and what he is and in time may become; we can say that the child creates his personal way and adds to his strengths.

Thus, over and over again Darlene repeated her effort to manage the jumping board at the preschool party until she finally succeeded and triumphantly shouted, "I jumped, I jumped!" (Murphy 1962, p. 170). Susan, still unable to sit up without support at the age of five after two years of slow recovery from polio, proudly exclaimed, "I can hold two things at once!" Terry during the preschool intelligence test asserted, "I know it, I know it!" The expectation of being able to handle new challenges is a major contribution of the preschool years that helps to dispel self-distrust and anxiety about not being able to manage. This mastery of early anxiety in turn contributes to the foundation for resilience.

This can be seen with transparent clarity as one works with children who have any handicap. With such a child anxieties about the differences between what can be accomplished and what difficulties are likely to remain unmanageable can be overwhelming. A major part of therapy is to help the child to sort out realistic versus unrealistic expectations of progress and to develop the ability to selectively respond to the manageable opportunities. Much of the stress experienced by the minimally brain-damaged child arises from unrealistic expectations of parents and others in the environment, who, seeing the child's success in certain areas, expect comparable achievement in all areas. Just as a child with widely varying innate abilities within the normal range has difficulty in developing a clear self-image that allows for variations from average to superior functioning in different areas, so the parents of the minimally brain-damaged child have even more severe difficulties in developing an accurate picture of what to expect from the child. Many of the child's secondary emotional difficulties can be reduced when the child and the parent have achieved an accurate view of the child's actual capacities, the zones that need special help, and those areas in which compromises with expected performance have to be accepted. Only when this realistic assessment is reached by the child and by the parent can the child's healthy pleasure in himself and his own functioning be evoked. In infancy this basic good feeling is dependent upon the experience of freedom from distress or pain and the pleasurable aftermath of good vegetative experience. For example, the earliest smiles often appear during or following a gratifying feeding experience or a bath or diapering, or while the baby is being pleasurably held or rocked. (Escalona and Leitch unpublished records, 1948–50).

The "good" feeling that becomes associated with the sense of well-being arising from good functioning of the body and that we assume to underlie the baby's investment in his body-self then becomes a motive (of the infant, growing person, or adult) to re-create, at each new phase of life, settings or stimuli comparable to those in which the earliest experiences of well-being were first evoked. Or else this good feeling reaches out for new stimuli and a configuration in which a similar sense of self and wholeness can be pleasurably realized. Normally, the range of such configurations evoking, enlarging, and elaborating the sense of well-being is expanded. New receptive and new active experiences carry the quality of pleasure in oneself, of one's first experiences in terms of the simplest comfortable vegetative functioning, which some infants express by contented coos or grunts or smiles. This early oral setting for the feeling of inner contentment and trust (Erikson 1964) is followed by primitive motor triumphs; exhilarated yelps or crows at standing up are a typical expression of this intensified delight in one's own functioning. Beaming self-satisfaction with successful performances on the potty or toilet then emerge. And parallel with or following these various motor developments is the child's delighted mastery of words, as he happily chants those he finds the most interesting or satisfying to hear himself say.

In numerous records of our Topeka sample at the preschool stage, we find excited outbursts of positive feeling or triumph in connection with successful coping in a situation where there is a threat of failure. There were moreover, positive correlations between the preschool children's ability to feel good about themselves and their responsiveness to the environment. The healthy narcissistic pleasure becomes a norm for the child to which he wishes to return, and when he does not feel good he is willing to struggle to reach this state again.

The capacity to seek help

The capacity to seek help was seen in Lennie, whose series of early illnesses had left him hard of hearing. This condition in turn led to speech problems (chapter 8, part II) and difficulties in concept formation; all these were followed by difficulties he experienced in his reading. This little boy, instead of vividly struggling, fighting for survival, and mastering tendencies as did Colin and Susan, very quietly asked for help, with utter trust that help would be given and constant cooperativeness in using it returned. This was also true with Terry, who at about the same age asked his mother to find a doctor who could help him with his enuresis. In these instances, the resilience and recovery were instituted by the child's insight, open trust, and initiative; the child sought out for himself the assistance needed in order to make recovery possible.

At the same time successful use of the adults' response to the child's plea for help reinforces his openness, his capacity to seek needed help in the future. This does not interfere with autonomy, as the request for help requires initiation, and we found positive relationships among autonomy and the capacity to seek help and other aspects of open responsiveness.

The children who lacked strong drive to recovery and mastery characteristic of resilient children had much less readiness for zest and delight; it took longer and more objective gratification to stimulate expressions of joy or satisfaction in Martin, Janice, Rachel, Daryl, and Darlene. For these children there had been prolonged or multiple stresses in addition to the mother's early tension; family stress and long drawn-out periods of suffering left emotional scars and decreased resilience. These were tense, pessimistic children. They did not lack strength—in fact, they were independent in certain situations. But they included stoics who did not have the ready joyfulness of Susan or Brennie. Some were controlling; all were cautious, if not suspicious. None of them took it for granted that a new challenge would probably be fun or that he could master stress. Rachel conveyed to more than one observer the impression that she expected nothing, that she did not believe the good things of life were for her. At parties when other children watched eagerly, hopefully, or impatiently for their take-home gifts, she sat passively waiting, betraying neither interest nor hope, a waiflike uncertainty in her eyes.

The drive to integration

We saw examples of disturbances of equilibrium, or disintegrative reactions, as Karl Menninger (1963) would say, when a child suffers from physical pain, from loss of mother, from threat to survival, from immobilization by an accident or handicapping illness, and from other stressful experiences. And we have also seen a rapid or gradual reintegration and recovery of equilibrium in response to one or all of the following: deeply satisfying stimuli from external play-objects or from loved persons; physiological therapy; cognitive mastery, fantasy, evoked perspectives; basic inner drives to mastery especially during a propitious phase.

The impressive progress most of the children made in recovery from disturbed episodes forces us to invoke a basic drive to integration along with the push to grow up which we can see as underlying and utilizing other drives—aggressive, dependent, loving, as well as cognitive and active. Progress in recovery, that is, resilience, utilizes all the relevant coping resources available to the child, fueled by this drive to integration.

Strengths contributed by this process include an extension of the trust and hope established in the early months of experience that one's needs are met by the environment, and that one can, through one's own efforts, both cope with the environment and evoke its help in ways that change pain to pleasure, frustration to satisfaction. Coping with stress and with their vulnerabilities brought greater reflectiveness and perspective in Lennie, Janice, Helen, Terry, Teddy and others among the children we watched; and so their coping resources were increased.

PART IV
OUTCOMES

11

The Development of a Vulnerable
but Resilient Child

Bad things can turn into good things.

Helen

Helen was one of a very few young adolescents who wrote helpfully and tenderly after the Kennedy funeral: "I felt as if I wanted to take Caroline, John, and Jackie into my arms and comfort them." The strength of this wish and capacity to comfort was demonstrated later at the time of a family tragedy when Helen physically supported her mother through the funeral of Helen's brother, who had been accidentally killed.

She has developed into a reflective, active young adult, sensitive to the meanings of her personal experience and also aware of the larger problems of the world. She is conscientious about her responsibilities; for instance, she has regularly taken care of the younger children after school while her mother worked. Helen is frank, warm, and able to communicate many insights and feelings, but this expressiveness is accompanied by a subtle distance and seriousness. Her poised distance conveys the impression to some observers that she may be trying to protect herself from disappointment in relationships.

She is of special interest because she was considered by Dr. Heider to be one of the most vulnerable infants in the Escalona–Leitch sample,[1] partly because of a tendency to become ill frequently. This poses many questions. How did she develop the strength we later saw? How did she avoid defeat and withdrawal? Can an understanding of her resilient

This abbreviated study is based in part on a much longer preliminary analysis by Vimla Gupta and me and has also made use of comments by several readers, especially Drs. Povl Toussieng, Alice Moriarty, Joan Davidson, H. Shevrin, Peter Hartocollis, Maria Dale, Peter Blos, Morton Leeds, and Pitsa Hartocollis. In addition, a preliminary report on Helen was presented at a staff session at the Menninger Foundation in 1960 and at a Hampstead Clinic Seminar in 1962. Anna Freud attended the staff conference at the Menninger Foundation where the account of Helen's development was presented and made important comments; Dr. Joseph Sandler and Dr. Humbert Nagera made a detailed assessment of Helen's early development following the Hampstead Profile.

development shed light on our initial question as to how children cope with their problems so as to remain "normal"? How did she develop her warm, active, sensitive, strong, and perhaps precociously mature adaptational style?

Her records from infancy on report interesting interactions between oral and contact needs and needs for autonomy, and between social sensitivity and aggression (in the sense of urgent assertiveness). These interactions, together with improved health, contributed to the evolution of her adaptational style, and to her mastery of the threat of personal inadequacy. After a preliminary review of the family setting in her preschool years, we shall focus on the beginnings of her development in infancy and proceed by successive stages to the present.

During Helen's early years her family lived in a somewhat shabby, but roomy, house with adequate yard space for growing children. In a neighborhood of well-kept homes, the old house, in need of paint and repairs, betrayed a gap between the financial resources of this family and their neighbors. The devoted father, a carpenter, had paneled the dining and living rooms with dark wood that "wouldn't show the fingermarks and scuffs of the children"—an example of the parents' tolerance and understanding of children's ways and needs for activity.

Helen's mother, like most of the mothers in our research group, did not work outside the home until after the youngest child was well along in school and Helen was mature enough to manage the brood in her mother's absence. Helen's mother was both a well-organized homemaker and an excellent seamstress; she provided pretty clothes for her two daughters as well as responsible, consistent care for her seven children. Helen's father was always stable and helpful; a mild permanent injury to his left arm did not interfere with his activity. At puberty, Helen remembered her father playing with her when she was small, tossing her up, tickling her. She also remembered his picking her up when she slipped and fell, and his comforting her when she knocked out a tooth; she remembered him as a warm, supporting father.

Grandparents helped in whatever way they could. Helen was especially fond of her paternal grandmother who came to baby-sit when the parents were absent and when the mother was hospitalized for a new baby. Helen's mother was not close to other relatives, although a cousin visited occasionally. There were family reunions at Thanksgiving but not frequent intimate contacts. Helen felt herself to be part of an extended family, yet, except for visits to her grandparents, she did not express delight in contact with them. This contrasted with the eager, excited sharing of information about uncles, aunts, and grandparents characteristic of several other children. There was thus a little more distance between Helen's family and both their neighbors and their relatives than was typical for this group. But Helen's family was active in a vigorous Protestant church circle.

Dr. Heider saw the mother "as a sensible if somewhat detached sort of mother who manages very well, and whose means, both financial and physical, are not too much strained even by the prospect of the seventh child. She is 'always there,' if at a somewhat self-protective distance. The family seems able to buy the necessities of life, and the television, for instance, was not something that required careful planning when the husband decided that he really wanted it. She does not impress one as a person of unusual vigor or energy and yet she must be unusually strong in some way . . . to be able to do everything that she does, and to keep her head, the way she seems to." But the mother remembered little about Helen ten years later, and Helen remembered less of her mother than of her father. In this brief vignette of the family situation as we began the preschool study, we have emphasized characteristics typical for much of our contact with the family. We now turn to Helen herself, as she was first seen at nearly five months of age.

Helen as a Vulnerable Baby

At the age of twenty weeks, Helen was first observed by Escalona and Leitch and their research team. The record of her prior experience comes from the mother's report in a home interview at that time and a home interview and an office interview with the research pediatrician when Helen was five years old.

Helen was the third living child and second daughter. A beautiful baby girl had died before Helen was conceived, a baby whose loss the mother still mourned. Anna Freud commented on the likelihood that the mother would be somewhat depressed, as is not unusual after such a loss, even after the birth of another baby. During one of the home visits Helen's mother showed the interviewers pictures of the two older children, a boy and girl, and also a picture of a beautiful newborn baby, which she still kept on her bureau mirror. This child died at the age of four days from a defect in her gastrointestinal system. The mother commented in low, intense, but gentle tones that this baby had looked just like their beautiful son. By contrast, Helen at first seemed "odd" to her mother; she did not resemble the beautiful baby who died, nor the attractive older children. (Ten years later, her mother considered Helen to be a "lovely girl.")

Two months after Helen's birth, her mother became pregnant again, and by the time Helen was six, three additional babies made a total of seven children. With one older brother and four younger ones, Helen's childhood was colored by contrasts between herself and the boys, as well as perhaps by the sense of difference conveyed in her mother's feeling that Helen was different from the preceding babies.

No pregnancy or birth difficulties were reported; labor was said to be smooth, spontaneous, and relatively short (four to five hours). Helen weighed 8.5 pounds at birth but did not seem to be a sturdy baby. There were some digestive and respiratory problems. Breast feeding was given up when the baby was four days old because of her mother's sore, cracked, bleeding nipples. No difficulty in the baby's acceptance of the bottle was reported, but her digestive troubles may have been related to this change, as well as to her extremely rapid pace of feeding. (At twenty weeks, she was observed to empty a six-ounce bottle in nine minutes.) She was said to have no difficulty in burping, but during the first three months of infancy she had colic attacks and would draw up her knees and cry. After some ten minutes, projectile vomiting occurred and she would go on to sleep. She had some diarrhea, but never constipation, the mother reported. Even in the early months, Helen suffered from colds, and she continued to have frequent upper respiratory troubles until her tonsils were removed when she was eight years old. These upper respiratory and gastrointestinal problems, though not dangerous, must have given considerable discomfort and irritation through her early months and years. Lacking close observations of Helen and her mother during the earliest weeks, we can only speculate that the combination of the loss of the previous beautiful baby, Helen's oddness and physical difficulties, and another pregnancy following so soon after Helen's birth, contributed to strain in the mother that probably affected her relationship with Helen. This in turn might have interfered with Helen's early adjustment and health.

The doctor said that at birth Helen's thumb was red, indicating she had been sucking it in utero, and throughout infancy thumb-sucking was a major comfort resource. At the age of twenty weeks, a conspicuous aspect of Helen's functioning was her sensitivity to touch: she seemed to have an urgent need for tactile gratification but at the same time she was very ticklish and turned away from too intense or prolonged contact. Thus she would swing from very positive to negative responses in the same zone of experience.

Some difficulty in response to sound was puzzling to her examiners. She responded well to human voices, and loud sounds wakened her when she was asleep. But in other ways she seemed singularly tolerant to sound; she was apparently not irritated or in any other way affected by sudden sharp or loud noises that were disagreeable to all the adults in the room. This tolerance to sound was striking in view of her quick expression of discomfort in response to overstimulation by tactile contact and other stimuli that contributed to heightened tension. It does not seem likely that her tolerance to sound should be seen as indifference, since she vocalized frequently and her infantile precursors of language were unusually good. (Moreover, musical interests became dominant by the time she was twelve years old.)

Prominent and highly variegated mouthing behavior with her wide, full lips, along with her avid, speedy sucking and evidence of thumb-sucking in utero reflected a strong oral drive in the judgment of all observers; it was probably reinforced by the frustrations in the tactile area. Stimulation by test objects was unpleasant and fatiguing. On the Gesell scale, motor and adaptive resources were lower than social functioning.

Along with gastrointestinal difficulties and upper respiratory infections, her autonomic reactivity reflected in flushing, circulatory changes, and her tendency toward cold hands and feet, led to Heider's rating of "low functional stability." She was thus seen as one of the most vulnerable infants in view of her early digestive difficulties, proneness to infection, autonomic lability; her high oral drive in contrast to low tactile responsiveness to impersonal objects; her fatigability, along with low motor adaptive resources (which made her less skillful than some other babies in making herself comfortable); her problem in protecting herself from excessive external stimulation; and the discrepancy between her own strong needs for contact and the meager gratification by her mother, all of which we shall discuss shortly.

Social qualities and experience of Helen at twenty weeks of age

Observers noticed that although Helen was not physically very attractive, her responsiveness invariably drew one toward her. She vigorously initiated and responded to social contacts, as we see in such remarks as: "[She] is so responsive to adult friendliness and has such a mobile face, that as soon as one talks with her, she seems very attractive and the earlier perception of homeliness is gone." "I regarded the baby as a pretty, though somewhat odd appearing youngster. The oddness is contributed largely by the bags of skin beneath her eyes, an unusually mobile lower jaw which tended to move at random, particularly when she was tired, with copious drooling and wide open mouth." In contrast to some other infants in the group whose appearance in itself charmed the observers, her interpersonal response—her "sending power"—was the important quality.

Although she was not considered *acutely* "sensitive" to social as opposed to nonsocial and object stimuli (in the sense of showing seemingly low thresholds), Helen was very responsive to social stimulation. She vocalized throughout the examination as if she enjoyed the attention. While she seemed to need and want social interaction, her responses did not appear to be as subtly varied as those of some other infants. "She smiled and cooed readily, but her facial expression, though appropriate, lacked finer degrees of differentiation to some extent."

Her mother reported that she rarely held her, but baby Helen was often held by her older brother and sister, who could be very affectionate, although they also teased her at times and the sister hit the baby once during an interviewer's visit. The maternal grandmother held and rocked Helen a good deal. In contrast with her lack of holding Helen, the mother held the beautiful twenty-two-month-old brother Ted closely and warmly at the time of one home visit. Although Helen seemed to the research group to lack sufficient contact with her mother, she seemed to receive and accept considerable compensation from other members of the family.

Developmental level and pattern

As rated on the Gesell Developmental Schedules, there was a slight imbalance in her developmental levels in different areas: while she was at the level of twenty weeks (C.A. 20 weeks) in the personal-social area, her language was four weeks *advanced*. By contrast, in the motor and adaptive areas she was a little less than three weeks *behind* her chronological age, and one observer noted a difference in coordination of her legs. This mild degree of imbalance, if continued or increased, might have contributed to some adaptational difficulties when social responsiveness involved her in stimulating situations with which she could not cope. The area of personal-social responsiveness and management, together with language and vocalized communication, was her major area of investment from this stage on.

In contrast to her strength in the area of interpersonal responsiveness, Helen's response to impersonal objects (such as test blocks, bell, and so on), their handling, and her management of them was regarded as an area of potential strain in adaptation. Observers commented that "she is a little immature in the coordinated, purposive use of her hands as well as in some postural aspects." "In response to object stimulation, she appeared to be quite a sensitive infant who experienced such stimulation as stress, and, after a short while, gave every evidence of fatigue." Also, it was observed that "her reaching for objects was often delayed and when she succeeded in obtaining objects, she tended to get them between the third and fourth fingers, or to press them with her fingers against the palm of her hand so insecurely that they dropped from her grasp." We shall see in tests some years later a similar discrepancy between higher "verbal" scores and lower "performance" scores.

Though she grasped most objects presented to her and manipulated a few briefly, her response was usually unenthusiastic. She fretted and turned away. Sometimes she flung objects from her. Even when initial response to a test object was positive she quickly became uncomfortable.

Her motor ineptness would be expected to involve frustration and also to make her either more dependent on help from adults, more intense in reaching and trying to grasp things, or less interested in things because they failed to be gratifying. In any case, this trouble in securing and holding onto things has to be seen in relation to other frustrations of infancy. "In bringing objects to her mouth, she frequently brought her thumb into her mouth and released the object as she began sucking." Oral satisfaction in sucking seemed to be a solace or a substitute for gratification from the manipulation of objects at this stage when she was so often frustrated. Besides showing this difficulty in hand coordination or firm grasp, we might see in her behavior the beginnings of an avoidance or rejection response, which was only partially successful: her delay did not contribute to a perfected response as it did with certain other infants, but seemed to reflect tension. Though she was not seen to deliberately turn away from any object that was proffered or was within reach, one also did not see the decided preferences and active reaching out for objects displayed by many other infants. Her use of the oral mode when frustrated in holding things evidently contributed to greater reliance on oral activities of many kinds.

Her development as a whole was within the average range; her IQ of 102 on the Cattell Infant Intelligence Scale was, however, in the low quartile of the infants in the group. The scatter in her general functioning was relatively narrow. This seems to be important: we ·assume that the task of achieving integration and ego-synthesis is probably not as difficult in children with a relatively narrow scatter, that is, a balanced range of resources.

Management of tension

In addition to her somewhat ineffective delay and avoidance when dealing with tension in relation to objects, Helen appeared "to be an infant to whom a heightened level of tension was distinctly displeasurable, and her facial expression as well as her total behavior suggested active discomfort when one persisted in presenting toys to her."

Regression was observed in the form of uncoordinated movements, eyes crossing, jaw moving at random, and, possibly, poor head control. Thus, we might infer that in infancy she had a relatively low tolerance and capacity to sustain tension.

However, she was not one of those infants who, in the face of such displeasurable heightened excitement, freeze or become immobile and impassive—a response that would not facilitate relief from such a situation, and is likely to be socially misunderstood. Neither was Helen overwhelmed by such tension to the point where she would explode in screaming, a response that would be more likely to draw attention to itself and not to the stimulus situation. Her reaction to such tension was one of discomfort, but expressively and fairly modulated. The mother also reported that Helen "only cried when she was really uncomfortable, wet, or very hungry." It would appear that overstimulation from the environment to the point of arousing affect storms was not frequent for Helen despite the sources of frustration we have noted. She was generally able to keep herself within limits—she was not overwhelmed. She made her feelings known in contexts that could be understood; she seemed to her mother to be "a reasonable baby."

Helen was also reported to be able to seek relief from any kind of tension in various ways involving different degrees of resistance and active response; none of them was very intense as compared with certain other infants, and yet they all were intense enough to be seen as an active, though not forceful, mode of reacting, in contrast to a passive orientation and way of coping. She was selective, and able to cope with the environment in several ways. Unwanted food was pushed out with her tongue; she could avoid looking at stressful objects, and she could evoke some playfulness from her mother.

When the speed with which Helen consumed six ounces of milk was commented upon, her mother said that Helen "never wastes time when she is hungry"; she got "very indignant" when the feeding was "interrupted for burping." We do not know whether her mother attempted to adapt the nipple to a less speedy tempo of feeding, which might have provided more gratification for sucking needs and prevented the colic as well.

According to her mother, only a short time before the observation Helen had begun to get interested in a wider range of things; for example, she began to show some interest in toys and to notice her feeding bottle. If she saw the bottle, but did not get it right away, she was liable to do a lot of kicking. No instance of prolonged or continued resistance in the face of an uncomfortable situation was reported; this would suggest that however vigorous her reactions to frustrations, in general Helen basically fitted into the environment with considerable flexibility. It was reported that she would fight against falling asleep only once in a while. Ordinarily, she fell asleep quite easily and did not need to be rocked or handled in a special way; she was just placed in her buggy. The transition from a phase of activity to passivity appeared to be smooth.

It is also important that Helen "tended to spontaneously alternate periods of activity with brief but frequent periods of relaxation." This is further evidence of her early capacity to seek and maintain within herself a modulated equilibrium. Unlike some other infants, she did not show a tendency to be overenergetic, or to indulge in driving to the point of exhaustion or absolute retreat.

Possible factors in Helen's infancy tension

While Helen was observed to be engaging and very socially responsive, there is a possible conflict involved between her social interests and her need to keep tension within limits. It was observed during the test as well as mentioned by the mother that "she seems happier alone." This does not seem exactly accurate, however, since she definitely liked to be held and played with, that is, up to a point where tension began to mount. Then she seemed to prefer to be put in the buggy, where she played with her toys and quieted down. There seemed to be a fine line between enough and too much.

The fact that the mother interpreted this socially responsive infant's need to avoid overstimulation as "preferring to be alone" may have led the mother to leave her alone more than Helen wanted to be left alone. The mother's need to protect herself from excessive demands from the environment, and possibly her own mildly negative feelings toward the baby she considered "odd" in the early months could have predisposed her to make this interpretation. If the mother was depressed, as Anna Freud and others felt she was, this could also have contributed to her distance from the baby.

We have seen that Helen attempted to maintain an inner equilibrium by mildly expressing discomfort in the face of overstimulation and heightened tension, by actively pushing unwanted food out of her mouth, by kicking for her bottle and giving it eager attention, by spontaneously seeking alternating periods of activity and rest, with smooth transitions from one to the other. Thus, though she was a baby who had weaknesses both in herself and in her relations with the environment, we do not get the impression of an infant who was a slave to the force of circumstances or to the force of her own drives. Her vulnerability was balanced by her active expressiveness and flexibility. However, there is one exception to this, and that is an area that must be dwelt on for some time in order to get a more complete idea of Helen's pattern of functioning.

Orality

Helen's oral expressiveness seemed to have a certain impelling urgency, force, or pressure. She chewed and chomped on her fingers, mouthed and sucked her hands, and also engaged in a "fascinating variety of tonguing motion." Mouthing behavior of various sorts was more prominent than it is even with most infants of the same age. There was hardly a time when she did not move the muscles of her mouth, actively moving the tongue both within the mouth and without; this latter activity occasionally approached tongue-sucking. Frequently, she licked and/or sucked objects (bedsheet), parts of her own body, or parts of someone else's body (hand or arm) that happened to come close enough to her mouth. "Both approaching objects with the mouth and bringing objects to the mouth were observed." Her mother frequently interrupted thumb-sucking, but Helen returned to it immediately. The observers also noted that Helen was a remarkably vocal infant who "accompanied almost all of her activities by expressive and quite well-differentiated sounds."

In the frequency and persistence of Helen's mouthing behavior, we find an urgent drive that repeatedly sought expression and had its own autonomy, that is, it was not just an outlet for tension aroused in other zones. Her large lips and active mouth were evidently predisposed to more than average intensity of oral experiencing. This may have been increased by her need to find her own gratifications, because of the limited gratification in her contact with her busy mother. The needs of the older children, the occurrence of another pregnancy so soon after Helen was born, as well as the mother's concern about the baby who died before, all diminished the attention available to Helen.

In addition, delays in gratifying Helen's hunger were evidently frequent; in the office, the mother recognized signs of hunger eight minutes before she decided to warm the bottle. In the elaboration of mouthing, we can see the beginnings of activity that could substitute for the needed sucking time as well as physical contact. We can assume that the need to suck would also have been reinforced by the limitation of sucking time when she was given bottles that could be emptied in less than ten minutes. The force in this area is apparent in another description: "The baby began to suck her thumb very vigorously and audibly, and all of us smiled at the baby's single-minded pursuit of this activity."

We cannot ignore, however, the potential tension in this mouthing activity that might have influenced the direction of Helen's interests and activities. While her mouthing did not seem destructive, it had a quality of intense demand. We do not know what else might have contributed to such an intense drive—whether constitutional factors chiefly,[2] or possible intrauterine stress, or a reaction to undernourishment as well as inadequate sucking time on the bottle. It is unfortunate that direct observations of Helen before her twentieth week are not available.

Summary of Helen as an infant

We saw that Helen was rated by Dr. Heider in the most vulnerable group of infants because of her early digestive problems, fatigability, proneness to infection, tendency to find object stimulation stressful, autonomic reactivity, tendency to some disorganization under stress,[3] apparently limited motor adaptive (problem-solving) resources as seen on the Gesell scale, some difficulty in protecting herself from external stimulation and pressures, and the meagerness of social gratification from her mother in relation to her strong needs for contact and social response. Her mother's relative detachment, whatever the reasons for it, was regarded by all observers as a factor in Helen's difficulties in managing her tensions and gratifying her strong needs. At the same time, she could not be considered a neglected baby. Basic needs were eventually met; her mother was responsible.

Helen's responsiveness to people, her flexibility, including her capacity to adapt to care-taking procedures, to accept substitutes, and to elaborate satisfying actions with her mouth were seen in retrospect as possible precursors of later strength. So were her actively expressive capacity to protest moderately, or to try to get rid of what she did not want, and her capacity to withdraw temporarily from stimulation excessive to her. At the time, however, the future of this sickly, contact-hungry baby with such an avid oral drive did not look too promising. The positive potentialities inherent in her capacity for multiple and varied oral satisfactions, her insistent drive, and her flexibility were not clearly glimpsed.

Helen as a Preschool Child

When she was five years old, Helen was examined by the pediatrician, psychiatrist, and several psychologists of the coping project. She con-

tinued to seem a vulnerable child, undernourished, particularly susceptible to infection, and also at this period extremely demanding. They were
again impressed with her responsiveness. "She is a very alive little girl,"
wrote Malhotra, "interested in the present situation, talkative throughout the examination. She seems to be an intelligent, responsive child,
fairly high in sensitivity. Her face is very expressive and mobile, changing
from moment to moment and never leaving any doubt about her feelings
at any given time. Her dark eyes frequently sparkle with pleasure and
interest in the environment." I described the expressiveness that was so
much a part of Helen: "I saw a very bright-eyed, subtle, changing
expression, successively hesitant, doubtful, expectant, appraising, as
Helen gazed at me from the front seat of the car, not committing herself
when I approached the car. . . . I had the feeling that she wanted me to
start something, to get us involved in interaction, to make something
happen, above all to have almost any kind of lively contact and
interpersonal activity. After an initial delay, she grabbed hold of the
wheel of the car, honking loudly."

She sometimes showed a modulation and delay in drawing others
toward her, but this was never so exaggerated as to appear inhibited or
restrained; it seemed to contribute to her stability and the distance she
was at times able to maintain with other people. In spite of this
occasional reserve, she was always alert and responsive to the environment and seemed to be one of the most active girls in the study.
Moreover, she could at times be quite impatient.

She warmly showed me "my church," which continued to be an
anchor throughout her growing up, and in adolescence the center of her
social life. Along with her initiative, sociability, and openness of
approach, her flow of language and mobile face were very expressive. In
order to understand her style, and to see how it reflected and was
integrated with other levels of Helen's personality, we have to look at it
in relation to other characteristics.

In spite of the social initiative and provocativeness that seemed to
express Helen's strong longings for contact, she was not very comfortable
with it. The first day she was to come for a test session, we are told that
she was so excited that she had thrown up her breakfast, an evidence that
early instability in gastrointestinal functioning had not been entirely
overcome and that tension was sometimes still discharged through this
zone. During a play session (MLT) I commented on another form of not
being able to hold excitement within her; provocative, exhibitionistic
impulses were expressed without inhibition. Her initial tensely quick
tempo quieted down as she got into the play session, though she never
seemed "contained." The psychiatrist got the impression in his play

interview that "as Helen became more familiar with me our relationship became warmer but only so long as she had me under complete control. Toward the end of the session, she gradually yielded some of the control and was able to accept limits."

At the preschool stage, Helen showed contrasting kinds of behavior—both stimulating others and yet at times being very controlled. One got the impression sometimes that her capacity to evoke a lively interaction generally elicited a favorable response from others, and that this role was assimilated into her self-image inasmuch as she wanted to appear lively and talkative. But at other times, one got the impression that this was not all of Helen, and perhaps not even her core aspect. She also seemed to cope with her difficulty in "containing excitement" or the danger of "losing control" of herself by periods of quietness. We are reminded that even as an infant of five months, she was observed to react with expressions of discomfort in the face of heightened tension and excitement and that she seemed to both hunger for contact and need to withdraw from it, apparently to avoid overstimulation. Her need to control situations may have been related, then, to this early need to avoid overstimulation. But she also had bladder difficulties and problems in achieving urinary control. Thus inner- and outer-directed control were areas of tension.

Sources of tension in infancy and early childhood

Before we elaborate on the nature of the excitement that Helen had to contain, we must consider other aspects of her difficulty in maintaining control. At the research center, she expressed a need to urinate much more frequently than did other children; at that time the research group saw this as a possible evidence of autonomic instability. But in the light of the later diagnosis of serious kidney infection, secondary to her nearly chronic upper respiratory infections, the role of irritation from these unrecognized infections may have been primary. Helen's mother reported that Helen was almost four years old before the mother stopped putting diapers on her at night. Her siblings made fun of her, and when her mother asked whether she did not want to be dry in the morning, Helen would answer, "I just don't want to, I don't care." Her mother was of the opinion that she was not able to keep dry through such long stretches. She did stop wetting herself when her parents adopted a routine of waking her just before they went to bed. Only later was the real kidney difficulty understood.

During her first three winters Helen had suffered from colds at weekly intervals; when she was three years old, she had penicillin several times because of this. In the same winter, her right eardrum ruptured spontaneously on two occasions with a purulent discharge for one day. It was also noticed then that she had temporary difficulty in hearing, but no definite hearing test was performed at that time. In view of her early respiratory infections, her tendency to vomit under excitement, and her persistent difficulties in achieving urinary control, it seems fairly clear that one source of her general tension and excitement might well have been the continual irritation in the respiratory, alimentary, and the urinary systems. At the age of five-and-one-half years, our research pediatrician reported her to be malnourished and strongly recommended tonsillectomy and adenoidectomy. Though she did not have as many colds then, she frequently gasped for breath, snored at night, and breathed through her mouth. The tonsillectomy and adenoidectomy were, however, not performed until three years later after more severe illnesses convinced the family doctor of its necessity.

The restlessness arising from these somatic problems, doubtless including her hunger from malnutrition, may have been intensified by, if not in part secondary to, Helen's affect-hunger. Her mother reported at this stage that Helen was very affectionate and "would take all the loving and attention you will give her." This need for contact in her first year was now referred to by her mother: "Even as a small baby she loved to be held and cuddled, and some of the others [her siblings] didn't care." This memory of her mother agrees with the observers' impression of Helen's early need.

By the time Helen was four years old, the mother worried that she might even be too affectionate; she wanted to "love" strangers such as delivery men. "One time when a salesman started up the sidewalk, she wanted him to pick her up and 'love' her." This disturbed the mother, and after she spoke to Helen quite firmly, it did not happen as often. At the research center Helen also expressed her longing for bodily contact in various ways. Once she asked if she could sit on Marie Smith's lap and, without waiting for a reply, she plopped herself down on her lap, and gave her "a resounding smack and a tight hug." Another time, with a warm smile, she affectionately but vigorously tapped Moriarty on the arm as she said, "I like you." This indiscriminate craving for physical contact and affection now seemed primitive and immature, as if basic processes of development of a selective relation to stable love objects had not taken place. Sometimes she projected her desires to the observer and remarked that she would not like to leave the room because the observer would feel lonely; she would like to come and live with "poor lonesome you" (Toussieng). At the end of the session, she could apparently take leave of the observer easily. Anna Freud commented that this aspect of her behavior somewhat resembled that of affect-hungry institutional children, who seek contact wherever there is an opportunity, without expecting continuity in the relationship. But while such indiscriminateness was characteristic of her at the preschool stage when her mother was busy with nearly annual babies, over the subsequent years we saw increasing evidence of Helen's deep loyalty and devotion to her family.

In these demands for affection, we got the same impression of a certain impelling drive that we saw in Helen's infant mouthing behavior. The intensity, frequency, and demand were similar. We would have to assume even without the earlier evidence that behind this intense need for physical contact and for "love" lay some dissatisfaction with the way the needs for nourishment, contact, and affection were met.

Guilty feelings and apparent conflict about her insistent efforts to gratify her desires were reflected in her remark that she got mad when her mother spanked her, and she was spanked " 'cause, I be naughty most of the time." Her mother, however, saw Helen as the most amenable of her children.

Helen's tension could have been aggravated by her respiratory troubles but perhaps it also contributed to the inner bodily irritation we noted above. Moreover, the need for "affect" and "contact" must have been accentuated by the combination of isolation and scattered attention that Helen doubtless experienced during her frequent bouts of illness while her mother was extremely busy with her six children. Illness added to the deprivation when Helen was unable to go out and find contacts for herself.

Later Forms and Elaborations of Responsiveness

With growth and age, as interpersonal situations became more and more important as sources for satisfying her needs of affection and hunger, the same intensity found in the mouthing behavior in infancy was extended to areas of social interaction. This, together with the relative strength in her social responses as observed in infancy and her use of language and the capacity for elaborating satisfactions seen early in her multiple mouthing patterns contributed to the large variety of social techniques she developed; the mixture of "aggressive" activity—in the sense of intrusive, insistent, demanding behavior—and the lonesome, hungry quality we saw in her social responses, her continuous chatter and conversation, and her way of stimulating a lively interaction. Her verbal skill was by now outstanding, characterized by her use of words that made feelings vivid. While her vocabulary and articulation were immature at times, she used highly differentiated expressions at other times. Her feelings also came across in her vivid pantomime. This range of social techniques seemed to have achieved a degree of "functional autonomy" at five years. Crystallized at an early age, it contributed an important part of Helen's adaptational style during her childhood.

Helen's use of assertiveness at the age of five

We have referred to Helen's vigorous way of dealing with her needs, but it is important to consider further the forceful assertiveness that was felt by some observers to be "aggressiveness." The following description of her reflects a main feature of her style: "In some ways, she seems rough and tumble, but this is in the direction of daring, much more than in the direction of controlling or hurting other people. Quite often, she alters the task or situation to make it more exciting and to provide a (startling) surprise for the other person," often teasing as an accepted form of arousing interaction. Sometimes one felt another kind of rivalry or role reversal breaking through in earnest, as when she asked Moriarty to answer the arithmetic problems.

She did not seem to be really aggressive in an angry or destructive way, but she seemed to be using vigorous behavior to give expression to her excitement and to be assertive in evoking responses from adults. A few examples show how she could use her resources to spring surprises or lend excitement to just routine things. Her mother reported with amusement an incident in which Helen's father was eating candy out of a bag, unaware that any of the children were around. Helen was nearby and suddenly asked, "Well, Daddy, what are you going to do, be a pig and eat it all?" It is possible here that her feeling involved some competition for the oral goodies or disappointment in not being noticed. During one session she pushed her hair under her hat gleefully and said, "That hat is a house and the hairs live in it. They have to go to bed. Hey, you! You go in, you go to bed." While many children at this age tend to animate objects, Helen used this device to have a little fun, to lift things above the matter-of-fact level.

However, annoyance or frustration did lead to occasional aggressive threats at a fantasy level. During the psychological tests she described her drawing to Moriarty and said, "It's a cockroach with mean snakes on it. I'm going to get these crayons off and let them bite you. They don't like to have you around here." Later, in the same session, she followed up this fantasy threat of oral aggression by saying, "Oh, my snakes aren't really going to bite *you*. I'll throw snakes at people." She explained that perhaps this would be reciprocated and this would not be pleasant, so perhaps she would not do it after all. Here we see evidence of aggressive thoughts, conflict about them, and modulation of the impulse to avoid retaliation—a pattern not typical of other girls in the study. This type of behavior may also have been a serious testing of the reactions of people. Helen seemed to have an exceptional capacity to absorb negative and aggressive feelings in fantasy and then to resolve her tensions. She freely made use of humor in expressing her aggression, but the closer the theme of conflict and aggression was to her person and her real life, the more the humor was tinged by a certain wistfulness.

At this age, Helen was already surrounded at home by brothers. At a later age, she referred to the one nearest in age as almost a twin. Hence, some of her rough and tumble and aggressive teasing may reflect the sibling play and rivalry, and also her need to be vigorously active in obtaining a share of the attention of her somewhat detached, extremely busy, though kind, responsible mother.

The early struggle for self-definition

The mixture of two seemingly opposite features was apparent in yet another area. The mother reported that "in some ways Helen is real feminine. In other ways she is a real tomboy. She gets dirtier than the boys, yet she doesn't want to wear jeans. . . . She likes sunsuits in the summer . . . but they must have a sash or a ruffle, and not look like boys' things." But the following are typical of the remarks by the female observers: "She was on and off her chair, constantly moving about in a free, easy manner, and her overall body movements appeared to be somewhat masculine in type." "Much of her behavior is tomboyish and her warm personal reactions partake of a certain competitiveness and aggression which she can and does control on a fairly logical basis." On the other hand, the male psychiatrist remarked that "her movements have a definite graceful and refined feminine quality, which sometimes shows evidence of being a little overdone, because of a slight but unmistakable self-consciousness. . . . She was somewhat overdressed in her session with me and though she never showed any hesitation in anything she did, she took good care that her clothes would not get messed up or too wrinkled." Then again, on her way to the drugstore, she announced, "I can walk like a lady."

This accent on differentiating her feminine identity had begun to play a crucial role in Helen's emerging self-image. Knowledge of her later development, interests, and behavior also suggests that a deliberate accent on maintaining distinctions was central: this emphasis on sharpening distinctions, keeping things separate, can almost be looked upon as a formal and structural feature of her functioning, and we may say her orientation is in the direction of differentiation at this stage rather than synthesis. This was also very conspicuous in her preschool Rorschach responses, which because of her very fine differentiations were unusually rich and delicate.

Whether this need to differentiate arose more from the fact that so many siblings were boys and she needed to maintain her separateness from them, or from the fact that the difference between herself and her next younger brother was only eleven months, we can only guess. Her mother attempted to increase the distance between them by sending the next brother to school a year later than he might have gone, so that he and Helen would not have to compete. This effort by the mother to differentiate the two children may have influenced both Helen's own efforts to differentiate herself and her tendency to use a process of differentiation as a method of control or of modifying negative experience.

Dr. Joan Davidson added another possibility, namely, that even more deeply, Helen's oral conflict (between hungrily taking in so much so fast and having to regurgitate) provided her with contrasts between experiences of getting "enough" versus "too much." We remind ourselves here of the problem we noted earlier in regard to enough contact versus too much. A sharper conflict in regard to functioning in the mouth–nose area could have arisen from the contrast between pleasurable sucking and unpleasant breathing—a contrast that may again have stimulated a differentiation between two experiences, good and bad, in the same zone. The repeated experiences of getting sick and recovering could make a similar contribution. It is very important to watch this emphasis on sharpening the boundaries and on contrasting unpleasant and pleasant in understanding the development of Helen's adaptational style and her ego identity.

Relationships and identification at the preschool stage

Even at this stage, in spite of having a mother and older sister, Helen looked outside the home for a model for identification. The mother said that she did not imitate anyone in her family, but she did imitate a little girl friend, Barby, three months older than herself, especially after Barby moved away. Helen thought that Barby was a little nicer than anyone else in the world. She mimicked everything that she saw Barby do, and once in a while she even played that she was Barby. The mother said that she did not copy Barby's clothes, but the way Barby played and talked, and added that Barby was small boned and dainty. This desire to replace her own basic identity is not unique at this stage. While it may happen frequently, its influence on a child's development is not to be minimized, and we need to explore contributing factors.

Her mother again described Helen at the preschool stage as "the odd one of the bunch," another fact that must have heightened Helen's awareness of distinctions. According to the mother, people thought that all the boys in the family were just like their daddy, and Betty (the oldest girl) was supposed to be the picture of her mother at her age. The mother and aunt believed that Helen was very much like her grand-mother, who in turn seems to have had a special feeling for Helen. This distinction made by the mother also seemed to contribute to her maintaining a subtle distance; years later, on being asked for her memories of Helen as a small girl, the mother remembered little about Helen and much more about her sister. At the preschool stage the research group felt that this distance probably contributed to some difficulty in Helen's identification with her mother. (Later, however, the identification seemed more complete.)

In order to round out the picture, we might combine several aspects of Helen: her hunger for receiving love and bodily contact, her accent on sharpening the distinctions between boys and girls, the contrast between her tomboyish activities and feminine clothes, some awareness that her mother thought her different from the other children, her experiences of being wet (bad) versus dry (good) and sick (bad) versus well (good). All these need to be seen along with another characteristic in order to suggest a possible combination of factors involved in the development of her relationships, and their connection with her needs. We saw that in infancy Helen showed a definite preference for people as contrasted with things and at five and a half years, this preference seemed to pervade her general behavior. In the play sessions, when confronted with a large variety of toys, paints, and playthings, she expressed herself mainly through the process of transference, always actively involving both or one of the observers. In the face of failure on the psychological test, she reversed the roles and assigned tasks to the examiner. For Helen, maintaining personal interactions remained a major need.

This lack of primary effort to engage herself with things was apparent in the formal quality of one of her MLT play sessions at the age of five. "Completely devoid of any concern with achievement in terms of organizing or constructing anything with toys, her play continued to move on in this fluid, emotional, adventuresome way, as a projection of moods and fancies, rather than an objective structuring of materials—the available stuff virtually became an extension of herself—or she projected herself through it." Anxiety about her behavior was reflected in quick reversals from aggression to punishment, from aggression toward others to self-aggression, from receiving aggression to retaliation, from aggression to affection, from aggression to helping or protection, from aggression to restoration or constructive activity—in other words, from "bad" to "good." Evidently, Helen's deep need for positive relationships overcame the aggressive impulses partly aroused by frustration, partly reinforced by her active brothers, partly intertwined with her drive to stir up some interactions with others in any way possible.

From all this we might expect that any investment in achieving, acquiring interests, expanding her knowledge, and developing her skills through the latency period and later would depend to a very large extent upon the value of the activity for relationships with people, or on the sublimation of her aggressive impulses, that is, her wish to be good (and loved) as opposed to being naughty (and rejected). Her deep social investments and related values would be expected to dominate her developing interests and her relation to herself and to the environment.

We have noted her mother's remark that Helen was the most amenable child of the bunch. The only incident of naughtiness mentioned was that Helen occasionally got into the bathroom and got water over everything. This was dealt with by asking her to clean it herself, but there was a prolonged struggle with the mother, reflected as one of the main themes in her fantasy material.

At home she did not openly express anger very often. She got angry when her brothers took things away from her, or shoved her, or went into the bedroom and dumped out all her dolly things. She would then "really tell them," but she had to be pushed pretty hard to hit back. If she did hit back, she always ran, because she did not want to be hit back again in turn.

She recovered quickly from such a disturbance. Usually if she was upset, she would cling to the available parent, hang her head, put her arms around the adult until the adult asked what was the matter. We find the same pattern of direct expression of aggression in her fantasy material, but even then hitting back was mainly resorted to as a form of self-defense, and the fear of retaliation was so strong that she had to escape from the conflict.

Interests at the preschool stage

At home she liked dolls and had a cradle, buggy, and toy dishes. She was fond of changing the dolls' clothes. Helen did not mind if her older siblings went to school as long as she had someone to play with. Already at this early stage, Helen liked music, had good rhythm, and enjoyed singing. But paper, pencil, and crayons held Helen's attention longer than almost anything else. This absorption with paper and pencil was the most remote from personal interaction and social response. Evidently, in research sessions the opportunity to maximize new relationships took precedence over other interests; at home, if social interaction was not available, she could use dolls and paper and pencil as substitutes. This interest in paper and pencil is common among children who have older siblings in school, and it often reflects a desire to achieve, to grow up, to be bigger (to have the bigger pencil of two, as she asked one of the observers) as well as to be part of the group able to write and read.

Management of energy in relation to her limits

As easily fatigued and as highly responsive to people as Helen was as an infant, she was reported to be able to take only a little social activity at a time and then to rest alone with her toys. At the age of five years and more, her mother said Helen never sat still for long periods. She often played in the room by herself, though never for more than an hour. Then she took off out of doors as fast as she could. They had a swing set and garden tools and "the dirtier she could get, the better." She did not really run enough to tire herself out, but "if she did get tired, she knew enough to sit down until she could get her wind back."

Thus, at the age of five and a half, we saw the same basic pattern of management of her energies that we saw in her as an infant. Although her predominant orientation was toward the social world, she possessed enough autonomy to withdraw from it to replenish her energy. This capacity to maintain her autonomy away from the social world when necessary probably helped her in obtaining relief from the danger of being overstimulated by constantly reaching out. It doubtless also contributed time to herself for development of her own ideas and fantasy and laid a foundation for sublimation.

Another important home experience had to do with bruises. Her motor ability was never, from infancy on, as adequate as her social and verbal abilities; at the age of five she still tumbled frequently and bruised her knees. Later, she remembered her father's comfort at such times, and this experience must have contributed very early to her feeling that a bad experience can turn into a good one. Thus, her very vulnerability itself (something bad) led to the experience of father's solace and warmth (something good).

Uses of fantasy

Many of the problems that confronted her in real life were vividly worked out in her play and fantasy. In addition, fantasy expression enhanced her mastery over these situations; we found her frequently using the reversal of roles—something she could not do in reality—thereby temporarily denying the threat involved in being the victim and also preparing herself inwardly for assuming an active adult role.

A preoccupation with defining her identity and sharpening the difference between boys and girls was characteristic in her fantasy, though it was not tackled with such conscious deliberateness and directness as some of the other themes we have discussed. In a play-interview she made a distinction between French and English, and remarked, "Smart snake, this is an English snake." There is here an attempt to emphasize the identity and perhaps to harbor a wish for a transformed identity. Frequently, in her stories on the CAT, one of the figures was perceived as belonging to a different species. Helen was one of the few children who noticed and remarked upon the chicken without a bib (evidently considered different or deprived, as she may have felt as a girl among so many brothers). The most likely figure of identification was perceived as a rabbit; one of the three bears was perceived as a kangaroo. Was the attraction of the kangaroo that it had both a large tail and a baby pouch?

We have traced some of the sources of Helen's emphasis on a sense of difference in the makeup, function, and even origin of her identity as an individual as compared with the rest of the family. This was related to her struggle with aggression and her way of modulating it with love and humor. The role of emphasis on difference and self-change was significant as a source of direction for some of Helen's interests, her preoccupation with appearance and with conforming and nonconforming aspects of behaving.

On the Rorschach Helen suggested that rabbits could be transformed to various colors under the influence of butterflies, and she inquired as to whether rain could not make different colors. These suggest a connection with her problem of difference, of identity, and of transformation at a deeper level, a concern with transforming unpleasant (rain) to something more attractive (colors). Very early she had been able to change certain situations—to push food out of her mouth if she didn't like it. By the preschool stage, she seemed to want to change her dark (naughty) self into a colorful (happy or acceptable?) self. Her mother reported that Helen had stopped bedwetting only a year earlier, a development of great import to a little girl so much teased by her brothers.

Helen's ways of coping with early limitations and conflicts

At five and three-quarter years, Helen showed a set of behaviors that might sum up the problems she faced with self-assertion and identity. At twenty weeks her motor ability had been observed to be less adequate than her social and other abilities. Later we saw her tendency to fall frequently and to get bruised knees, although she never had a serious accident. The impression at that time was that, apart from poor coordination or bidding for sympathy, these difficulties might be connected with her feelings of inadequacy in relation to her brothers and sister. One seemed to be that she fell because she was running fast, trying to keep up, and so got tripped. Or some of her trouble could be due to the fact that she hurt herself somewhat on purpose because "of guilt about her naughtiness, which seems to be so openly admitted and accepted along with the spanking which it brings." Often Helen mentioned a doll in the play, or a rabbit (on the Rorschach) that was all cracked up and smashed to pieces. In relation to a male investigator, Helen showed considerable preoccupation during play with differences in size, but mainly in a negative way. Most of the time the distinctions were wiped out in some way; she was, for example, vague about her sister's age, also about whether her older sister could run faster, and replied that her sister ran "almost faster."

Her *control* of the psychiatrist (who had not had access to any other data on Helen from any source) was also, he felt, aimed at "eliminating activities which would put her at a disadvantage as the smaller one. Her wishes to deflate Bobo and Bugs Bunny [large inflated plastic dolls] seemed to be partially motivated by these concerns." Her desire to be in an advantageous position in relation to a male observer and her concern about damage and injury suggest that this problem of wanting a transformed identity might have been in some way related to the body injury which she, as a recurrently ill girl with several healthy brothers, may have imagined herself to have suffered. Her rivalry with an older, prettier sister who looked more like her mother could also contribute to a wish for a changed self. She kept things in control so as to keep herself from carrying through aggressive impulses. She did not at this time sublimate in construction, achievement, or absorption in nonpersonal objects except in her value on "being smart" or "tricky."

At this stage, the general impression of the psychiatrist as well as of the other observers was that though on the surface "Helen appears to have made a very comfortable feminine identification and to be very much at ease with herself and the world around her, on closer investigation her self-concept is not nearly as comfortable, as she appears quite concerned about being handicapped. This was partly expressed in terms of being smaller than others and being a girl. With hidden but unmistakable resentment, and with considerable energy, she fights against these 'handicaps,' hiding her struggle behind a facade of seemingly competent and confident social poise."

In infancy, at the age of five months, we saw her great susceptibility to infection; and Helen was a sensitive and easily fatigued baby, along with her strong social and oral needs. She accepted the environment relatively easily. Along with an active orientation, she showed some modulation and lack of destructive reactions to frustration; her multiple forms of mouthing behavior probably provided considerable release of tension. We find now that the struggle for "holding her own" had become more marked. She was actively oriented toward patterning herself to the "conforming" aspects of being a girl, but the accent on this adaptation became somewhat exaggerated. This overemphasis may have risen from the disparity that existed among her intense needs for contact and for love, her strong assertiveness, and her orientation toward conforming. This exaggeration suggested the energy she was expending to cope with stress related both to her vulnerabilities and to developmental conflicts regarding her place in her family.

In general, however, she was functioning well and showed good judgment. She was very quick. She performed tasks within the overall average range and showed many ways of coping with interpersonal situations and with her needs, both through her active efforts and her rich fantasy, which kept so close to her real life problems. But her persistent health problems, intense affect-hunger, reactivity, and difficult family situation led Dr. Heider (1966) to rate her as higher than average in vulnerability at this stage, although somewhat less vulnerable than she had been at the infancy phase. It was still uncertain what her school years might bring.

Helen in Latency[4]

Latency changes: illness and sequelae of special care

When she was between seven and eight years old, Helen was again seen at the research center. Health problems had become more acute at this time; she had serious bladder trouble and had to be in the hospital for three and a half days for a series of tests. When this difficulty was at its height, Helen needed to urinate very often, and had some pain; though she had been dry for several years, she began to wet her bed, sometimes two or three times a night. Helen hated this, and the wetting seemed to have developed into a fairly stressful situation; Helen's mother reported that it got "really disgusting" and that she herself could hardly stand it.

During the hospital examination her mother said Helen was "hopping around and having a big time" until the final stages of the examination when they gave her a hypo or two, and she "did not care for that." They put her to sleep for the painful part of the examination and she was "deathly sick" afterward; Helen couldn't hold her head up and she cried, but she did not really vomit because they had kept her without food for a number of hours in advance. She had a little soreness from the examination for several days. The doctor had thought that there was some kind of "kink in the tube leading to the bladder" which the examination might straighten out, but after he probed he realized that this was not the difficulty and that she did have an infection. Medication was given to control the problem. Following this examination Helen had two further sieges of bladder trouble, but the medicine helped a great deal. Helen took the pills willingly; even when her mother forgot, she remembered to take them. Later the difficulty was recognized to be related to lowered resistance to infection resulting from chronically infected tonsils. These were finally removed when she was eight years old on another visit to the hospital. The stressful aspects of this entire experience are obvious, in terms of both physical discomfort and the self-value conflict involved in the apparently infantile wetting behavior.

The gratifying aspects were also important. From indirect evidence obtained through Helen's own reports, fantasy material, and later memories, we seem justified in inferring that this prolonged physical discomfort brought more than usual nurturance and attention from the mother and also the grandmother, and this and her improved health may have contributed measurably to her subsequent relaxation and increased security. A major compensation was a trip to California and Disneyland provided by her grandmother after the tonsillectomy and perceived by Helen as her grandmother's way of making up for the bad time in the hospital. Later Helen looked back on this sequence of experiences as a major example of how "bad can turn into good."

Social behavior in latency

During the bladder difficulties Helen's physical appearance suffered. According to one observer, Helen was at that time one of the least attractive girls seen in the study, sallow and unhealthy looking. Her heavy breathing seemed to create some problems with the other children. Another observer felt that her appearance when she came directly from play at home was more like that of a little "urchin" than that of a well-cared-for little girl. "Her hands and nails were dirty and so was her smudged face." But an examiner who saw Helen at a later time found her to be "a slim, rather attractive child whose short dark brown hair was very neat and quite in the modern mode." Probably Helen felt better at some times than others, and these variations may have contributed to variations in the level of her self-care.

Socially, Helen showed essentially the same picture seen earlier: directness and openness in contacting adults; freedom to express her own needs; awareness of refined affective shifts in her own behavior; and a brash earthiness in her rough, too quickly affectionate approaches, her teasing and jockeying for status. Her vigorous oral activity and her control of impulses on a logical cognitive basis were both observed. Only the fact that her mood was a little subdued seemed different.

This subdued quality was more apparent after than before the hospitalization described above. Still friendly, open, and spontaneous, Helen seemed to have developed certain social controls and was able to maintain some distance, at least until she wanted to be involved. There was more subtlety in her moving close, though she was at times provocatively and exhibitionistically feminine when a male observer was present. Just before the hospitalization, Helen had shown a good deal of insecurity in facing a new and unfamiliar situation. She clung to one examiner, holding her hand and leaning against her, obviously maintaining the familiar contact until she saw what was to be done next. Several times during the trip from her house she wondered aloud if Moriarty really remembered where she lived and would be able to find her home. It appeared as if "she hung on for dear life." All this suggested that Helen was much more anxious and insecure during the period when she was facing hospitalization than she was afterward. Her greater control after the hospitalization could have been the result, in part, of her decreased bodily irritation and therefore lessened restlessness, and, in part, to the final achievement of sphincter control with which she had had such difficulty. It must have been a great satisfaction to feel that now she _could_ control herself.

But she still continued to chatter and talk a great deal. She entered easily into interaction, and with definite awareness of her talkativeness: "I used to be a nice quiet little girl, but now I am a chatterbox." On seeing that she was accompanied on her trip from home by another child from the study who had to use crutches, she asked why this was necessary and made efforts to engage her in conversation. She freely said that she did not find school too pleasant herself, and that recess was the most pleasant period of the day for her. She also talked about wanting to "do some tricks" when she got to the research party.

Her intrusiveness and demandingness were also seen in relationships with her peers, and it was not clear whether it arose from her preoccupations with her body due to illness or had its basis chiefly in a more primitive or infantile urge for bodily contact, or both. Even though she expressed much affection, it seemed to some observers that she was relating on a superficial level, not taking time to develop any meaningful relationship at the party as some other children did. One instance of intrusiveness occurred when Helen went to Daryl in order to lift up her bouffant skirt and look at the fluffy petticoats under it. When Daryl shrank back, Helen went back to Vivian and tried to lift her, as she had done once before. This time Helen did not hold her by the waist, but grabbed her between the legs. After this initial struggle was somehow resolved, the three girls spent the rest of the afternoon sticking rather close to one another.

In a fairly successful way Helen handled her need to be assertive, and the anxiety associated with it, by playful, controlling behavior toward the adults, so that she was not rejected but continued to be reassured. One of her games combining these elements is instructive for the dynamics of her relationship with a mother figure. Helen would climb up on the seesaw on her hands and knees until she reached the height of the observer. She then lay down on her stomach and turned her head over to the side, telling the observer that she was going to pretend to go to sleep, and ordered, "You be the mommy." The observer was asked to tell her to take a nap, and then to look away. Meanwhile, Helen would slide away; noticing that she was gone, the observer was supposed to start spanking and ended up by spanking the board, thus hurting her own hand instead of Helen. Helen thought this was quite funny; she laughed long and loud and exclaimed, "I'm tricky, ain't I?" This game, which revolved around the situation of being disciplined or punished by the mother, evidently provided a considerable release of tension for Helen. It was a way of tricking adults as children of this age like to do, but Helen decidedly had the upper hand. The act of spanking involved enough conflict that it had to be disguised in the form of patting the baby to sleep. Helen was, however, like many children during the latency stage, very open about much of her manipulation, and playfully triumphant in outwitting the adult. (Note latency riddles and jokes typical of many children.)

After her recovery from illness, Helen was also reported to have more of a temper than formerly and "showed her spunk," doubtless in part because she was in better health. She enjoyed running, wrestling, and rough activity and made sure that she came out on top. As at the preschool stage, she was reported to get angry when the boys messed up her dolly things, but she did not hesitate so much to hit back. She also got "put out" if she wanted her mother to come and play with her but the mother did not find this convenient. She would pout in her room; but in about fifteen minutes all was forgotten and everything was well. The mother reported that Helen still liked her share of attention, was affectionate, and also craved affection. It was as if she could never get enough. All in all, Helen seemed freer, placing less accent on dresses and indulging in tomboyish activities with greater vigor than before her recovery from the prolonged infection.

Increasing freedom, competitive drives, and interest in achievement were also reflected in her mental development. As compared with the preschool period, Helen showed greater differentiation and maturity in cognitive processes, concomitant with greater autonomy of cognitive functioning. On the Stanford Binet (see discussion in Moriarty 1966, pp. 98–104) at seven years, ten months, she obtained an IQ of 117, fifteen points higher than at the preschool stage on the same test. In keeping with her better language functioning in the infancy test her verbal score (116) was higher than her performance score (101) on the WISC.

Memory varied from average to superior; though potentially good, particularly in her capacity to perceive and to recall visual stimuli, her broad interests in all aspects of the situation sometimes distracted her. Problem-solving was consistently direct, realistic, and practical, but she usually moved into a task a little too rapidly (just as she had consumed her bottle too quickly in infancy). She was quite unconcerned about time limits. Her planning was vague, and she was always surprised when her plans did not exactly work out. She was all smiles when she met with success. Her drawings also reflected more definitive and differentiated affect.

Helen was reported to be enjoying school and doing well there. Her best subject was spelling and she got mostly A's and B's. School was beginning to provide opportunities for sublimation as well as an area for achievement. Helen's responsiveness and adaptability, and the controlled order of a traditional school that protected her from overstimulation evidently contributed to the positive development of her cognitive capacities.

Helen also had a perceptive, understanding way, which had been noticed earlier. She alone among the children remarked at the age of seven, "I know what you're doing. You're finding out what we do so you'll know what the sick children should be doing." Another expression of Helen's awareness was a remark about her family at this period: "We haven't much money, and we have a lot of children." This understanding quality seemed to some observers to imply a level of insight and integration beyond what had been indicated in her test scores.

Ways of dealing with conflicts in latency

Helen went to some length to avoid getting involved in any conflict situation, even in fantasy, with the mother-figure. Aggression toward female adults was inhibited compared to the preschool period, and Helen had not yet become very comfortable with this. Though the inhibition was effective, in the face of such a conflict stress was reflected in her lower performance score on the intelligence test and in generally fragmented organization. A solution seemed to be emerging in the direction of identification with an adult role, anticipation and eager orientation toward the future and growing up, with hints of a possibility of earlier maturing than other girls of her age—all of which seem congruent with her increased verbal score.

She was, as before, largely oriented toward adapting to the pattern of things, and even in her fantasy material and play she was largely reacting to her current situation. While drawing a turkey (in November) and enthusiastically, but with much difficulty, elaborating it into a comic strip, she suddenly disclosed, "It's not very funny to go to the hospital. I was there two times, once when I was a baby and now when I had kidney trouble. I still have a little bit . . ." She seemed to associate both the hospital and the turkey with the possibility of dying and assured the turkey, which she had some conflict about killing, that it would be all right.

Her continued problem in getting sufficient love was reflected in various comments: to the psychiatrist, in an offhand manner, she remarked, "Do you know what I keep thinking? Nobody likes me—at night," and once she had said this, she passed on to something else. On another occasion, she said that she liked her little brother Tommy the best, because he jumped on her and clung to her like a pup. In the same session, she said that she wished she had a white poodle; "I want an itty-bitty white one that will come and jump on me." Later, after a move to the country, the family did get a dog which Helen enjoyed very much. She liked to romp with, nuzzle, and caress the puppy.

Here we see a number of strengths in the devices Helen used for coping with her affect-hunger. We have the impression that she was somewhat more cautious about her impulses, just as in infancy she had developed a pattern of needing to have some distance at times from excessive external stimulation. Even though she wanted to be like the pup, playful and abandoned in his affection, she dared not be so free; and so, perhaps, she wished to possess such an animal. This reveals again her acceptance of substitutes and the capacity to project sources of satisfaction to the outside.

It was noted that Helen was the only child in the group who had expressed a positive feeling of looking forward to going to the next higher grade. This suggests that she looked forward to better times ahead. Further questioning revealed that she would perhaps like to have a house, some children in it, and then make them go to school. This emphasis on growing up, and her new demand for achievement, while progressive in direction, seemed, however, to be slightly exaggerated or forced. Facing growth might have been slightly conflictual for Helen; perhaps she was unsure about her ability to transform the unpleasant aspects of present reality into something better.

We found a good deal of fear at this time, released in various dreams and fantasies, and an increased anticipation of possible punishment. A number of times, sometimes jokingly and sometimes seriously, Helen asked the examiner, Moriarty, to put her in jail because she was "shooting firecrackers in the city." Under the impact of certain events in the environment, especially concern about her brother's peccadilloes, issues of naughtiness were magnified. In dreams, her fears of punishment were considerably exaggerated; she said that she mostly had bad dreams. In one of them, she got killed in a fire in her bed while she was asleep and everyone else was outside. This was followed by another bad dream in which everyone in the world was killed in a fire while at church. In association with this, she mentioned her little brother who woke up screaming and went downstairs, yelling for his daddy. Again we see how a threat to another was sufficient to make Helen anxious, and stimulated her to mobilize her defenses.

We also found an achievement-orientation emerging in Helen at this time, and concerns about her inadequacy to achieve. (Later, achievement took the form of winning—"getting" by earning multiple prizes at local fairs. She also won a number of scholarship awards for college.)

In contrast to what we saw at the age of five and one-half, at the age of eight we saw a shift in Helen in the direction of seeking a dependent, protective relationship with a father-like figure, and a struggle to be independent of the fantasied inadequate mother by overidentification with the fantasied protective mother. She more often acted out the roles of the good and protective mother; in a very concrete and obvious manner she was trying to overcome her fears and to assure herself that everything would be well when she grew up.

Other latency anxieties

Threatening situations in her latency play also included illness and hospitalization. There was considerable integration in themes of a wish to be affectionately handled and to have bodily contact: one theme dealt with getting a shot, while she played the reassuring nurse, perhaps reliving the comfort she was given in her own stressful hospitalization. Or, she may again have been reflecting about the balancing or compensating and good aspects of unpleasant experiences.

Her preoccupation with big and small sizes and reversal of roles had been seen even at the preschool stage. Whereas at that time Helen took care to avoid situations where she might be at a disadvantage because she was small and did not want to get involved in competition, Helen now was facing the issue more openly and was trying to come to grips with it, at a level not too far from herself. She was bigger now, and stronger. Perhaps, also, with an increase in social control there was a simultaneous increase in ability to come to grips with this problem of sizes. Earlier this was more evident in a distant medium like the CAT stories; now Helen grappled with it in a face-to-face interaction. In one play-interview close to her eighth birthday, she directed the two observers to pretend that they were scared of being examined by a doctor. Helen then consoled them that it would not hurt and gave one of the observers a "shot" in the buttocks, then went over to the other observer and said, "You laugh, he's scared; you're three and he's five." Note the emphasis on the ages; the younger of the two was not scared. Another time, she picked up a smaller doll to represent the father and a bigger one to represent the brother; also, she took the father doll to the observer and emphasized this issue by saying, "Here's the father. Wow, *you're* big." Later in the same session she inquired, "Wouldn't it be strange if the baby was bigger than the father?" Asked whether this was so in the case of her brother, she said, "No" but added that her sister was bigger than her aunt. For Helen, sizes and ages (and space and time by analogy) were very important reality issues along with problems of control, weakness, fatigability, and being loved. It is important to keep these issues in mind for understanding the progress in her ways of dealing with her vulnerabilities, disappointments, and aggressive impulses.

The transformation of role in creating her sense of identity

In addition to the progressive control in Helen's handling of her aggressive or "bad" impulses, and of her identification with a protective role, we saw at latency a marked increase in themes pertaining to sexual roles, identity, and adult relationships. At the preschool stage, a large number of sexual symbols and conflicts appeared in her MLT and other fantasy material; we noted her heightened consciousness of her feminine role in the presence of a male examiner. At latency we saw clearer role-playing of the sexes in her play, and her themes were conveyed at a deeper and more symbolic level in a recurrent and significant dynamic pattern. Earlier Helen showed a predominant orientation toward receiving and taking affection and was less giving. At latency, we saw an extreme swing to the other side, where she took the role of one who gives; in fantasy she had to make the other partner helpless, deprived, and ill ("poor") so that she was justified in continuing to give. This might suggest unresolved feelings with regard to giving and taking, with underlying feelings of deprivation and dissatisfaction. It may not be wrong to assume that she faced some stress in dealing with conflicts about giving affection.

In contrast with coping devices where she differentiated, she was likely to appear indiscriminate and aggressive in her giving; similarly she seemed insatiable in her receiving. Here the mingling of themes continued from her oral needs of infancy. But conflict, competition, and anger were also directly expressed by adults or age-mates in her fantasy. Her wish to be different from what she was, to be transformed and to change her identity, still strikes us as a core of her personality and seems closely related to her way of coping with her vulnerability, that is, to change bad to good, illness to health, demanding to giving.

In contrast to the preschool stage, where feelings of difference, rejection, and isolation were more predominant, at latency these feelings of difference were integrated to the extent that they were now expressed on the cognitive level. In a play session, she wrote on the board: "Let's play her name was Heather Jones," referring to an actual girl in class who had some very pretty dresses and bracelets.

Summary of early latency

At this stage, Helen responded to the demands of school by managing them well on the surface, adapting to the school situation, and getting good grades. She had some friends. Her health problems were finally being clarified. Yet inwardly she was struggling hard with (1) the persistent needs for contact, affection, and care that had been rein-tensified by her chronic illness and physical difficulties; (2) "bad," aggressive impulses; and (3) resentment of parent figures. These resentments doubtless stemmed from a continued underlying sense of deprivation of contact, which was reinforced by her feelings about being poor as well as by her wishes to be a boy, or to be different, in a positive instead of negative way, and related doubts about growing up, among other conflicts. She was probably helped by her ability to use culturally available story themes to deal with these problems, by her ability to project to others the difficulties she felt, or conversely, to give to others what she craved for herself, as well as to involve others in actively playing out her problems. Yet this was done at a price—at least, there was more to be integrated than she could manage at that time. She still controlled herself sufficiently to avoid both delinquent behavior and affect storms. But her cognitive functioning on the projective tests showed the strain, despite the fact that on the structured tests her verbal level rose. On the whole, she kept actively trying, while relegating her old demands and needs to covert realms as far as possible. She was trying to be good.

Development from Eight to Eleven Years

Helen and her mother were approached for another round of observations when Helen was eleven years old. Her mother reported that Helen had been feeling "real well" ever since the tonsillectomy. There had been no recurrence of her kidney trouble and Helen "had not had even a bad cold since." Physically she seemed to be in such good condition that, even when the whole family suffered from flu, Helen got only a slight touch of it and recovered rapidly. This implied that she had successfully disposed of a major source of almost continuous somatic discomfort, irritation, and excitement—a source that had recurrently precipitated a good deal of anxiety and fear about bodily harm. But the question of "good" and "bad" was still in the foreground, this time with sexual implications. Helen had a frightening experience at the age of ten, when, if she had not been rescued by her brothers, she would have been molested by a threatening older boy. She was able to talk about this with her mother after the first shock, and after this she became more cautious with strangers.

In reaction to this and other threats, the parents decided to move to a nearby smaller town where they would have more space for the children to play. In addition, tensions were also reduced for all the family by the fact that now the socioeconomic status of the family resembled that of their neighbors.

The stressful events had mobilized certain reactions of defense and protection and further heightened Helen's consciousness of "good" and "bad" and the conforming and nonconforming aspects of behavior. Helen's behavior at the research center indicated that her new inhibitions and sharpened cautiousness had not detracted from her spontaneity with (safe) old acquaintances. She seemed to have developed a greater tolerance for dissonance and a possible strengthening or protection of herself by sharpening such nonconforming and tension-arousing forces, and differentiating herself from them.

Evidences of modulation and maturity at puberty

Helen's subsequent transition to early adolescence was relatively smooth. From an undernourished, "skinny" child in her early years she grew into a graceful teenager. She was neither ahead of nor behind her age-mates in the growth spurt, and she went through no embarrassing deviant phase such as the "fat stage" suffered by some pubertal children. Menstruation came easily and was "less trouble than she expected," uncomplicated apparently by tensions often experienced by other girls. She enjoyed food and did not have to diet, nor were there at this time any obvious residues of her earlier respiratory, gastric, or kidney vulnerabilities. She often seemed radiant and joyfully attractive in teenage clothes. Altogether she was a changed girl in health and appearance.

During the next two years Helen was seen repeatedly in psychological, pediatric, and psychiatric examinations, and she was observed at her school. Later she was included in a study of religion in young adolescents (Stewart 1967), which involved two testing and interview sessions with her, and interviews with her mother and pastor; a study of speech and hearing (chapter 8, pt. II); and other studies of cognitive style (Gardner and Moriarty 1968), memory, ESP, and creativity (Moriarty and Murphy 1967), and reactions to the Kennedy assassination (chapter 9). Results of these sessions are reported separately as indicated in the references above, and will not be included here in detail. In addition, special visits and interviews took place within a short time after the accidental death of her brother.

The emphasis in all reports was the unalloyed delight she provided to the other person; an observer who had contact with her for the longest period of time said, "This session with Helen was undoubtedly one of the most delightful and interesting in which I have participated this year. . . . I experienced her as a warm, bubbling, gay child with considerable insight into affective processes, and remarkable social skills. . . . Helen's aggressive affection has become modulated and her flighty movements have almost entirely disappeared. . . . there was no need to draw Helen out, because practically from the moment we met, she initiated conversation at a mature level."

We found her making an increased effort to define the nature of things; she also attempted to seek solutions for the problem of defining her own identity. And we found stronger achievement-orientation. Not only was she doing well in school, but she was a leader in her church youth group, eagerly using new opportunities to satisfy both social and achievement needs in constructive ways. She received four prizes at annual fairs in one year, for instance.

At a party at the Murphy home she was notably ready for pleasure, enjoying the surroundings, wall-hangings, textiles, and other appurtenances of the setting, whereas some other pubertal children were indifferent or too shy to stop and look. She readily made friends with a girl of similar interests.

As always, Helen used language freely and to advantage. She talked about a wide variety of things and initiated topics on her own, such as her current pleasure in her new home and school. Although the first days at the new school were difficult, she had made friends with two other girls who were also new at the school. Though she would have to share a room with her sister in the new house, she looked forward to the time when her sister would go to business school, so that she could have a room of her own. In other topics of conversation Helen was also oriented toward the future and what she would like to do. She talked about wanting to teach school, preferably the first or the second grade because young children were "less sassy," more easy to manage, and more interesting than older children. She wanted to travel to Hawaii, which she considered an exotic paradise, and to Russia, which she realized was a country of great importance in world affairs. She wanted to talk with Eisenhower and Khrushchev and with vigorous interest indicated that she would ask Khrushchev, "Why do you want all those countries and what would you do with them, if you have them?" She was curious about what children are like in different parts of the world.

She initiated a discussion of race attitudes with me, stating that she felt differently from the way her mother did, citing the Bible and the Constitution in support of her equalitarian ideas. It was as if by her social skills Helen was developing an interpersonal approach as a basis from which she could establish her own autonomy. Also, by clarifying cognitively the structure within which others function, Helen seemed to be seeking new principles of organization of her own identity. Not totally absorbed by her plans for the future, she talked about some past happenings, including her past contact with the research project, and she inquired about specific people with whom she had associated during her visits. She also talked with considerable enthusiasm about watching the election returns together with the rest of the family. She then asked for my political preferences, and even though these were different from her family's views, Helen accepted this difference as a right and privilege inherent in and important to our form of government. We did not find here the reflections of Helen's earlier anxiety about certain situations of conflict or dissonance, nor an attempt to reconcile quickly.

Interests, activities, sublimation, and self-control

In talking about a number of interests and plans for her immediate future, Helen mentioned elaborate plans for a garden in which she wanted to raise tomatoes and flowers. She discussed sports and group activities provided by the school, her enjoyment of the school assemblies and of the bus rides, to which she looks forward. She did not talk about her own boyfriends, but about her sister's boyfriends, and expressed various degrees of fondness for a large number of them. A closer examination showed that many of Helen's interests contained her strong social orientation, consistent from infancy.

At this stage, Helen showed another group of strong interests and skills that seemed to have channeled her boyish activities to a significant extent; these also helped to satisfy her earlier competitiveness, which now seemed modulated and less aggressive. In school Helen was reported to be very active in games on the playground, and in one particular running game she was the "hardest girl to catch." Her mother reported that Helen liked to roller skate and do all sorts of tricks on roller skates. During the summer she played with the girls in the neighborhood and went skating; and she learned how to ride very fast on a bicycle with her brothers. They were all surprised at how rapidly she learned to ride, because earlier she had been a little timid and afraid of getting hurt.

Her competitiveness was now reflected in her response to the vocabulary test. Though Helen picked at her fingers nervously when the items became more difficult, she was quite poised and did not seem to be greatly embarrassed by her failure to point out "similarities" in another test. Apparently, in spite of some fluctuations, Helen had always been at least a high average student in school, achieving somewhat better grades than her earlier average intelligence scores would lead one to expect. This, too, was perhaps an example of successful sublimation of the aggressive aspects of her competitive drive.

Peer-group stress

But Helen was now observed not to mix well in spontaneous casual encounters with the other children in her school, and whenever she was observed talking to them she seemed businesslike and controlled.

Her mother also reported some difficulties with peers; once, after a square dancing class, Helen told her mother that there had been more girls than boys that day, and though there were several boys from her own school, none of them asked her to dance though they asked some other girls who didn't even know how to dance. Helen was hurt and decided that she was not going to the dances any more. However, she soon recovered from this feeling and had forgotten all about it by the next week. She went to the next square dance and "had a wonderful time." This sequence indicated that while Helen was sensitive to rejection by her peers, she was resilient and had not isolated herself from them to any serious degree. She was reported to be playing with the girls in the neighborhood, to attend choir on Saturday mornings, and Girl Scout activities on another afternoon.

Although she was a leader in serious church activities, her mother reported that Helen did not go along with the boys of the fifth and sixth grade when they were acting silly; she "did not like the giggling and the yelling." This distance from her peers contrasted with her earlier behavior when, with one or two children of her age, Helen had always showed initiative in bringing them into the conversation, or in sharing her activity. Earlier, Helen had been more brash and competitive in a group setting. Now she seemed to protect herself by a mild detachment. As part of this, she sometimes appeared overabsorbed in a particular activity, but with less evidence of concern to produce results. For instance, Helen worked very intently at her desk and was not distracted by the noise or commotion going on around her; she continued reading a book while most of the children were working at other things. It seemed then that Helen used this absorption in books to minimize the pressure of the "silly" behavior of her surrounding peers, in which she hesitated to become involved. Helen's heightened consciousness of conforming and nonconforming behavior at this time, and perhaps a confusion of being "good at" with "being good," may have contributed to some difficulty in spontaneous relationships with other children. In her decreased fantasy material at this stage we have to see her control as carried beyond modulation to the point of reaction-formation, in some areas. Yet she could be warmly spontaneous with adults; with them she was never stiff or inhibited as were certain children who developed a more generalized and rigid construction.

Helen's initiative is illustrated by her suggestion to her teacher to "invite Dr. Murphy to come and talk to the class and show her pictures of her trip around the world." Helen proudly reported, "I'll have to introduce you because I'm your only friend at this school."

Self-awareness at puberty

Helen was growing fast; the changes in her physical development and bodily makeup could have increased her awareness of herself, especially in relation to her peers. Helen was reported by her mother to have been especially interested in her appearance since her eleventh birthday; she put pincurls in her hair every night and felt badly if she had to miss a night. Though she had outgrown "the ruffle stage," she was even more interested in clothes than she had been earlier; the only thing that worried her mother was Helen's slowness in getting dressed in the morning. Her sister commented that if a dress shown on TV was cut too low, or a couple was embracing, Helen got very embarrassed; her face would get red and she would hang her head. This embarrassment reflected her increased awareness of her own bodily changes and sexual development and perhaps some covert feeling of shame associated with it.

Helen has appeared to be the only girl in the study group who looked forward to each new grade in school and did not hanker for the old one. Perhaps there was some overemphasis on this device, which was partly defensive and concealed her hopeless wish to be small and cared-for like the recurring babies in her family. This struggle did not stir excessively turbulent or resentful feelings in Helen, nor did it make her resist the challenge of growth; rather, she may have pushed herself to grow up a little too early. But in general, she was increasingly oriented toward progress, stability, lack of tumult, reflectiveness, and a quiet sense of humor.

The emergence of a credo

Unique in this group and typical of Helen was her formula of faith that "bad things can turn into good things." This was unconsciously implied in her preschool concept that dark rain can turn into colors, and we saw repeated hints of this orientation in succeeding years. When she was twelve years old and we asked her where this conviction came from, she mentioned her memory of the wonderful trip to California with her grandmother after her tonsillectomy, and her thrill at looking out the window at the beautiful lights of Hollywood. It is interesting to see that in this memory of an event four years earlier, by no means just a screen memory—although it condensed experiences from infancy onward— both the pain and the transforming compensation were implied. What was not explicit was the slow sequence of her childhood experience, from illness to health, from feelings of deprivation to the capacity to meet her own needs, from naughty, brash demandingness to modulated and socially acceptable assertion, from being an odd-looking, vulnerable baby and sickly child to becoming a lovely and healthy teenager. Her image also contained her ego-ideal of the giving grandmother with whom she had evidently deeply identified, even while at puberty she increasingly identified with her own mother as well. Her general attitude of faith was further expressed in strong religious interests, a deep sense of the support of God, and emotional response to church ritual, hymns, and the personality of her pastor.

Finally, she was able, by adolescence at least, to expand her philosophy that "bad things can turn into good things" to "bad people can also be good people"—that is, she was tolerant and accepting even of the people who were quite deviant from her own strong religious viewpoints. In this, she differed from Darlene who still had a good deal of missionary zeal. Helen was more able to take people as they are and did not need to reform them.

At college Helen was "the outstanding candidate for a music scholarship." After graduation and a year of internship, she married and taught music in the public schools.

12

L'envoi: Overview

Throughout this book we have shared specific observations, statistical analyses, and case excerpts. The time has come for us to share an overview of child development in this ecological and cultural setting. From the top of a mountain one sees the surrounding peaks, the main rises of land. What are some of these?

The Development of the Concept of Coping

We began by confiding in our readers our early dissatisfaction with adultocentric labels such as "withdrawn," "resistant," "aggressive," and dichotomous categories such as "pathological" versus "normal." It seemed to us that children were seen through special glasses, constantly judged in relation to their conformity to adult demands, expectations, and pressures. And it seemed to us that this led to misunderstanding and an intrinsic generation gap. It seemed to make adults blind to the child's own experience of a given situation, his feelings about it, his efforts to deal with it in a way that could make him comfortable. During World War II I regularly read the Hampstead Nurseries reports by Anna Freud and Dorothy Burlingame on children's ways of coping with bombs, separation from mother, and other stresses of their lives.

The concept of coping seemed right for describing children's ways of dealing with challenges, and I decided to focus on children's coping methods in the next research. The opportunity came in 1952 at the Menninger Foundation.

As soon as we began to visit the Topeka children's homes, take them to the research setting, test and examine them, and watch them play we found that practically every new situation, every demand, stress, and even opportunity for fun involved coping problems. And, despite our intentions to avoid categorizing, we could not avoid talking about "good copers" when we came to the point of sharing our carefully guarded independent observations. We were impressed with their wide range of coping devices, from offering substitutes when they could not provide exactly what was asked, to reorganizing the situation, or putting an end to what they did not like. Coping with the environment was referred to as Coping I for short; then we found ourselves watching the children's ways of keeping comfortable, or maintaining internal integration, which we referred to as Coping II. Coping styles varied from child to child, and all children used some defense mechanisms temporarily—regression especially—as part of this coping.

Conditions Contributing to Coping Capacity

The space, safety, and freedom of this Kansas town gave many children opportunities to explore, to discover the world for themselves, to exercise their autonomous resources, to come to their own conclusions, to establish a realistic basis for evaluating opportunities and threats they might encounter.

Along with this went opportunities to develop motor skills, to let off steam or discharge tensions ("If you can't be quiet in the house, get out and run!").

While the climate provides many days of sunshine good for outdoor activity, Kansas is "tornado country" and children grow up "knowing what to do if a tornado hits"—and thus absorb a model for coping.

Extremes of poverty and wealth were not experienced by these children, and in the relatively secure economic climate of the town most families were free from economic stress.

Solid realism went along with a commitment to a religious orientation: grace at meals, bedtime prayers, church and Sunday School, and parents' reminders of God's will and of the Lord as a source of help in trouble as well as a judge of right and wrong made religious faith an important part of everyday life. This faith supported successful problem-solving and coping with stress.

Family closeness and respect for individuality bolstered the children's self-confidence and pride; mastery of skills and development of coping resources were stimulated by opportunities to watch skillful fathers and to do a share of the family chores.

Clear limits and expectable discipline were generally accepted by the children overtly; the fact that parents' comfort and help were offered when children were disappointed or frustrated strengthened the children's sense of being cared for. While parents demanded frankness and obedience, they did not impose pressures for outstanding achievement or judge their children by external norms. They expected children to grow in the children's own way.

Preschool Coping

All the children had ways of coping; no child left any of the situations in which he was observed. In keeping with the outdoor freedom they had enjoyed, most of the children were autonomous and assumed that adults would respect their autonomy, opinions, and wishes. At age four and older, all were able to go to new places and were able to cope with a variety of challenges. Most, even the more vulnerable children, used a large number and variety of coping devices. They had a clear self-image and sense of identity.

Autonomy was usually balanced by cooperativeness and compliance with mandatory requests. Thus autonomy was flexible—available when the situation permitted, in abeyance when the situation required.

Sex differences: Boys were more active, with more motor skills and initiative out of doors. More freedom had been permitted them by parents. But at two to three years of age, certain boys clung more to their mother when in new places.

Variability: Often there was a combination of defensive behavior with direct coping efforts oriented toward saving face or maintaining the level of self-feeling while at the same time directly attempting to get the help that would make it possible to function more effectively and realistically.

Coping with adults: Various approaches in dealing with adults were seen in different children. There were those to whom it was important to sustain interpersonal relationship through talking or interaction. The tendency to draw people into their world appeared to have the value of enriching their experience. Several of these children were also children who identified with adults—who tended to reverse roles in experiments and games.

Others entered into competition with adults, trying to test the possibilities of extending their power, expanding their own area of control. Though these efforts to find or maintain an equal level in their relationship with grown-ups may have contributed to the uncertainty that their tension reflected, we cannot say that an attitude of identification with and competition with grown-ups inevitably threatened the child's security at this stage.

Still others looked for or followed adult cues, complied with adults' commands, offered deference to authority.

There is evidence (from the Children's Apperception Test) that the children experienced themselves unconsciously, if not consciously, as little people surrounded by a world of big and powerful grown-ups with whom they could, however, deal and compete.

The Comprehensive Coping Inventory

The CCI is a list of coping devices, related dispositions, and observed aspects of the home environment. These items come from clinical observations as well as psychological, psychiatric, and pediatric examinations, medical history, observations in the home and at parties and excursions. We found both active and passive coping devices and also defense mechanisms and did not imply judgments of success. Not all coping *efforts* succeed. While some combinations, or overuse, of defense mechanisms may interfere with healthy coping, flexible use of defense mechanisms were part of coping.

Two global concepts were formulated:

Coping I — capacity to cope with opportunities, challenges, frustrations, threats in the environment.

Coping II — maintenance of internal integration; capacity to manage one's relation to the environment so as to maintain integrated functioning (thus contrasted with vulnerability).

The entire list of coping items was correlated with Coping I and Coping II; by implication the correlations in essence reflected the examiners' implicit evaluation of the contribution of specific coping techniques to overall coping effectiveness.

Some motor variables correlated higher with Coping I for girls than for boys, which reflected the girls' wider range (from good to poor) in this area. Some affective, sensory, and cognitive variables gave higher correlations with Coping I for boys than for girls; these reflected a wider range of levels of functioning in these areas among boys.

The best copers among boys and girls, those with the widest range of coping resources, were those who had both "masculine" and "feminine" skills or resources.

There is some overlap in items correlating significantly with Coping I and Coping II. The ability to control the impact of the environment implies autonomy, but in this case the child's efforts are oriented toward maintenance of integration. A balance of autonomy with sufficient dependency to be able to get and use help contributed to Coping II.

The line between coping devices and dispositions may sometimes be hard to draw, as with capacity to delay, tolerance of frustration, "sending power," and "healthy narcissism"—liking oneself (a dynamic generative response to life characteristic of some of these children).

Coping styles must be seen in relation to types of situations as these are experienced by the child. Coping techniques and styles evolve and change over time.

The coping patterns of children probably differ in other American subcultures as well as subcultures in other nations. Children in other cultures would not have the same experiences, challenges, frustrations, or supports. Their experiences could contribute different coping orientations from those of the children in Topeka.

Coping with vulnerability (susceptibility to deterioration of functioning under stress). At the preschool stage, any deterioration, disorganization, or inhibition of cognitive, affective, motor, or integrative functioning pointed to vulnerable areas, as did extreme autonomic or affective reactivity to stimulation, and other disturbances in functioning.

Some children developed self-protective preventive devices or compensatory measures to manage such problems: timing rest; ability to limit or fend off excessive stimulation; ability to control the impact of the environment through strategic withdrawal, delay, and caution; and the ability to select, to restructure the environment. Involved here as prerequisites were realistic appraisal of the environment, acceptance of people, clear differentiation of fantasy from reality, and many cognitive coping capacities.

Tolerance of temporary regression protects against stress by reducing tension.

Some aspects of the child's self-feeling and relation to his home helped the child cope with vulnerability. These included the adequacy of the child's self-image, security, and positive orientation to life along with related items; the mother's enjoyment of the child, encouragement or support of the child, and active help to the child in coping were also significantly related to coping capacity.

Early Influences on Coping

Mothers and infants' response. While mothers were typically responsible, family-centered, and devoted, as stimuli for their babies they were infinitely varied: speedy or easy-going, colorful or monotone, vigorous or gentle, talkative or quietly observant, humorous or sober, relaxed or tense, rigid or flexible, warmly intimate or a bit distant. They also varied in perceptiveness of their babies' needs, and as judged by Grace Heider, in their "fit" with their equally varied babies.

Even though there were no extremely neglectful mothers, there were differences in the impact of their handling of the babies; in some cases this was related to the "fit" between mother and baby. A very gentle mother did not provide a rugged, active baby with the vigorous play such babies like, and a very energetic mother seemed over-stimulating to a quiet, sensitive baby. The amount of attention (talking to the baby, smiling at the baby, watching the baby) contributed to good development up to a point; *too much* attention and *too little* attention were alike detrimental (cf. p. 60). These correlations were curvilinear, but correlations of infant functioning with mothers' adjustment were consistently positive.

The mother's respect for the baby's natural pace and rhythms evidently avoids irritation and autonomic excitation, which can interfere with good digestion and oral gratification.

The autonomy allowed by the mother in the feeding situation correlates significantly with the infant boy's own termination capacity and capacity to resist and protest. Evidently the boy's decisiveness evoked the mother's respect for the baby's autonomy. To give autonomy to the infant, the mother had to be free from anxiety, to have a style of her own that did not conflict with the baby's style. And she probably had had sensitive mothering herself. (A mother orphaned in infancy lacked the more typical intuitive responsiveness to the baby's pace and style.)

Mother–child viability (compatibility of mother and infant) correlates with mother's respect for baby's autonomy, the mother's level of adjustment, and with the baby's vegetative functioning and capacity to use support from others. The mother's adjustment may be facilitated by this compatibility, but the mother's adjustment has little relation to the infant's activity level and sensory reactivity; the latter seem to be determined by constitutional dispositions. However, there is a reciprocal relationship between the infant's drive level and the mother's responses through speech and facial expression. The evocative, responsive baby draws responses from the mother that in turn stimulate the baby.

Dynamics of individuality in the infants. Even within the first month the baby has had such a multitude of important experiences that we cannot assume any characteristics reflect purely genetic influences. When we speak of constitutional differences we never forget that we are talking about dispositions influenced by pregnancy and birth experiences and the entire range of interactions with the total environment in contact with the baby.

Activity level refers to all movement, both goal-oriented efforts and impulsive reactions to release tension. Activity includes locomotion and motor exploits, social interaction, manipulation of toys, and problem-solving. A high activity level may contribute to the capacity for mastery of motor skills and greater exposure to the environment. A wider range of manipulative experiences stimulates cognitive development and leads to development of coping resources.

Possible reasons for low activity level include constitutional tendency toward low activity, great visual or sensory interest that is better sustained in conditions of motor quiet, and self-protective controls to avoid overstimulation.

To what extent is activity a reflection of internally generated impulses as contrasted with a marked tendency to react to external stimuli by motor activity? To what extent is it a reciprocal relationship between the two? (An active baby encourages the mother's stimulation, to which the baby reacts.)

Sensory reactivity varied greatly among the babies. Support for the infant's sensory preferences (re contact, lights, colors, sounds, temperatures, and so on) contributes to a feeling of acceptance and gives the child freedom to pursue drives oriented to the external world and a steadiness of goal orientation.

Management of the excitation aroused by sensory stimuli depends both on the baby's resources for motor discharge of tension and his inner resources for processing and integrating perceptions evoked by stimulation. When thresholds for loss of coordination under stress are low, increased stimulation and resulting heightened activity level result in decreased smoothness of motor functioning.

Precursor to ambivalence. Some infants responded to stimulation in the same modality (especially tactual stimulation) with strong positive reactions under certain conditions, and strong negative reactions under other conditions; both quantitative and qualitative variations in stimuli are involved here. This precursor to ambivalence can color the relationship with the mother and to others, can contribute to conflicts that stimulate coping, as well as shape the amount and style of social participation, development of selected few versus many varied relationships, and so forth.

Visual differences. Mild visual defects can contribute to slow orientation patterns and sensitivity to strangeness. The outcome of experiences affected by visual "sensitivity" either in terms of low thresholds or of high reactivity need not be accompanied by integrative difficulties or social inadequacies, but depends on the balance of capacities of the child. A child with relative emotional and autonomic stability and rapid processing of visual impressions can integrate these into his information bank to develop coping resources. *Differences in early capacity to differentiate objects* contribute to differences in reactions to strangeness, the ability to accept substitutes, and the tendency to cling to the familiar.

Oral drives and their integration in coping. Differences were found in the intensity of certain aspects of oral functioning that are involved in oral drive (that is, oral demand, gratification, autonomy in satisfying oral need, capacity to protest or terminate unsatisfying oral situations), and these are not necessarily parallel. The oral zone provided a pattern that contributed to a sense of being able to communicate a need, obtain a response, control the input, and experience gratification.

Developmental balances and imbalances affect coping capacity. Individual babies exhibited a wide range of maturity of functioning in different areas. Imbalances can contribute to coping problems. For instance, an infant with advanced responsiveness and sending power is apt to evoke much social interplay from others. If such an infant is immature in processing stimulation, or in motor coordination required for active interplay, or if the infant has a high level of autonomic reactivity, he may not be able to cope with the stimulation evoked by his own responsiveness. Other consequences of developmental imbalances can be observed.

Differences between level of activity, coordination, and capacity to process stimulation can be expected to contribute to coping problems. This is conspicuous in a child of high activity level with poor coordination and/or slow capacity to process stimulation.

Developmental imbalances often occurred in a context of poor vegetative functioning, which added discomfort and increased coping difficulties.

A balanced pattern of development—one in which social, language, motor, and adaptive functions all mature at a comparable rate—contributes to smoother development and more effective patterns of coping with the environment.

Problems in maintaining internal integration result from high sensory reactivity and difficulties in vegetative functioning and contribute to vulnerability. Vulnerability varies also with the infant's resources to restore stability and maintain integration. (Compare Teddy and Roddy.) *Individual differences in some integrative functions* are reflected in decisiveness of preferences, ease of control of impulse or inhibition, capacity to delay, synthesizing capacities, and imitating and identifying.

Capacity for self-regulation. Conditions for recovery of energy and of equilibrium vary for different infants. Aspects of self-regulation capacity include regulation of activity and rest rhythms, self-regulation of the intensity of stimulus to which the infant will expose himself (this varies both from infant to infant and within an individual infant from one zone of sensitivity to another), and infant's tempo of mastery and level of integration. In situations that arouse acute anxiety or severe threats—where the infant cannot select, measure, or time the quantity, quality, or tempo of stress—the self-regulating capacity may break down.

Resilience, recovery and stress management. The infant's foundation for resilience is related to the resources of self-regulation. The model for recovery and resilience is the loss of integration under stress and the regaining of smooth functioning and energy with relief from stress.

Aspects of resilience include the infant's tempo of arousal and speed of decline after arousal, responsiveness to objects, intensity of drive, and available preferred gratifications.

Infant's devices for letting go of tension and stress include crying, fussing, screaming; turning away from overstimulating objects, spontaneous pacing (alternating activity with rest) pleasurable sensory gratifications initiated by baby (thumb-sucking, turning toward potentially gratifying objects). Certain of these capacities were related to the infant's age.

A combination of renewed metabolic activity (result of rest, sleep, food), alleviation of tension and pain (result of comfort by mother or by self), pleasurable affect and renewed drive (result of object-stimulation), helps reestablish the dynamic balance.

Mothers had a variety of ways of helping to soothe their babies and restore the baby's equilibrium: talking to, patting, stroking, rocking, holding the baby to the mother's shoulder; offering a toy, pacifier, drink, or food; laughing with the baby. These involved different combinations of tactile, kinesthetic, rhythmic, visual, auditory, oral stimuli to induce pleasure and relaxation.

Continuity and change. The primary adaptational styles of the infants varied in degree of balance, organization, consistency or variability (and thus degree of fixedness), and range of potential future developments. A well-knit, balanced, and consistent pattern in the baby, when the baby is cared for by a mother who respects and thus reinforces his pattern, can be seen to provide a foundation for a later consistency and thus continuity in development.

In general, cognitive and motor characteristics such as quality of attention and smoothness of motor coordination were more predictable from infancy to the preschool stage than were aspects of social behavior.

Balance contributed freedom from the kind of variation in capacities that would be upsetting or that would subject the child to endless frustration: the well-balanced infant is not driven to pursue goals beyond his or her reach and skills. The well-balanced baby does not evoke or provoke more stimulation from other people than the infant can absorb and respond to.

By contrast, a child with marked imbalances and much variability within the range of observed behaviors and thus less firm organization of tendencies is likely to change much more as changing environmental experiences block, deflect, or reinforce different features of his early adaptational style. Moreover, when the imbalances occur in the form of marked variations in the intensity of different drives, or in relative age and drive strength, conditions exist that are likely to contribute to conflicts. The outcome will depend on subtle variations in the child's ways of struggling with these conflicts as well as the specific kinds of environmental exacerbation of them or efforts to help resolve the conflicts.

These outcomes include creative modulation of impulsiveness, sublimation, and channeling controlled aggressive energy into socially useful roles such as teacher, mechanic, musician. Early balance and minimum stress or conflict contribute more to stability than to creativity.

It is not surprising, then, that we found continuity in some motor and cognitive zones of the personality to be consistent with *plasticity* in the child's overall adaptational pattern: a stable core permits flexibility of response to changing pressures. But also variability, imbalances, and moderate early instabilities and difficulties are balanced by coping efforts leading to creative integrations, reflectiveness, and insight. Mild vulnerabilities stimulate coping efforts.

In keeping with their greater predictability we found that some children show more continuity than others, and also that some behavior patterns show more continuity than others in most children. We also found contrasting directions of change characteristic of two groups of children: one group changed from early inhibition to later increased spontaneity, while the other group changed from early impulsiveness to greater control (which is what we usually expect as children grow from the preschool level to latency or school age). When infants with extreme patterns were exposed to stable, consistent environmental influences the extreme pattern is apt to be exposed to pressure toward modulation toward the mean: for instance, Terry was outstanding for his high activity level, high tonus, high vocalizing, and so forth, but also for his high responsiveness to the social environment. His wish to remain a part of it, to identify with it, helped him to learn to control his restlessness, talkativeness, and so on, especially after entering school.

Later Developments from Early Coping Tendencies

Surprising to us was the correlation between the children's infant capacity to terminate, protest, resist unwanted food or other stimuli and their preschool ability to structure new situations, fend off pressure, and in other ways act decisively in their dealings with us. Equally impressive was the correlation between infantile gratification in feeding and later strength and range of interests and gratification.

We saw the creative outcomes of coping with external and internal problems, and the modulation, compromise, sublimation, and transformation of extremes of activity, impulsiveness, and aggressiveness when confronted with environmental limits.

We also discovered new dimensions of feeling evoked by mastery of challenges: Darlene's glow of triumph after she overcame her fear of jumping; Susan's radiance with progressive steps in mastery of locomotion after her long illness with polio. These expressions of delight and pride added vividness to each child's personality, as well as adding strength, confidence, and greater self-respect.

Variability of IQ

In recent years, new data and new ways of scrutinizing old data have been challenging the long-standing and ferociously defended assumption that consistency in average IQ of *large groups* tested over a limited period of time implied stability of IQ in *individuals* regardless of the other sources of stability or instability in the individuals, and over the entire developmental period. Longitudinal studies of individual children from infancy to adulthood and the study of specific groups under changed conditions have shown fallacies in such assumptions. By now, the evidence is overwhelming that IQs change in certain children whose *cognitive* functioning is evidently more subject to influence by autonomic and affective factors than is that of some other children.

An intensive, primarily qualitative approach to issues usually approached only singly and statistically led to Moriarty's conclusion that variations in IQ were also related to varying conditions of health, emotional comfort, family and other stress, the child's orientation toward growth and progress, as well as to transitory aspects of the test situation and variations in cognitive functions studied at different levels of development. Children whose IQs varied were often sensitive and more easily aroused. Children with the most stable IQs included some who reacted to stress in motor areas. We have to agree with Macfarlane's (1972) statement that no single IQ test at a given time can be regarded as an adequate picture of a child's potentialities.

The data from our records of children from infancy into the latency period also call for revision of certain widely accepted concepts in the field of child development and of mental health. The recognition of sequences (McGraw, Gesell, Macfarlane, Bayley, etc.) and of stages of development (Freud, Erikson, Heinz Werner, Piaget) seems to carry along with it an assumption of irreversibility of the sequence under normal conditions. But Moriarty observed that the most effective children, the best copers if you like, allowed themselves leeway for regression to infantile sorts of gratification under the pressures of the intelligence test situation. Regression is a defense mechanism used not only by neurotic children, but by other healthy children whenever they need to let down, to balance up the efforts involved in meeting the adult-imposed challenges that are so often irrelevant to the spontaneous goals formed by the children themselves. Regression occurred in these children not only under frustration, as Barker, Dembo, and Lewin (1943) showed (true of ⅔ of the children in their sample), but also under conditions of success when this involved focused effort, as with Trudy and others. Regression took the form of nonfunctional irrelevant uncoordinated motor outlets, oral and other primitive tactual and messing activities, amorphous affective discharges through nonverbal vocalizations of an animal-like and infantile quality, among others.

In other words, with these children, and perhaps with most people, regression may go hand in hand with progress and the effort to make progress; in short, as Ernst Kris pointed out, some regression may appear in the service of the ego.

Thus we saw that active coping efforts often go hand in hand with defense mechanisms. We saw no child in this demonstrably normal group who did not include temporarily useful defense mechanisms as part of his overall coping pattern. Moriarty's record of the children's reactions to the shock of President Kennedy's assassination included illustrations of initial denial and projection (as did reports of many adult reactions).

Vulnerability

While we were impressed by the wide individual differences of the children in their responses to all situations, we soon became interested in the relation of these differences to the variations in zones of vulnerability of the children: some of them reflected stress by tightening muscles or becoming rigid, "freezing," or more mildly tensing up. With other children speech became slow, fuzzy, stammery, or deteriorated in other ways. Growing pale or flushing or—with boys—having an erection, sometimes along with increased rapidity of breathing, pulse, or heart-rate could occur with or without motor or speech changes.

Approaches to the study of vulnerability. At an early stage of our studies I began to explore vulnerability in terms of extremes, deviations, and imbalances in the child's equipment, and the zones in which the child tended to lose smooth functioning under stress. Grace Heider evaluated vulnerability in terms of the gestalt of the child in his situation—both his own vulnerable zones and balancing resources and the stress and support in the environment. Povl Toussieng evaluated strengths and weaknesses in ego functioning, including evidence of conflicts and symptoms. Alice Moriarty, with Clyde Rousey, made an intensive study of speech as a major zone reflecting vulnerability to stress.

No child was invulnerable: some loss of their best functioning occurred in all children in the face of one or another experience evidently felt as threatening or stressful.

Furthermore patterns of recovery from a disturbed state varied from child to child as did children's own ways of coping with disequilibrium—by retreating to safety, taking time out, using self-comfort devices. And typically mothers tried to help children by comforting reassurances and encouragement.

Yet of the children considered by Heider *most vulnerable* in the preschool years, eight out of eleven needed special help of one kind or another at a later stage, and even infantile vulnerability was reflected in the reactions of certain children to the sudden stress of the assassination of President Kennedy when they were thirteen to fifteen years of age.

Exploring resilience. Just as patterns of vulnerability varied among the children, so also did patterns of recovery. At a physiological level, different tempos of reduction of tension or recovery of equilibrium were seen. Children responded to different kinds of distraction from pain. The ability to evoke help and to respond to help, including help in understanding, help in working through loss, help in restitution and compensation, and in making efforts needed for recovery were seen in resilient children, along with the capacity to identify with resilient care-givers. Fantasy, denial, regression, and repression all had a place at certain times, while at a propitious phase children used emerging energies to master inadequacies occurring as residue of illness.

The role of stress as a challenge evoking added energy—the "inoculation" effect of mastering stress or desensitization or "getting used to" stress—and the resulting strength were illustrated in a number of episodes. We also saw the contribution of coping with stress and with vulnerability to the child's integration of a personal view of life; in Helen's summary, "bad things can turn into good things."

"Adaptation" by children in this context is not seen as simple compliance with adult demands, but as coming to terms with them in such a way as to get along with the adults while meeting their own needs as children. None of the children in this intensive study sample became a "delinquent," none became "schizophrenic" or "psychotic." Their prepuberty scores on the Holtzman Inkblot Test were comparable to those of a sample of 400 Texas sixth-graders. Insofar as the constriction and anxiety often documented at this stage is considered "neurotic," it has to be recognized as typical for our culture with its stressful pressures (such as shifting to a large impersonal junior high school at the time when bodily changes are producing inner disequilibrium and insecurity). Continuous smooth functioning as a goal of adequate adaptation is unrealistic.

Looking back over the years during which these children were growing up, and taking into account the variations and changes in their coping patterns, we encounter some haunting questions. Where do the children get the capacity for effort and struggle, the determination to reach goals and to overcome obstacles? We saw this in baby Ronald's thirty-five-minute struggle to raise himself on all fours, in baby Terry's persistence in reaching a toy that he wanted, in Susan's commitment to conquering deficits from polio, in Darlene's determination to overcome her fear of jumping. This is not merely a matter of high activity level, for many active children do not show such a focused capacity for coping, and some relatively quiet—even frail—children are extremely determined. Nor is it an expression of aggression, although aggression may be used in the process of coping. Even the general concept of mastery does not explain it, since mastery may serve to dominate others or to achieve expertise in skills and yet not ensure coping with a crisis, challenge, or threat. In these children the drive to mastery was directed toward coping with life's challenges; how did this come about?

Since we were not equipped to make intensive physiological and biochemical studies of factors in energy, we can point to only part of the answer—the cultural tradition as conveyed by the family and as evoked and supported by various ecological aspects of the setting. We saw the assumption that children could cope with tornadoes and their success in doing so. Part of the cultural tradition was the maxim that God helps those who help themselves. We saw too how children watched resourceful coping by parents. And we saw parents' encouragement of children's independent coping efforts from early infancy. Here we have ecologically conditioned, general cultural and individual parental reinforcement of children's spontaneous efforts and expressions of determination. And so the answer to the question Where does coping capacity come from? is not simple. It involves drive within the child, supported by the need and the freedom to cope with real challenges, with multiple supports from the environment.

A related and equally puzzling question is What accounts for the resilience we saw in many contexts? The capacity to make a comeback after frustration, discouragement, defeat, as well as from weakness due to illness varied among different children. This may well be related to the flexibility we found emerging among our correlations. Flexibility was reflected in freedom from the tendency to get stuck, bogged down, or frozen into a self-defeating attitude, and, as part of this, the development of a wide *range* of coping resources, ideas for problem-solving, growing out of a variety of experiences and observation of coping efforts of others.

At a physical level, recovery from disturbed autonomic nervous system reactions gives a foundation—however unconscious—for recovery of a sense of equilibrium and energy available for coping. Thus a rapid pace of autonomic recovery contributes to the maintenance of coping capacity.

We saw disintegrative reactions to pain shift to a positive integrative response when Richard turned from sobbing helplessness in the hospital to eager activity ("forgetting his pain") when interesting play materials were brought to him. Here the pleasure competes with and, as we say, "distracts from" or decathects from pain.

The role of constant loving care is implied in Susan's revelation in a play session that "the nurses loved the sickest child best" and in the record of her parents' indefatigable devotion throughout her illness and convalescence. Coping and resilience can be evoked by qualities of response that psychology has not begun to study adequately.

Child-rearing

We were surprised to learn that support for the child's spontaneous coping efforts can begin at birth, and that coping capacity develops along a continuum from, let us say, 90 percent helplessness at birth to 90 percent autonomy in maturity. (The figures may be wrong, but the point is important.) And we were also surprised to find that coping in the first six months is correlated with coping resources and techniques several years later.

Child-rearing then is not just a matter of taking care of the baby and the young child—whether with a philosophy of permissiveness or of discipline—but of supporting the child's efforts to take care of himself. This implies respecting the baby's signals as to what is comfortable, what is enough or too much, what is too hot or too cold, what tastes good or tastes bad, what feels good to the touch. It implies respecting the baby's efforts to look and scan, reach, push away, turn over, move toward something. There are many times when mother knows best, to be sure, but much of the time the child knows what it needs, what it is ready for.

At the toddler stage, when autonomy blossoms and the child incessantly pokes and peeks into every space available, eyes, ears, touch are being exercised more than ever, and "safe freedom" is needed to permit the development of a cognitive map of the environment and skills in using it. It is important to provide the child with opportunities for watching the activities of older children and adults, for managing small responsibilities as well as self-care. This is important even when at first feeding is messy, buttons are missed, the washcloth drips water on the floor.

When new challenges are feared—as in going to school, moving to a new home, going to the hospital—parents can help not by forcing the child to cope alone, but by the reassurance of their presence and help and by allowing the child to show how much can be managed independently.

The parents of good copers neither indulged their children nor overprotected them. They respected their children's capacities, encouraged and rewarded their efforts, and offered reassurance in times of frustration and failure.

Need for Further Study and Research

All through these chapters we have pointed to or hinted at the need for further research on issues and hypotheses growing out of our studies of the Topeka children. We cannot review all these now, but we can underscore certain questions that demand further study most urgently. Many hypotheses are implicit in the Vulnerability Inventory (Appendix 8).

Studies of babies and children in their home settings are too rare, and only in these natural habitats can our records of spontaneous coping efforts be adequately extended: struggling to get thumb to mouth, to perfect sucking, to wiggle to a comfortable position in mother's arms or in the crib, to terminate unwanted feeding. Later, to insist on feeding oneself, to experiment with latches to get out of enclosures, to invent new activities when bored (such as drawing on the window with toothpaste), to fend off unwanted intrusions, to satisfy curiosities by exploration. These are only a few of the coping efforts observable chiefly in open-ended home records.

The area of sensitivities with related problems of needs or adequate stimulation and difficulties from overstimulation, as well as ambivalence related to positive and negative responses to the same types of stimulation, need study especially in relation to later sequelae of early experience.

Early autonomic instability and reactivity, coupled with high activity level and sensitivity should be studied in relation to early thresholds for frustration and both regressive and aggressive reactions to frustration—and the patterning of aggression.

Zones of disintegrative responses to stress (cognitive, as in IQ changes; motor, as in the loss of control, including speech problems) call for study in relation to patterns of coping with resulting difficulties.

Can the complex interacting factors contributing to variability of IQ in our Topeka group be found in other children studied longitudinally? In particular, can more intensive studies of prenatal and birth influences (along with experiences affecting integration in the earliest months) illuminate vulnerability in perceptual—cognitive functions and coping capacity?

Under what conditions do vulnerabilities evoke vigorous coping efforts such as those we saw in Lennie and others of our group and have read about in accounts of the development of two great Roosevelts, Theodore and Eleanor?

Related to these questions are others calling for further study: in the absence of mother-love (due to her physical or mental illness or other unavailability) does father-love tend to be intensified, and if so, does it contribute to greater vigor and drive to mastery?

Can we verify in other groups the intensified coping energy we saw emerging at "propitious phases" for mastering crises? It is apparent from our records that wide variations in how critical a critical phase actually is can be seen in different children. Can we identify contributing factors such as the general equilibrium of the child, autonomic and other somatic reactivity, the tempo of emergence into a new phase (abrupt or gradual), the relevance of environmental support, the congruence between the child's emerging needs and capacities and the environmental pressures and opportunities?

We saw contrasting patterns of change in different children: from quiet control to active expressive responsiveness with some, and from effervescent impulsiveness to reflective modulation of activity in others. How can we learn to predict such changes? Can they be related to changing balances in equipment and physiological functioning?

Contemporary social and economic conditions (such as unemployment, housing problems, bussing children to achieve school integration, migratory work patterns, changing locations of army, navy, and corporate personnel, ministers, foreign service workers, and others) all confront children with a series of new coping problems. More study is needed of the ranges of coping efforts of parents, children, and community members facing these challenges. We also need to compare the deeper levels of mental and emotional integration in the child who struggles with these complexities as compared with children developing within a stable coherent cultural unit such as an Israeli kibbutz or one of the healthier villages of India.

Since our sample of children was small and came from one ecological and cultural setting of a population predominantly Nordic, it is important to explore other groups of children from other settings. Is the continuum of vulnerability we found in our group characteristic of all ethnic and geographic areas? Do isolated groups with highly integrated experience during the growing-up period and freedom from complex mixed heredity show a narrower range of vulnerabilities (for example, Hutterites, Mennonites, the long-lived mountain peoples of Ecuador)? Are the patterns of vulnerability more varied in groups of widely mixed heritage? Are they decreased among groups which long ago practiced infanticide for fragile or defective infants and increased as a consequence of modern methods of saving lives of premature and birth-damaged infants?

Can we learn more about ecological settings that stimulate or fail to arouse coping efforts? Might we find that optimal—not too much, not too little—stress from forces of nature contributes to development of effective coping patterns in the culture?

APPENDIXES

Appendix 1: Staff at Each Phase of the Study

Infancy Staff

Sibylle Escalona, Ph.D., psychologist, codirector
Mary Leitch, M.D., psychiatrist, codirector
Sylvia Brody, Ph.D., psychologist
Margaret McFarland, Ph.D., psychologist
Grace Heider, M.A., psychologist
Irene Weimers, M.A., psychologist

Preschool Staff

Lois B. Murphy, Ph.D., director
Nelly Tibout, M.D., child analyst, co-director

Examiners and Interviewers
Grace Heider, Ph.D., psychologist
Walter Kass, Ph.D., psychologist
Alice Moriarty, Ph.D., psychologist
Paul Pulver, Ph.D., psychologist
Patricia Schloesser, M.D., pediatrician
Povl Toussieng, M.D., psychiatrist

Observers
Baljeet Malhotra, M.A., psychologist
Wilma Miller, Ph.D., psychologist
Lila Weissenberg, Ph.D., psychologist
Beatrice Wright, Ph.D., psychologist

Secretary and Research Assistant
Marie Smith

Consultants
Gardner Murphy, Ph.D., Director of Research, Menninger Foundation
Philip Du Bois, Ph.D., psychologist, statistician
Wayne Holtzman, Ph.D., psychologist
Walter Raine, Ph.D., psychologist, statistician

Latency Staff

Lois B. Murphy, Ph.D., director

Examiners and Interviewers
Keith Bryant, M.D., psychiatrist
Grace Heider, Ph.D., psychologist, interviewer
Baljeet Malhotra, M.A., study of play style

355

Alice Moriarty, Ph.D., psychologist, examiner
Paul Pulver, Ph.D., psychologist, Rorschach analysis

Observers
Alice Moriarty, Ph.D., psychologist
Lila Weissenberg, Ph.D., psychologist

Statistician
Walter Raine, Ph.D.

Collaborators
Mary Engle, Ph.D., insight tests
Carol Dyer, M.A., Witkin battery

Consultants
Gardner Murphy, Ph.D., Director of Research, Menninger Foundation
Sibylle Escalona, Ph.D., psychologist
Robert Holt, Ph.D., psychologist
Wayne Holtzman, Ph.D., psychologist
George Klein, Ph.D., psychologist
Martin Mayman, Ph.D., psychologist
Margaret Mead, Ph.D., anthropologist

Prepuberty Staff

Lois B. Murphy, Ph.D., director

Examiners and Interviewers
Mildred Faris, PSW—interviews with mothers
C. Joseph Morgan, M.A.—special studies of boys
Alice Moriarty, Ph.D.—intelligence tests, TAT, 1960–62
Pitsa Hartocollis, M.A.—Rorschach
Rosemary Mayman, HIT test
Patricia Schloesser, M.D.—pediatric examination
Povl Toussieng, M.D.—psychiatric examination

Data analysts
Betty Faulk, Ph.D.—study of the defense maneuvers of a child recovering
from polio, in relation to her problems of identity
Sylvia Ginsparg, Ph.D.—analysis of Rorschachs at preschool and latency
Ralph Sherfey—a study of Ray
Paula van der Waals, M.D.—analysis of pediatric data
Irene Wiemers, Ph.D.—analysis of infancy data

Assistants
Mary Cook, psychology
Diana Dolgoff, psychology
Beth Koropsak, psychology
Julie Palmquist, psychology

Consultants
    Maria Dale, M.D.
    Anna Freud, LL.D.
    Margaret Lowenfeld, M.D.
    Tarlton Morrow, M.D.
    Donald Winnicott, M.D.

Adolescence Staff

    Povl Toussieng, M.D., psychiatrist, codirector
    Alice Moriarty, Ph.D., psychologist, codirector

Consultant
    Lois B. Murphy, Ph.D.

Secretary
    Marie Smith

Note: Dr. Lolafaye Coyne was statistical consultant for the latency, prepuberty, and adolescent studies.

Appendix 2: Subjects of the Coping Study ("Intensive" Group) at the Preschool Stage

Pseudonyms	Age Seen in Infancy (in weeks)	Age at First Test**	Religion	Father's Employment	Siblings (y: younger, o: older)	Grandparents (gg: great)
Barbie Howard	24	4:11	Protestant	banker	1-o	2
Brennie Leonard	28	3:5	Protestant	executive	1-y	3 (1 gg)
Chester Cooper	12	4:11	Protestant	laborer—Santa Fe	2-o 5-y	4
Cynthia Burns	16	5:8	Protestant	architect	2-o 1-y	2
Darlene Lowell	8	3:5	Protestant*	laborer	1-y	4
Daryl Howe	24	4:5	Catholic	real estate	3-y	4
Diane Raylor	28	3:10	Orotestant	telephone repairman	3-o 1-y	3
Donald Dickinson	16	3:5	Protestant*	flour packer	2-o	3
Gordon Spencer	24	5:2	none	used-car salesman	none	3
Greg Gregory	8	5:5	Protestant	(physician—dead)	none	2
Helen Harris	20	5:4	Protestant	linoleum layer	2-o 4-y	4
Janice Timberlake	28	5:4	Protestant	owner of business	4-o	3
JoAnne Jackson	4	4:1	Catholic	Deliveries		2
Lennie Wilkins	4	3:5	Protestant	policeman—now with General Motors	2-y	4
Martin Saunders	20	5:5	Catholic	mailman	1-o	3
Molly Thornton	8	3:8	Protestant	psychologist	3-o	3
Patsy Lake	32	4:10	Catholic	budget manager	2-o 1-y	4
Rachel Hall	20	4:3	Catholic	maintenance	2-o 1-y	1
Ralph Burns	12	4:0	Protestant	architect	2-o 2-y	2
Ray Cooper	16	3:3	Protestant	laborer—Sante Fe	3-o 4-y	4

* Churches in which revivals play an important role.

** Subjects were interviewed in fall of 1953; testing began some months later.

Roddy Nash	20	4:11	Protestant	Goodyear		1-y	4
Ronald Holt	28	4:1	Catholic	insurance office		2-y	1
Sally Thompson	28	3:10	Protestant	machinist—Santa Fe	1-o	2-y	3
Sheila Ramsey	4	2:9	Protestant	salesman	3-o		3
Steve Ramsey	6	5:1	Protestant	salesman	2-o	1-y	3
Susan Stevens	28	5:2	Protestant	optometrist		1-y	4
Teddy Layton	20	5:5	Protestant	army		1-y	4
Terry Bowen	32	5:8	Catholic	winter V.A. aidf		2-y	4
Tommy Chase	32	4:1	mixed	machinist	1-o	1-y	6 (2 step)
Trudy Thornton	(not seen in infancy)	6:4	Protestant	psychologist	1-o	2-y	3
Vernon Rogers	28	4:8	Catholic	carpenter	2-o	1-y	3
Vivian Howe	4	3:1	Catholic	real estate	1-o	2-y	4

Family Status:

In all but one family both parents were alive and well during the children's preschool stage.

In one family the father died before the child was born (mother remarried later).

In one family there was a divorce and the mother remarried later.

In two families the mother was ill for extended periods of time.

Only ten families were living in the same houses at the beginning of the coping study that they were living in during the infancy study (three more moved later).

Basic Ratings of the Coping Group

Pseudonym	Preschool CA	MA	IQ	Latency CA	MA	IQ	Tentative Sheldon Ratings (1955)		
Barbie Howard	4–11	6–6	132	7–5	9–8	130	3.5	3.5	3.5
Brennie Leonard	3–6	4–1	117	7–0		116*	4	4	3
Chester Cooper	4–11	6–2	125	7–6	9–6	127	4	5	2.5
Cynthia Burns	5–9	6–3	109	9–3	10–2	110	3	4.5	4
Darlene Lowell	3–11	4–5	113	6–1	8–0	132	4	2	5
Daryl Howe	4–6	5–1	113	Incomplete			4	3	3
Diane Taylor	3–11	4–9	121	7–1	9–2	129	4	3	4
Donald Dickinson	3–5	4–5	129	6–2	7–6	122	3	5.5	1.5
Gordon Spencer	5–2	6–6	126	8–5	10–2	121	3.5	4	4
Greg Gregory	5–5	7–0	129	8–1	11–0	136	2	4.5	4
Helen Harris	5–3	5–4	102	7–10	9–2	117	2.5	3.5	5
Janice Timberlake	5–5	6–7	122	8–1	9–8	120	2	1.5	6
JoAnne Jackson	4–3	4–3	100	6–10	6–6	100	3	5	2
Lennie Wilkins	3–6	3–3	93	7–1	7–6	106	4	5.5	2.5
Martin Saunders	5–7	6–4	113	8–5	9–10	117	1.5	4.5	4
Molly Thornton	3–3	4–7	141	5–6	7–8	139			
Patsy Lake	4–11	5–3	107	7–11	9–2	116	4	3.5	3.5
Rachel Hall	4–4	4–9	110	6–10	6–8	98	3.5	4.5	2
Ralph Burns	4–1	4–6	110	7–5	10–2	137	3.5	5	2.5
Ray Cooper	3–3	3–0	92	5–9	5–11	103			
Roddy Nash	5–0	5–0	100	8–3	9–0	109	3	4.5	2.5
Ronald Holt	4–1	4–8	114	7–1	7–10	111	2	4.5	4
Sally Thompson	3–11	5–4	136	6–6	7–8	118–121			
Sheila Ramsey	2–8	3–1	116	5–10	6–8	114	6	4	2
Steve Ramsey	5–0	5–0	100	8–2	8–8	106	3	5.5	3.5
Susan Stevens	5–4	6–4	119	7–10	9–8	123			
Teddy Layton	5–5	6–10	126	Not available			6.5	4	1.5
Terry Bowen	5–9	7–2	125	8–6	10–6	124	3	3	5
Tommy Chase	4–2	3–10	92	7–10	8–10	102	2.5	4	3.5
Trudy Thornton	5–9	7–0	122	8–1	11–10	146			
Vernon Rogers	4–9	6–6	137	7–4	9–6	130	4	4.5	3.5
Vivian Howe	4–0	4–8	117	6–2	7–4	119	4.5	3.5	1.5

Note unusual IQ increases in four children (Darlene Lowell, Helen Harris, Ralph Burns, Trudy Thornton) and one marked decrease (Sally Thompson, whose mother has been disturbed).

* Child given only WISC because of time limitations. Other scores are on Stanford-Binet, form L.

Correlations between Boys' Preschool Behavior and Infancy Oral
Termination, Protest, and Resistance to Disliked Foods

Preschool Behavior	r	p
Speed of orientation, grasp of situation, task	.67	.01
Mastery: drive for, struggle capacity, determination	.54	.05
Ability to organize, provide own structure	.55	.05
Ability to control impact of environment	.62	.05
Ability to restructure environment, create new patterns	.51	.05
Can forestall danger—knowing when to stop	.78	.001
Uses strategic withdrawal	.62	.05
Impulse control	.67	.01
Clarity regarding own identity	.57	.05
Reality testing, accuracy of perception	.62	.05
Loss of perceptual clarity under stress	−.67	.01
Overall ability	.60	.05
Developmental level of speech	.55	.05
Level of drive: narcissistic	.53	.05
Stubborn: maintaining a stand despite consequences	.50	.05

All but three of these correlations were in the same direction for girls but did not reach the criterion for significance. These correlations imply for boys at least considerable continuity of active mental and motor coping from the first six months of infancy to the preschool level, and the contribution of these to clarity about self at the preschool level.

Significant Correlations between Boys' Preschool Behavior and Infancy Oral Gratification

	r
Loss of perceptual clarity under stress (PT)	−.75
Separation of self and others	.71
Critical of people	−.70
Strength of interests	.64
Support from siblings	.62
Sense of self-worth	.61
Clarity of perception	.61
Feeling of being rejected	−.60
Adequacy of the child's self-image	.60
Uses strategic withdrawal	.60
Masculine attitude: assertiveness	.59
Clarity in sex role	.56
Ability to mobilize energy to meet challenge or stress	.54
Controlling others	.53
Tendency to be demanding	.53
Ability to control the impact of the environment	.53
Security	.52
Tendency to get fatigued	−.52
Ability to limit or fend off excessive stimulation	.51

Appendix 3: Child-Rearing Emphases Rated by Topeka Mothers

In 1964 Topeka mothers were asked to rank the list of child-rearing emphases presented in the 1924 Middletown questionnaire (Lynd and Lynd 1929). Topeka mothers were asked to rate the three most important traits "A," the five next in importance "B," those of lesser importance "C," and those of no importance "D." In order to maximize the more positive values, we combined A and B ratings. The ratings are in percent.

	A	B	C	D	A + B
Good manners	29.5	56.8	13.7	0	86.3
Tolerance	50.0	34.1	15.9	0	84.1
Loyalty to church	43.1	36.4	13.6	6.9	79.5
Frankness	50.0	25.0	22.7	2.3	75.0
Economy in money matters	11.3	52.3	34.1	2.3	63.6
Patriotism	9.1	50.0	38.6	2.3	59.1
Independence	29.5	29.5	36.4	4.6	59.0
Social-mindedness	25.0	29.5	34.1	11.4	54.5
Appreciation of art, music, poetry	4.5	47.9	45.3	2.3	52.4
Concentration	4.5	40.9	54.6	0	45.4
Strict obedience	18.1	27.2	34.1	20.6	45.3
Knowledge of sex hygiene	9.1	25.0	63.6	2.3	34.1
Curiosity	9.1	22.7	61.3	6.9	31.8
Desire to make a name in the world	9.1	9.1	38.6	43.2	18.2
Good grades	0	18.1	72.8	9.1	18.1

Appendix 4: Preschool Data

Data Collecting and Summarizing Sessions at Preschool Level
(1 September 1953–1 January 1956)

	No.
Parent interviews (Heider plus 6 Tibout interviews)	52
Pediatric examinations (Schloesser)	30
Psychiatric sessions (including 11 medical)	45
Sessions with Dr. Kass	55
Sessions with Dr. Moriarty	83
MLT sessions with Dr. Murphy and assistants	88
Parties (attended by all testers; 5–6 children each)	6
Somatyping sessions and trip to zoo (each attended by 6 testers and 5–8 children)	4
"To-and-fro" reports	301
Staff conferences for summary and analysis of child	20
Child discussed in conferences with Dr. Escalona	5
Planning conferences (two hours each)	c. 20
Consultation conferences with Drs. Gardner Murphy, George Klein, and Robert Holt	8

Comprehensive Coping Inventory (CCI) *

Variable No.	*Variable*
1	Neighborhood—economic level
2	" —space
3	" —safety
4	" —privacy
5	" —other children available
6	Kind of house
7	Condition inside house
8	Condition outside house
9	House size in relation to family size
10	Aesthetic values
11	Cleanliness of house
12	Order of house
13	Orientation (child/adult)
14	Equipment—television
15	" —gadgets
16	" —separate play room
17	" —dining room
18	" —piano
19	Child's living space—room size
20	" " " —occupants in room
21	" " " —equipment in room
22	" " " —sleeping arrangements
23	" " " —space for toys
24	Parents' room: location
25	Parents' room: occupancy
26	Possessions: toys
27	Possessions: clothes
28	Physique (robust/fragile)
29	Vegetative functioning
30	Sensory threshold overall
31	Activity level overall
32	Developmental level—degree of balance
33	Vocalizations: frequency
34	Drive level
35	Autonomic-affective reactivity
36	Tendency to delay in response
37	Awareness of infant's needs
38	Mother–child viability
39	Degree of acceptance of infant
40	Skill in handling infant

* Items assembled from records and summaries by all examiners.

Variable No.	*Variable*
41	Acceptance of infant's own development pace
42	Amount of attention given
43	Speech–facial expression
44	Mother's level of adjustment
45	Feeling about own competence with infant
46	Acceptance of natural functions in general
47	Ease of pregnancy
48	Ease of delivery
49	Variability of Gesell ratings
50	Religion
51	Father's occupation status
52	Number of older siblings
53	Number of younger siblings
55	Number of grandparents
56	Restrictiveness of mother toward child
57	Gesell Language 3
58	" " 2
59	" " 1
60	Gesell Personal-Social 3
61	" " " 2
62	" " " 1
63	Gesell Motor 3
64	" " 2
65	" " 1
66	Gesell Adaptive 3
67	" " 2
68	" " 1
69	Family unity
70	Mother's enjoyment of the child
71	Mother's encouragement or support of child
72	Cleanliness, neatness in the home
73	Satisfying mothering (directed to child's needs)
74	Optimism of mother vs. doubts, fears, etc.
75	Maturity and stability of mother
76	Temperamental compatibility of parents
77	Success in breast feeding
78	Amount of contact
79	Degree of respect for infant's autonomy needs
80	Utilization of support from own functioning
81	Ways of handling self and the world: protests
82	Oral activity
83	Ways of handling self and the world: avoids
84	Utilization of support from mother

Variable No.	Variable
100	Child order number
101	Pregnancy: complicated or uncomplicated
102	Nausea during pregnancy
103	Bleeding during pregnancy
104	Other complications during pregnancy
105	Delivery (complicated or uncomplicated)
106	Anesthesia
107	Feeding at hospital
108	First six months
109	Feeding at home
110	Length of nursing, breast
111	Length of bottle feeding
112	Age at weaning
113	Age at sitting
114	Age at walking
115	Measles
116	Chicken pox
117	Tonsillectomy and adenoidectomy
118	Tonsillins
119	Ear trouble
120	Deformities
121	Other illnesses
122	Skin disorders
123	Mumps
124	Sleep (reaction to illness)
125	Activity (reaction to illness)
126	Eating (reaction to illness)
127	Relation to others (reaction to illness)
128	Physiological reaction (reaction to illness)
129	Height (in cm.)
130	Height (in percentile)
131	Weight (in pounds)
132	Weight (in percentile)
133	Chest (in cm.)
134	Chest (in percentile)
135	Pelvis (in cm.)
136	Pelvis (in percentile)
137	Pulse, early
138	Age at talking
139	Activity level
140	Phenotype
141	Nervous habits
142	Mother–child relationship

Variable No.	*Variable*
143	Sensitive system
144	Pulse rank
145	Blood pressure: systolic (rank order)
146	Blood pressure: diastolic (rank order)
147	Blood pressure: systolic and diastolic
148	Pulse and blood pressure: systolic and diastolic
149	Differences in variability: systolic and diastolic
150	Rank 2: systolic and diastolic
151	Rank of pulse
152	Maximal reactivity: pulse
153	Maximal reactivity: blood pressure, systolic
154	Maximal reactivity: blood pressure, diastolic
155	Maximum autonomic reactivity: Lacey type T-score
400	U.A.
401	Mental age
402	Preschool IQ
403	Patterning of structured test responses—visual
404	" " " " " —visual motor
405	" " " " " —verbal
406	" " " " " —memory
407	" " " " " —comprehension
408	" " " " " —information
409	" " " " " —number concepts
410	Variability of Sheldon ratings
450	Overall level of activity
451	Variability in activity level
452	Loss of motor control under stress
453	Motor inhibition resulting from stress
454	Motor coordination
455	Smoothness in movements
456	Purposefulness of movements
457	Pleasure in movement for its own sake
458	Fineness of coordination
459	Ability to remain quiet when attention is engaged
460	Changes of motility resulting from affect
461	Variability in activity level depends on affect
462	Freedom to translate ideas into action
463	Speed or tempo
464	Energy level
465	Special vulnerability in the motor area
466	Alertness to details of environment
467	Enjoyment of intense stimulation
468	Tendency to be overwhelmed by strong stimulation

Variable No.	Variable
469	Length of attention span
470	Pleasure in sensory stimulation for its own sake
471	Response to color
472	Responsiveness to a wide range of stimuli
473	Tactile sensitivity
474	Auditory sensitivity
475	Visual sensitivity
476	Tendency to seek oral satisfaction
477	Enjoyment of fine nuances of sensation
478	Clarity of perception
479	Attention attracted to objects more than people
480	Tendency to develop strong attachment to physical objects
481	Constricted in using space in play and other activity
482	Pleasure in cognitive functioning
483	Interest in what makes things work
484	Overall ability
485	Creativeness and originality
486	Directs his attention to his own inner state
487	Eagerly explores the environment in a new situation
488	Makes a preliminary survey before engaging in new situation
489	Preference for highly structured situations
490	Imposes his own structure on a situation
491	Loss of perceptual clarity under stress
492	Good spatial orientation
493	Stereotyped use of toys
494	Involvement in the play activities
495	More apt to look than to do
496	Achieving clear structure has priority over experiencing effect
497	Realism
498	Degree of fantasy elaboration
499	Tendency to aggressiveness and destructive activity
500	Appropriateness of affective response to the situation
501	Forcefulness of affective expression
502	Degree of differentiation of affect
503	Amount of latent aggression
504	Tendency to fears and anxieties
505	Tendency for clearcut shift of affective state
506	Range of affect shown
507	Affect is easy to relate to observable conditions
508	Impulse control
509	Pleasure outweighs frustration experience
510	Depth of affect
511	Tolerance for situations that do not please child

Variable No.	Variable
512	Capacity for pleasure
513	Feelings readily reflected in facial expression
514	Tempo of recovery from emotional state
515	Time taken to reach an emotional state
516	Impulsive
517	Tendency to present management difficulties
518	Faces the world with open anticipation
519	Pleasure in own body
520	Pleasure in handling materials or objects
521	Rigidity of expressive patterns (posture, gesture)
522	Vividness of expression
523	Autonomic reactivity
524	Warmth
525	Tendency to be sober and not gay
526	Tendency to avoid or evade in the face of threat
527	Tendency to use forthright protest to dislikes
528	Typically uses restriction as a defense
529	Typically uses inhibition as a defense
530	Typically uses projection as a defense
531	Compulsive
532	Tendency to regress
533	Tendency to defend his own position
534	Ability to solve problems directly
535	Positive self-appraisal
536	Self-awareness
537	Pride in own possessions
538	Anxiety over own body
539	Tendency to be exhibitionistic
540	Feeling of being rejected
541	Pleasure in concrete results of own activity
542	Ease of ability to ask for help when needed
543	Autonomy
544	Capacity to mobilize resources under stress
545	Tendency to be devious rather than forthright
546	Tendency to give up easily at failure
547	Values success
548	Tendency to impose own ideas on reality
549	Tendency to take cues from others (to imitate)
550	Identification with own sex
551	Degree of conflict regarding sex role
552	Flirtatious or seductive with persons of opposite sex
553	Difficulty in relating to others
554	Difficulty in relation to peers

Variable No.	Variable
555	Enjoyment of social contacts
556	Tendency to be reserved with strangers
557	Tendency to be socially charming with adults
558	Tendency to function as a leader in a peer group
559	Intrusiveness in relating to people
560	Social sensitivity
561	Tendency to exploit vulnerabilities in others
562	Tendency to make his presence felt with peers
563	Tendency to be demanding with relation to others
564	Selectiveness in response toward people
565	Tendency to relate to others on own terms
566	Ability to accept warmth and support from others
567	Gives warmth and support to others
568	Is stimulating to others
569	Autonomic sensitivity
570	Thumb-sucking
571	Nail-biting, nose-picking
572	Other regressive tension relieving activity
573	Tendency to get fatigued
574	Oral behavior conspicuous
575	Tendency to hurt himself
576	Tendency to play realistically
577	Clarity of distinction between fantasy and reality
578	Use of fantasy to solve reality problems
579	Use of fantasy as an escape from reality
580	Reality testing
581	Developmental level of speech
582	Tendency for verbal fluency to surpass other intellectual abilities
583	Special vulnerabilities in the speech area
584	Realism-imagination balance
585	Drive level: orality
599	Overall variability of activity, mood, etc.
600	Range of affect
601	Threshold for frustration
602	Tension level
603	Breadth of perceptual field
604	Variety of orientation adjustment procedures
605	Ego-images: inferior/adequate
606	Autonomy
607	Naturalness vs. artificiality
608	Carelessness, roughness, impulsiveness
609	Inhibition of impulse
610	Clarity of focus

Variable No.	*Variable*
611	Orientation problem
612	Initial contact: handling of problem variability
613	Freedom from inhibitions or rigidity in thinking
614	Attention span
615	Speed (affect)
616	Goal direction
617	Coherence of thinking
618	Attention to fine detail
619	Attention to uses/functions of whole details
620	Frustration tolerance
621	Initial contact: handling of problem
622	Neatness, cleanliness, form rigidity
623	Methods of dealing with threatening stimuli as in I
624	Methods of dealing with threatening stimuli in terms of society
625	Manipulating
626	Controlling others
627	Aggression
628	Tempo (affect)
629	Spread of affect
630	Strength of affect
631	Reality level
632	Judgment
633	Operational functions
647	Maintenance of self-regard in the face of difficulty
648	Competence, although it may not be highest level
650	Tolerance for obstacles, difficulties
651	Covertly hostile, antagonistic
652	Resilience, recovery rate from embarrassment
653	Determination
654	Active orientation, acting on, doing to
655	Feeling one's way along, using a third ear
656	Capacity for freewheeling attention
657	Resistances (to us or to situation)
658	Strength of interests
659	Knowing the score, grasping sequences
660	Pleasure in tactile experiences
661	Resilience following disappointment, defeat, etc.
662	Capacity to use substitute gratification
663	Fantasy in everyday life
664	Pleasure in form, pattern
665	Drive level: nurturing, taking care of
666	Can tolerate or contain negative feelings
671	Reaction formation MLT

Variable No.	Variable
672	Frustration leads to aggression
673	Motor tension-release
674	Available neutral energy
675	Fears
676	Freedom from doubt and ambivalence
677	Regression for tension-release
678	Ability to accept substitutes
679	Integrative capacity, MLT
680	Differentiating capacity, MLT
681	Able to fix and fit things together
682	Shyness
683	Level of drive: narcissistic
684	Identification and imitation (of adult)
685	Fitting into expected image or role of child
686	Separation problem (initial)
687	Control in handling things
688	Initiative
689	Communication
690	Use made of watching, observing
691	Level of aggressive drive
692	Drive level: erotic, sexual
693	Evidence of conflicts in response to structured test
694	Pride
695	Courage
696	Likes self
697	Range of areas of enjoyment, gratification
698	Good–bad concerns, moralistic
700	Range of fine-muscle skills, competence
701	Range of larger muscle skills competence, mastery
702	Ease of feeling threatened by specific events
703	Love-affection-warmth, giving to staff
704	Aggression drive (overall, covert or overt)
705	Ability to discharge aggression within limits
706	Ability to reconcile differing identifications
707	Persistence in working toward a goal-action
708	Psychichally active orientation: having opinions
709	Substitutions (offering a substitute)
710	Ability to control the impact of the environment
711	Ability to wait, postpone, control timing of gratification
712	Love–aggression balance
713	Use of external control, impersonal
714	Coping concepts, ideas, solutions
715	Orientation toward long term goals

Variable
No.   *Variable*

716   Repression (as a psychic defense)
717   Maintains self-regard in the face of difficulty
718   Tension with siblings; siblings a source of difficulty
719   Support from siblings
720   Mother proud of infant
721   Tension with extended family: male and/or female
722   Support from extended family: grandparents
723   Family stress at preschool level
724   Accepts people as they are
725   Drive level: fear, caution (drive toward security)
726   Satisfaction in mastery, competence, skill
727   Gratification and pleasure observed in structured test
728   Definiteness of choices, confidence in choices
729   Flexibility in adapting means to a goal
730   Impulse to grow (grow up)
731   Impulse to stay dependent, to remain a child
732   Uses trial-and-error methods consciously
733   Ability to postpone, wait for, gratification
734   Ability to use social outlets in ego syntonic ways
735   Imitation
736   Following the line of least resistance, compliance
737   Perseveration of anxiety in structured tests
738   Ability to synthesize thinking, affect, action
739   Ability to ask for, or get, help when needed
741   Craving for power or dominance
742   Keeping one's distance temporarily (out of caution)
743   Dependency (at first)
744   Affectionateness, warmth
745   Competitiveness, outdoing
746   Strength of task-involvement
747   Typical mood level position
748   Receptivity to environmental cues, moods, qualities
750   Cooperation with authority demands B (new)
753   "   "   "   "   " (difficult)
754   "   "   "   "   " (total)
755   Reaction to the adult as a person B (new)
758   "   "   "   "   " "   "   " (difficult)
759   "   "   "   "   " "   "   " (total)
760   Overt tension or anxiety (new)
763   "   "   "   "   (difficult)
764   "   "   "   "   (total)

Variable No.	Variable
765	Autonomy expression (new)
768	" " (difficult)
769	" " (total)
770	Cooperation with authority demands A (new)
773	" " " " " (difficult)
774	" " " " " (total)
775	Accepting own limits (new)
778	" " " (difficult)
779	" " " (total)
780	Help: will ask for help in clarifying directions (new)
783	" " " " " " " " (difficult)
784	" " " " " " " " (total)
785	Self-feeling (new)
788	" " (difficult)
789	" " (total)
790	Motor and visual motor control (new)
793	" " " " " (difficult)
794	" " " " " (total)
795	Orientation: speed with which child was aware (new)
798	" " " " " " " (difficult)
799	" " " " " " " (total)
800	Reaction to adult as a person A (new)
803	" " " " " " " (difficult)
804	" " " " " " " (total)
805	Coping I (AM)
806	Coping II (AM)
807	Affective coping capacity (AM)
808	Motor coping capacity (AM)
809	Cognitive coping capacity (AM)
810	Combined Coping I (LBM & AM)
811	Combined Coping II (LBM & AM)
812	Coping capacity I (LBM)
813	Coping capacity II (LBM)
814	Sensitivity balanced by ability to control subject's preschool environment
815	Number of mechanisms used in most preferred mechanism
820	Supply of energy
821	Sensitivity of affective response
822	Planning, looking ahead, looking before you leap
823	Creative potential (including structuring capacity)
824	Tact
825	Sense of fitness, social appropriateness
826	Accepting limits: knowing how far one can go—social

Variable No.	*Variable*
827	Ability to integrate modalities
828	Ability to limit or fend off excessive stimulation
829	Has insight into situations, realistic appraisal
830	Ability to restructure environment, create new patterns
831	Speed of orientation, grasp of situation, task
832	Psychically active orientation vs. let life happen
833	Interest in people vs. not concerned with others
834	Interest in mastering space (physically)
835	Enjoys newness, discovery
836	Positive orientation to life
837	Intensity of interests, enthusiasm, etc.
838	Has emotional sending power—reaches others
839	Range of moods in reaction to stimuli
840	At times overwhelmed by strong stimulation
841	Awareness of feelings of others
842	Flexibility of emotional management and control
843	Resistance to discouragement
844	Security
845	Ability to protest
846	Capacity for fun, zest, delight, pleasure
847	Invites intimacy
848	Appropriateness of degree of affect
849	Appropriateness of quality of affect
850	Adequacy of expression of affect—open vs. poker-faced
851	Reactivity—set off easily
852	Use of pleasure in structured situations
853	Always seems to have good luck
854	Pride (unassailability)
855	Clarity regarding own identity
856	Independence, self-reliance, autonomy
857	Self-awareness, self-insight, awareness of limits
858	Vitality
859	Narcissism, pleasure in being oneself, healthy
860	Sincerity
861	Ability to positively assert own needs, preferences
862	Ego involvement in own activity
863	Ability to harmonize goals, reconcile diverse goals
864	Flexibility of energy distribution
865	Ability to facilitate resilience by timing rest
866	Ability to balance dependence and independence
867	Ability to synthesize drives: affective, aggressive
868	Ability to balance gratification and frustration
869	Capacity to use delay for appraisal

Variable No.	Variable
870	Strategic withdrawal to safety vs. being caught in situation
871	Can forestall danger—knowing when to stop
872	Maintaining physical safety by refusal to take risks
873	Self-value maintenance capacity
874	Positive friendly social relationship maintenance capacity
875	Ability to mobilize energy to meet challenge or stress
876	Asperation level
877	Ability to control the impact of the environment
878	Adequacy of discharge of tension
879	Uses environmental areas selectively
880	Adequacy of self-image in child's social milieu
881	Sense of self-worth, comfortable relation to ego ideal
883	Capacity to sustain effort toward completion of task
884	Mastery: drive for, struggle capacity, determination
885	Constructive use of one's anxiety
886	Child's ability to sublimate aggression
887	Constructive use of external control
888	Sense of importance, being taken seriously
889	Uses of strategic withdrawal
890	Clarity in sex role
891	Masculine attitude: assertiveness, forthright
892	Feminine attitude: sensitivity to people
893	Ability to lead others
894	Ability to elicit desired response
895	Tendency to make presence felt with peers
896	Sensitivity to criticism in relation to achievement
897	Able to elicit warmth (preschool level)
898	Separation of self and others
899	Desire to please
900	Intensity of relatedness to people
901	Differentiated social relationships
902	Ability to take different roles (freedom to shift)
903	Reversal of roles
904	Insightfulness into social situations
905	Critical of people, depreciates others
906	Active interaction with others in group
907	Bravado, puts on a front
908	Considerateness, adapts own needs to others
909	Realistic evaluation of people
910	Can fend off demands, pressures from people
911	Social skill with adult
912	Competes with adult, "raise you one" situation
913	Degree of social capacity, range of social skills

Variable No.	*Variable*
914	Communication
915	Stubborn: maintaining a stand despite the consequences
916	Tension load carried
917	Differentiated response to stress
918	Degree of disintegration under stress
919	Frequency of disintegration under stress
920	Immobilized by stress (externally)
921	Copes by changing environment
922	Tolerance for frustration vs. hard to please
923	Stimulated to greater effort by failure
924	Social "distancing" (actively putting off)
925	Denial
926	Displacement
927	Compensation—of all test
928	Reaction formation
929	Noninvolvement, detachment, apt investment
930	Escape from external pressures, demands, threats
931	Ego restrictions
932	Provocative (not merely irritating)
933	Crying-communication-manipulating
934	Discharge efficiency for child who has discharge residue
935	Mother's acceptance of major coping devices
936	Family situation grew more difficult infancy to preschool
937	Family situation, atmosphere, security, improved
938	Mother's active help to child in coping
939	Siblings a source of difficulty—preschool
940	Mother's acceptance of child's coping style
941	Difficulties created for child by mother
942	Difficulties created for child by father
943	Total environmental difficulties for child, not social
944	Amount of stress child experiences
945	Liveliness of family atmosphere (open feelings)
946	Degree of religious control of family behavior
947	Social-status anxiety influencing behavior
948	Amount of shared fun in the family
949	Degree of disorganization in family life
950	Parents' emphasis on fairness to each child
951	Use of motor skills for coping with environmental demands
952	Problem-solving attitude toward life (implies mastery)
953	Supply of energy
954	Ability to use vision to master the environment
955	Pleasure in tactile experience
956	Curiosity, finding out

Variable No.	Variable
957	Places high value on knowledge
958	Reality testing, accuracy of perception
959	Eliciting desired response from others
960	Confidence, ability to do
961	Definiteness with attitudes, opinions
962	Self-feeling level, it feels good to be
963	Ability to balance self and social demands
964	Uses delay for appraisal, planning
965	Balance of ego strengths and instinctual strength
966	Ability to protest actively
967	Identifies with examiner
968	Selective responses toward people
969	Talkativeness
970	Tension
971	Ability to organize, provide own structure
972	Anious response to the new, the strange
973	Receptive to emotional impressions from environment
974	Responds contagiously, tends to be carried away by feelings
975	Explosiveness, tantrums, tendency to outbreaks
976	Tolerance of temporary regression
977	Degree of help in coping from father
978	Success gratification
979	Success—active autonomy
980	Success—passive autonomy
981	Success—anxiety
982	Failure—active autonomy
983	Failure—passive autonomy
984	Failure-defense—realistic
985	Failure anxiety
986	Coping techniques used in response to difficulty (cognitive)
987	Coping techniques used in response to difficulty in structured test (motor)
988	Coping techniques used in response to difficulty in structured test (independence)
989	Coping techniques used in response to difficulty in structured test (refuge)
990	Coping techniques used in response to difficulty in structured test (affect)
991	Coping techniques used in response to difficulty in structured test (escape)
992	AM's efficiency statistical regression scores
993	Efficiency table I (AM)

Variable No.	*Variable*
994	Average scores of satisfaction efficiency (AM)
995	Average scores of integration efficiency
996	Average scores of objectivity efficiency
997	Ratings on satisfaction
998	Ratings on integration
999	Ratings on objectivity (AM)

Relationships between Coping Items and Resilience

Preschool resilience (as rated by the consensus judgment of Moriarty, Murphy and Heider) correlated positively at a .001 level of significance with:

Coping I (LBM & AM)
Coping II (LBM & AM)
Cognitive Coping (AM)
Affective Coping (AM)
Range of areas of enjoyment
Self-feeling level (it feels good to be me), healthy narcissism
Realistic evaluation of people
Insight into social situations
Reality testing
Capacity for free-wheeling attention
Flexibility in adapting means to a goal
Ability to synthesize thinking, affect, and action
Freedom to translate ideas into action
Feeling one's way, intuitive
Creativeness and originality

Other correlations between preschool resilience and coping variables significant at the .01 level included:

Overall level of activity
Speed of orientation
Clarity of perception
Freedom from rigidity or inhibitions in thinking
Ability to accept substitutes
Ability to accept warmth
Pleasure in own body
Positive self-appraisal
Impulse to grow (grow up)

But significant correlations between preschool resilience and prepuberty ratings by Moriarty included only Coping I at the .01 level, and Reality testing and Ability to provide own structure at the .05 level. (The prepuberty phase is an anxious phase for so many children that differences are reduced.) Suggestive correlations congruent with those at the preschool stage but significant only at a .01 level at the prepuberty stage included:

Affective coping capacity
Pleasure in own body
Flexibility in adapting means to a goal
Frustration tolerance
Uses environmental areas selectively
Ease of ability to ask for help when needed
Impulse to grow (grow up)

Appendix 5: IQ Data

Intelligence Quotients at Five Age Levels (Moriarty)
(Age is in weeks for infancy and years and months for others.)

Pseudo-nym	Infancy: Cattell IQ	Preschool: Binet IQ	Latency: Binet IQ	Prepuberty: WISC Full-Scale IQ	Adolescent: WAIS Full-Scale IQ
Trudy	*	122 (5–9)	146 (8–1)	132 (13–0)	
Molly	105 (8)	141 (3–3)	139 (5–6)	134 (10–5)	
Sheila	200 (4)	116 (2–8)	114 (5–10)	111 (9–10)	112 (17–1)
Steve	121 (6)	100 (5–0)	106 (8–2)	108 (12–2)	
Cynthia	109 (16)	109 (5–9)	110 (9–3)		
Ralph	120 (12)	110 (4–1)	137 (7–5)		
Roddy	122 (20)	100 (5–0)	109 (8–3)	127 (12–8)	121 (16–1)
Teddy	132 (20)	126 (5–5)		135 (12–1)	139 (18–3)
Susan	116 (28)	119 (5–4)	123 (7–10)	107 (12–1)	115 (18–6)
Gordon	117 (24)	126 (5–2)	121 (8–5)	114 (12–1)	110 (17–9)
Greg	100 (8)	129 (5–5)	136 (8–1)	115 (12–1)	120 (18–3)
Tommy		92 (4–2)	102 (7–10)		107 (18–8)
Patsy	104 (32)	107 (4–11)	116 (7–11)	108 (12–6)	
Terry	112 (32)	125 (5–9)	124 (8–6)	115 (12–4)	119 (18–5)
Darlene	144 (8)	113 (3–11)	132 (6–1)	125 (10–2)	122 (17–1)
Diane	121 (28)	121 (3–11)	129 (7–1)	114 (11–10)	117 (17–8)
Chester	121 (12)	125 (4–11)	127 (7–6)	120 (11–7)	108 (17–6)
Ray	126 (16)	92 (3–3)	103 (5–9)	109 (10–0)	101 (15–11)
Sally	120 (28)	136 (3–11)	121 (6–6)	106 (10–6)	106 (17–8)
Vernon	129 (28)	137 (4–9)	130 (7–4)	127 (11–3)	124 (17–4)
Janice		122 (5–5)	120 (8–1)	116 (12–2)	115 (18–2)
Daryl	99 (24)	113 (4–6)		103 (10–11)	118 (17–1)
Vivian	147 (4)	117 (4–0)	119 (6–2)	108 (9–8)	109 (15–10)
Rachel	110 (20)	110 (4–4)	98 (6–10)	105 (10–11)	
JoAnne	164 (4)	100 (4–3)	100 (6–10)		
Martin	111 (4)	113 (5–7)	117 (8–5)	124 (12–1)	120 (18–1)
Brennie	121 (28)	117 (3–6)		120 (10–7)	
Lenny	145 (4)	93 (3–6)	106 (7–1)	120 (10–7)	119 (17–4)
Donald	140 (16)	129 (3–5)	122 (6–2)	117 (10–0)	119 (16–0)
Helen	102 (20)	102 (5–3)	117 (7–10)	110 (11–10)	121 (18–1)
Barbie	113 (24)	132 (4–11)	130 (7–5)	117 (11–8)	115 (17–5)
Ronald	109 (20)	114 (4–1)	111 (7–1)	110 (10–10)	119 (17–8)

* Blanks represent lack of test record because of unavailability of child for test at certain age levels.

Intelligence Quotient Variations

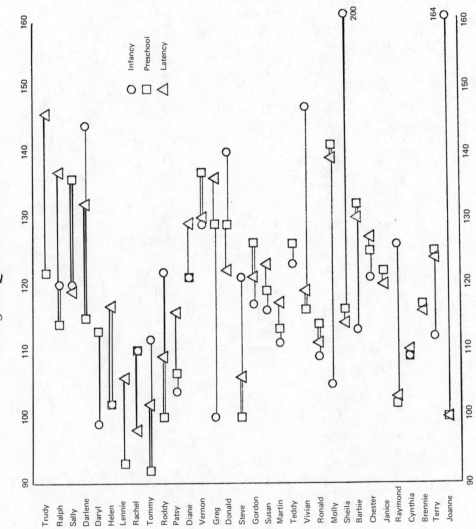

Infancy ○
Preschool □
Latency ◁

IQ Test Constancy and Variability in Relation
to Defense Structure (Moriarty 1966)

Intensive Coping Group (beginning preschool)

Stable	*Accelerating*	*Slow*	*Erratic*
Terry	Ralph	Tommy	Chester
Cynthia	Karen	Ray	Greg
Ronald	Roddy	Donald	Rachel
Vivian	Trudy	Lennie	Barbie
JoAnne	Darlene		Daryl
Steve	Martin		Patsy
Sheila			Brennie
Teddy			Vernon
Molly			Gordon
			Susan
			Diane
			Sally
			Janice

Additional Group (beginning at early latency)

Stable	*Accelerating*	*Slow*	*Erratic*
Richard	Mitch	Stanley	Tony
Brenda	Julia	Bertha	Delbert
Jennifer	Jack		Simon
Sylvia	Claudia		Dennis
Sherry	Adele		
Melvin	Norma		
Stewart	Russell		
Silas	Jay		
Melba	Rupert		
Paula	Leigh		
Maurice			
Cassy			
Jeff			
Corliss			

Appendix 6: Outline of Aspects of
Orality Observable in Escalona–Leitch Records
(Murphy in consultation with Grace Heider)

I. Infant's primary experience
    A. Nutritive oral functioning
        1. Demand pattern: level of intensity, frequency; choosiness; preference pattern; active oral seeking vs. passive receiving
        2. Sucking efficiency and style in feeding: quick coordination or slow learning; steady sucking or intermittent; rhythmic or jerky, etc.; "efficient" or "lazy"
        3. Pleasure: intensity; quality; contentment, satisfaction vs. active sensuous delight, smacking, "purring"
        4. Termination and rejection patterns: letting go, pushing out, closing lips, spitting out; protest; resistance
        5. Autonomy permitted by mother: mother respects preferences, rhythm, pace, etc.
        6. Frustration due to: mother pushing beyond satiation; low supply; interruptions; autocratic timing (mother decides time of feeding, pace of feeding, etc., regardless of baby's rhythm; forcing); intensity of frustration
        7. Gastrointestinal ease vs. colic, pain, etc.
    B. Non-nutritive activities in the oral zone
        1. Play: bubbling, mouthing, etc.; quantity, intensity, etc.
        2. Sensuous need: sucking thumb, pacifier, etc.; style, duration, frequency, intensity
        3. Use of the above for comfort, restoration of equilibrium; sucking thumb (breast in India, e.g.) pacifier, etc. (This may induce priority of oral gratification over pain, or screen out external stimuli, but in either case appears to be important in maintaining a pleasure–pain balance.)
    C. Mouth as organ for exploring (cf. antennae, feelers), tasting, feeling, biting: toes, objects, toys, part of crib, of mother's body, etc.
    D. Vocalization
        1. Discharge: quantity; differentiation—types of crying: "neonatal squall"; scream of pain or terror; yell of protest; begging cry, etc. Also as part of overall activity in tension discharge
        2. Pleasure: calling, babbling, chuckling, cooing
        3. Expression: distress, delight, excitement, fear, rage
        4. Communication: cries differentiated for pain, fatigue, hunger, etc.; provocative vocalizing; playful communication, symbolic communication; "smile of recognition" (cf. Erikson, 1950)

II. Infant's secondary oral experience
   A. Pleasure perceived, felt, in mother's handling of feeding and her feeling about it; in the interplay between mother and baby, etc. Gratification at mother's pleasure in baby's expressiveness, communications, etc. Baby may be gratified that (a) mother talks back, (b) mother smiles, is gay, playful, pleased.
   B. Displeasure in reaction to mother's tension, anxiety about quantity or pace of feeding; disapproval of sucking thumb or playing with food; disgust at spitting up, or anger at baby's biting or chomping the nipple (mother may be disturbed at libidinal quality of baby's orality)

III. Oral hazards in the first weeks of life
   A. Difficulties in integration of the sucking mechanism with obtaining and holding the nipple
   B. Difficulties in maintaining one's own rhythms due to poor coordination in sucking, taking in air, or tendencies of the mother either to interrupt or to force continuity
   C. Difficulties due to colic or other gastrointestinal pain and discomfort associated with feeding
   D. Threats to gratification due to incomplete satisfaction of the sucking drive although appetite and hunger are satisfied, or due to insufficient energy to continue working long enough to satisfy hunger drive
   E. Distaste and resistance aroused by forcing of new or disliked foods
   F. Weaning difficulties from breast to bottle or from bottle
   Note: The outcome of the baby's own efforts to deal with these hazards with whatever degree of support and insight available from his mother have much to do with the capacity or orality to provide a permanent resource of gratification during the vicissitudes and frustration of other needs and drives in the development of the child, and a comfortable organismic setting for all aspects of ego development.

IV. Types of oral orientation for intensive study of individuals (examples only)
   A. High gratification: moderate to high demand with gratification
   B. Moderate demand, gratified
   C. Low demand, gratified: easily satisfied, interests in other areas, etc.
   D. Frustrated, negativistic: baby too often frustrated as in III; mother rigid, inattentive, irregular, interrupting, or in other ways interfering with gratifying oral experience
   E. Insatiable: high demand with frustration; may seek multiple sources of oral gratification at different levels
   F. Ambivalent: early pain in oral experience balanced by maternal soothing with later gratification and parallel resentments
   G. Disturbed: extreme pain, unassuaged, interfering with organismic internal integration and serene experience as background for ego development (seen in pathological cases, cf. Melanie Klein et al.)

Appendix 7: Definitions of
Prepuberty Variables*
(Moriarty)

Ability to accept substitutes:	Willingness to give up an idea or object and to develop or adopt a new approach; to use makeshift or alternate equipment; or to accept a substitute gratification as gift, reward, or edible if the desired one is not available.
Ability to accept warmth and support from others:	Responsiveness to affection and encouragement from others.
Ability to organize, provide own structure:	Ability to systematize, arrange, plan or to set up a framework for one's activities.
Ability to positively assert own needs, preferences:	Capacity to express one's wishes, usually verbally, to be assertive in regard to feelings, opinions, etc.
Ability to synthesize thinking, affect, action:	Capacity for integrative behavior in which ideation, feelings and motor skills are effectively directed toward self-expression.
Acting out (low)—Overcontrol (high):	Behavioral expression of needs or wishes vs. constriction. (Acting out implies impulsiveness in contrast to spontaneity.)
Active orientation, acting on, doing to:	Degree to which child possesses an attitude and approach of actively doing to or acting upon his environment.
Adequacy of expression of affect (open expressiveness vs. poker face):	Open expression of feelings (high) vs. concealing, minimizing or distorting feelings (low).
Affective coping capacity:	Range and appropriateness of feelings (includes subtlety, differentiation, complexity).
Attention to fine detail:	Awareness of and focus on parts, aspects, qualities, or characteristics of a whole. (Contrasts with tendency to generalize, to perceive globally, but does not necessarily imply compulsiveness.)
Available neutral energy:	Reserve capacity for mental or motor activity prior to definitely established cathexis.
Avoidance:	Tendency for child to evade or bypass ongoing procedures. (Clinically, one often observed delay as a form of avoidance in contrast to delay to clarify.)
Capacity for freewheeling attention:	Capacity to take account of peripheral activity or detail, to carry on parallel association.

* Adapted from definitions by Moriarty in Gardner and Moriarty 1968.

Capacity to mobilize resources under stress:	Capacity to use cognitive, affective, and motor skills under pressure (of difficulty, threat of failure, frustration, apprehension, etc.).
Capacity to sustain effort toward completion of a task:	Persistence or perseverance.
Capacity to use delay for appraisal:	Capacity to wait in order to observe and plan (contrasts with rapid moving into a situation without fully understanding it).
Clarity of distinction between fantasy and reality:	Differentiation of the real and unreal, implying good reality-testing and also tolerance for unreality.
Clarity of perception:	Capacity to perceive clearly, to achieve definite and sharp percepts.
Clarity regarding own identity:	Definiteness, stability, and unity of self-concept.
Clings to realism:	Tendency to stay concrete, to adhere to reality, to avoid fantasy.
Cognitive coping capacity:	Effective employment of cognitive resources (at whatever level they exist); efficiency in use of capacity to focus, perceive, conceive, organize, integrate, etc.
Confidence in ability to handle the demands of a test situation:	Feeling capable or adequate in meeting and interacting with an adult and in handling imposed demands of an adult.
Cooperation with authority demands:	Willingness to follow instructions and to participate in adult-directed activity.
Coping I:	Active problem-solving; use of opportunities; effective response to environmental demands, challenges, obstacles, etc.
Coping II:	Internal equilibration, balance; resources for maintaining internal integration under stress.
Creativeness and originality:	Capacity to perceive relationships in new ways, to express impressions in novel or fresh terms, to seek out and develop new ideas or ways of handling things, to form new organizations of available facts and techniques.
Critical of people, depreciates others:	Excessive derogation, censure, or undervaluation of others.
Curiosity, finding out:	Eagerness to know about or to find out about people or objects.
Degree of differentiation of affect:	Degree of subtlety in affective expression; capacity to show many nuances in feeling-tone.
Degree of disintegration under stress:	Degree to which skills fall off or become less effective when child feels under pressure. (Loss of coordination or smoothness in speech, gross motor or visual–motor coordinations or capacity to solve problems, etc.

Denial:	A defensive process in which intensity of negation suggests deep underlying feelings (as in a child who denies all negative feelings toward parents).
Determination:	Quality of being resolute in working toward or accomplishing a goal. (Differs from stubborness in permitting more flexibility in means used to reach a goal.)
Displacement:	Attachment of strong feeling to objects or people other than that which initially aroused the feeling.
Ease of ability to ask for help when needed:	Freedom to look to an adult when assistance is appropriate.
Ego restriction:	Inhibitive or blocking of ego functions (high) in contrast to freedom to mobilize and enhance adaptive forces of ego (low).
Energy level:	Forcefulness and vigor of motor activity.
Fearfulness:	Degree to which child shows fear or apprehension.
Feeling one's way along, using a third ear, being intuitive:	Capacity to react without excessive reflection or analysis, to react to minimal cues without conscious consideration.
Flexibility in adapting means to a goal:	Capacity to shift plans or to change behavior to achieve a goal.
Freedom from doubt and ambivalence:	Singleness of purpose without opposing drives or lack of conviction (implies self-confidence).
Freedom from inhibitions or rigidity in thinking, conceptualizing:	Freedom from blocking; freedom to accept new ideas or to reformulate ideas already held.
Freedom to translate ideas into action:	Capacity to think through problems and act accordingly without delay; effective realistic cognitive functioning.
Frustration tolerance:	Capacity to accept frustrating circumstances (disagreeable, difficult, etc.) without disruption of behavior or disorganizing tension.
Good-bad concerns, moralistic:	Hyperdevelopment of superego; excessive emphasis on naughtiness or evil, or rigid self-limitation by religious teaching.
Hostile (low)—Friendly (high):	Antagonistic vs. affable, cordial. (Doubt that any of our children were really hostile, though friendliness varied and many children were sometimes opposed to handling specific tasks.)
Identification with own sex:	Acceptance of the values and behavior patterns of one's own sex; assuming appropriate role for one's sex.
Impulse to grow (grow up):	Impulse to achieve maturity, to become independent.

Independence, self-reliance, autonomy:	Freedom to act on one's own without seeking direction or reassurance when one feels competent and confident.
Inhibition (low—Spontaneity (high) (Stiffness and restraint vs. free and natural behavior):	Capacity for self-expression without undue restraint from inner anxiety or blocking. (Does not imply impulsiveness but rather ingenuous self-initiation.)
Insightfulness into social situations:	Sensitivity to implications of social interaction capacity to behave appropriately in social situations.
Isolation (obsessive–compulsive:	A defensive process in which behavior and feelings are separated or segmented, resulting in hyperattention to detail in such a way as to interfere with affective culmination of a task or goal.
Knowing the score, grasping sequences:	Capacity to grasp and understand directions, sequences, implications.
Length of attention span:	Length of time one can attend to one object or purpose.
Love, affection, warmth; giving to staff:	Open expression of positive feelings toward adults.
Mastery:	Drive to master or to learn about and understand.
Meticulousness:	Emphasis on neatness and precision. (Observable in speech and in careful, orderly manipulation. May also be apparent in grooming.)
Openness to new experience:	Receptivity to and enjoyment of new experiences. Implies appropriate response.
Overall level of activity:	Quantity and extent of motor activity whether functional or not. (Contrast with *Energy level*, which refers to the quality of vigor in activity and endurance.)
Overt or observable tension:	Discomfort, as observed in verbalization, voice quality, facial expression, autonomic reactions, body part movements, etc. Registration in facial expression and manner, or motor activities, feelings of discomfort, strain, anxiety.
Pleasure in own body:	Healthy narcissism, satisfaction in one's own physical development, appearance, and acquired skills.
Pleasure in tactile experiences:	Obvious satisfaction in touching, being touched. Noting textures: softness, hardness, smoothness, roughness, etc., associating these qualities with pleasant experiences.
Pleasure in the situation:	Tendency to be pleased, gratified with the situation.

Positive self-appraisal:	Capacity to view oneself (assets and limitations) realistically, without undue self-depreciation, etc.
Preference for highly structured situations:	Preference for situations where demands are explicit (as in structured tests) vs. preference for situations that permit or require more self-expression or more opportunity to organize the situation (as in projective tests or play).
Projection:	A defensive process in which one's own feelings are attributed to others. (Usually accompanied by feelings of personal inadequacy and suspiciousness.)
Range of areas of enjoyment:	Scope of activities, hobbies, or pleasures available to the child, range of stimulation to which the child responds pleasurably.
Rationalization:	A defensive process in which more acceptable motivation is substituted for less personally agreeable or socially commendable motivation.
Reaction formation:	The establishment of a trait or consistent pattern of behavior that is opposed to an unconscious trend (as, for example, excessive cleanliness in a child for whom messiness and sloppiness are appealing).
Realistic evaluation of people:	Capacity to understand and empathize with others, to recognize and accept assets and limitations in skills and feelings of other people.
Reality testing:	Capacity to check against reality, to use past experiences for verifying and clarifying precepts and concepts.
Receptive to emotional impressions from the environment:	Openness feelings of others, implying capacity to understand, accept, and interact.
Repression:	A defensive process in which anxiety is avoided by excluding unacceptable feelings from consciousness.
Rigidity of expressive patterns (posture, gesture):	Limitations in quantity or variety of self-expressive maneuvers (high) vs. mobility in facial expression, gestures, stance, posture, etc. (low).
Self-feeling level; it feels good to be:	Sense of well-being, reflected in pride and self-confidence.
Separation of self and others:	Clarity in regard to self-image as a unit and as distinct from others; a sense of personal integrity; freedom from tendencies to confuse one's own feelings with those of others, or overidentification with others.
Spatial orientation:	Awareness of position, size, direction, distance of objects or locations. Ease in finding one's way

around new places or recognizing familiar locales.

Speed of orientation, grasp of situation, task: Alertness in understanding, absorbing directions, seeing implications.

Stubborn; maintaining a stand despite the consequences (Move me if you can): Stubbornness is a special form of determination insofar as it includes resoluteness, but it also involves a quality of obstinacy in clinging to ideas and behavior whether or not they seem practical and functional.

Talkativeness: Quantity of verbal communication, from little or none to much.

Task involvement: The extent to which the child is involved in the tasks presented. (This implies satisfaction or pleasure in participating, not just compliance.)

Tendency to regress: Tendency to react in ways that are more appropriate for younger age levels (for example: babytalk or finger-sucking beyond presschool).

Tendency to take cues from others (to imitate: Tendency to be alert to minimal stimuli, to recognize and act upon clues or suggestions, to follow a pattern or model of behavior.

Trust: Faith in the integrity of people and things.

Uses environmental areas selectively: Capacity to respond to cues in a differentiated way, implying preferences or choices.

Variability: The extent to which a child fluctuates or shifts in mood, style, or quality of relating or functioning.

Appendix 8: Vulnerability Inventory
(Murphy)

This inventory is based on data on normal infants and children and does not include children with gross damage, disease, or severe congenital or acquired defect.

Combinations and interactions of the following with each other and in the child's interactions with the environment contribute to frustrations and anxiety and various adaptational problems and difficulties in coping with them. The outcomes depend on the child's strengths and resources and the relation of stress or support from the environment to the pattern of vulnerability and strength in the child at any time. Vulnerability may increase as a result of cumulative stress, trauma, conflict, illness, growth irregularities, or the interaction of these; or it may decrease with improved health, skills, resourcefulness in solving problems, and understanding.

Secondary vulnerability of the child may also add to difficulties in resolving typical developmental conflicts: for example, the highly vulnerable child may be realistically more dependent upon the mother, or may have more realistic problems in peer-group competition and membership, and thus have difficulty in achieving independence.

Coping strategies, defense mechanisms, and coping styles may be largely influenced by the vulnerabilities with which the individual struggles: for example, the too easily overstimulated child may need to avoid noise, large groups, highly competitive situations, and so forth.

Aspects of vulnerability:
I. Primary vulnerability (constitutional or early vulnerability acquired in the first six months)
   A. Defects (mild to severe)
      a) Visual (e.g., myopia, hampering quick orientation)
      b) Hearing (partial loss affecting communication)
      c) Manual (contributing to awkwardness, poor fine coordination)
      d) Gross motor difficulties due to flat feet, club foot, knock knee, or poor coordination (interfering with running, jumping, games and sports)
      e) Balance (making bicycle riding, etc., difficult)
   B. Unusual structure and/or developmental pattern
      a) Body build
         1. Extreme ectomorphic (often a poor fighter, feels he can never win)
         2. Obese tendency (often slow, cannot keep up)

3. Low center of gravity, short legs, etc. (limits skills in games)
   b) Peculiar appearance, asymmetrical face or head, conspicuous ears, stigmata (contributing to teasing or to withdrawal by others)
   c) Constitutional deviation from appearance and/or body build expected for own sex and family pattern (contributing to ambivalence in parents' or relatives' response)
   d) Extreme or sudden changes in body build, as at puberty, creating problems for child in maintaining the accustomed peer-group role and in accepting a changed self-image (20% of all children go through a "fat stage"; some grow four to six inches in one year)
   e) Slow or rapid growth: of boys the 20% that mature latest and of girls the 20% that mature earliest have more problems

C. Sensitivities
   a) General tendency to extremes: inadequate stimulus barrier, hyper-input proneness leading to easy overstimulation and resulting loss of integration; hypo-input proneness or failure to obtain sufficient stimulation
   b) In specific zones
      1. Tactile: skin sensitivities contributing to complex, ambivalent, or anxious reactions to contact; thus withdrawal from contact sometimes combined with longing for it
      2. Temperature: sensitive to (uncomfortable with) heat, cold, or sudden temperature shifts; lowered resistance to infection when exposed to heat or cold
      3. Auditory: sensitivity to loud sounds or special qualities, which are experienced as unpleasant (child may be easily "hurt" by harsh voice of adult)
      4. Visual: painful or excitable reactions to bright light, colors, or other visual stimuli
      5. Pain: child may experience inoculations or other treatment as more painful than others do; or the child may suffer more at minor injuries, insect bites, etc.
   c) To specific qualities, e.g., shiny surfaces, rough textures may be unpleasant
   d) To general stimuli, e.g., new situations, strangeness, sudden change. Some infants as young as two months old showed distress in strange situations or at the approach of strange people. Some are disturbed by any dissonance, while others are interested

D. Imbalances—tendencies for
   a) Motor response tempo more rapid than perceptual–cognitive appraisal leading to poor integration and adaptation
   b) Perceptual–cognitive pace more rapid than motor response may contribute to greater intake than can be acted upon and result in difficulty in integration
   c) Verbal–social areas (Gesell) outreaching coping and discharge capac-

ities may lead to overstimulation, flooding, etc., as the environment
responds to the infant's vocalizations and social excitement

    d) Drives stronger than control capacities may result in impulsiveness
leading to accidents

    e) Aggressive drives stronger than capacity for love may lead to
difficulties in modulation of aggression

    f) Sensitivities greater than protective and coping resources may be
disorganizing

E. Temperamental vulnerability: low threshold for irritability, displeasure,
hostility, anxiety (e.g., infants who seem to experience nearly every stimulus
as an insult)

F. Deviant arousal patterns: exceptionally slow or fast arousal may contribute to inadequate interplay and cooperation with others

G. Lability

    a) Autonomic lability as indicated by marked variability in pulse, heart
rate, respiratory rate, flushing, paling, tendency to urinate, defecate
under stress may contribute to internal discomfort and coping
difficulties

    b) Tendency to frequent disturbances of vegetative functioning: colic,
diarrhea, vomiting, respiration, etc., may lead to frequent or chronic
distress and difficulty in achieving equilibrium

    c) Somatic reactions to stress such as headaches, stomachaches, etc.,
may add physical stress to initial stress reactions

    d) Susceptibility to infection, colds, ear infections, and other respiratory
illnesses occurring during a period of emerging autonomy and
initiative may reinforce passivity

    e) Allergies, eczema, skin rashes, etc., may interfere with activity and
opportunities to develop coping capacity

H. Perceptual–cognitive vulnerability: tendency to loss of integration or of
optimal level of functioning in cognitive areas under stress; fluctuating
differentiation of fantasy and reality may interfere with development of
cognitive coping resources

I. Motor vulnerability: tendency to disorganized motor reactivity or marked
inhibition under stress may interfere with successful motor adjustments

J. Speech: tendency to loss of smooth speech under stress may interfere with
communication

K. Social: tendency to loss of trust with loss of direct contact; need for more
support than average

L. Lack of constitutional bases for flexible, active coping due to

    a) Constitutional passivity

    b) Predisposition to restriction, inability to adapt body to environment
or to use environment for own comfort or satisfaction

    c) Low "sending power": limited vocalization, mimetic, affectionate,
and other expressive capacities to evoke response, support, help

    d) Tendency for wide diffusion and overflow of affect (vs. containment or confinement to specific time, space stimulus, and appropriate differentiation), interfering with appropriate cognitive and motor response

e) Tendency to direct impulse-expression at the expense of delay, orientation, planning, sublimation, etc.

f) Lack of flexible response to cues and comfort from caretakers

II. Acquired predispositions developed in reaction to birth and early infantile distress (during the period of patterning of perceptual-cognitive-affective functioning and later)

A. Acquired predisposition to anxiety over

a) Own body self-functioning,

b) Object relationships (separation, loss, rejection, etc.)

c) Failure or challenge

B. Predisposition to hostility and aggression (in reaction to interfering, frustrating, or painful handling)

C. Predisposition to ambivalence and conflict rooted in

a) Strong positive and negative reactions to the same stimulus

b) Early strong positive and strong negative tendencies in the mother, strongly satisfying combined with strongly frustrating ways of handling

c) Pain experienced in connection with pleasurable stimulus (as with a toy causing injury)

D. Fatigability related to

a) Low energy reserve

b) Poor energy management

c) Inability to alternate activity and rest

d) Excessive intensity or drive to mastery

III. Later outcomes of total infantile experience (evolved after the first six months)

A. Failure to develop

a) Trust sufficient to withstand rebuffs and disappointment

b) Nonverbal and verbal communication, imitation, identification

c) Stable, flexible relationships; capacity to communicate, cooperate, fight, love in the setting of the relation with the mother

d) Resources for discharge of tension, resolution of anger, mastery of anxiety

e) A range of affect, including capacity for fun, joy, interest in new experience play, creativity

f) Capacity to satisfy needs, or expectation of ability to, along with a capacity for delay

g) Ability to express drives through socially acceptable motor efforts (to avoid hurting self or others, which could evoke punishment or lead to conflict)

h) Reinforced capacity to exert effort or capacity to struggle against obstacles, to keep on trying after failure, etc.

      i) Capacity to "forgive and forget," tolerate frustration, renew positive relationships or let go and begin new relationships

      j) Recovery patterns through temporary regression or withdrawal, self-comfort, compensation, etc.

      k) Ability to consolidate positive coping attitudes and resources with healthy defense mechanisms

      l) Clear verbal concepts of objects, space, time relationships in the immediate and broader environment

      m) Autonomy appropriate to the developmental stage and resources

      n) Balance of control and spontaneity

      o) Capacity to use the environment selectively, to achieve goals, obtain substitutes, structure or restructure the environment

B. Residues of illness, accidental or operative damage contributing to vulnerabilities

      a) Temporary hearing defects, etc., interfering with speech development, communication, and concept development

      b) Dizziness or other anxiety-evoking reactions

      c) Sensitivities

      d) Motor or adaptive difficulties

C. Cumulative conflicts arising from interaction of any of the above with problems of control in relation to early feeding, or cleanliness, or toileting, or pressure for motor control, etc.

D. Depressive, retreating reactions to loss, separation, frustration, illness, which inhibit coping efforts

E. Persistent anxiety regarding separation from mother, home; potential pain in treatment by doctors; other stimuli experienced in a traumatic context

IV. Any of the above may be expressed in acquired vulnerability in one or more zones

  A. Motor

      a) Disorganization of motor control under stress: jerkiness, tremor, decreased accuracy and coordination

      b) Inhibition, immobility or paralysis of action, stiffening rigidity

      c) Loss of impulse control or other difficulties

  B. Speech

      a) Loss of smooth functioning under stress (stammer, etc.)

      b) "Whistling *s*" under stress; infantile speech

      c) Inhibition of speech under stress; chronic speech inhibition

  C. Perceptual:

      a) Loss of perceptual clarity under stress, vagueness, confusion, perceptual distortion due to projection, displacement, etc.

      b) Narrowed range of perceptual response; withdrawal, turning away, loss of curiosity, interest, response to environment

      c) Loss of control of attention, capacity to select

  D. Affect:

      a) Loss of appropriateness of affect; extreme diffuseness, intensity, or extreme flattening

      b) Eruption of overwhelming affect; affect-storm

      c) Loss of affective investment in people, objects, activities, learning

E. Loss of integrative functioning

      a) Decreased investment in the environment, loss of clarity of orientation, initiative, problem-solving

      b) Decreased cognitive efficiency as tested or in school; decreased general adaptational adequacy

Appendix 9: Vulnerability Correlations

Positive Correlations of CCI with PVR (Murphy)

Variable	Boys' r	Girls' r
At times overwhelmed by strong stimulation	.51	
Reactivity—set off easily	.53	
Loss of motor control under stress	.60	
Special vulnerability in the motor area	.51	
Tendency to fears and anxieties	.53	
Carelessness, roughness, impulsiveness	.54	
Spread of affect	.72	.61
Frustration leads to aggression		.58
Restrictiveness of mother toward child		.59
Feeling of being rejected	.56	.70
Tendency to give up easily at failure	(.45)	.68
Degree of conflict regarding sex role	.54	.50
Difficulty in relation to peers	.73	.53
Tendency to be demanding with relation to others	.53	(.40)
Tendency to get fatigued		.58
Tendency to hurt oneself	.63	.87
Evidence of conflicts in response to structured test	.52	
Good–bad concerns, moralistic		.56
Impulse to stay dependent, to remain a child	.55	
Tension load carried		.82
Degree of disintegration under stress	(.46)	
Frequency of disintegration under stress	(−.40)	.61
Difficulties created for child by mother		.58
Total environmental difficulties, not social		.71
Explosiveness, tantrums, tendency to outbreaks	.54	

Negative Correlations of CCI with Vulnerability
(Contributes to Positive Development)

Variable No.	Variable	Boys' r	Girls' r
6	Kind of house	−.65	
69	Family unity		−.54
70	Mother's enjoyment of the child		−.70
71	Mother's encouragement or support of child		−.50
73	Satisfying mothering (directed to child's needs)		−.70
121	Other illnesses	−.67	
403	Patterning of structured test responses—visual		−.75
408	Patterning of structured test responses—information		−.54
409	Patterning of structured test responses—number concepts		−.55
455	Smoothness in movements	−.59	−.78
456	Purposefulness of movements	−.53	
459	Ability to remain quiet when attention is engaged	−.50	
466	Alertness to details of environment		−.53
469	Length of attention span		−.55
478	Clarity of perception	−.65	−.62
484	Overall ability	−.57	(−.36)
492	Good spatial orientation	(−.39)	−.50
494	Involvement in the play activities		−.57
508	Impulse control	−.57	
509	Pleasure outweighs frustration experience		−.64
511	Tolerance for situations that do not please child	(−.40)	−.71
518	Faces the world with open anticipation		−.50
520	Pleasure in handling materials or objects		−.60
535	Positive self-appraisal	−.54	−.64
543	Autonomy	−.75	
544	Capacity to mobilize resources under stress	−.67	
576	Tendency to play realistically	−.64	
577	Clarity of distinction between fantasy and reality	−.79	
580	Reality testing	−.79	
581	Developmental level of speech	−.55	−.51
584	Realism–imagination balance		−.59
601	Threshold for frustration	−.78	−.79
605	Ego-images—inferior/adequate	−.71	−.70
607	Naturalness vs. artificiality		−.58
613	Freedom from inhibitions or rigidity in thinking	(−.43)	−.63
614	Attention span	(−.49)	(−.40)
620	Frustration tolerance	−.65	−.61

Variable No.	Variable	Boys' r	Girls' r
623	Methods of dealing with threatening stimuli in terms of self	−.66	−.78
632	Judgment	(−.49)	−.58
650	Tolerance for obstacles, difficulties	−.73	−.49
658	Strength of interests	(−.48)	−.50
661	Resilience following disappointment, defeat, etc.	−.62	−.64
662	Capacity to use substitute gratification	(−.44)	−.80
674	Available neutral energy	−.51	−.52
675	Fears		−.54
676	Freedom from doubt and ambivalence	(−.47)	−.52
678	Ability to accept substitutes	−.63	−.68
687	Control in handling things	(−.40)	−.69
695	Courage	−.59	−.55
696	Likes self	−.64	−.53
700	Range of fine-muscle skills, competence	−.54	−.68
707	Persistence in working toward a goal-action	−.60	
708	Psychically active orientation: having opinions	(−.38)	−.52
711	Ability to wait, postpone, control timing of gratification	(−.37)	−.75
712	Love–aggression balance		−.69
724	Accepts people as they are		−.61
725	Drive level: fear, caution (drive toward security)	−.53	
730	Impulse to grow (grow up)	−.71	
733	Ability to postpone, wait for, gratification	−.58	−.79
736	Following the line of least resistance, compliance		−.70
746	Strength of task-involvement	−.53	
768	Autonomy expression (on difficult test)	−.57	
798	Orientation: speed with which child was aware (difficult)	−.64	(−.39)
806	Coping II (AM)	−.60	(−.43)
809	Cognitive coping capacity (AM)	−.61	
811	Combined Coping II (LBM & AM)	−.88	−.76
812	Coping Capacity I (LBM)	−.62	(−.40)
814	Sensitivity balanced by ability to control S pres. -env.	−.60	−.51
824	Tact	(−.40)	−.74
826	Accepting limits: knowing how far one can go—social		−.61
828	Ability to limit or fend off excessive stimulation	−.62	−.82
829	Has insight into situations, realistic appraisal	−.67	(−.44)
830	Ability to restructure the environment, create new patterns	−.56	
836	Positive orientation to life		−.71

Variable No.	*Variable*	*Boys' r*	*Girls' r*
843	Resistance to discouragement	$-.57$	$-.63$
844	Security		$-.74$
849	Appropriateness of quality of affect		$-.86$
853	Always seems to have good luck	$(-.40)$	$-.67$
855	Clarity regarding own identity		$-.60$
856	Independence, self-reliance, autonomy	$-.52$	
859	Narcissism, pleasure in being oneself, healthy	$(-.34)$	$-.61$
860	Sincerity	$-.52$	$-.59$
863	Ability to harmonize goals, reconcile diverse goals		$-.52$
864	Flexibility of energy distribution		$-.50$
865	Ability to facilitate resilience by timing rest	$-.78$	E.69
866	Ability to balance dependence and independence		$-.87$
868	Ability to balance gratification and frustration		$-.55$
870	Strategic withdrawal to safety vs. being caught in situation	$-.53$	$-.50$
871	Can forestall danger—knowing when to stop	$-.55$	$-.68$
875	Ability to mobilize energy to meet challenge or stress	$-.64$	
877	Ability to control the impact of the environment	$-.69$	$-.69$
878	Adequacy of discharge of tension		$-.65$
879	Uses environmental areas selectively	$-.53$	
880	Adequacy of self-image in child's social milieu		$-.63$
881	Sense of self-worth, comfortable relation to ego ideal	$-.51$	$-.70$
885	Constructive use of one's anxiety	$-.64$	$-.52$
887	Constructive use of external control	$-.69$	$-.65$
892	Feminine attitude: sensitivity to people		$-.69$
897	Able to elicit warmth (preschool level)		$-.63$
917	Differentiated response to stress	$-.55$	
922	Tolerance for frustration vs. hard to please	$-.61$	$-.84$
938	Mother's active help to child in coping		$-.58$
940	Mother's acceptance of child's coping style		$-.64$
954	Ability to use vision to master the environment	$-.57$	
958	Reality testing, accuracy of perception		$-.54$
959	Eliciting desired response from others		$-.65$
962	Self-feeling level, it feels good to be		$-.61$
964	Uses delay for appraisal, planning		$-.54$
965	Balance of ego strengths and instinctual strength	$(.47)$	$-.60$
971	Ability to organize, provide own structure	$-.63$	
976	Tolerance of temporary regression		$-.75$
993	Efficiency table I (AM)	$-.53$	
998	Ratings of integration	$-.60$	

Appendix 10: The Prepuberty
Speech Examination
(Moriarty 1974)

Without knowledge of the results of previous psychological, psychiatric, or physical examinations, or of social or developmental history, Dr. Rousey individually examined and tape-recorded the speech of twenty-four eleven to fourteen-year-old children from the larger group studied earlier. His examination included the following standard procedures.

1. Interview to determine a child's experiences and feelings about speech development, and capacity for and interest in verbal communication
2. Hearing assessment by a puretone audiometer
3. Assessment of capacity to differentiate common speech sounds by the Wepman Articulatory Discrimination Test
4. Physical examination of peripheral speech mechanisms
5. Measure of rate and accuracy of sound production in repetitive articulation of single sounds (diadochokinetic rates)
6. Oral reading of sentences for evaluation of pitch, intensity, voice quality, and accuracy of speech sounds in a meaningful context

The recorded sessions were summarized and behavioral pre- or postdictions made by Dr. Rousey were assessed by me for accuracy against clinical data. Of 233 pre- or postdictions, 85 percent were judged to be accurate; 8 percent inaccurate; and 9 percent not verifiable. For individual children, accuracy ranged from 50 to 100 percent, though for 83 percent of the children, 75 percent of the statements made were found to be accurate.

Ratings were made on severity of speech and hearing problems and on effect on communication.

For the first of these variables, "Objective evaluation of severity of speech and hearing problems," the scale points were described as follows:

1. None
2. Few or infrequent, that is, no more than two observable speech symptoms
3. Numerous and definite, that is, at least three speech problems that are clear-cut and persist over time
4. Many and severe, that is, more than three speech symptoms that are distinct and serious distortions in communication
5. Total communication breakdown

A rating of 5 on this scale would imply speech distortions serious enough to result in difficulty on the part of the observer to understand the child. For example, very severe stuttering, blocking, or gross articulatory distortions would have been given a rating of 5.

The second variable rated at prepuberty was called "Effect on emotional relationships of communication." Scale points were as follows:

1. None
2. Mild
3. Mildly severe
4. Severe
5. Total disruption

A rating of 5 on this scale would imply complete rejection of communication through verbal terms or the inability to receive verbal communication through heard speech symbols. (Inability to receive verbal communication as we conceived of it also implied inability to differentiate sound when there was no indication of organic hearing loss.)

Table A: Speech and Hearing Problems in Prepuberty*
(N = 24)

Group A: Children who exhibited the poorest speech and who seemed to be most handicapped in interaction as a result of the problems that existed. In each of these children at least three speech symptoms were observed and were present persistently. Effect on interaction was in each case judged to be severe or mildly severe.

	Rating on Severity or Frequency	Rating on Effect on Interaction	
Greg	4.5	(>	?)
Rachel	4	=	4
Lennie	4	=	4
Donald	4	=	4
Vivian	4	>	3.5
		>	3
Martin	4	>	3
Terry	4	>	3
Roddy	3.5	>	3

Group B: Children who exhibited definite speech problems, but whose communication was only mildly affected by the problems that existed.

	Rating on Severity or Frequency	Rating on Effect on Interaction	
Sally	3.5	>	2.5
Daryl	3.5	>	2.5
Gordon	3	>	2.5
Darlene	3	>	2.5
Diane	3	>	2.5
		<	2.5
Amy	3	>	2
Helen	3	>	2
Vernon	3	>	2
Sheila	2.5	>	2
Steve	2	(<	2.5)

Group C: Children who exhibited the clearest, most "perfect" speech or who showed only minor, infrequent problems that had minimal effect on communication.

	Rating on Severity or Frequency	Rating on Effect on Interaction	
Barbie	2	>	1.5
Ronald	2	>	1.5
Chester	2	>	1.5

* Adapted from Moriarty, A. E. 1974. Vulnerability and tension outlets reflected in the speech of normal children. In *Psychiatric assessment by speech and hearing*, ed. Clyde Rousey. Springfield, Ill.: Charles C. Thomas.

	Rating on Severity or Frequency	*Rating on Effect on Interaction*
Ray	2	> 1.5
Susan	1.5	> 1
Janice	1.5	> 1

Of the eight children who were judged to exhibit significant speech problems at prepuberty, five had previously been assessed as vulnerable in speech or vocalization in infancy and in their preschool years. For comparative purposes, these more vulnerable children were contrasted with six children who showed little or no evidence of vulnerability in the speech area in their prepuberty years. However, two had been assessed as vulnerable throughout their infancy and preschool years, and one was said to be vulnerable in the preschool years only.

The ten other children whose speech showed only mild deviations that did not in our speech pathologist's judgment affect communication, have not been evaluated for the purposes of this summary report.

Table B: Children Most Vulnerable in the Speech Area at Prepuberty
(x = problems in oral-vocalization areas as assessed by Dr. Heider;
0 = no problems in oral-vocalization areas as assessed by Dr. Heider.)

	Infancy Vulnerability	*Preschool Vulnerability*
Greg	0	0
Rachel	x	x
Lennie	x	x
Donald	x	x
Vivian	0	0
Martin	x	0
Terry	x	x
Roddy	x	x

Table C: Children with Clear Speech at Prepuberty

	Infancy Vulnerability	*Preschool Vulnerability*
Barbie	0	0
Ronald	x	x
Chester	0	0
Ray	0	x
Susan	x	x
Janice	x	0

Tables B and C suggest that speech may reflect both special developmental problems at certain times and better or poorer overall mental health over time. It also suggests that when speech is in any way distorted, there is likely to be clinical evidence of stress. However, in some children with known difficulties, speech was not affected.

Appendix 11: JFK Questionnaire, November 1963

(Moriarty, Ginsparg, Morgan)

Young People's Feelings about the President's Death

We know that young people have opinions about right and wrong, how they and their parents should behave, and how the government should be run. Great men of the nation and the world, as well as the "man on the street" have been asked for their opinions and feelings about the President's death. We would like to know how you feel about it.

Name_____ Sex: boy_____girl_____ Age_____

Father's occupation_____ School_____ Grade_____

What church do you attend? _____

1. How and when did you first hear that JFK was shot?
2. (a) How did you feel about the news that JFK was shot?
   (b) How did you feel when you later learned that JFK was dead?
3. How did the student sitting next to you or the first person you met feel upon hearing the news?
4. How do you think Mrs. Kennedy and the children feel?
5. (a) What do you think should have been done with the killer?
   (b) How did you feel when you learned that he had been shot?
   (c) How should the killer's assassin be treated?
6. Did you listen to T.V. and/or radio broadcasts? How much? (Estimate the number of hours)
7. How did you feel when many usual programs or activities were cancelled?
8. What do you think will be the effect of the President's death:
   (a) On you?
   (b) On our country?
   (c) On the world?
9. Did you feel that you wanted to do something after hearing of the death of the President? If so, what?
10. Do you think the President's death could have been prevented? If so, what could have prevented it or what should have been done?
11. Were there things about Mr. Kennedy as a person which you did not like to see in him?
12. Give one word or a short phrase which best describes Kennedy as you saw him.

Appendix 12: Outline for Study
of the Development of a Child
(Murphy)

The present (still tentative) outline has developed out of earlier formulations in my *Social Behavior and Child Personality* and *Personality in Young Children*. It makes use of concepts formulated by G. Murphy, E. Erikson, K. Menninger, S. Escalona, G. Heider, A. Freud, Federn, Hartmann, Kris, and others. In particular, the effort to integrate psychoanalytic and developmental concepts was assisted by the thinking of N. Tibout, who presented her comprehensive outline of development in psychoanalytic terms at our preparatory conferences in 1953. The present outline reflects certain differences between data obtainable from observations as compared with data from intensive analytic treatment. It is not possible to keep each area mentioned here separate from the rest. The child is developing as a total unit, with all aspects interacting with the others throughout the course of development.

Environment

Ecological setting and architectural factors related to development: physical aspects of the environment (city, neighborhood, home), climate, density of building versus spaciousness, freedom to roam and to master the physical environment and other opportunities for motor discharge of tension. Safety and threat aspects. Quantity and quality of stimulation. Cultural resources, and material for sublimation. Size of home, type of room arrangements, privacy of adults' and children's living space. Aesthetic aspects of home individually and in comparison with others in the neighborhood.

Relation of all of these to family interaction and to ego and drive development of the child; ease of functioning at the child's pace versus chronic pressure for control in the neighborhood.

Social institutions with their supporting and threatening aspects

Well-baby clinics and associated clarity, support, anxiety. Relation of family to church and its supporting, stimulating, threatening aspects at different stages of child's development and for different members of the family. Religious ideology as it promotes or conflicts with drive expression, ego development, etc. Types of superego influence, resources for discharge of tension and for coping. Schools and their adequacy to the child's ego and drive needs and to special problems. Athletic organizations (Little League), social and recreational organizations (TARP, YMCA). Supporting or helping organizations (speech clinics, Family Service, etc.). Cultural organizations and resources.

Family's attitude and relation to different resources, and use of them at different stages.

Congruence versus conflicted heterogeneity of child's social environment (neighborhood versus home, school, and church, etc.).

The family and other persons involved with the family

Extended family including supportive and stress aspects of relationships with grandparents, other relatives, close friends. Community members: "family doctor," minister, neighbors, and other persons influencing, helping, or disturbing the family.

Family structure: supportive and stress aspects of sibling family. Relation with each parent, especially with relation to "fit" of child to parents' wishes and hopes; demand, comfort and interplay of parents with children, identification process. Interplay, support, identification, and conflict aspects of sibling relationships.

Ideology of each parent and relevant relatives, influencing home atmosphere and attitudes toward life demands, as well as those bearing on child development (e.g., God helps those who help themselves). Orientation toward progress, disaster, changes, values in child-rearing. Tendencies making for tolerance or recovery versus disintegrative forces in the family.

Constitution and Equipment in Infancy and Childhood

Body build: appearance, growth pattern (even or by spurts); style of functioning; energy, fatigability; consistency or variability; satisfaction versus ambivalence of child in regard to own body.

Vegetative functioning: gastrointestinal; respiratory, cardiovascular, and other evidences of autonomic functioning (reactivity, variability); persistence versus recovery from automatic upheaval. Results for child's body experience, sense of comfort or irritation.

Developmental balance: areas of acceleration or retardation (and shifts in these in response to what changes in hierarchy of drives and interests, health, external stimulation). Frustrations and interests related to balances or imbalances.

Sensory thresholds and affective responses in different zones: resultant "sensitivities." Zones of ambivalently strong positive and negative or pleasure and pain response and reactions to these.

Orienting, coping and learning capacities from birth: zones of rapid or slow coping, fixation of learnings or integrations. Zones of accelerated ego functioning. Sequences of emergent ego functions, their relation to each other, their relation to drives, impulse-control, social interaction.

Cognitive resources: pace of emergence of "autonomous ego functions," qualities of attention, "perceptiveness," memory, associating; pace of differentiation; recognition of familiar versus strange, of mother versus strangers; style of integrating, organizing; "insight," understanding; capacities for anticipating, preventing, planning; ease of translating ideas into action; persistence of learned or evolved integrations; level, range, and stability; tendencies to or resistance to disintegrative reactions in cognitive functioning (to what sorts of inner or outer stress). Uses of cognitive resources in direct coping with the environment. Child's perception of his cognitive capacities. Balance of cognitive development with other aspects of development; sources of precocity or retardation in certain areas or generally, and resultants for object-relations and interactions with the environment as a whole.

General drive tendencies: intensity, variability, receptivity, activity, modifiability, and controllability versus unmanageability; tendencies toward fusion versus keeping drives separate.

Infantile orality: smoothness of oral functioning. (See Appendix 6.)

Consistency or ambivalence of contact needs: resources for eliciting response or managing amount and quality of stimulation, level of gratification or frustration, ways of coping with results of deprivation or overstimulation. Effects on object-relations, self-image.

Sexual, erotic reactions: associated with what zones at different phases; intensity, persistence, residual effects; relation to somatization, fantasy, etc.

Anal drives: note type of excretory functioning: tendencies to diarrhea or looseness versus constipation; comfort or discomfort of elimination; skin pleasure or irritation associated with excretion; effort or ease in evacuating; pleasure in effort or pain, etc. Base of control, timing, and training. Relation of these to tendencies to withhold, mess, be clean, neat, and to enjoyment or disgust with anal experiences.

Motor drives: zones, vigor; coping uses; sources of gratification; frustration or conflict; effects of the latter in modifying drive.

Aggression: intensity, variability, thresholds for arousal associated with what libidinal and motor zones, what affects, what stimuli, rewards, punishments, conflicts, anxiety associated with destructiveness.

Narcissism: level at successive phases from birth as influenced by quality of vegetative functioning, drive gratification, achievement, object-relations, etc.; later childhood expressions in pride, confidence, pleasure in own functions and growth.

Mastery drive and coping capacities: infant's capacity to cope with difficulties, obstacles, pressures, or idiosyncrasies; autonomy, initiative, determination: level of gratification, frustration, pain, conflict. Separation or diffusion of conflicts. Residual for persistent aspects of ego functioning of coping at successive stages; zones of flexibility.

Affects and investments of interest: range, ease, frequency, vividness, duration of expression of affect; uses of affect, expression for discharge, enhancing pleasure, communication, etc. Perseveration of affect and tendency for affects to become attached to specific stimuli. Preferences and expression of; sequences of interests. Predisposition to specific affect-tendencies, delight, affection or warmth, or anxiety, hostility, or ambivalence (and factors contributing to these); tendencies to disturbance in response to strangeness, change, strong stimulation, etc. Capacity to modulate affect appropriately.

Interests: interaction of drives, cognitive and motor resources in development of interests; use as coping resources; control and integrative difficulties and zones of these. Tendencies toward selective interaction with the environment. Flexibility, freedom to appropriately respond to change versus rigidity of interests.

Mother–Child Relation and
Other Object-Relationships

"Viability" of mother–child relation in terms of mutual tempos, needs, resources, gratification, etc.; balance of autonomy and support offered by mother from birth; mother's handling of basic infancy needs for contact, stimuli, protection, feeding, cleaning, activity; communication at nonverbal and verbal levels; pleasure in mother–child relation.

Interaction of each of the tendencies of the infant suggested under constitution and equipment (above) with mother's capacities, needs, limits, goods, problems.

Impact on the mother–child relation of changes within the mother at different stages, and of changes in drives and ego development of the child, especially: increasing overt aggression and activity with the development of motor skills and drive; loss of intimacy and libidinal gratification from the child with latency and departure to school; hostility and rivalry emerging with the birth of new siblings, etc.

Impact on mother and other members of the family of changes in the child, and child's reaction to family changes, birth of siblings, departure of siblings or parent, divorce, death, etc.

Selective and changing patterns of identification in the child.

Experiences Significant at Successive Stages
and Their Interaction with Development at That Stage

Major recurrent gratifications, frustrations, deprivations, separations, losses; illness, operations, accidents, other traumas; special gratifications and integrating events. Developmental retardation or acceleration in different functional areas as influenced by experiences; interaction of experiences with drive and ego development reported especially at critical stages. Stress factors chronic or recurrent other than the above, observed or potential in the environment, and their interaction with intrinsic sources of conflict within the child and persistent relations with the environment.

Subjective experience of a child: in all of the above as perceived by the child, reflected in projective tests, etc. Resultant stoicism, pride.

Ego and Drive Integration

Emergent ego structure and coping tendencies in successive stages of psychosocial development and stages in the development of aggression; influence of these on motor resources, social interactions, object-relations, integration of selective identifications.

Coping Patterns and Defense Mechanisms

Coping with the environment: development of range of ways of dealing with the environment; obtaining and limiting stimulation, forestalling danger; adapting oneself and adapting the environment to one's own needs through restructuring, maximizing, or minimizing maneuvers.

Coping with the fantasies, wishes, needs, anxieties, conflicts, and other aspects of the internal world.

Ways of using coping devices and defense mechanisms, and their efficiency in discharge of tension, prevention of stress, containment of tension and avoidance of being overwhelmed; furthering the insight of the child, supporting relationships with the environment; selectivity of repression, reaction-formation, displacement, projection etc.; degree to which regression under different conditions is in the service of the ego.

Evolution of the somatic organization: of organism, environment, and psychic life, and of ego, drives, and superego growing out of all of the above interactions; success or failure of maintenance of autonomous ego functions. Patterning of losses or gains of ego integration, rigidity, flexibility, and modifiability of superego; influence on coping style. Acceptability of the child's spontaneous coping style to the family and to the culture.

Resulting narcissism: self-image, sense of identity in terms of the present and the future, and the place of the ego, id, superego in relation to the self and major object-relations.

Summary of Strengths and Weaknesses
of the Child's Personality Structure

In relation to the potentialities of the child and to the specific demands and challenges of the expected future environment. Sources of danger, types of conflict, zones of disintegrative reactions to stress, possible pathology, probable symptoms and their dynamics. Resources for resilience and growth, probable types of help or support to which child will respond.

Notes

Chapter 1

1 Erik Erikson (1964) documented the relation of ecology and culture to child development in *Childhood and Society*, focusing on life themes rooted in ecological experiences. Haggard and von der Lippe (1970) studied the isolation imposed by rugged mountain ecology in Norway and the relation of this to the personalities of these remote people.

2 The Murphys enjoyed the gentle Hawaiians during a summer on Oahu; Norman Douglas described in *South Wind* (1946) the ambience of life in the trade-wind area. Not all South Sea natives are gentle, as we learn in *Sorcerers of Dobu* (Fortune, 1932).

3 A Nigerian baby carried in a wide protective sash on the mother's back could see everything as she moved about the village or city and also experienced a rich combination of tactile, kinesthetic, and rhythm sensations from its closeness to the mother's body.

4 The "intensive" group included thirty-two preschool children in twenty-seven families; thirty-one of these children had been subjects of the Escalona–Leitch infancy study.

5 Whyte (1956) emphasized the repeated problems and efforts of adjustment to mores of new communities as families are sent to new locations.

6 The range of effects on personality of relatively homogeneous as compared with heterogeneous community experiences has not been adequately studied. Certainly the latter must place the greater burden of inner integration on the child.

7 While Oscaloosa, the small Kansas town studied by Barker and Wright (1954), does not compare in size with Topeka, many values and child-rearing patterns are similar.

8 U.S. Department of Commerce, Bureau of the Census, *1970 Census of Population*, vol. 1, pt. 1, table 7.

9 Children in large cities across the nation sing "O beautiful for spacious skies, for amber waves of grain" in school with hardly a passing thought that these spacious skies (of unpolluted azure) are not often seen through the smog that hovers over their cities, nor that what they are singing about is precisely the midwestern spaces which their parents too often downgrade as "flat" and "uninteresting."

10 Many lakes were created by the government-financed work of the depression era, such as the CCC and WPA programs.

11 The city of Topeka was founded in 1854. In 1950 the city comprised 12.5 square miles with 6,303 people per square mile, in contrast to New York City with 25,046 people per square mile.

413

12 The flood of 1951 inundated areas along the north side of the river, where many homes of relatively poor families were located.

13 Census figures for 1950 were 78,791; for 1960, 119,484.

14 Fathers involved in construction were unemployed for limited periods of time during the winter months; the Santa Fe Railroad shops had occasional temporary layoffs.

15 There were no high-rise apartments in Topeka in 1950 and no urban renewal such as took place in metropolitan cities in the sixties and early seventies.

16 Pianos were present in a few homes that usually contained other cultural resources as well. One musical child learned to play the piano by practicing on a friend's piano; another was given permission to use the organ and phonograph records of the church their family attended.

17 The fact that both of the poorest families in this sample were not "culturally deprived" is reflected in the fact that both mothers read to their children and one taught catechism.

18 The families in our group can be usefully divided as the Lynds (1929) divided their middle-western group, into "working class" and "business and professional" families, roughly "blue collar" and "white collar" workers. But (with the possible exception of two families each containing a large number of children, and each having a father whose income was not adequate to clothe and feed the children without substantial help from relatives, community agencies such as the church, and, at times when the father was out of work, county relief), the working-class families often overlapped in style of life, standards, and tastes with families at a modest economic level in the business group. The boys in one of these poor families, however, always wore immaculately clean clothes, however faded and worn they might be.

19 TB deaths in 1950 in Topeka, 8; in New York City 2,518. New York City would have had about 800 deaths instead of 2,518, if the rate had been the same as that of Topeka, since New York's population was at that time over 100 times as great: 7,891,957 vs. 78,791 (National Office of Vital Statistics, *Vital Statistics of the U.S.*, vol. 3, 1950).

20 Mental health resources included, in addition to the Menninger Clinic, the State Hospital, VA Hospital, County Guidance Clinic, and Family Service.

21 There were three conspicuous exceptions to this, and all occurred in families belonging to fundamentalist Protestant churches. In the most extreme instance the mother did not permit her little girl to play with any other child who "did not go to a church like ours." The sturdy and independent child protested so vigorously that the mother, after first talking to us about it, consulted her minister, who urged that she be more flexible and assured her that God did not intend that the friendships of little girls should be limited to other children of only one church.

22 Certain general characteristics of the Topeka homes contrasted with homes of destitute families seen in the Parent–Child Center program: no homes lacked indoor plumbing; none had filthy, broken floors too dangerous for a baby to be allowed to crawl around and explore, none had piles of dirty

clothes, bedding and mattresses, or loose debris. None was isolated from neighbors.

23 In her book, *On the Banks of Plum Creek*, Laura Ingalls Wilder described the sod hut her father built in Minnesota. In the latter half of the nineteenth century and even in this century, a sod hut was the first shelter built by a homesteader.

24 At the age of seven, sensitive Steve remarked to me when directing the route to his home on the return from the research center, "Our house is kind of shabby." However, a little later his family moved to a better house in a better neighborhood two miles away. At the same age Helen commented, "We haven't got much money in our family." Their family was almost unique in being surrounded by more well-to-do families.

25 In order to evaluate how typical this Rorschach pattern was for Topeka children in general, Pitsa Hartocollis tested 100 sixth-grade children and found that their "W" percentage was, again, lower than that of Pittsburgh and New Haven children, as reported respectively by Ledwith and by Ames et al. (1952).

26 My forebears, pioneers in Iowa in the nineteenth century, participated in such cooperative efforts and care. Like many children at the turn of the century, I was told of this with pride and respect by my parents.

27 Different personalities emerged by the end of adolescence, but no child became a delinquent and only one became a state hospital patient.

Chapter 2

1 Less disturbance at separation was shown by infants separated from initial foster families that included other children, according to Yarrow's (1972) study of adoption. Since two-thirds of our infants had one or more older siblings, we would expect a similar pattern.

2 The observations in this section are summarized from the original detailed records of home visits by the staff of Escalona and Leitch. I visited India in 1950, 1955, and 1960; USSR in 1960; Nigeria in 1963. Observations in "ghetto" homes in New York were made in connection with teaching at Sarah Lawrence College in the 1930s and 1940s; those in Topeka and the "northern kingdom" of Vermont were made in connection with consultation for Head Start and Parent Child Centers between 1966 and 1970.

3 While reaction to strangers and to strange places is often believed to appear in the second half of the first year, it is occasionally seen as early as twelve weeks. In this group, Donald and Molly were both disturbed by strangers at this age. See also Katherine Wolf (1952, pp. 97–137) and Décarie et al. (1973).

4 I have observed the absence of vocalization toward the babies and by them in deprived institutional settings and it has been discussed by several investigators. See Stone, Smith, and Murphy (1973, pp. 1004–05; 1214–30). I observed infants in foundling hospitals in New York, Tokyo, Athens, and Nigeria.

5 The concepts of "good breast–bad breast" or "good mother–bad mother" as developed by Melanie Klein, H. S. Sullivan, and others are too narrow in their emphasis on the infant's feeding experience. The extent to which the mother gives support for exercise of all the baby's earliest drives and needs must be assumed to be important in the development of the infant's perception of mother or care-giver.

6 While autonomic reactivity has been measured and studied (e.g., Richmond and Lipton 1959), its relation to gastrointestinal functioning and oral gratification has not been adequately studied.

7 Howard A. Moss (1967) found that mothers held male infants "about 27 minutes more per 8 hours than they held females," and other measures of contact showed from 20 to over 50 percent more time given to boy babies.

8 Margaret Mead has documented cultural differences in adaptational style in studies with her collaborators in Manus (1930), among the Arapesh (1935), in Bali (1942), and other cultures.

Throughout, she has observed the association between experiences, such as the mother's handling of the baby and the patterns of adult ritual. She observed the feeding and also the bathing, play, and discipline experiences of the baby, noting the influence of intimate pleasurable and unpleasurable skin and body contacts, stimulation of motor achievements, as well as the interactions in vegetative and eliminative spheres. She perceives such coherences among the varieties of behavior at different developmental phases to be the outcome of both simple, elementary behavior patterns and complex interactions that provide the tool behavior for coping with the environment, including the pressures, intrusions, or challenges of people—whether these coping styles are active, aggressive, or cooperative, or in contrast, withdrawn, passive, or compliant. Her approach describes a wider arc than that implicit in the "core culture" concept. Her persistent concern in research has been with the meaningful interrelatedness of widely disparate aspects of any culture.

Chapter 3

1 No other investigators of behavior in a large sample (128 infants) have produced comparably detailed records by simultaneous observers as have Escalona and Leitch. Very detailed observations of each infant in a very small sample over a much longer period of time have been made by P. H. Wolff (1959), and more limited observations on substantial samples were made by Gesell (1928), Bühler (1930), Bayley (1956) and others. (See reports in Stone, Smith, and Murphy 1973.) Thus, the Escalona–Leitch records provide a unique source for varied analyses of infant behavior and mother–infant interactions and for studies of continuity and change (see Appendix 6).

Macfarlane's studies (1939) were based solely on mothers' reports of *infant* behavior, as was the study of behavioral individuality by Thomas et al. (1963). Kagan and Moss's (1962) longitudinal report gives no data on infancy as such (the first year of life) but uses ratings on behavior over the span of the first three years as a basis for comparison with later stages of development.

There are differing limitations and contributions in each approach; here the mature experience and breadth of professional orientation of the major investigators contribute unique richness and sensitivity to their records, while the presence of three simultaneous observers provides a special protection for reliability of observations. In addition, standard tests offer the advantage that individual patterns can be looked at in relation to data on other samples. Since all test norms (Cattell, Gesell) are based upon the success of a given number of children—always a majority but never all the children to whom the tests were originally given—we have for every item of behavior included on the tests a certain "normal" range. The range of individual differences for each item, however, is generally not available in research reports. Shirley (1933) does give the interquartile range of ages at which each behavior first appeared in her Minneapolis sample of twenty-five babies.

2 Among the early investigators who documented individual differences in infants were Gesell and Ames (1937). Ames identified fifteen traits from cinema records, including "energy output," "motor demeanor," "self-dependence," "social responsiveness," "communicativeness," "adaptivity," "emotional expressiveness," and others. Some follow-ups of differences in infants were made by Gesell's (1939) group emphasizing the persistence of "alacrity."

Mary Shirley (1933) recorded differences in irritability, tone and timbre of cry, activity, muscle tone, and quality of reactions to test situations. In addition, she charted differences in the age of appearance of each of these functions; she gave 1st and 3rd quartiles as well as medians. Such differences could be expected to influence the course of development of relationships with the mother: for instance, an early smiling baby might tend to evoke more response from the mother, more stimulation, more interaction, thus gaining more social experience and skill. Similarly, a baby who developed the capacity to grasp objects early might evoke more attention from the mother to his interest in objects; this could lead her to provide more toys and other objects, and his greater time with them could lead to earlier mastery and concept-formation.

Ruth W. Washburn (1929) focused on differences in expressiveness, differentiating infants who frequently laughed or cried as multi-expressive, while those who laughed or cried little were parvi-expressive; a third group who smiled or laughed little, while they were sober or cried much, were called depressor-expressive. These were considered temperamental differences.

The work of Margaret Fries and Paul Woolf (1953) on activity level has stimulated more subsequent research than any of the other early studies of individual differences. Also, see chapter 1 in Stone, Smith, and Murphy (1973). This contains excerpts from early and recent studies of individuality in infancy, as well as discussions of *possible contributions* of the interaction of individual characteristics to development.

Variations in the range of individual differences in infants from birth can be expected in different samples: infants from heterogeneous samples of mothers with widely different genetic, health, nutritional backgrounds, as well as wide differences in pregnancy and birth stress would reflect these differences. Infants from homogeneous samples of mothers (with similar genetic, health, nutritional backgrounds and similar levels of freedom from pregnancy and birth stress) could be expected to show less variation.

David M. Levy (1943, 1966) saw differences in the handling of babies by overprotective mothers; these differences related to the passivity vs. dominance of the babies. Overprotective mothers dominated passive babies but yielded to active, dominant babies. Mary D. S. Ainsworth and collaborators (1971); Stayton et al. (1971) have emphasized the degree of mothers' responsiveness to the cues given by the baby as a source of differences in infants' behavior. Anneliese Korner (1971) in an extensive review of relevant research emphasizes, as does Escalona, ways in which individual differences at birth shape the infants' early experience and later development.

Lacey (1959), who has studied individual differences in degree of cardiac rate response to stress situation in fetuses as well as children found differences in cognitive style, ways of perceiving and thinking, between strong and weak reactors. Other early investigators who found variations in response among newborn infants include M. C. Jones (1926); K. C. Pratt, A. K. Nelson, H. H. Sun (1930); E. S. Bryan (1930). These and others are briefly summarized in Murphy, Murphy, and Newcomb (1937, 1964). We have not yet had a thorough comprehensive study of the effects of such newborn differences on interactions between adults (nurses and mothers) and the newborn, and sequelae of these interactions between newborn differences and differences in care-givers.

3 In addition to the running records of three simultaneous observers and the psychological and pediatric test records, Escalona made a summary sketch of each infant as it appeared when observed. We are drawing upon these rather than formulating our own second-hand summary.

4 In order to have an adequate study of factors in activity level, we would need a study of internal sources of irritation or stimulation, and physiological factors involved in motor versus internal responses to stimulation, as well as a thorough study of all immediate and distal stimuli impinging on the baby and his differential reactivity to these. Samples in differing ecological settings (quiet vs. noisy, crowded vs. spacious, large family vs. small family, colorful vs. drab) and also samples differing in expectable pregnancy experiences of mothers affecting the prenatal experience of the baby would be needed. In addition, differences in early tendencies to defensive or self-protective inhibition of activity (for reduction of stimulation) would be needed, along with the opposite tendency to escalate activity in order to evoke greater stimulation.

The apparent increase in high activity levels or "hyperactivity" in American children is concomitant with the environmental increase in multisensory stimulation in urban areas: noise, crowding, air pollution, speeded tempos, as well as the increase in disrupting and anxiety-provoking experiences such as moving (being uprooted) and divorce. One does not see many hyperactive children in villages of India or rural areas of the USA.

5 Three of the coping sample babies were reported by their mothers to have been disturbed at ages from eight to twelve weeks by a woman who was a stranger, just as "Christina," the baby girl described by Katherine Wolf (1952), was frightened by a visitor at this early age. In each instance the stranger either looked strikingly different (dark hair in contrast to mother's blonde hair; gray hair in contrast to mother's dark hair); talked loudly; and/or handled the baby roughly. These babies were apparently disturbed by the degree of *dissonance* between the visitors' stimulus pattern and that of mother, since they were not said to be afraid of all strangers, and we would not expect them to be at such an early age. Just once have I had the experience of taking a three-month-old baby in my arms only to be greeted with crying; that baby has grown into a young lady who is on her way to being an anthropologist—who will presumably make a life work of differentiating peoples.

6 This section is based on my analysis of test records of the thirty-one coping infants, in which the scores on different test areas were compared. Heider (1966) was concerned with balance and consistency of scores on different items within test areas.

7 See my (1972 b) discussion of developmental aspects of integration. Factors such as extreme autonomic lability, susceptibility to infection, difficulties in digestion and elimination probably contribute most to internal discomfort, while imbalances in development contribute to frustration. Integrative problems from early infancy arising from such sources present challenges met in different ways by different infants.

8 Wide individual differences in degree of activity of infants were found by Weiss (1929), and these are consistent with the differences in activity level documented and studied longitudinally by Margaret Fries and Paul Woolf (1953) in terms of their implications for personality development. Mittelmann (1954) documented individual differences in style and in many formal and functional aspects of motility in the first three years. He defined a motor urge comparable in intensity to other instinctual drives; this is described as reaching a peak at the time of emerging locomotion during the second year of life when it largely dominated the child's interest and attention. With increasing priority of motor drive, the interest in improving motor skills leads to extensive efforts to practice and master a wide variety of motor coordination. The motor drive remains strong with many children through the entire period of childhood and into adolescence.

The two babies we saw above, Vernon and Brennie, were rated low (5) and moderate (3) respectively by Heider on the basis of evaluations by the original observers. The distribution of Heider's ratings on *activity level* for the 31 babies in our intensive sample who were at three different phases of development were as follows:

Activity Level in 31 Infants in the Coping Sample

Rating	4–12 Weeks	16–24 Weeks	28–32 Weeks	Total
High 1	2	3	3	8
Moderate 3	4	4	5	13
Low 5	4	4	2	10

9 Initially Heider attempted to rate "sensitivity" to stimuli in different sensory modalities. However, in response to discussions with William Goldfarb, it was recognized that since the evidence for sensitivity was simply the infant's reaction to stimulation, we could in fact rate only reactivity to sensory stimulation.

Sensory Reactivity of 31 Babies

Rating	4–12 Weeks	16–24 Weeks	28–32 Weeks	Total
High 1	4	6	3	13
Moderate 3	4	2	2	8
Low 5	2	3	5	10

10 "Gating" is in use in psychology to refer to a person's capacity to take in stimulation at a slower or faster pace.

Chapter 4

1 For extensive descriptions of the preschool children's ways of coping with new or challenging or stressful situations, see Murphy and Associates (1962). Relevant descriptions of preschool children's ways of responding to opportunities for play with miniature life toys, sensory toys, and others and also to ego-blocking and aggression challenges are found in Murphy (1956). Responses to dilemmas inviting sympathetic behavior by preschool children are described in Murphy (1937).

2 The companionable loquacity of the majority of these children was conspicuous to me. Westchester and New York middle-class children from small nuclear families (without the grandparents, relatives, or siblings) were in general not so naïvely open and communicating with me. A few children seemed to identify at least Grace Heider and myself as belonging to the grandparent category. But they were equally expressive with other staff members, including the male psychiatrist, Dr. Toussieng. All of this implies their assumption that grown-ups would be interested in their observations and thoughts. This sociable conversation was characteristic even of Terry and a few other children with speech problems (see chapter 8, pt. II). In some families children were punished for "talking back" or "sassing their mother," but this has to be seen in the context of family communication, which was a nearly constant part of life in the home. The fact that children did not expect

to be excluded from parents' conversations with visitors was implied in the great difficulty their mothers had in making them stay out of the room where the home visit to the mother was made.

3 In noting that girls had some characteristics generally regarded as "masculine," we do not imply lack of feminine identity or appearance. No girl was mistaken for a boy. JoAnne and Sally, both forthright, motorically skillful—and in Sally's case—good at "fixing things," were slender, curly-haired little girls who took pride in their hair ribbons and feminine attire. However, Sally remarked at the prepuberty examination, "I was half-boy and half-girl for a long time. At eight I decided to be a girl." She gave up "tomboy" behavior and even some aspects of intellectual functioning considered masculine by her mother (see p. 189). She continued to cope well with a variety of life demands.

This overlap between boys' and girls' coping resources is similar to the overlap discussed by Terman and Miles (1936) in their study of masculinity and femininity.

4 JoAnne, Janice, Teddy, and others were open in their protests, corrections, directions given to adults. These coping methods occasionally carried a slight tone of defiance, but often a tone of treating the adult as an equal, while at the same time accepting adult direction, as in the structured tests.

5 My records of the children's handling of MLT provided instances of the children's capacity to organize, impose a structure on unstructured materials, integrate modalities, be flexible in adapting means to a goal, accept substitutes, as well as use environmental areas selectively.

6 At the time of this early work in 1953–55, no published formulations of coping devices or strategies were available to us; our work was therefore exploratory and had both the advantages and disadvantages of any pioneer work. The advantages were that we were unburdened by frozen concepts, as some of the American work on intelligence and assessment of mental illness has been. The disadvantage was that, inevitably, our conceptualizations were rough or loose at times.

7 "Strategic withdrawal" is used by children who step aside or retreat temporarily in order to visually appraise the possible gratifications and/or dangers in a new situation and/or make a plan for action before entering into participation. This contrasts with the exploratory "casing the joint" approach to new situations in which the child goes over the ground surveying, testing, sizing up the available resources before he settles down to actual use of the opportunities present.

8 A "psychically active orientation to life" is distinguished from the motor "activity level." "Activity level" refers to the amount, scope, vigor of movement as such. A person may have a psychically active orientation to life in terms of the capacity to change his situation, influence others, restructure the environment and the like, while at the same time he is economical in body movement. One of the most "quiet" boys in our Sarah Lawrence Nursery School group became an engineer.

9 In contrast to the greater communication of the Topeka children, they produced fewer and less complex organizations of toys. This is in line with their decreased "W"% responses on the Rorschach (as analyzed by Pitsa Hartocollis) compared with metropolitan children in New Haven and Pittsburgh, and is generally interpreted to imply less ambition. As we have noted, ambition, whether in terms of getting good grades in school or making a name for oneself, was not high on the list of emphases in child-rearing. Frankness, loyalty to the church, tolerance were rated higher.

> This sample of the Topeka children show less W% and higher D% than in children on whose records Ames and Ledwith based their norms; namely the means on W for the Topeka children are at 10 years 26.6% against 51.4% of Ames; 11 years 29.9% against 43.8%; 12 years 33.1% against 46.9%; 13 years 26.1% against 46.2%. The means on D are: 10 years 69.6% against 41.3%; 11 years 73% against 43.9%; 12 years 63.3% against 45%; and 13 years 69.5% against 45.9%.
>
> The Topeka sample is found to differ consistently from the comparison of norms in the area of perceptual approach. It seems to focus more upon the practical concrete aspects of daily living (high D) and showed less inclination toward abstract or theoretical thinking. They did not favor use of organizational and integrative skills (low W).
>
> It is interesting to note that our children gave a higher H% and a lower A% than the children in the Ames sample at all ages. At the same time our children are found to be more constricted (higher F%) and they also gave a considerably lower F+% at all age levels.—Pitsa Hartocollis

10 By "cultural relativity" we mean to imply that the range of coping items seen in these Topeka children would not necessarily duplicate what would be seen in a group of deprived rural or metropolitan American children, much less children in widely different cultures. For instance, children in villages in India might not exhibit the capacities to "restructure the environment" shown by some of these children who watched their fathers build another room or two or a porch onto the house or even raise the roof to add a second floor. And they might not show the tendencies to "fend off pressures from the environment" by protest and other means. I did see "strategic withdrawal," as for instance a new child in a rural basic education center preoccupied himself with painting during the early weeks of getting oriented to the new setting.

11 "Maintaining internal integration" is a broad variable that refers to the child's capacity to keep free of the "disintegrative tendencies" discussed by Karl Menninger (1954). The latter include both disturbing vegetative reactions (wetting, nausea, headaches, etc.) and interferences with customarily smooth perceptual, cognitive, speech, and motor functioning.

12 "Healthy narcissism" is a term used by Hermann van der Waals in his lectures at the Topeka Psychoanalytic Institute during the 1950s and 1960s.

13 The phrase "most children in our culture" may need some qualification. Since the major studies of children's fears have been carried out on children

in New York, New Haven, Oakland, California, and other urban centers, we do not know whether children on a Texas ranch, for instance, would show the same or as many fears as we find in these urban children. Macfarlane and her staff (1954) demonstrated that many fears of the preschool period are outgrown by the time children are established in elementary school.

14 We assume that all young children are vulnerable to some degree, in the sense of experiencing some threat to adequate functioning in stressful situations. This does not imply that such vulnerability results in trauma with permanent negative effects; rather, the child's zones of vulnerability present coping challenges in addition to those presented by adaptational tasks at different stages of growing up.

Chapter 5

1 See also Rousey and Moriarty (1965), Gardner and Moriarty (1968), and Stewart (1967).

2 In view of our observations of a frightened reaction to a stranger seen in certain babies three months old or younger (and Wolf's [1952] similar observations), along with preschool fearfulness of strangers, we can infer that chance experiences of fright may contribute to subsequent fearfulness toward strangers and in new situations. These chance experiences could not be predicted. Similarly, unpredictable events and changes in the environment could contribute to other patterns in this list.

3 Our prepuberty study included the HIT, the results of which were analyzed by Holtzman's staff. They found that the test results on our small sample were comparable to those obtained on their large sample of Texas schoolchildren. Wayne Holtzman reported:

Normative characteristics of the 50 children from Topeka who were given the Holtzman Inkblot Technique by Riley Gardner and Alice Moriarty:

I have just reread Chapter 7 in *Personality Development at Preadolescence* which discusses the HIT, and I have examined again the percentile norms for the 50 cases as they were produced by our computer. I think that the comments made by Riley and Alice on pages 120–22 are accurate assessments of the general characteristics of these 50 children as compared with our earlier normative samples of children in the first through seventh grade. They tend to fall near the middle on:

Reaction Time	Human
Location	Animal
Form Definiteness	Anxiety
Movement	Hostility
Pathognomic Verbalization	Penetration
Integration	Popular

They appear to have significantly lower scores on: Form Appropriateness, Color, Shading, Barrier.

In this sense they are a little more like some of the Mexican children in our cross-cultural sample, although I certainly would not make that comparison on a serious scientific basis for many obvious reasons. In any event I am sure you could characterize them as well within the normal range on any of the more important variables. Of course there are single individuals within the group that stand out markedly in their individual patterning of scores, but the group as a whole would have to be characterized as a normal group of schoolchildren rather than a group of emotionally disturbed children as in the new norms prepared at Johns Hopkins Medical School using the HIT.

We must also note the findings on a random sample of Oakland children studied by Macfarlane's staff: transitory constriction on the Rorschach test at the prepuberty stage was typical for the group (McFate and Orr 1948). In our sample, however, it is noteworthy that prepuberty disturbance was most apparent in children earlier evaluated as vulnerable.

4 Several children commented during senior year in high school that their research contacts had "helped them to think things through" for themselves, or in some other way had been experienced as supportive. It is impossible to tell what part their sense of our interest in their development helped them. Insofar as it did, we have to include this as one example of the capacity of individual children to use brief recurrent friendly contacts for resilient growth.

5·At the prepuberty phase of our studies a list of variables was selected by Moriarty, Riley Gardner, and me in conference, primarily for the Gardner-Moriarty (1968) study of cognitive style at prepuberty. These were selected from the list already found to be highly correlated with Coping I and Coping II (see Appendix 4). The list as finally selected is given in Appendix 7 and is discussed at length in Gardner and Moriarty (1968). These items were rated by Dr. Moriarty on the basis of her own observations during intelligence tests and Dr. Toussieng's observations during his psychiatrically oriented interviews. Subsequently, I enlisted the cooperation of Lolafaye Coyne to explore the possible relationships between infancy/preschool and prepuberty items.

Our infancy ratings did not include an item on timidity or fearfulness, but it is conceivable that activity level could be reduced in some babies by fearfulness, although anxiety could also be reflected in either restless agitation or inhibition.

6 Harlow (1975) has commented on his daughter's refusal at a very early age to be held supine; this position provoked crying which stopped only when she was held so that she could look around at the world. This drive to sit up seems to evoke more effort to sit up and success in sitting up early. This difference between the experience of an early-sitting versus an early-walking baby deserves further exploration and could be managed by a study of selected samples of babies observed in the first year and three to five years later. Available techniques make it possible now to study in detail what the sitting baby does with his eyes, hands and body, as compared with the range

of experiences the mobile baby discovers. The relationships between these differences and later cognitive, perceptual-motor and cognitive skills could then be analyzed.

7 In addition to the relationships mentioned in the text, a series of correlations logically congruent with these were significant at an .05 level; speed of orientation, freewheeling attention, a capacity to use delay for appraisal, clarity regarding the distinction between fantasy and reality, selectivity, self-feeling level (positive), positive assertion of own needs, capacity to sustain effort toward a goal, stubbornness, insightfulness into social situations, affective coping, ability to mobilize resources under stress. Reactivity to sensory stimulation includes evidences of both autonomic and motor responses, that is, any change in response to any sensory stimulus.

8 Infancy autonomic reactivity and curvilinear relations with prepuberty coping:

reality testing
awareness of fine details
capacity for freewheeling
   attention
"knowing the score"

clarity regarding own identity
separation of self and others
self-feeling level (it feels good
   to be)
positive self-appraisal
drive to grow and grow up

freedom from rigidity of expressive
   patterns
freedom from doubt and ambivalence
hostile-friendly attitudes
pleasure in (the examining) situation
spontaneity (versus inhibition)

availability of energy
task involvement

tendency to use denial

9 The correlations between infant vegetative functioning and prepuberty functioning included the following items at an .05 to .001 level:

flexibility in adapting means to a goal (.01)
spontaneity vs. rigidity of expressive pattern (.001)
freedom from inhibition and rigidity in thinking (.05)
ability to organize and provide own structure (.025)
capacity to use delay for appraisal (.025)

We would expect that good vegetative functioning would contribute to a relaxed state conducive to flexibility, and this is congruent with spontaneity and freedom from rigidity.

10 Spitz's discussion of "fundamental education" (at the April 1970 meeting of the American Academy of Pediatrics, Washington, D.C.) explicated the contribution of mother–infant interplay to the development of cognitive-affective-motor integrations. See also Spitz's chapter in Maria Piers, ed., *Play and Development: A Symposium* (New York: Norton, 1972). Experimental studies provide ample evidence of the contribution of maternal stimulation to the baby's smiling and talking. (See Stone, Smith, and Murphy 1973, pp. 1070 ff.) But the mother's contribution to alertness, responsiveness, alacrity, eagerness, and enthusiasm has not been adequately studied.

11 Mothers' enjoyment of the infant and prepuberty functioning:

	r
Coping I	.48
Cognitive Coping	.49
Capacity to mobilize resources under stress	.49
Freedom to translate ideas into action	.53
Flexibility in adapting means to a goal	.52
Uses environmental areas selectively	.51
Clarity regarding own identity	.55
Positive self appraisal	.55
Separation of self and others	.50
Freedom from doubt and ambivalence	.56
Realistic evaluation of people	.48
Independence, self-reliance	.57
Confidence in ability to handle the demands of a situation	.54
Pleasure in the situation	.49
Openness to new experience	.51
Repression	− .50

12 "Family unity" correlated with prepuberty:

Capacity for freewheeling attention, preferring lightly structured situations, capacity to use delay for appraisal, creativeness and originality, freedom from inhibitions or rigidity in thinking, being intuitive.

Clarity regarding own identity, separation of self and others; self-feeling level, ability to positively assert own needs and preferences, uses environmental areas selectively, impulse to grow (grow up).

Range of areas of enjoyment, pleasure in own body.

Realistic evaluation of people, ease of asking for help when needed, insight into social situations.

Freedom from doubt and ambivalence, availability of energy.

Curiosity, active orientation, knowing the score.

Autonomy, confidence in ability to handle the demands of a situation.

These can be seen as aspects of cognitive flexibility, orientation to self, pleasure resources, social capacities, decisiveness, cognitive mastery, independence.

Chapter 6

1 The concepts of coping and defense mechanisms have been used differently by different writers. Anna Freud (1937), Rapaport (1951), Hartmann (1951),

and others have discussed the role of defense mechanisms in normal character development. Norma Haan (1963) and some others have opposed defense mechanisms as "pathological" to coping as "normal." In our usage here, defense mechanisms are unconscious processes that in different ways may successfully drain tension as in healthy regression (Moriarty 1966, A. Freud 1937) or may protect the child from overstimulation as with a defensive use of the stimulus barrier (S. Freud 1955). No child in our normal sample was without defense mechanisms. When the latter are used to the extent that perception of reality is seriously distorted, pathology may ensue. But pathology is not an inevitable consequence of mechanisms of defense. Coping efforts (devices, strategies) may be either successful or unsuccessful, healthy or unhealthy. For instance, excessive and inappropriate use of aggression (direct violent assault against the environment, however justified the protest may be) brings child as well as adult into court or mental hospital. In war or peace, coping strategies may or may not work, may be useful or pathological (Murphy 1970).

2 *Balance* of developmental levels needs to be studied more fully than has been possible here. In my experiences in testing schoolchildren, I encountered such imbalances as: outstanding insight and creativity with mediocre or even below average capacity to handle mechanical operations or mathematical problems which would have to be managed for use of the insight and creativity; outstanding subtlety and complexity of thought with extreme slowness of communication; high drive with low endurance, etc. Such imbalances present children with basic difficulties in developing a clear self-image.

3 In the 1940s Max Wertheimer used to illustrate the concept of a "radix" or dominant, organizing characteristic of a personality in little games: at a party he would play different tunes with varying tempi, staccato or legato quality, rhythm, etc., and ask the group to identify the person represented by a given tune, then tell why the tune expressed the quality of that person.

4 Since we have so much evidence on variability of tested IQ from different longitudinal studies (Skeels and Skodak 1938; Bayley 1949; Macfarlane 1963; Sontag 1958; as well as Moriarty 1966), there is an urgent need for deeper analysis of processes involved. Moriarty (1966) and others have discussed variations in physical condition, rapport with the tester, motivation, differences in content of tests at different levels, etc., but it seems likely that other factors are also involved: changes in the zones of functions and specifically, cognitive functions unconsciously cathected and/or decathected; changes in the meaning of taking a test; changes in self-image and expectation related to energy mobilizable in the test. Studies of details of variation in cognitive functioning noted in test records during a period of time when the subject is undergoing analysis would add much to our understanding of processes underlying changes in IQ.

5 The concept of "invulnerability" has been used by Garmezy and Nuechterlein (1972) to highlight the contrast between those severely deprived and

stressed disadvantaged children who grow up to be adequate or even creative citizens in contrast to those who fail to develop adequately (become very neurotic or psychotic or delinquent, etc.). In our use of "vulnerability" there is no completely invulnerable child—we are concerned with the degree and the locus of vulnerability in relation to the intensity and quality of the stress. When the child's most vulnerable area is confronted by severe stress for that area, *some degree* of breakdown (somatic or psychological "disintegrative reaction") is likely to occur even though the child does not become delinquent or mentally ill. From another point of view everyone may be said to be vulnerable to the hydrogen bomb. Vulnerability to poverty conditions, then, will vary with the individual child's constitutional strength, the strengths in the family (which vary widely even in the ghetto), specific supports the child may find in the neighborhood (as two children in our sample "adopted" other mothers who gave them much support), and the particular pattern of stress to which the child is exposed. Eleanor Pavenstedt (1967) and Robert Coles (1967) have documented strengths in some children and their families that made it possible for them to cope with stress. Pavenstedt also described the characteristics of the most stressed and most vulnerable children and families.

Chapter 7

1 Several trends have contributed to an assumption of permanence of traits genetically determined, foremost, the gulf between experimental and longitudinal research. Experimental research generally assumes the permanence of behavior recorded at a given time in a given situation (no matter how strange, inhibiting, or unintelligible to the child). This has also been true by and large of assumptions about the results of intelligence testing despite the mass of evidence from Klineberg's (1935) study of effects of improved schooling on Negro intelligence, Skeels and Skodak's (1938) study of changes in IQ after improved stimulation, through Bayley's (1949), Sontag, Baker, and Nelson's (1958), and Moriarty's longitudinal studies of changes in IQ over years. Misuse of statistics as discussed by R. Rao has also contributed to support of the myth of permanence of the IQ: subgroups, one of which changes in an upward direction while another changes in the opposite direction, are ignored when heterogeneous groups are massed into one large group. Resistance of experimentalists to far more intensive (and extensive over time) data on changes in IQ from therapy cases is also involved.

2 Regression in the sense of disintegrative reactions to stress occurs in some infants who are neurologically immature or physiologically unstable. Some children "outgrow" this tendency whereas it persists or even worsens in others.

3 Harlow's work on the tactile element in love between mother and baby monkeys was important for its effect in correcting an overemphasis on oral aspects of the mother–baby relationship. But it is far from the comprehensive

formulations of either Bowlby (1958) or Murphy (1964) and others. (See chap. 6 in Stone, Smith, and Murphy (1973.)

4 See Stone, Smith, and Murphy 1973, p. 984, for a brief discussion of separation. An individual infant's reaction to separation is influenced by many conditions: realistic dependence on the mother related to maturity of self-management; range of experience with other caregivers; attendant circumstances such as simultaneous removal from the familiar setting of home and degree of strangeness of the new setting; previous experiences with strangers and strangeness, and so on.

5 Mittelmann's discussions of motility in *Psychoanalytic Study of the Child,* vol. 9, have brought the motor urge to a level of emphasis parallel to the classic emphasis on the oral drive. Erikson's discussion in *Childhood and Society* focuses attention on the contributions to the ego—the achievement of autonomy—contributed by motor mastery as well as achievement of sphincter control.

6 The views expressed here owe much to the work of the Berkeley studies including my own brief participation in the summers of 1938 and 1947. Especially relevant are the reports by Herbert and Lois Stolz (pp. 27 ff.), Jean Macfarlane (pp. 426 ff.), and Mary C. Jones and Paul Mussen (pp. 156–64) in Jones, Bayley, and Macfarlane's *Course of Human Development.*

7 Little attention has been given to the discovery of new talents as the child matures and the release of energy as well as improved self-image that may result.

8 Gesell long ago emphasized alternations of equilibrium and phases of disequilibrium, but these were seen too narrowly in our opinion.

9 The sometimes temporary fat stage at the time of puberty is generally not understood, although Stolz and Stolz documented and discussed this a generation ago (1944, *Adolescent problems related to somatic variation,* Yearbook of the National Society for the Study of Education, 43, pt. 1, pp. 81–99).

10 Situational variations in behavior were discussed by G. and L. B. Murphy in 1935 in C. Murchison, ed., *A Handbook of Social Psychology.* Also, in 1937 I documented a rather dramatic case of variation in behavior of a preschool girl in *Social Behavior and Child Personality.*

11 Shy Joyce was observed over a period of three years at the Sarah Lawrence Nursery School, then interviewed by me when she was fourteen, a leader in high school (see Murphy 1941).

12 Dr. Donald Winnicott demonstrated his "Squiggle" interview method in a session with Chester when he visited the Menninger Foundation in 1961.

Chapter 8 (Part I)

1 Virginia Apgar's 1953 scale is an appraisal of five easily checked aspects of functioning at birth: heart rate, respiration, muscle tone, reflex responsiveness, skin color. The overall score on this scale has been found useful in

predicting, for instance, later attention. Hoopes (1967) found no one symptom significantly differentiating between vulnerable and invulnerable children, but groups of more than three symptoms did differ significantly. Relevant here is the otherwise healthy and well-equipped blind or deaf child who with adequate external supports becomes competent and happy—a picture I have personally observed in good schools for deaf children. Chapter 2 in Stone, Smith, and Murphy (1973) reviews prenatal and perinatal development, with selected reports on human and subhuman newborns. Steinschneider's discussion of developmental psychophysiology (chap. 1 in Brackbill and Thompson 1967) emphasizes the importance of physiological factors in selective responses to the environment. Sontag's (1963) discussion of somatopsychic aspects of personality and body function reviews research findings on the physiological basis of psychological functioning.

2 Our concept of vulnerability has evolved by a series of steps beginning with my observations in 1932–34 at Speyer School (Murphy 1937); continuing in greater detail at the Sarah Lawrence Nursery School, especially from 1937 to 1944 (Lerner and Murphy 1941; see my outline of temperament in the chapter on sensory play); and finally in Topeka the observations of a group of children from infancy to adolescence.

At the beginning of our preschool study, we had not formulated our plans in terms of studying "vulnerability, stress, and resilience." We wanted to study children's ways of coping, of dealing with their problems, recognizing that all children have developmental problems, obstacles, challenges, and difficulties. These we saw as contributing to anxiety, which could in turn add to the problems with which some children had to cope; anxiety pushed some children to seek new solutions. Our own studies of East Coast middle-class children and Macfarlane's studies on the West Coast (1971) had shown the universality of problems and the frequency of temporary symptoms.

During the 1930s and 1940s, in medical discussions of childhood and adult disturbance, normality was seen as a polar opposite of pathology; the normal was as a rule not seen on a continuum at one end of which was what we call pathology, with a series of steps between the ends of the scale. There was thus a conceptual gulf between normal and disturbed adaptation. However, parallel with our studies in Topeka during which time we began to think in terms of a continuum of vulnerability, other investigators using widely different observations and approaches contributed to a concept of a continuum of deviation that included both the normal range and the range of pathology in an overlapping area. Among these important contributions was Roger Williams's (1956) discussion of biological individuality, Knobloch and Pasamanick's (1960) continuum of organic threat, the Leightons' (1963) gradient of degrees of mental illness related to different socioeconomic levels, and Karl Menninger's (1958) unitary concept of mental illness.

Our observations directed our attention to the importance of both an "economic" and a "dynamic" approach to the problem of vulnerability, and even more to the interaction between these, as implied in Bergman and

Escalona 1949. Mary Shirley (1939) had previously pointed to the effects on social behavior of sensitivities in premature infants; and these can now be seen in relation to other evidences of integrative difficulties related to behavior problems appearing in the development of premature children, especially when they were poorly cared for or living in a depriving environment, as Drillien (1964) has shown.

3 Interrelations between physical and emotional development are illustrated in K. M. B. Bridges's (1931) report on the social and emotional development of the preschool child. Along with group findings, she describes the transition of a seclusive and inhibited emotional child into a normal sociable and expressive child, simultaneous with weight gain and a surge in physical development. Even at the Fels Institute, where outstanding pioneer studies of development of intelligence (Sontag, Baker, and Nelson 1958), individual patterns in autonomic functioning (Lacey et al. 1962), and influences of parental behavior (Baldwin et al. 1945) have been carried out during the last thirty years, we have not yet been provided with studies in which the physiological, psychological, and environmental factors are analyzed in dynamic relation to each other.

4 Colicky and crying babies are often seen in relation to maternal handling (Stewart 1953). But other relevant factors, such as gastric hypersecretion, are discussed by Mirsky (1953).

5 The tendency toward variability in the level of quality of cognitive integration as well as vulnerability to loss of integration in other zones was discussed a generation ago by Bender (1953) in her reports on characteristics of children later diagnosed as schizophrenic. She described the general "maturational lag" and the pathology or lack of integration in behavior "at every level and in every area of patterning within the central nervous system," including the vegetative, motor, perceptual, intellectual, emotional, and social zones. While Greenacre's (1952) concept of a "predisposition to anxiety" was tied to birth trauma, we believe this predisposition may result from any combination of prenatal or perinatal factors contributing to functional difficulties, imbalances, or instability, including high autonomic reactivity as discussed above (see also Stone, Smith, and Murphy 1973, pp. 468–84).

6 Cross-sectional studies of single variables or small groups of variables provide concepts whose implications can be seen only in studies of the total development of the personality. For instance, studies of autonomic reactivity do not generally include data on subjective concomitants of different expressions of autonomic variability or the relations of these to behavior. But Lacey et al. (1963) have indicated some correlates of autonomic response patterns.

7 Donald had highly selective responses to different degrees or qualities of stimulation in the same zone. Ambivalence developed from the simultaneous presence of positive and negative responses to the same modality of stimulation can contribute to conflict (Shevrin and Toussieng 1962).

8 Ritvo (1963) and his colleagues presented the most comprehensive research report on interactions of multiple constitutional and environmental factors in development.

9 High sensitivity may be coupled with high activity level and drive to mastery, as with Terry (who majored in psychology in college) or high fantasy, as with Greg (whose main interests later were in art and literature), or with tendencies to motor inhibition when exposed to stimulation excessive for his tolerance, as with Donald.

10 Bergman and Escalona's (1949) discussion of unusual sensitivities deals with records of therapy patients and was paralleled by Escalona's observations of sensitivities in normal infants. Escalona (1968) focused on the differences in experience that are characteristic of high-activity and low-activity infants.

11 The procedure here was as follows: since the psychiatrist had limited available time, I reviewed in detail his reports of the children, then ranked the children on global vulnerability in terms of his reports. These rankings were then checked carefully in consultation with the psychiatrist who had seen the children, and revisions were made to conform to his judgment of the overall vulnerability of each child.

12 It may be a matter of chance that in this sample there were more emotional disturbances among mothers than among fathers.

13 Many important clinical observations have a bearing here: Spitz noted in his study, *Anaclitic depression* (1946) that *different infants reacted with different degrees of severity and reversibility to separation from the mother,* and that the most severe reactions were among the infants who had had the "best" mothering. Moreover, in certain traditional foundling homes where infant mortality rates are usually high, there are still infants who survive, or do not develop marasmus or other pathology. In such instances we may be seeing *adaptational differences* related to previous experience ("good" or "less good" mothering); differences in strength of autonomy; and also in basic equipment, sturdiness, drive, etc.

14 Why should we go to the trouble of exploring vulnerability in these different ways? Why it is not enough to rely solely on the evaluation of inadequacies in the integrative functioning of the ego, since it tells us so much? We have found that the needs of a child within the normal range, as well as the needs of a disturbed child can be better understood and therefore better met if we can understand not only the factors in vulnerable ego functioning at a given age, but also the difference between acquired (and possibly reversible) deficiencies or disturbances, and persistent primary factors in vulnerability. Limitations in understanding have arisen from lack of recognition of an enormous range of *early tendencies that increase the child's problems in any or most environments.* Similarly, it is necessary to understand the interplay of these constitutional patterns with the family and specific aspects of the mother's style, strengths, and limitations.

Chapter 8 (Part II)

1 Prior to joining the Menninger Foundation staff, Dr. Rousey had formulated a series of hypotheses suggesting systematic and predictable relationships between a number of developmental and/or environmental conflicts and misuse of speech sounds. These hypotheses were subsequently validated by me against clinical data summarized from observations by independent examiners that were unavailable to Dr. Rousey when he made his predictions. Dr. Rousey's hypotheses and details of a validation study are presented in Rousey and Moriarty 1965.

2 In her earlier study of vulnerability on infants and preschool children, Dr. Grace Heider (1966) observed that vulnerability could be seen in different aspects of behavior and in different functional areas, most frequently in speech and motor performance. Problems or deviance in infant vocalization were reflected in relatively lower scores on verbal tasks of the Gesell Developmental Schedules, in unusual oral activity of a nonvocal nature, in slow speech acquisition, and in a distinct preference for self-expression of needs through motor channels. Such infants were also likely to show high drive and high sensory sensitivity. In those with such a combination of behavioral traits, vulnerabilities were likely to persist over time, being seen in the preschool years in articulatory, voice, or rhythm deviations, and in motor inhibition and/or loss of motor coordination at times of emotional stress. Ordinarily perceptually alert, eager, active youngsters, such children appeared to suffer from conflict between their urgencies for self-expression and their capacities to organize and control their behavior. Dr. Heider pointed out that vulnerability arose from both internal constitutional or dispositional and environmental handicaps or stresses, and from management of the interaction between the two.

3 This typical or normal sequence of developing vocal, verbal, speech, and language skills is lucidly described by Daniel Boone (1965), and is now generally accepted by most experts in the speech field, as is indicated by discussion in most basic texts on speech development, such as Van Riper (1954) and others.

4 Rousey and Toussieng (1964, p. 4) differentiated between speech and language as follows: "Speech is meant to refer to sounds as they are technically called phonemes, which when used together in certain accepted ways then produce verbal language. Verbal language refers to the symbolic meanings attached to the same groupings."

5 Drive level or external cathexis was defined as "the degree to which an infant was reaching out perceptually or physically toward the external world; the extent of his interests in bodily activity, for example in the use and mastery of a new locomotor skill, and the extent of his interests in his body as a perceptual object." Even Vivian, though rated low in drive level, was perceptually alert and could at times be motorically vigorous when she was not overwhelmed by her more dominant older sister.

6 This is not to deny that in at least two cases there was in later years considerable friction between mother and child. The point here is that there was apparently enough continuity and warmth in the early years within the family circles so that speech was not impaired, perhaps because in both cases, the children themselves were inclined to temper realistic stress by stoical acceptance.

Chapter 9 (Part II)

1 Differences reported here were significant statistically when the Mann-Whitney U Technique was applied. This was impressive, especially since the numbers of children were very small, and the ratings on which the statistics were based were made by several different members of the project staff at several different developmental periods in the children's lives.

2 This analysis was made by Dr. Sylvia Ginsparg.

3 These ratings were made earlier as a part of a study of the relationship between ESP potential and creativity. See A. Moriarty and Gardner Murphy, "Some thoughts about prerequisite conditions or states in creativity and paranormal experience," *Journal American Society for Psychical Research* 61, no. 3 (July 1967).

Chapter 11

1 The sample, as noted, excluded all infants with evidence of defect or retardation. Thus Helen's vulnerability was mild compared with what would be found in an unselected sample.

2 Dr. Joan Davidson noted the extensive representation of the mouth, tongue, and glottis in the sensory cortex of the cerebrum and wonders whether there might not have been a larger area of this cortex than was typical for other infants.

3 Dr. Morton Leeds suggested that several tendencies implied neurological immaturity or problems.

4 This phase of observations continued over seven months and included a second party organized for the children in this study; a series of sessions with several psychologists, during which a number of structured and nonstructured projective tests were given (AM); a series of MLT play sessions (LM); three play-interviews with a psychiatrist (KB); a couple of interviews with Helen's mother (GH); and incidental observations. Additional sessions with the Engel Insight Test for Children and the Witkin Perception test were also included at this phase.

References

Ainsworth, Mary D. S., and Bell, S. M. 1969. Some contemporary patterns of mother–infant interaction in the feeding situation. In *Stimulation in early infancy*, ed. J. A. Ambrose. London: Academic Press.

———; Bell, Silvia M. V.; and Stayton, Donelda J. 1971. Individual differences in strange-situation behavior of one-year-olds. In *The origins of human social relations*, ed. H. R. Schaffer. London: Academic Press (excerpted in Stone, Smith, and Murphy 1973, pp. 1150 ff.).

———; Bell, Silvia M. V.; and Stayton, Donelda J. 1972. Individual differences in the development of some attachment behaviors. *Merrill-Palmer Quarterly of Behavior and Development* 18, no. 2.

Alpert, Augusta. 1959. Reversibility of pathological fixations associated with maternal deprivation in infancy. *Psychoanalytic Study of the Child* 4. New York: International Universities Press.

———; Neubauer, Peter B.; and Weil, Annamarie P. 1956. Unusual variations in drive endowment. *Psychoanalytic Study of the Child* 11. New York: International Universities Press.

Ames, L. B.; Learned, J.; Metraux, R. W.; and Walker, R. N. 1952. *Child Rorschach responses: Developmental trends from two to ten years.* New York: Hoeber.

Apgar, Virginia. 1953. A proposal for a new method of evaluation of the newborn infant. *Anesthesia and Analgesia* 32: 260–67.

Baldwin, Alfred L. et al. 1945. Patterns of parent behavior. *Psychological Monographs* 58, no. 3.

Barker, Roger G. 1968. *Ecological psychology.* Stanford, Calif.: Stanford University Press.

———; Barker, Louise S.; and Ragle, D. D. M. 1967. The churches of Midwest, Kansas, and Yoredale, Yorkshire: Their contributions to the environments of the towns. In *Change in the small community*, ed. W. Fore and L. Hodapp. New York: Friendship Press, pp. 155–89.

———; and Wright, Herbert F. 1954. *Midwest and its children: The psychological ecology of an American town.* Evanston, Ill.: Row, Peterson.

———; Wright, Herbert F.; Nall J.; and Schoggen, P. 1950. There is no class bias in our school. *Progressive Education* 27: 106–10.

———; Dembo, T.; and Lewin, K. 1943. Frustration and regression. In *Child behavior and development*, ed. R. G. Barker, J. S. Kounin, and H. F. Wright. New York: McGraw-Hill.

Barron, Frank X. 1968. *Creativity and personal freedom.* Rev. ed. Princeton, N.J.: Van Nostrand.

Bateson, Gregory. 1965. *Naven: A survey of the problems suggested by a composite picture of a New Guinea tribe drawn from three points of view.* 2nd ed. Stanford, Calif.: Stanford University Press.

435

Bayley, Nancy. 1949. Consistency and variability in the growth of intelligence from birth to eighteen years. *Journal of Genetic Psychology* 75: 165–96.

―――. 1956. Individual patterns of development. *Child Development* 57: 45–74.

Bender, Lauretta. 1953. Childhood schizophrenia. *Psychiatric Quarterly* 27: 663–81.

Benjamin, John D. 1959. The innate and the experiential in child development. In *Lectures on experimental psychiatry, Western Psychiatric Institute and Clinic*, ed. Henry J. Brosin. Pittsburgh, Pa.: University of Pittsburgh Press.

Bergman, Paul, and Escalona, Sibylle, K. 1949. Unusual sensitivities in very young children. *Psychoanalytic Study of the Child* 3 and 4. New York: International Universities Press.

Bernardez, Teresa. 1965. The feminine role. *Bulletin of the Menninger Clinic* 29: 198–205.

Bernfeld, Siegfried. 1929. *The psychology of the infant.* New York: Brentano's.

Bettelheim, Bruno. 1950. *Love is not enough.* Glencoe, Ill.: Free Press.

Biber, Barbara et al. 1952. *Life and ways of the seven-to-eight year old.* New York: Basic Books.

Birch, Herbert G., and Gussow, Joan D. 1970. *Disadvantaged children: Health, nutrition, and school failure.* New York: Grune and Stratton.

Boone, Daniel R. 1965. Infant speech and language development. *Volta Review* 67: 414–19.

Bowlby, J. 1958. The nature of the child's tie to his mother. *International Journal of Psychoanalysis* 34: pt. 5, 1–23.

Brackbill, Yvonne. 1970. Continuous stimulation and arousal level in infants: Additive effects. *Proceedings, 78th Annual Convention, American Psychological Association* 5: 271–72.

―――, and Thompson, G. G., eds. 1967. *Behavior in infancy and early childhood.* New York: Free Press.

Brazelton, T. Berry. 1961. Psychophysiologic reaction in the neonate. *Journal of Pediatrics* 58: 513–18.

―――. 1969. *Infants and mothers: Differences in development.* New York: Delacorte.

Bridges, K. M. B. 1931. *The social and emotional development of the preschool child.* London: Routledge.

Brody, Sylvia. 1956. *Patterns of mothering: Maternal influence during infancy.* New York: International Universities Press.

Bruner, Jerome S. 1968. Volition, skill and tools. In Bruner, *Processes of cognitive growth: Infancy, Heinz Werner Lecture Series, no. 3.* Worcester, Mass.: Clark University Press with Barre Publishers.

Bühler, Charlotte. 1930. *The first year of life.* New York: John Day.

Caldwell, Bettye M. 1962. Assessment of infant personality. *Merrill-Palmer Quarterly of Behavior and Development* 8, no. 2: 71–81.

Coelho, George; Hamburg, David; and Adams, John. 1974. *Coping and adaptation.* New York: Basic Books.

————, and Hamburg, D. A. 1968. Coping strategies in a new learning environment. *Archives of General Psychiatry* 9: 433–43.

Coles, Robert. 1967. *Children of crisis.* Vol. 1: *A study of courage and fear.* Vol. 2: *Migrants, sharecroppers, mountaineers.* Boston: Little, Brown.

Davidson, Joan. 1967. Infantile depression in a "normal" child. *Journal of the American Academy of Child Psychiatry* 7: 522–35.

Davis, A. 1948. *Social class influence upon learning* (The Inglis Lecture). Cambridge, Mass.: Harvard University Press.

Décarie, Thérèse G. 1965. *Intelligence and affectivity in early childhood.* New York: International Universities Press.

———— et al. 1973. *The infant's reaction to strangers.* New York: International Universities Press.

Despert, Louise. 1970. *The emotionally disturbed child.* Garden City, N.Y.: Doubleday.

Douglas, Norman. 1946. *South wind.* London: Secker and Warburg.

Drillien, Cecil M. 1964. *The growth and development of the prematurely born infant.* Baltimore: Williams and Wilkins.

Ekstein, Rudolf, and Motto, Rocco L. 1969. *From learning for love to love of learning.* New York: Brunner/Mazel.

Erikson, Erik H. 1959. Identity and the life cycle. *Psychological Issues* 1, no. 1.

————. 1964. *Childhood and Society.* Rev. ed. New York: Norton.

Escalona, Sibylle K. 1952. Emotional development in the first year of life. In *Problems of infancy and childhood: Transactions of the sixth conference, 1952.* New York: Josiah Macy, Jr. Foundation.

————. 1968. *Roots of individuality: Normal patterns of development in infancy.* Chicago: Aldine.

————, and Heider, Grace M. 1959. *Prediction and outcome: A study in child development.* New York: Basic Books.

————; Leitch, Mary; et al. 1952. *Early phases of personality development: A non-normative study of infant behavior.* Monograph, Society for Research in Child Development 17, no. 1, ser. no. 54.

————, and Leitch, Mary. Unpublished records of infant behavior, 1948–50.

————, and Moriarty, Alice E. 1961. Prediction of school-age intelligence from infant tests. *Child Development* 32: 597–605.

Fantz, Robert L. 1963. Pattern vision in newborn infants. *Science* 140: 296–97.

Federn, Paul. 1952. *Ego psychology and the psychoses.* New York: Basic Books.

Fischer, John L., and Fischer, Ann. 1963. The New Englanders of Orchard Town, U.S.A. In *Six Cultures: Studies of child rearing,* ed. Beatrice Whiting. New York: Wiley.

Fortune, Reo. 1932. *Sorcerers of Dobu: The social anthropology of the Dobu islanders of the western Pacific.* London: Routledge.

Frank, Lawrence K. 1957. Tactile communication. *Genetic Psychology Monographs* 56: 209–55.

————. 1966. *On the importance of infancy.* New York: Random House.

Freud, Anna. 1937. *The ego and the mechanisms of defense.* London: Hogarth Press.

Freud, Sigmund. 1953. *Three essays on the theory of sexuality* (1905). In *The standard edition of the complete psychological works of Sigmund Freud,* vol. 7. London: Hogarth Press.

———. 1955. *Beyond the pleasure principle* (1922). In *The standard edition of the complete psychological works of Sigmund Freud,* vol. 18. London: Hogarth Press.

Fries, Margaret E. 1944. The psychosomatic relation between mother and infant. *Psychosomatic Medicine* 6: 154–62.

———, and Woolf, Paul J. 1953. Some hypotheses on the role of the congenital activity type in personality development. *Psychoanalytic Study of the Child* 8: 48–62. New York: International Universities Press.

Fuller, Dorothy. 1974. Martha. In *Growing up in garden court,* ed. Lois B. Murphy and R. E. Switzer. New York: Child Welfare League of America.

Gardner, R. W., and Moriarty, Alice. 1968. *Personality development at preadolescence: Explorations of structure formation.* Seattle: University of Washington Press.

Garmezy, N. 1971. Vulnerability research and the issue of primary prevention. *American Journal of Orthopsychiatry* 41, no. 1: 101–16.

———, and Nuechterlein, Keith. 1972. Invulnerable children: Fact and fiction of competence and disadvantage. Unpublished paper presented at the Forty-Ninth Annual Meeting of the American Orthopsychiatric Association, 5–8 April 1972.

Gesell, Arnold. 1934. *Infant behavior: Its genesis and growth.* New York: McGraw-Hill.

———. 1943. *Infant and child in the culture of today.* New York: Harper.

———, and Ames, Louise B. 1937. Early evidences of individuality in the human infant. *Scientific Monthly* 45: 217–25.

———; Amatruda, Catherine S.; et al. 1939. *Biographies of child development; the mental growth careers of 84 infants and children.* New York: Hoeber.

———, and Ilg, Frances. 1940. *The first five years.* New York: Harper.

———, and Ilg, Frances. 1946. *The child from five to ten.* New York: Harper.

Gewirtz, Jacob L. 1965. The course of infant smiling in four childrearing environments in Israel. In *Determinants of infant behavior, III,* ed. B. M. Foss. New York: Wiley.

Gordon, Norma S., and Bell, Richard Q. 1961. Activity in the human newborn. *Psychological Reports* 9: 103–16.

Greenacre, Phyllis. 1952. *Trauma, growth and personality.* New York: Norton.

Guernsey, Martha. 1951. *Eine Genetisch Studien über Nachamung.* Summarized in C. Bühler, *Kindheit und Jugend* (1931), pp. 28–39, and in Murphy, Murphy, and Newcomb 1964.

Haan, Norma. 1963. *Proposed model of ego functioning: Coping and defense mechanisms in relation to I.Q. change.* Psychological Monographs 77, no. 8: 1–23 (whole no. 571).

Haggard, Ernest A., and von der Lippe, A. 1970. Isolated families in the mountains of Norway. In *The child in his family.* Vol. 1 of *International*

Yearbook of Child Psychiatry, ed. E. J. Anthony and C. Koupernik. New York: Wiley, pp. 465–88.

Halverson, Charles F., Jr., and Waldrop, Mary F. 1974. Relations between preschool barrier behaviors and early school-age measures of coping, imagination, and verbal development. *Developmental Psychology* 10, no. 5: 716–20.

Hamburg, David A.; Hamburg, Beatrix; and deGoza, Sydney. 1953. Adaptive problems and mechanisms in severely burned patients. *Psychiatry* 16: 1–20.

Harlow, H. 1975. Quoted in Gardner Murphy, and Morton Leeds, *Outgrowing self-deception*. New York: Basic Books, p. 19.

Harris, Thomas A. 1973. *I'm o.k., you're o.k.* New York: Avon Books.

Hartocollis, Pitsa. Rorschach responses of Topeka ten-year-olds. Unpublished paper.

Hartshorne, Hugh; May, Mark A.; and Shuttleworth, Frank K. 1930. *Studies in the nature of character.* Vol. 3 of *Studies in the organization of character.* New York: Macmillan.

Hartmann, Heinz. 1951. Ego psychology and the problem of adaptation. In *Organization and pathology of thought: Selected sources*, ed. and trans. David Rapaport. New York: Columbia University Press.

Heider, Grace M. 1966. *Vulnerability in infants and young children: A pilot study.* Genetic Psychology Monographs 73, no. 1: 1–216.

Hess, R. D. 1970. Social class and ethnic influences on socialization. In *Carmichael's manual of child psychology*, ed. P. H. Mussen. 3rd ed. New York: Wiley, 2: 457–557.

Hilgard, E., and Bower, G. 1974. *Theories of learning.* 4th ed. New York: Appleton-Century-Crofts.

Holtzman, Wayne et al. 1961. *Inkblot perception and personality.* Austin, Texas: University of Texas Press.

Honzik, Marjorie P.; Macfarlane, Jean W.; and Allen, Lucille. 1948. The stability of mental test performance between two and eighteen years. *Journal of Experimental Education* 17: 309–24.

Hoopes, Janet L. 1967. *An infant rating scale: Its validation and usefulness.* New York: Child Welfare League of America, Inc.

Hunt, J. McV. 1966. Intrinsic motivation and its role in psychological development. In *Nebraska Symposium on Motivation*, ed. David Levine. Lincoln: University of Nebraska Press.

Inkeles, A. 1968. Society, social structure, and child socialization. In *Socialization and society*, ed. J. A. Clausen. Boston: Little, Brown, pp. 73–129.

Jacobson, Edith. 1954. The self and the object world. *Psychoanalytic Study of the Child* 9: 75–127. New York: International Universities Press.

Jahoda, Marie. 1958. *Current concepts of positive mental health.* New York: Basic Books.

James, William. 1962. *Psychology: Briefer course.* New York: H. Holt and Collier Books. Originally published in 1892.

Jersild, A. T., and Holmes, F. B. 1935. *Children's fears.* Child Development Monographs, no. 20. New York: Bureau of Publications, Teachers College.

Jones, H. E., AND Jones, Mary C. 1938. Adolescent study. Unpublished case study prepared by Lois B. Murphy.

Jones, Mary C. 1924. The elimination of children's fears. *Journal of Experimental Psychology* 7: 382–90.

———. 1926. The development of early behavior patterns in young children. Pediatric Seminar and *Journal of Genetic Psychology* 33: 537–85.

Kagan, Jerome. 1969. Continuity in cognitive development during the first year. *Merrill-Palmer Quarterly of Behavior and Development* 15: 101–19.

———, and Moss, Howard A. 1962. *Birth to maturity: A study in psychological development.* New York: Wiley.

Kessen, W.; Haith, M. M.; and Salapatek, Philip H. 1970. Human infancy: A bibliography and guide. In *Carmichael's manual of child psychology,* ed. Paul H. Mussen, vol. 1. New York: Wiley.

Khan, Masud M. M. R. 1964. The concept of cumulative trauma. *Psychoanalytic Study of the Child* 18. New York: International Universities Press.

Klein, C. Melanie. 1932. *The Psychoanalysis of children.* New York: Norton.

———. 1936. Weaning. In *On the bringing up of children,* ed. J. Rickman. London: Kegan Paul, pp. 31–56.

Klineberg, O. 1935. *Negro intelligence and selective migration.* New York: Columbia University Press.

Korner, Anneliese F. 1971. Individual differences at birth: Implications for early experience and later development. *American Journal of Orthopsychiatry* 41: 608–19.

Krech, D.; Rosenzweig, M. R.; and Bennett, E. L. 1966. Environmental impoverishment, social isolation, and changes in brain chemistry and anatomy. *Physiological Behavior* 1: 99–109.

Lacey, John I. 1959. Psychophysiological approaches to the evaluation of psychotherapeutic process and outcome. In *Research in psychotherapy,* ed. E. A. Rubinstein and M. B. Parloff. Washington, D.C.: American Psychological Association, pp. 160–208.

———; Kagan, Jerry; Lacey, B. C.; and Moss, Howard A. 1962. The visceral level: Situational determinants and behavioral correlates of autonomic response patterns. In *Expression of emotions in man,* ed. P. J. Knapp. New York: International Universities Press.

———, and Van Lehn, Ruth. 1952. Differential emphases in somatic response to stress. *Psychosomatic Medicine* 14, no. 2.

Lambo, Thomas A. 1961. Growth of African children. In *Pan African Psychiatric Conference,* ed. T. A. Lambo. Abeokuta, Nigeria: Government Printer, Hadan.

Lazarus, Richard S. 1966. *Psychological stress and the coping process.* New York: McGraw-Hill.

Leighton, Dorothea C. et al. 1963. *The character of danger: Psychiatric symptoms in selected communities.* The Stirling County Study of Psychiatric Disorder and Sociocultural Environment, vol. 3. New York: Basic Books.

Leitch, Mary, and Escalona, Sibylle K. 1949. The reactions of infants to stress.

Psychoanalytic Study of the Child 3/4. New York: International Universities Press.

Lerner, Eugene, and Murphy, Lois B., eds. 1941. *Methods for the study of personality in young children.* Monograph, Society for Research in Child Development 6, no. 4.

Lester, Marianne. Personality patterns in Rorschachs of women college freshmen. Unpublished manuscript.

LeVine, Robert A. 1970. Cross-cultural study in child psychology. In *Carmichael's manual of child psychology,* ed. P. H. Mussen. 3d ed. New York: Wiley, 2: 559–612.

Levy, David M. 1966. *Maternal overprotection.* 2d ed. New York: Norton.

Lewis, C. 1946. *Children of the Cumberland.* New York: Columbia University Press.

Liss, E. 1937. Emotional and biological factors involved in learning processes. *American Journal of Orthopsychiatry* 7: 483–88.

Lorenz, Konrad. 1950. The comparative method in studying innate behavior patterns. In *Society for Experimental Biology, physiological mechanisms in animal behavior.* New York: Academic Press, pp. 221–68.

Lynd, Robert S., and Lynd, Helen M. 1929. *Middletown.* New York: Harcourt.

McCarthy, D. 1954. Language development in children. In *Manual of child psychology,* ed. L. Carmichael. 2d ed. New York: Wiley.

Macfarlane, Jean W. 1939. The guidance study. *Sociometry* 2: 1–23.

––––––. 1963. From infancy to adulthood. *Childhood Education* 39: 336–42.

––––––; Allen, Lucille; and Honzik, Marjorie P. 1954. *A developmental study of the behavior problems of normal children between twenty-one months and fourteen years.* Berkeley, Calif.: University of California Press. Also in *The course of human development* (1971), ed. Mary Jones et al. Waltham, Mass.: Xerox College Publishing, pp. 183–88.

McFate, Marguerite Q., and Orr, Frances G. 1948. Through adolescence with the Rorschach. *Rorschach Research Exchange and Journal of Projective Techniques* 13, no. 3: 302–19.

Mattick, Ilse. 1967. Children of disorganized lower-class families. In *The drifters,* ed. E. Pavenstedt. Boston: Little, Brown.

––––––, and Murphy, Lois B. 1971. Cognitive disturbances in young children. In *Cognitive deficits,* vol. 2, ed. Jerome Hellmuth. New York: Brunner/Mazel.

Mead, Margaret. 1930. *Growing up in New Guinea.* New York: Morrow.

––––––. 1935. *Sex and temperament in three primitive societies.* New York: Morrow.

––––––. 1942. Balinese character. In Bateson, Gregory, and Mead, Margaret, *Balinese character.* New York Academy of Sciences.

Menninger, Karl. 1954. Psychological aspects of the organism under stress. *Journal of the American Psychoanalytic Association* 2: 67–106.

–––––– et al. 1958. The unitary concept of mental illness. *Bulletin of the Menninger Clinic* 22: 1–12.

–––––– et al. 1963. *The vital balance.* New York: Viking.

Mirsky, I. A. 1953. Psychoanalysis and the biological sciences. In *Twenty years of psychoanalysis*, ed. F. Alexander and H. Ross. New York: Norton.

Mittelmann, B. 1954. Motility in infants, children and adults. *Psychoanalytic Study of the Child* 9. New York: International Universities Press.

Morgan, C. J. 1964. An individual action-research method for intensive exploration of adaptive difficulties in the prepuberty stage. *The Journal of Psychology* 58: 439–58.

Morgan, George A., and Ricciuti, Henry N. 1969. Infants' responses to strangers during the first year. In *Determinants of infant behavior*, vol. 4., ed. B. M. Foss. New York: Wiley.

Moriarty, Alice E. 1961. *Coping patterns of preschool children in response to intelligence tests demands*. Genetic Psychology Monographs 1964: 3–127.

———. 1966. *Constancy and IQ change: A clinical view of relationships between tested intelligence and personality*. Springfield, Ill.: Thomas.

———, and Murphy, Gardner. 1967. An experimental study of ESP potentiality and its relationship to creativity in a group of normal children. *Journal of the American Society of Psychical Research* 61: 326–38.

———, and Toussieng, Povl. 1976. *Adolescence in a time of transition*. New York: Grune & Stratton.

Morrow, J. T. 1965. Providing growth experiences. *Bulletin of the Menninger Clinic* 28: 309–23.

Moss, Howard H. 1967. Sex, age, and state as determinants of mother–infant interaction. *Merrill-Palmer Quarterly of Behavior and Development* 13: 19–36.

Murphy, Gardner; Murphy, Lois B.; and Newcomb, Theodore M. 1964. *Experimental social psychology*. Reprint. Westport, Conn.: Greenwood Press.

Murphy, Lois B. 1937. *Social behavior and child personality: An exploratory study of some roots of sympathy*. New York: Columbia University Press.

———. 1940. Interiorization of family experience by normal preschool children, as revealed by projective methods. *Journal of the Psychological League* 4: 3–4.

———. 1941. Joyce from two to five. *Progressive Education* 18: 46–53.

———. 1956. *Colin: A normal child*. Vol. 1: *Methods for the study of personality in young children*. Vol. 2: *Personality in young children*. New York: Basic Books.

———. 1961. Preventive implications of development in the preschool years. In *Prevention of mental disorders in children*, ed. G. Caplan. New York: Basic Books.

——— and Associates. 1962. *The widening world of childhood: Paths toward mastery*. New York: Basic Books.

———. 1964. Some aspects of the first relationship. *International Journal of Psychoanalysis* 45: 31–44.

———. 1970. The problem of defense and the concept of coping. In *The child in his family*, ed. E. James Anthony and Cyrille Koupernik. New York: Wiley.

———. Later outcomes of early infant and mother relationships. Paper presented at 1971 Annual Meeting of American Orthopsychiatric Association.

———. 1972 a. Infant play and cognitive development. In *Play and development*, ed. Maria Piers. New York: Norton.

———. 1972 ᵇ. Developmental integration in childhood. *Annals of the New York Academy of Sciences* 192: 253–59.

———. 1973 ᵃ. Some mutual contributions of psychoanalysis and child development. In *Psychoanalysis and contemporary science*, vol. 2, ed. Benjamin G. Rubinstein. New York: Macmillan.

———. 1973 ᵇ. The variability of infants' reactions to pain. *Clinical Proceedings, Children's Hospital National Medical Center* 29, no. 1: 3–7.

———. 1974. Coping, vulnerability, and resilience. In *Coping and adaptation*, ed. D. Hamburg and G. Coelho. New York: Basic Books.

———, and Gupta, Vimla. Vulnerability, stress and resilience. In process.

———, and Murphy, Gardner. 1935. The influence of social situations upon the behavior of children. In *Handbook of social psychology*, ed. C. Murchison. Worcester, Mass.: Clark University Press.

Neilon, Patricia. 1948. Shirley's babies after fifteen years: A personality study. *Journal of Genetic Psychology* 73: 175–86.

Olson, W. C. 1959. *Child development*. Boston: Heath.

Pasamanick, Benjamin. 1954. The epidemiology of behavior disorders of childhood. In *Neurology and psychiatry in childhood, Proceedings of the Association for Research in Nervous and Mental Diseases* 34: 397–403.

———, and Knobloch, Hilda. 1956. Pregnancy experience and the development of behavior disorder in children. *The American Journal of Psychiatry* 112, no. 8: 613–18.

Pavenstedt, Eleanor, ed. 1967. *The drifters: Children of disorganized lower-class families*. Boston: Little, Brown.

Piaget, Jean. 1952. *The origins of intelligence in children*. New York: International Universities Press.

Proshansky, Harold M.; Ittelson, William H.; and Rivlin, Jeanne G. 1970. *Environmental psychology: Man and his physical setting*. New York: Holt.

Provence, Sally, and Lipton, Rose E. 1962. *Infants in institutions*. New York: International Universities Press.

Rapaport, David, ed. and trans. 1951. *Organization and pathology of thought: Selected sources*. New York: Columbia University Press.

Raushenbush, Esther, and Murphy, Lois B., eds. 1960. *Achievement in the college years: A record of intellectual and personal growth*. New York: Harper.

Rheingold, Harriet L. 1961. The effect of environmental stimulation upon social and exploratory behavior in the human infant. In *Determinants of infant behavior*, ed., B. M. Foss. New York: Wiley, pp. 143–77.

Richmond, J. B., and Lipton, E. L. 1959. Some aspects of the neurophysiology of the newborn and their implications for child development. In *Dynamic psychopathology in childhood*, ed. Lucie Jessner and Eleanor Pavenstedt. New York: Grune and Stratton.

Richmond, B., and Lustman, S. 1955. Autonomic function in the neonate. I. Implications for psychosomatic theory. *Psychosomatic Medicine* 17: 269–75.

Ritvo, Samuel et al. 1963. Some relations of constitution, environment, and personality as observed in a longitudinal study of child development: Case

report. In *Modern perspectives in child development*, ed. Albert J. Solnit and
Sally A. Provence. New York: International Universities Press.

Robertson, James. 1970. *Young children in hospital.* 2d ed. with a postscript.
London: Tavistock Publications; 1st ed., 1958.

Rousey, Clyde L. 1971. The psychopathology of articulation and voice disorders.
In *Handbook of speech pathology and audiology*, ed. L. E. Travis. New York:
Appleton-Century-Crofts, pp. 816–19.

———. Forthcoming. *Psychiatric assessment by speech and hearing behavior.*
Springfield, Ill.: Charles C. Thomas.

———, and Moriarty, A. E. 1965. *Diagnostic implications of speech sounds.*
Springfield, Ill.: Charles C. Thomas.

———, and Toussieng, Povl. 1964. Contributions of a speech pathologist to the
psychiatric examination of children. *Mental Hygiene* 48: 566–75.

Rust, Metta. 1932. *The effect of resistance on intelligence test scores of young
children.* New York: Teachers' College Contributions to Education.

Sandler, Joseph. Trauma, strain, and development. Unpublished paper.

Schachtel, Ernest C. 1959. *Metamorphoses.* New York: Basic Books.

Scheibel, M. E., and Scheibel, A. B. 1964. Some neural substrates of postnatal
development. In *Review of child development research*, vol. 1, ed. M. L.
Hoffman and L. W. Hoffman. New York: Russell Sage Foundation.

Sheldon, William J. 1940. *The varieties of human physique.* New York: Harper.

Shevrin, Howard, and Toussieng, Povl. 1962. Conflicts over tactile experience in
emotionally disturbed children. *Journal of the American Academy of Child
Psychology* 1, no. 4: 564–89.

Shirley, Mary M. 1930. *The first two years of life.* New York: John Day.

———. 1931–33. *The first two years: A study of twenty-five babies.* Vol. 3.
Minneapolis: The University of Minnesota Press.

———. 1938. Development of immature babies during their first two years.
Child Development 9: 347–60.

———. 1939. A behavior syndrome characterizing prematurely-born children.
Child Development 10: 115–28.

Skeels, H. M., and Skodak, H. 1938. *Study of environmental stimulation: An
orphanage preschool project.* Studies in Child Welfare, vol. 15, no. 4. Des
Moines: University of Iowa Press.

Solnit, Albert J., and Provence, Sally, eds. 1963. *Modern perspectives in child
development.* New York: International Universities Press.

Sontag, Lester W. 1963. Somatopsychics of personality and body function. *Vita
Humana* 6, nos. 1–2: 1–10.

———; Baker, C.; and Nelson, V. 1958. *Mental growth and personality development.* Society for Research in Child Development Monographs 23, no. 2.

———, and Kagan, Jerome. 1953. The emergence of intellectual achievement
motives. *American Journal of Orthopsychiatry* 33, no. 3: 532–35.

———, and Wallace, R. F. 1935. The movement response of the human fetus to
sound stimuli. *Child Development* 6: 253–58.

Spitz, René A. 1945. Hospitalism. *Psychoanalytic Study of the Child* 1. New
York: International Universities Press.

————. 1946. Anaclitic depression: An inquiry into the genesis of psychiatric conditions in early childhood. *Psychoanalytic Study of the Child* 2. New York: International Universities Press.

————. 1972. Fundamental education. In *Play and development*, ed. Maria Piers. New York: Norton.

————; Emde, Robert N.; and Metcalf, David. Further prototypes of ego formation: A working paper from a research project on early ego development. Excerpted in Stone, Smith, and Murphy 1973.

Spock, Benjamin. 1946. *Common sense book of baby and child care.* New York: Duell.

Srole, Leo et al. 1962. *The midtown Manhattan study.* Vol. 1: *Mental Health in the Metropolis.* New York: McGraw-Hill.

Stayton, Donelda J.; Hogan, Roberta; and Ainsworth, Mary D. 1971. Infant obedience and maternal behavior: The origins of socialization reconsidered. *Child Development* 42: 1057–69.

Steinschneider, Alfred. 1967. Developmental psychophysiology. In *Infancy and early childhood*, ed. Yvonne Brackbill. New York: Free Press.

Stevenson, Harold W. 1970. *Learning in Children.* In *Carmichael's manual of child psychology*, ed. Paul H. Mussen. New York: Wiley, 1: 849–938.

Stewart, Ann. 1953. Excessive crying in infants—a family disease. In *Problems of infancy and childhood, transactions of the sixth conference, 1952*, ed. Milton J. E. Senn. New York: Josiah Macy, Jr. Foundation.

Stewart, Charles W. 1967. *Adolescent religion: A developmental study of the religion of youth.* Nashville: Abingdon Press.

Stolz, Herbert R., and Stolz, Lois M. 1971. Somatic development of adolescent boys. In *The course of human development*, ed. Mary C. Jones et al. Waltham, Mass.: Xerox College Publishing, pp. 27–42.

Stone, L. Joseph; Smith, Henrietta T.; Murphy, Lois B., eds. 1973. *The competent infant: Research and commentary.* New York: Basic Books.

Sullivan, Harry S. 1953. *The interpersonal theory of psychiatry.* New York: Norton.

Tavistock Study Group on Mother–Infant Interaction. 1959. *Determinants of infant behavior*, vol. 2, ed. B. M. Foss. New York: Wiley, 1961.

Tennes, K. H. et al. 1972. The stimulus barrier in early infancy; An exploration of some formulations by John Benjamin. *Psychoanalysis and Contemporary Science* 1: 206–34.

Terman, Lewis M. 1925. *Genetic studies of genius.* Vol. 1. *The mental and physical traits of a thousand gifted children.* Stanford, Calif.: Stanford University Press.

————, and Miles, Catherine C. 1936. *Sex and personality.* New York: Russell and Russell; 2d ed., 1968.

Thomas, A.; Birch, H. G.; Chess, S.; Hertzig, M. E.; and Korn, S. 1963. *Behavioral individuality in early childhood.* New York: New York University Press.

Thompson, William D., Jr., and Sontag, Lester W. 1956. Behavioral effect in the offspring of rats subjected to audiogenic seizure during the gestational period. *Journal of Comparative and Physiological Psychology* 49: 454–56.

Toynbee, Arnold. 1972. *A study of history.* New York: McGraw-Hill. Abridged ed., London: Oxford University Press, 1960.

Tuddenham, Read D., and Snyder, Margaret M. 1954. Physical growth of California boys and girls from birth to eighteen years. *Child Development* 1, no. 2: 183–364. Berkeley, Calif.: University of California Press.

Van der Waals, Hermann. 1965. Problems of narcissism. *Bulletin of the Menninger Clinic* 29: 293–311.

Van Riper, C. 1954. *Speech correction: Principles and methods.* Englewood Cliffs, New Jersey: Prentice-Hall.

Washburn, Ruth W. 1929. A Study of the smiling and laughing of infants in the first year of life. *Genetic Psychology Monographs* 6, no. 5: 397–535.

Weiss, L. A. 1934. Differential variations in the amount of activity of newborn infants under continuous light and sound stimulation. *University of Iowa Studies in Child Welfare* 9, no. 4.

Weissenberg, L. Unpublished paper.

Werner, Heinz. 1957. The concept of development from a comparative and organismic point of view. In *The concept of development,* ed. D. Harris. Minneapolis, Minn.: University of Minnesota Press.

———. 1964. Comparative psychology of mental development. Rev. ed. New York: International Universities Press.

White, Burton. 1969. The initial coordination of sensorimotor schemas in human infants—Piaget's ideas and the role of experience. In *Studies in cognitive development: Essays in honor of Jean Piaget,* ed. David Elkind and John H. Flavell. New York: Oxford University Press.

———; Castle, P. W.; and Held, R. 1964. Observations on the development of visually-directed reaching. *Child Development* 35: 349–64.

White, Robert W. 1974. Strategies of adaptation. In *Coping and adaptation,* ed. George V. Coelho; David A. Hamburg; and John E. Adams. New York: Basic Books.

Whiting, Beatrice E. 1963. *Six cultures: Studies of child rearing.* New York: Wiley.

Whiting, J. W. M., and Child, I. 1953. *Child training and personality: A cross-cultural study.* New Haven, Conn.: Yale University Press.

Whyte, William H., Jr. 1956. *The organization man.* New York: Simon and Schuster.

Wilder, Laura Ingalls. 1937. *On the banks of plum creek.* Rev. ed., 1953. New York: Harper.

Williams, Roger J. 1956. *Biochemical individuality.* New York: Wiley.

Wolf, Katherine M. 1952. Observation of individual tendencies in the first year of life. In *Problems of infancy and childhood: Transactions of the sixth conference, 1952,* ed. Milton J. E. Senn. New York: Josiah Macy, Jr., Foundation.

Wolff, Peter H. 1959. Observations on newborn infants. *Psychosomatic Medicine* 21: 110–18.

————. 1966. The causes, controls and organization of behavior in the neonate. *Psychological Issues* 5, no. 1.

Yarrow, Leon J. 1963. Research in dimensions of early maternal care. *Merrill-Palmer Quarterly for Behavior and Development* 9: 101–14.

————. 1964 [a]. Separation from parents during early childhood. In *Review of child development research*, vol. 1, ed. M. Hoffman and L. Hoffman. New York: Russell Sage Foundation.

————. 1964 [b]. Personality consistency and change: An overview of some conceptual and methodological issues. *Vita Humana* 7: 67–72.

———— et al. 1971. Infancy experiences and cognitive and personality development at ten years. Paper presented at the Annual Meeting of the American Orthopsychiatric Association, Washington, D.C.

————. 1972. Dimensions of early stimulation and their differential effects on infant development. *Merrill-Palmer Quarterly of Behavior and Development* 18: 205–18.

Bibliography of Coping Studies
and Related Discussions

Books and Monographs

1959   Escalona, Sibylle, and Heider, Grace. *Prediction and outcome: A study in child development.* New York: Basic Books.

1961   Moriarty, Alice E. *Coping patterns of preschool children in response to intelligence test demands.* Genetic Psychology Monographs, vol. 64:3–127.

1962   Murphy, Lois B. and associates. *The widening world of childhood: Paths toward mastery.* New York: Basic Books.

1965   Rousey, Clyde L., and Moriarty, Alice E. *Diagnostic implications of speech sounds: The reflections of developmental conflict and trauma.* Springfield, Ill.: Charles C. Thomas.

1966   Heider, Grace M. *Vulnerability in infants and young children: A pilot study.* Genetic Psychology Monographs, vols. 73–74: 265.

1966   Moriarty, Alice E. *Constancy and IQ change: A clinical view of relationships between tested intelligence and personality.* Springfield, Ill.: Charles C. Thomas.

1967   Stewart, Charles W. *Adolescent religion.* Nashville: Abingdon.

1968   Gardner, Riley, and Moriarty, Alice E. *Personality development at preadolescence: Explorations of structure formation.* Seattle, Wash.: University of Washington Press.

1970–73   Murphy, Lois B., and Leeper, Ethel. *Caring for children: Ten guidelines for day care.* Prepared for the Office of Child Development. DHEW Publication No. (OCD) 72-15, 74-1031, 1032, 1033, 1034, 1035.

In process   Wiemers, Irene H., and Murphy, Lois B. Individual differences at four weeks and four months of age. (monograph)

Symposia

1957   Murphy, Lois B. Cultural sequences, expectancies and patterns in relation to childhood stress. *Human Development Bulletin,* pp. 44–71. Eighth Annual Symposium, University of Chicago.

1957   Murphy, Lois B. A longitudinal study of children's coping methods and styles. *Proceedings of the Fifteenth International Congress of Psychology, Brussels,* pp. 433–36.

1958   Murphy, Lois B. What is an emotionally disturbed child and how does he get that way? *The emotionally disturbed child*, pp. 11–35. Fourth Annual North Carolina Conference on Handicapped Children, Duke University.

1960   Murphy, Lois B. (with Gardner Murphy). *The Child as potential.* One of 31 studies included in *The nation's children*, an outgrowth of White House Conference on Children and Youth. Vol. 2, *Development and education*, pp. 207–24. New York: Columbia University Press.

1960   Murphy, Lois B. Preventive implications of development in the preschool years. *Prevention of mental disorders in children*, ed. Gerald Caplan, pp. 218–59. New York: Basic Books.

1963   Murphy, Lois B. Self-management capacities in children. ASCD (a department of the National Education Association), *New insights and the curriculum. Yearbook 1963*, pp. 107–21.

1964   Murphy, Lois B. Factors in continuity and change in the development of adaptational style in children. *Vita Humana, the International Journal of Human Development* 7:96–114.

1965   Ginsparg, Sylvia; Moriarty, Alice E.; and Murphy, Lois B. Individual differences in young teenagers' responses to the assassination of Kennedy and their relation to previous experience. In *Children and the death of a president*, ed. Martha Wolfenstein and Gilbert Kliman, of the Albert Einstein College of Medicine. New York: Doubleday.

1965   Murphy, Lois B. Psychoanalysis and child development, Parts I and II. In *Psychoanalysis and the study of behavior*, ed. Irwin G. Sarason, pp. 134–165. New York: Van Nostrand.

1968   Murphy, Lois B. Individualization of the environment: Vulnerability Inventory. In Lourie, Reginald, and Chandler, Caroline, *Early Childhood Care*, ed. Laura Dittman. New York: Atherton.

1970   Murphy, Lois B. The problem of defense and the concept of coping. In *The child in his family*, ed. E. James Anthony and Cyrille Koupernik, pp. 65–86. New York: Wiley.

1971   Mattick, Ilse, and Murphy, Lois B. Cognitive disturbances in young children. In *Cognitive deficits*, ed. Jerome Hellmuth. Vol. 2. New York: Brunner/Mazel.

1972   Murphy, Lois B. Developmental integration in childhood. *Annals of the New York Academy of Sciences* 192:253–59.

1972   Murphy, Lois B. Infant play and cognitive development. In *Play and development*, ed. Maria Piers. New York: Norton.

1972   Murphy, Lois B., and Chandler, Caroline A. Building foundations for strength in the preschool years. In *Handbook of community mental health*, ed. Stuart Golann and Carl Eisdorfer. New York: Appleton-Century-Crofts.

1973   Murphy, Lois B. Some mutual contributions of psychoanalysis and child development. In *Psychoanalysis and contemporary science*, vol. 2.

1973   Murphy, Lois B., Basic determinants of coping style (pp. 76–77); Development in the first year of life: Ego and drive development in relation to the mother–infant tie (pp. 468–84); Later outcomes of early infant and mother relationships (pp. 1111–14); Sex differences in coping and development (pp. 1268–74). In Stone, L. Joseph; Smith, Henrietta T.; and Murphy, Lois B. *The competent infant.* New York: Basic Books.

1974   Murphy, Lois B. Coping, vulnerability and resilience in childhood. In Coelho, George V.; Hamburg, David A.; Adams, John E., *Coping and adaptation.* New York: Basic Books.

Articles

1956   Murphy, Lois B. Effects of child-rearing patterns on mental health. *Children* 3, no. 6:213–19.

1956   Murphy, Lois B. Emotional first aid for the normal child. *Childhood Education* 32:105–207.

1956   Murphy, Lois B. Emotional first aid for the young child. *Menninger Quarterly* 10, no. 1:19–22.

1957   Murphy, Lois B. Learning how children cope with their problems. *Children* 4, no. 4:132–37.

1957   Murphy, Lois B. Psychoanalysis and child development. *Bulletin Menninger Clinic.* Part 1, 21, no. 5:177–259. Part 2, 21, no. 6: 248–59.

1960   Heider, Grace M. Vulnerability in infants. *Bulletin Menninger Clinic* 24, no. 3:104–15.

1960   Heider, Grace M. What makes a good parent? *Children* 7, no. 6:207–13.

1960   Moriarty, Alice. Children's ways of coping with the intelligence test. *Bulletin Menninger Clinic* 24, no. 3:115–28.

1960   Murphy, Lois B. The child's way of coping: A longitudinal study of normal children. *Bulletin Menninger Clinic* 24, no. 3:97–104.

1960   Murphy, Lois B. Coping devices and defense mechanisms in relation to autonomous ego functions. *Bulletin Menninger Clinic* 24, no. 3:144–54.

1960   Murphy, Lois B. Pride and its relation to narcissism, autonomy and identity. *Bulletin Menninger Clinic* 24, no. 3:136–44.

1960   Toussieng, Povl W. The psychiatric examination as part of the coping study. *Bulletin Menninger Clinic* 24, no. 3:128–36.

1961   Heider, Grace M. Vulnerabilities, sources of strength, and capacity to cope in the "normal" child. *Proceedings of the XIV International Congress of Applied Psychology,* pp. 79–94. Copenhagen: Munksgaard.

1961   Moriarty, Alice E. (with Sibylle Escalona). Prediction of school-age intelligence from infant tests. *Child Development* 32:597–605.

1962   Murphy, Lois B. Needs of infants and young children: Implications of current research. *Bulletin Merrill-Palmer Institute,* pp. 37–54. From the Fourth and Fifth Annual Merrill-Palmer Conferences on Infant Development.

1962   Murphy, Lois B. World implications of early childhood needs. World Organization for Early Childhood Education (OMEP). *Report of the 9th World Assembly,* pp. 19–23. London, England.

1963   Murphy, Lois B. Problems in recognizing emotional disturbance in children. *Child Welfare* pp. 473–88.

1963   Murphy, Lois B. Review: *The development of the psychoanalytic child. The Psychoanalytic Study of the Child. Contemporary Psychology,* pp. 439–43.

1964   Morgan, C. J. An individual action-research method for intensive exploration of adaptive difficulties in the prepuberty stage. *The Journal of Psychology* 58:439–58.

1964   Murphy, Lois B. Adaptational tasks in childhood in our culture. *Bulletin Menninger Clinic* 28:309–23.

1964   Murphy, Lois B. Continuity and change in coping resources of preschool children. *The Journal of Nursery Education* 19, no. 2:78–88.

1964   Murphy, Lois B. Some aspects of the first relationship. *International Journal of Psychoanalysis* 45:31–44.

1964–65   Murphy, Lois B. Children's stresses and distresses. *PTA Magazine.* (October).

1965   Bernardez, Teresa. The feminine role. *Bulletin Menninger Clinic* 29:198–205.

1965   Morrow, J. Tarlton. Providing growth experiences. *Bulletin Menninger Clinic* 29:177–89.

1965   Murphy, Lois B. Learning through feelings. In *Feelings and learning.* American Association Childhood Education.

1967   Davidson, Joan. Infantile depression in a "normal" child. *Journal of the American Academy of Child Psychiatry* 7:522–35.

1967   Murphy, Lois B. Spontaneous ways of learning in young children. *Children* 4, no. 6:211–16.

1968   Murphy, Lois B. Child development—then and now. *Childhood Education* 44, no. 5:301–06.

1968   Murphy, Lois B. The role of the consultant in the day care center for deprived children. *Children.*

1969   Murphy, Lois B. Children under three: Issues in research. *Children* 16, no. 2:47–52.

1973   Murphy, Lois B. The stranglehold of norms on the individual child. *Childhood Education* (April 1973), pp. 343–49.

1973   Murphy, Lois B. The variability of infants' reactions to pain. *Clinical Proceedings, Children's Hospital, National Medical Center* 29, no. 1:3–7.

Index

Activity level: and cognitive development, 79; factors in, 79–80, 177, 340, 421; and stimulation, 79, 80–81; and internal integration, 79, 85; and coping, 79, 339–40, 347; individual differences of in infancy, 79, 419–20 n8; and vulnerability, 206–08; and passivity in dealing with stress, 258; need for further studies of, 418 n4

Adaptation: not as compliance, 346

Adaptational style: source of evidence for study of, 76–77, 151; in two infants, 152–53; stability of, 153–55, 162–65; factors shaping, 155–57; role of balance in, 158; and changes in IQ, 159; changes in, 165–68, 178–80; prediction of, 175; and mother–child relationship, 175, 187, 188; revision of, 178; adaptational crisis, 186; in infants, 188–89, 342; aggressiveness in, 310–11, 314

Aggression: in coping, 272, 347; in adaptational style, 310–11, 314, 347

Ainsworth, M. D. S., 47, 154, 418

Allen, L., 11, 123, 285

Alpert, A., 204, 281

Amatruda, C. S., 11, 76

Ambivalence, 83, 340

Ames, L., 417, 422

Anxiety, 204, 431

Apgar, V., 201, 429

Assassination of a president, 249–62; feelings about reactions of Kennedy family, 253

Autonomic reactivity, 143, 425 n8

Autonomy: related to ecology, 103; flexible use of, 114–15; as criterion for mental health, 121

Autonomy in infants: need for, 61; and mother's personality, 62; and later coping capacity, 62, 146–47, 150; consequences of respect for, 63; and vegetative functioning in girls, 67; in feeding, 137; and changes in adaptational style, 179; of ego, 429 n5

Balances and imbalances: in community life, 38–39; between gratification and frustration, 71; in infancy and later behavior, 174; in infant functioning and vulnerability, 223–24

Balances and imbalances in development: as factors in coping problems, 84–85, 341; and overstimulation, 85; as precursors of vulnerability, 85; areas of, 99; and adaptational difficulties in one child, 300; outcomes of, 342–43; and later difficulties, 427 n2

Baldwin, A., 29, 125, 481

Barker, L., 9, 12, 23

Barker, R., 9, 12, 23, 345, 413

Barron, F. X., 174

Bateson, G., 125

Bayley, N., 7, 158, 416, 427–29

Bell, R., 47

Bender, L., 134, 138, 158, 174, 206, 416, 427–29, 431

Benjamin, J., 76

Bergman, P., 430, 432

Berkeley studies, 429

Bernardez, T., xx

Bernfeld, S., 90

"Bible" (list of all scores and ratings), xvi. *See also* Comprehensive Coping Inventory

Birch, H., 47, 76

Blos, P., 295

Boone, D., 433

Bowlby, J., 429

Brackbill, Y., 430

Bridges, K. M. B., 431

Brody, S., 40 n, 68, 137

Bryan, E. S., 418

Bryant, K., xviii

Bühler, C., 285, 416

Burlingame, D., 334

Challenge in coping, 69, 70–71, 284

Chandler, C., xxiii

Change in continuity: in cultures and individuals, 7; and role of vulnerability in coping, 171; and integration of personality, 193; in functioning style, 195–98, 342

Children in this study: ages at beginning of study, xiv; IQs, xv

Coelho, G., xxi

Cognitive functioning, 204; predictability of, 342

Coles, R., 286, 428